CITIZEN DIPLOMATS

CITIZEN DIPLOMATS

Pathfinders
In Soviet-American Relations
∽ And How You Can Join Them

Gale Warner & Michael Shuman

FOREWORD BY CARL SAGAN

CONTINUUM · NEW YORK

1987
The Continuum Publishing Company
370 Lexington Avenue, New York, N.Y. 10017

Printed in the United States of America

Designed by Tom Mellers

Library of Congress Cataloging-in-Publication Data

Warner, Gale.
  Citizen diplomats.
    1. United States—Relations—Soviet Union.
2. Soviet Union—Relations—United States.
I. Shuman, Michael. II. Title.
E183.8.S65W37 1987   303.4′8273′047   87–308
ISBN 0–8264–0382–4

MacNelly cartoon p. 298, reprinted by permission: Tribune Media Services

Lyrics to "Riding for Peace" copyright 1984. Music and lyrics by Tom O'Neill and Michael Terry, Pearl Street Publishing ASCAP

For our parents
Louise and Jack Warner
Bernadine and Jack Shuman
with love and gratitude

CONTENTS

PHOTOS BETWEEN PAGES 188 AND 189

FOREWORD

"UNLOCKING THE DEADLY EMBRACE"

by Carl Sagan
David Duncan Professor of Astronomy and Space Sciences
and Director, Laboratory for Planetary Studies
Cornell University

Despite earnest protestations of their peaceable intent and solemn treaty obligations to reverse the nuclear arms race, the United States and the Soviet Union somehow manage to add to the existing strategic arsenals enough new nuclear weapons each year to destroy every city on the planet—something they can already do twenty times over. When asked for justification, each earnestly points to the other. And, indeed, each side has a list as long as your arm of deeply resented abuses committed by the other. Some abuses are imaginary; most are, in differing degrees, real. Every time there is an abuse by one side, you can be sure of some compensatory abuse by the other. Both nations are full of wounded pride and self-righteous indignation. Each knows in excruciating detail the most minor malefactions of the other, but hardly even glimpses its own sins and the worldwide suffering its policies have caused.

On each side, of course, there are good, honest and patriotic people who see the grave danger that their national policies have created— people who long, as a matter of elementary decency and simple survival for themselves and their descendants, to put things right. But there are also, on both sides, people gripped by a hatred and fear intentionally fanned by the respective agencies of national propaganda, people who believe their adversaries are beyond redemption—people who welcome an occasional confrontation. Indeed, sometimes they are spoiling for a fight. The confrontationists on each side are indebted to one another. They encourage one another. They need one another. They would not be nearly so powerful without one another. The relation between the nations fluctuates. In certain years the Americans are reasonable and the Soviets obdurate and intransigent; a few years later the positions reverse for a while. But by and large, jingoism, fear and hatred dominate.

It is a little like an old married couple, perhaps in their youth forced to marry. They are unable to separate or divorce—perhaps because of religious scruples or social stigma, or because of the children. And so every day, grumbling, they have to deal with one another. They must live with one another. Their better natures know it would be better to be kind or at least civil, and occasionally they manage to do so. But they are so outraged by past and present grievances that they cannot help themselves. One of the problems with rare interludes of amity is that neither can bear to see the other happy. And so even their most minor interactions are fraught with anxiety and hostility.

We all know such married couples. They cannot resolve their problem because each is unable to recognize his or her own contribution to the failure of the relationship. Indeed, they project onto one another the most unwholesome facets of their own characters—character flaws which at best they rarely glimpse, much less acknowledge. A part of their being knows they should stop, and longs for an end to the fighting. But they do not know *how* to stop. Their rational faculties are exquisitely vulnerable to the next outrage. And so they devote vast emotional and intellectual resources to the conflict. They are locked in a deadly embrace.

One possible solution, of course, is to go to a competent marriage counselor. But the mere act of jointly consulting a therapist is tantamount to confessing that the problem is mutual. One of the first tasks of the therapist would be to get both parties to admit their contributions to the failure of the marriage. If you've invested a lifetime in self-justification and insensitivity, you are likely to resist any third-party meddling, to say nothing of a close examination of root causes. And, anyway, who could serve as marriage counselor to the superpowers? It will be a long time, unfortunately, before any other nation has both the military and economic strength and the moral credibility to mediate between the United States and the Soviet Union. As far as I can see, this leaves only one alternative: The people.

Just as war is too important to be left to the generals, so the relation between the superpowers is too critical to be left to the bureaucrats. The people of both nations, by and large, receive only the picture of the potential adversary that their own government presents. The governments, of course, have a vested interest in justifying the confrontation and especially their own doctrinal position; it is the work of decades, involving a long succession of presidents, party chairmen, and other national leaders. It is not to be abandoned lightly.

The governments, both governments, have a near-stranglehold on what their people are permitted to know about the adversary nation. The rhetoric is different—and there is a significant range of opinion available in the United States to those who know how to find it—but the results are often remarkably similar. Obeisances to the ideal of free exchange of views are made in the United States, but the range of opinion given general prominence on commercial television and the leading newspapers and newsmagazines is extremely narrow. For example, most people on the planet Earth consider themselves socialists. When is the last time that a program has appeared on one of the major television networks in the United States that provides an extensive and sympathetic presentation of socialism by one of its adherents? Capitalism is by far the most powerful economic force in the world. When is the last time that a program has appeared on an all-union network in the USSR that provides an extensive and sympathetic presentation of capitalism by one of *its* adherents?

From the grand design of social systems to the minutiae of everyday life, the mass media of both sides strain information through a fine-gauge ideological filter. Why? Why not permit advocates of the contending systems to take their best shots? The two governments (and their captive editors and media executives) must be afraid that their citizens will defect, at least emotionally, when presented with another point of view. They fear to make alternative opinions available. They do not seem confident—despite their near monopoly of the information resources—of the validity of their own doctrines. Neither side trusts its own people with all the facts and all the arguments.

Many citizens of both countries, of course, recognize this. They know they are being lied to. They know the news is managed. They want to come to their own conclusions. This sort of critical thinking is fundamental to the scientific method. It is also courageous in the face of the certain knowledge that their search will be dismissed by some as the efforts of dupes or fools or worse. But because of advances in and the steadily declining cost of transportation and communication, it is increasingly difficult to isolate the populations of the two countries from each other. Sooner or later they will begin to see for themselves.

This book describes what happens when the filters become more porous, when not only information, but people, start trickling through the boundaries. It is about nine Americans—many of them typical, some not—who visited the Soviet Union out of curiosity, or because they were skeptical about the information available in the United States, or as businessmen eager to make a profit, or out of concern for the health of the planet. We trace, on these pages, not only their official Soviet contacts, but also a wide range of spontaneous, unplannable encounters with ordinary Soviet citizens. Here are the experiences of a medical doctor; the organizers of mountain climbing and bicycle racing expeditions for Soviet and American youngsters; a Midwest farmer; a billionaire; a magazine editor; a sweet but resolute grandmother; and a young girl from Maine who wrote a letter to the General Secretary of the Communist Party of the Soviet Union politely upbraiding him for wanting to conquer the world. Not one of them came away with a view that falls squarely into either ideological camp. They made up their minds for themselves.

There are also many Soviet citizens who visit the United States every year, many on official business. There is good reason to believe that most of them come away with attitudes that also are profoundly changed. It will be a hopeful day when *their* memoirs are as freely published as in the American accounts in this book. But it does not so much matter which country the interaction is in as that it takes place at all. Every bilateral exchange of opinion, every shared nonbureaucratic experience brings the quarrelsome nation states closer together.

Herein are committed, imaginative, resourceful people who did not despair at the state of the world, but thought to do something about it. They found ways. They are unlocking the deadly embrace, and replacing it by something better. We had better figure out how to encourage many more such people—and in all nations. Our civilization and our species depend on it.

❧❧❧
ACKNOWLEDGMENTS

Our first thanks must go to the citizen diplomats themselves. Their cheerful, prompt cooperation and willingness to talk about their lives and their work made writing this book a joy and an adventure. Each chapter is based upon personal interviews with the citizen diplomats and their colleagues conducted between December 1984 and May 1986. These interviews were supplemented by written correspondence, telephone calls, library research, and, when possible, direct participation in the citizen diplomats' activities.

This book has been a special project of the Center for Innovative Diplomacy (CID), a nonprofit research organization dedicated to preventing nuclear war by encouraging direct citizen participation in foreign policy. We owe special thanks to CID's staff, trustees, and members—particularly Meg Bowman, Dwight Cocke, Anne Ehrlich, Alex Kline, Hal Harvey, Eric Horvitz, and Lynn Squires—for more than three years of unwavering support.

The other individuals who have contributed their criticism, ideas, and other forms of input to this book are too numerous to name, but we are especially grateful to: Bob Allen, Bruce Allyn, John Barton, Don Bates, John J. Berger, David Brower, Martha Collins, Gordon Feller, Jim Garrison, Nancy Graham, Steven Haft, Bill Haneman, David Hunt, David Landau, Harold Lee, Ted Levin, John Mack, William Mandel, John Marks, Bob Pickus, Holt Ruffin, Sid Shapiro, Bill Shaw, and Paul von Ward. Jean Anderson, Maureen Eichmann, Kate Garst, Virginia Inglis, and Dorothy Mulder were especially helpful with setting up interviews. Sarah Braun, Carrie and Doug Brumer, Liz Garst, Meredith Heiser, Jennifer Kreger, Jonathan Kreger, Dan Meek, and Salee and Paul Stanfield offered roofs over our heads at needed moments.

Seth Zuckerman wrote the first draft of the chapter on Sharon Tennison and contributed in numerous other ways. Alice Peters, Jonathan Wald, and Jane West provided extra research help at crucial times. Amy Kelly and Andy Kanter donated valuable technical assistance.

David Kreger was a constant support, a sharp-eyed editor, an emergency researcher, a shoulder to cry on—everything Gale's "significant other" needed to be.

Acknowledgments

Special thanks go to Craig Comstock, our agent, and Michael Leach, the associate publisher of Continuum, for their sustained enthusiasm and encouragement. Evander Lomke, our editor, shepherded the manuscript through production with tremendous patience and competence.

While this book was a shared venture from the start, our roles were quite different. Gale conceptualized and wrote the nine major profiles after interviewing the citizen diplomats and researching their stories. Michael originally conceived of the project, took an active editing role, and researched and wrote the final "what you can do" section. The introduction was a joint undertaking.

As is customary for contemporary books that mention Soviet citizens, we have sometimes changed names and other small identifying details. In general, identification by first name only indicates that the name has been changed; when first names and surnames are given, the names are real.

The citizen diplomats' inclusion in this book should not imply their endorsement of the positions and initiatives of one another, the authors, or the Center for Innovative Diplomacy. We alone bear responsibility for the accuracy, tone, and editorial slant of the book.

Most of all, we want to thank each other for bearing with the challenges of coauthoring a book on a controversial, rapidly changing field while three thousand miles apart and absorbed in a myriad of other tasks. It has been a tremendous, sometimes difficult, often joyous learning experience for us both.

Gale Warner
Gloucester, Massachusetts
Michael Shuman
San Francisco, California
December 1986

CITIZEN DIPLOMATS

INTRODUCTION

WHO ARE THE CITIZEN DIPLOMATS?

What images come to mind when one thinks about the Soviet Union? For many Americans, these images include processions of tanks and rockets rolling through Red Square on a gray October day, long lines of peasants queuing up to buy meager rations of food, and Siberian labor camps where dissidents lift bricks at gunpoint. For many Soviets, the first images that come to mind about America include factories cranking out endless supplies of missiles and warheads, streets overflowing with drugs and pornography, and prisons crowded with oppressed blacks and Indians. Americans and Soviets alike may suspect these images are incomplete and misleading, but they are still the landmarks of our psyches, the mental filters through which we process geopolitical facts.

These are the images of the Cold War, the perpetual state of fear, suspicion, and mistrust that has characterized Soviet-American relations. The Cold War has persisted even though the United States has never been in an armed conflict against either Russia or the Soviet Union. The only territorial dispute ever to arise between the two countries—over Alaska—was resolved through a peaceful purchase. During both world wars, the Soviet Union was one of America's most important allies.

But shortly after World War II, Soviet-American cooperation disintegrated into a fierce global competition for allies, resources, and military superiority—a competition that has kept superpower relations on the verge of collapse. The fear and distrust perpetuated by the Cold War have promoted worst-case analyses by both superpowers' generals, war strategists, and weapons designers—analyses that have persuaded leaders to continue expanding, diversifying, and modernizing their military arsenals. Afraid of appearing "weak," both American and Soviet leaders have, with only minor interruptions, continued accelerating the arms race, causing even more distrust and reactive weapons building. Since 1945, when two American nuclear bombs incinerated the cities of Hiroshima and Nagasaki, the United States and the Soviet Union have accumulated more than fifty thousand nuclear weapons—enough to fuel a Hiroshima-sized blast every second for nearly twelve days. As evidence mounts that even a limited nuclear exchange would precipitate a "nuclear winter," the stakes of the Cold War have grown to encompass human survival.

For nearly four decades, the superpowers have coexisted uneasily in a state of "mutually assured destruction," better known as "MAD," in which each has threatened to respond to any act of nuclear aggression with a devastating "second strike." Over the past decade, the stability of deterrence has gradually eroded as both nations have built more accurate nuclear weapons with shorter flight times. Superpower leaders now have less than ten minutes to decide whether to launch their nuclear missiles after they receive warning of an attack, lest an enemy "first strike" should wipe out their retaliatory forces. As the time for life-and-death judgments shrinks, the possibility of nuclear war—whether initiated by another "Cuban missile crisis," an erroneous computer message, or an unidentified act of nuclear terrorism—increases.

In the early 1980s, the Cold War intensified as President Ronald Reagan declared that the Soviets were "the focus of evil in the modern world" and the Soviet press began comparing Reagan's foreign policies to Hitler's. Official American castigations of the Soviet Union for its invasion of Afghanistan and role in suppressing the labor union Solidarity in Poland were blunt and belligerent. Official Soviet denunciations of the United States' invasion of Grenada, military involvement in Central America, and deployment of intermediate-range cruise and Pershing II missiles in Western Europe were no less harsh.

By 1984, relations had become so strained that three of America's most renowned experts on the Soviet Union—the late W. Averell Harriman, Clark M. Clifford, and Marshall D. Shulman—were moved to write: "Our situation has become deeply troubling: there has been a total breakdown in negotiations with the Soviet Union while we have rushed into the largest peacetime military buildup in our history. Some regard these developments with complacency, even satisfaction, but ignoring the lessons of history, they are blind to the dangerous trends now set in motion."

Millions of alarmed citizens throughout the world began pressing national leaders for an immediate halt to the arms race. Thousands of peace groups sprang up and launched educational and lobbying campaigns that emphasized the disastrous consequences of nuclear war, the enormous financial, social, and psychological costs of the arms race, and the need for a bilateral nuclear freeze and other arms control measures. In the United States, the peace movement succeeded in highlighting the public's latent fear of nuclear war and thrusting it into the mainstream of American political debate. According to a 1984 poll by Daniel Yankelovich's Public Agenda Foundation, 89 percent of Americans believe nuclear war is mutually suicidal and 68 percent believe that war will result if the arms race continues without arms control negotiations.

Yet these sentiments have not led to significant changes in either superpower's arms policies or to a diminution of the Cold War. What the peace movement did not successfully address were Americans' fears of the Soviet Union. The 1984 Public Agenda Foundation poll showed that Americans also believe: "If we are weak, the Soviet Union, at the right moment, will attack us or our allies in Europe and Japan" (65 percent); "The Soviets lie, cheat and steal—do anything to further the cause of communism" (61 percent); "The Soviets respond only to military strength" (61 percent); "The Soviets have cheated on just about every treaty and agreement they've ever signed" (61 percent); and "The Soviet Union is like Hitler's Germany—an evil empire trying to rule the world" (56 percent).

The American public is caught in a dilemma between its fear of nuclear war and its fear of the Soviet Union. Afraid that political rivals might accuse them of being "appeasers" or "soft," American leaders have been reluctant to take significant initiatives to halt and reverse the arms race. Until Americans' fears of the Soviet Union are dealt with directly, serious arms control and increased cooperation will always be vulnerable to new demagogues playing upon old Cold War fears. The Cold War must be replaced with a fundamentally different kind of relationship between nations; otherwise, nuclear war will never be more than a misunderstanding, crisis, or computer error away.

In recent years, more and more Americans have begun taking responsibility, as private citizens, to promote healthier relations between the United States and the Soviet Union. While recognizing that foreign affairs are the traditional province of governments, they are convinced that leaders alone are incapable of melting the Cold War. They believe the risk of nuclear war is too high for citizens to wait passively on the sidelines and merely hope for the best. They have been unsure of what they could accomplish, but absolutely certain that doing something is better than doing nothing.

They have traveled to the Soviet Union and met with members of every stratum of Soviet society, from Politburo members to peasants. They believe that expanding the dialogue between the countries at every level is valuable and stabilizing. Some simply seek to learn as much as possible through direct observation and personal experience, and then communicate to other Americans what they have learned. Others try to develop cultural exchanges, joint scientific projects, and trade agreements. Still others work to open new forums of political dialogue that might directly affect the opinions of policymakers in both countries. All of them focus on such questions as: What is the Soviet Union really like? Its people? Its government? How can the United States transform its relationship with the Soviet Union? What can American citizens do?

These are the people known as "citizen diplomats."

In this book, we profile nine of these Americans. Their ages range from thirteen to eighty-eight. Their walks of life include law, medicine, psychology, journalism, business, education, nursing, farming, and junior high school. Their politics range from liberal to conservative, with some considering themselves apolitical. We chose these nine for their diversity, the pioneering nature of their initiatives, and the drama of their stories. But they are hardly alone. In a final section of the book, we summarize the activities of literally thousands of other Americans working to transform the relationship between the superpowers.

Although there are many citizen diplomats from other countries trying to mend East-West relations and many other citizen diplomats working on other international conflicts, we have made no attempt to include them in this book. The field of Soviet-American citizen diplomacy alone is enormous, and expanding so rapidly that, at times, writing this book has resembled documenting the progress of a forest fire.

The term "citizen diplomats" is appropriate because these Americans, unlike many of the tourists who travel by the thousands to the Soviet Union each year, are *deliberately* trying to improve nation-to-nation relations and reduce the risk of war—the essential task of diplomacy. Hans Morgenthau, one of America's foremost international-relations scholars, has defined diplomacy as the method governments use for "establishing the preconditions for permanent peace." Traditional diplomats serve as the nation's legal representatives who can negotiate and enter treaties; they serve as symbolic representatives who can show respect for other nations' diplomats through lavish ceremonies and parties; and they serve as "the nerve center of foreign policy, . . . [the] outlying fibers maintaining the two-way traffic between the [home country] and the outside world."

The citizen diplomats serve analogous functions. While they cannot undertake the quest for a "permanent peace" on behalf of the United States government, they often can claim to represent smaller chunks of America—churches, businesses, civic groups, local governments, or other Americans of like mind. On behalf of their constituencies, the citizen diplomats often negotiate and enter into agreements with Soviets. They demonstrate their respect and goodwill for Soviets through singing, dancing, feasting, and toasting. And they maintain their own two-way traffic of information and impressions by reporting at home on their view of events in the Soviet Union and conveying to Soviets the views of Americans.

In short, while traditional diplomats serve as conduits between American and Soviet leaders, citizen diplomats serve as conduits between the American and Soviet people. Yet citizen diplomats affect both nations' leaders as well. Sometimes they do this by working alongside the traditional diplomats. More often, however, they affect the political context in which leaders operate by spreading information and forming people-to-people relationships.

Strategy #1: Influencing Leaders

Some of the citizen diplomats attempt to influence both American and Soviet leaders directly. In a seminal article on this type of citizen diplomacy in the Winter 1981–1982 issue of the quarterly *Foreign Policy,* Joseph V. Montville, a Foreign Service officer in the State Department, in collaboration with William D. Davidson, a psychiatrist specializing in foreign affairs, defined the official channel of government-to-government relations as "track one diplomacy" and the unofficial channel of people-to-people relations as "track two diplomacy." Montville argued that the second track is "a supplement to the understandable shortcomings of official relations." In track one diplomacy, national leaders "must assure their followers they will defend them against enemies—other tribes or nations—who want to conquer or destroy them." Unfortunately, this "necessary and predictable leadership function often gets tribes—and countries—into conflict."

To defend their nation's interests, track one diplomats must make worst-case assumptions about an adversary's intentions, but these very assumptions may set in motion a chain reaction of mutual distrust, threats, and hostilities that can culminate in war. In track two, Montville argued, new types of relationships are possible that can prevent a chain reaction of escalating hostilities:

5

Track two diplomacy is unofficial, nonstructured interaction. It is always open minded, often altruistic, and . . . strategically optimistic, based on the best case analysis. Its underlying assumption is that actual or potential conflict can be resolved or eased by appealing to common human capabilities to respond to good will and reasonableness.

When track one diplomacy gets stuck, as it often does, citizen diplomats try to uncover new avenues for accommodation that can be developed, negotiated, and finalized by the traditional diplomats. "Both tracks," Montville concluded, "are necessary for psychological reasons and both need one other."

Track two diplomacy has had concrete results. The off-the-record Dartmouth Conferences initiated by Norman Cousins have enabled influential Soviets and Americans to set the stage for track one agreements to ban aboveground nuclear tests, install the original "hot line," expand trade, and allow direct flights between the United States and the Soviet Union. In the late 1970s, when seven dissident Pentecostalists took refuge in the American embassy in Moscow, track one negotiations over their safe release were deadlocked until Olin Robison, a college president with special ties to Soviet religious communities, was called in to mediate. And thanks in part to the creative lobbying of the members of the Harvard Nuclear Negotiation Project, the superpowers have agreed to upgrade the "hot line" from a crude teletype machine to a modern two-way data transmission link capable of rapidly sending messages, charts, and maps. In each of these instances, citizen diplomats have helped identify new areas of cooperation that culminated in important formal agreements.

Strategy #2: Spreading Information

A second technique citizen diplomats employ to improve superpower relations is helping both Americans and Soviets learn more about the viewpoints, politics, culture, and lifestyles of "the other side." They aim to close the enormous information gap between the United States and the Soviet Union—a gap that fosters mutual fear, suspicion, and mistrust.

Soviet images of the United States, for example, are simultaneously too glorious and too critical. Many Soviets admire and mimic American art, film, literature, fashions, and music, and yet they also believe that America is a virtual war zone, inundated with race riots, massive poverty, handgun anarchy, and political corruption. According to *Los Angeles Times* Moscow correspondent Robert Gillette, when residents in the Soviet province of Taganrog were recently asked to list the "most developed democracy" outside the Soviet Union, their most frequent answers were Czechoslovakia, France, Bulgaria, and East Germany. Their candidates for the worst violators of human rights were Greece, the United States, Spain, and West Germany.

Yet most Soviets are also highly skeptical of their sources of information and are eager—indeed, often ecstatic—to learn more by meeting and speaking with Americans. An afternoon with an American is like a taste of a forbidden fruit. Comments Michael Murphy, cofounder of the Esalen Institute and an active citizen diplomat: "Every day the Soviet media is pounding in how absolutely awful life is in the West—massive unemployment, unjust poverty, dreadful insecurity. It's like a Catholic girls' school where the nuns pound in day after day after day how awful and evil and sinful sex is—it gets the girls so steamy they can't wait to get out and try it." To many Soviets, every visiting American is a walking banned book, containing facts and opinions at odds with prevailing "party lines." And in fact, citizen diplomats sometimes carry with them books, magazines, or news clippings containing information that Soviets might otherwise never see.

Little as the average Soviet may know about the United States, the average American may know even less about the Soviet Union. Noting the Soviets' voracious appetite for any and all uncensored information about the United States, columnist Ellen Goodman writes: "In the United States, it is private citizens who self censor Russian language, literature, politics. . . . Maybe the notion that our shelves are full of facts dulls our appetite." Senator Dan Quayle, a conservative Republican from Indiana, has remarked that the US Congress is pervaded by an "incredible lack of knowledge about the Soviet people and Soviet history." A November 1985 *New York Times* survey revealed that 44 percent of all Americans did not know that the Soviet Union fought against Nazi Germany in World War II. In contrast to the more than four million Soviets currently studying English, only about twenty-five thousand Americans are studying Russian. An oft-cited statistic is that there are more Soviets teaching English than Americans learning Russian.

The information gap is both compounded by—and, in turn, feeds—Cold War images of an absolute enemy. According to psychiatrist Ralph K. White, "the diabolical enemy image, like the moral self-image, which is its constant counterpart, . . . means that all of the guilt in the situation is imputed to the enemy and none to oneself." Margaret Mead once stated that she and her fellow anthropologists had found "no justification for the statement that man is a killer. But we see great justification for emphasizing man's ability to define half the human race as not human."

"All nations have a way of demonizing their adversaries," writes *New York Times* reporter David Shipler. "And so do we, picturing our values as antitheses of the Russians'—our freedom, their slavery, our wealth, their poverty, our honesty, their deceit, our righteousness, their subversion, our peaceful intentions, their warlike militarism." The same demonizing is undertaken by the Soviets, too, who often portray Americans as the impoverished slaves of multinational corporations and the promoters of bloody imperialism in the Third World. In both the United States and the Soviet Union, the institutions that provide citizens with information—the press, the entertainment media, and the schools—frequently become Cold War prisms that project and reinforce enemy images.

"In recent years," writes Princeton Sovietologist Stephen F. Cohen, "the quality of American newspaper coverage [of the Soviet Union] has been as bad as I can remember. Too much of it is one-dimensional, distorted, and factually wrong." An April 1983 survey by the Public Broadcasting Service (PBS) found that 80 percent of all Soviet-related stories originated in the United States. The rest of the news comes from a small pool of two to three dozen resident journalists in Moscow, only a handful of whom speak Russian fluently and have academic training in Soviet studies. While many make a conscientious effort to be balanced and complete, the difficulties inherent in being a Western journalist in Moscow often tempt the best-intentioned reporters into a simplistic "us-versus-them" mentality. Their attitudes toward the Soviet system harden in part because the Soviet government automatically suspects them to be spies and subjects them to harassment. Reporters also become frustrated by the difficulty of obtaining solid news. Official Soviet information is often shallow, self-congratulatory, and unreliable; press conferences are rare (though now on the rise); reporters have little personal access to high-level officials; and most other Soviets are afraid to talk with correspondents for fear that incautious words will end up in print. Many of the Soviets who do actively seek out Western journalists are dissidents eager to share their stories of injustice and disillusionment. Because most Western editors expect their journalists to cover news from the Kremlin and because these editors create, in Cohen's view, "a persistent anxiety on the part of many journalists . . . that they might appear to be too soft on the Soviet system," Western journalists seldom write stories describing the lives of ordinary Soviets.

Much of America's cinema, television, and school curricula also reinforce stereotyped images of a subhuman, diabolical enemy. The 1984 film *Red Dawn* portrays American high school students resisting a brutal invasion by Soviet paratroopers. The 1985 film *Rambo* depicts Soviets as sadistic torturers in Vietnam who are ultimately massacred by a heroic anti-Communist veteran. The American Broadcasting Company's television series *Amerika,* slated for broadcast in early 1987, will depict life in the United States after a bloodless Soviet conquest. Often schools offer few alternatives to these images; many American high-school history texts downplay the Soviets' role in defeating Hitler and pass over the fact that twenty million Soviets died during World War II.

Similarly skewed and dehumanized images of the United States are presented in Soviet news media, films, and schools. Almost every day, Soviet newspapers carry cartoons of American businessmen and generals conspiring to build and use deadly weapons against innocent civilians. Soviet reporters based in Washington, DC, pepper their dispatches with comments from the "dissident" American Communist Party and deliberately slant their news to fit the views of the Soviet government. A 1984 ten-part Soviet television series called *Tass Is Authorized to State* pitted clever and daring Soviet intelligence agents against a group of ruthless CIA spies. On the streets and in the classroom, "peace" billboards and posters portray Uncle Sam or caricatures of America's leaders as demonic militarists.

The information chasm between the superpowers is so wide that even if the citizen diplomats' missions were simply to take some notes, snap some photographs, speak with several Soviets on the streets, and share their experiences with friends and family after their return, they would be helping to bridge the gap. But many citizen diplomats take this a step farther by conveying their experiences to Americans through public speeches, slide presentations, radio and television shows, and local newspaper articles. Many citizen diplomats have also addressed large public crowds in the Soviet Union, had their points of view reported in Soviet newspapers, and appeared on Soviet radio and television.

Citizen diplomats are also trying to close the information gap by taking advantage of a host of increasingly inexpensive and accessible communications technologies. Through satellite linkups, Columbia University, Emory University, and Stanford University now enable their students and faculty to watch live Soviet television, including Soviet news, movies, drama, and music. "Space bridges" have brought American and Soviet audiences together through gigantic video screens that carry simultaneous images of each audience. Television broadcasts of these space bridges on the *Phil Donahue Show*, PBS specials, and network news shows have reached tens of millions.

Besides using advanced technologies, citizen diplomats have helped spread them to the Soviet Union in the hope of substantially expanding channels of communication between the superpowers. Some citizen diplomats have facilitated the importation of personal computers into the Soviet Union. Others have shown top Soviet scientists how to communicate with Americans through international computer networks. For the time being, personal computers and computer networks are under strict Soviet government control. But in the years ahead, as machines multiply and get smaller, as diskettes move in and out of the country, and as computer networks begin connecting to satellites instead of telephones, it is conceivable that a whole generation of young Soviet "hackers" may be able to communicate with one another and with foreigners in ways their parents never dreamed possible.

All of this information sharing is enabling citizens of both countries to depend less and less on their governments and their professional journalists as their sole sources of information about "the other side." Jeremy Stone, director of the Federation of American Scientists, writes:

> Americans travelling to the USSR generally return with a more realistic view of the Soviet economy and military; historically, those on the left become disillusioned with the degree of regimentation, while those on the right experience the Soviet horrors of war . . . and lose some of their exaggerated fear of unchecked Russian military might. By contrast, Soviet officials are typically sobered by our economic strength and social stability. Yet they are also reassured by our intentions which differ dramatically from simplistic Soviet propaganda.

As Americans' and Soviets' enemy images give way to more complex and nuanced pictures of one another, both peoples can develop what Stanford political scientist Alexander Dallin calls "an instinct . . . to make confident judgments about what is ludicrous." In leaders, this instinct enables them to understand and react to one another's behavior more wisely. In citizens, this instinct denies superpower leaders the opportunity to portray one another as evil enemies and puts pressure on them to transform demagoguery into diplomacy.

Strategy #3: Forming Relationships

The citizen diplomats' third strategy is based on the concept that the best defense against nuclear warheads may well be a strong, complex, and durable web of relationships between the peoples of the Soviet Union and the United States—and indeed between all nations. Few Americans fear the nuclear weapons possessed by Great Britain or France, even though their weapons could wipe us off the map, because of the numerous ties linking our countries. Even China, a nuclear-armed country widely regarded as a "yellow menace" as recently as the late 1960s, has since become a friend, in part because of what Arthur W. Hummel, Jr., the US Ambassador to China in the early 1980s, has called "an amazing web" of relationships. "We no longer need to plan for the possibility of a war with China," writes Hummel. "The multiplicity of relationships which we have—perhaps the majority of them having nothing to do with the US government—is a genuine stabilizing force and a force which through the decades will produce much better understanding." The citizen diplomats aim to build personal, cultural, scientific, and economic relationships with the Soviet Union so that a Soviet-American war becomes as unthinkable as a Franco-American war or a Sino-American war.

It is true that in the past, economic and other ties between nations have not always been adequate to avert warfare; numerous links among the French and German peoples, for example, did little to halt the Franco-Prussian War and two brutal world wars, and strong trade relations between Japan and the United States prior to World War II did not prevent Pearl Harbor. But the invention of the atomic bomb has irrevocably changed the nature of warfare. While decisionmakers once regarded war as an acceptable instrument of policy, today there is a growing realization that no policy objective can be furthered by a war that is as likely to destroy the aggressor as the victim. And unlike many other historical conflicts driven by tangible disputes over territorial or economic claims, the Cold War is largely driven by an intangible clash of ideologies. Citizen diplomacy addresses the intangibles of perception and belief, and thus may be more well-suited for affecting the current East-West conflict than other historical clashes.

Americans and Soviets tend to regard the true source of "evil" as one another's leaders. In a 1983 *Time*/Yankelovich poll, nearly 90 percent of the American public agreed that "the Russian people are not nearly as hostile to the U.S. as their leaders are and, in fact, the Russians could be our friends if their leaders had a different attitude." Similarly, travelers to the Soviet Union are struck by the high regard most Soviets have for the American people, whom they remember as reliable war allies. *New York Times* correspondent Serge Schmemann writes, "Hostile receptions [for Americans] are virtually unknown; on the contrary, Russians often joke that the Soviet Union is the last bastion of pro-Americanism in the world."

Many Americans and Soviets have a strong desire to meet one another, and personal bonds are often formed with surprising swiftness and intensity. These bonds usually begin with a profoundly shocking, visceral, and even euphoric revelation: the once dark, mysterious "enemy" really looks, talks, thinks, dresses, worries, and behaves in familiar ways. Both Americans and Soviets are relieved to learn how much "the enemy" shares their fear of nuclear war.

Yet citizen diplomats have discovered that recognizing their common humanity with Soviets is only a first step in building successful relationships. A second step is learning about and coming to terms with their significant cultural and political differences with Soviets, and this step can be as painful and confusing as the first step was euphoric and clarifying.

A turning point often comes when, after the handshakes, toasts, speeches, and agreements, Americans criticize their own government and expect the Soviets to reciprocate by criticizing theirs. In nearly all formal settings (and even many informal ones), the Soviets will simply agree with the Americans' criticisms and say nothing critical about their own government. If the Americans have not yet come to appreciate that most Soviets will only criticize their government in a private, nonthreatening atmosphere, they may feel betrayed and frustrated, and conclude: "They really are government propaganda mouthpieces, after all." If the Americans keep pushing—cross-examining the Soviets and trying to trap them into contradictions and concessions—the Soviets then may feel betrayed as well, and conclude: "They're really just trying to subvert our government, after all."

As in marriage, both an appreciation of similarities and a respect for differences are necessary for a long-term relationship between the American and Soviet peoples. If a relationship is to last beyond the honeymoon, each partner must accept the other's imperfections, unpleasant mannerisms, and differing beliefs, while still, perhaps, not giving up entirely a secret hope of eventually changing the other.

While every individual Soviet-American relationship may itself have little effect, the cumulative impact of these ties can improve the overall state of relations between the nations in two ways. First, such relationships may help weave a sturdy fabric that no single international incident can rip apart. The citizen diplomats sometimes use the image of the Lilliputians tying down the giant Gulliver with thousands of tiny strands. As more and more Americans and Soviets become closer friends, plan cultural exchanges, take on joint research projects, and enter into business contracts, the possibility of the nuclear giant stirring becomes more and more remote. Recognizing the personal, political, and economic value of these relationships, citizens can effectively lobby their national leaders to strengthen relations when they are good and to repair relations when they are bad.

In the 1970s American farmers eager to sell grain and farm technology to the Soviet Union were among the beneficiaries of détente. After President Carter responded to the Soviet invasion of Afghanistan by embargoing American grain sales, these farmers—who, by conservative accounts, lost more than thirteen billion dollars in sales—helped pressure President Reagan to scrap the embargo in early 1981 and, two years later, sign a new five-year contract with a guarantee against interruption for political reasons. Events like these put national leaders on notice that, if they cut off relations with the other superpower, they will face stiff political costs.

A second way such relationships can make a difference is that they force us to come to grips with the "mad" aspects of mutually assured destruction (MAD) and to identify on a human level with the intended victims of our weapons. By creating relationships in which more and more Americans and Soviets understand, empathize, and care for one another, citizen diplomacy is gradually transforming the act of launching nuclear weapons into an act of murdering friends. British historian E. P. Thompson has written:

> What is unthinkable is that nuclear war could happen to *us*. So long as we can suppose that this war will be inflicted only on *them*, the thought comes easily. . . . We *think* others to death as we define them as the Other: the enemy: Asians: Marxists: non-people. The deformed human mind is the ultimate doomsday weapon—it is out of the human mind that the missiles . . . come.

If citizen diplomacy helps Americans and Soviets to recoil from the thought of using nuclear weapons, then more and more citizens in both countries may begin searching for less dangerous ways of resolving the conflict between their nations.

HOW HAVE GOVERNMENTS REACTED TO CITIZEN DIPLOMACY?

Throughout history, governments have held on tightly to their national sovereignty, especially their exclusive right to conduct foreign affairs. Consequently, governments have sometimes viewed foreign policy initiatives by citizens with suspicion and alarm. Yet democratic traditions in the United States have given American citizens freedom to undertake increasingly creative foreign policy initiatives.

American citizen diplomacy goes back to 1798, when a Philadelphia Quaker named George Logan traveled to Europe in a last-ditch effort to prevent the United States and France from going to war. France, which was then battling Britain, had begun attacking American ships because of growing US political cooperation with Britain. To the amazement of everyone, Logan returned to the United States with a decree from France indicating its willingness to end its trade embargo and to free all captured US seamen. Instead of receiving a hero's welcome, Logan was castigated for his "usurpation of executive authority" by a decidedly pro-British American Congress and President John Adams, who were gearing up for a fight with France and hastily passed a law criminalizing any direct interventions of citizens in foreign affairs.

The Logan Act is still on the books, but it represents only one American political philosophy toward citizen diplomacy. Another philosophy, expressed in the US Constitution and two centuries of court opinions, is that Americans have full rights to travel abroad and speak with foreigners about anything they choose, including relations between nations. The strength of this second philosophy is underscored by the fact that the Logan Act has never been enforced. The government's misgivings about letting its citizens "meddle" in foreign affairs has been generally outweighed by a laissez-faire attitude toward the travel and activities of its citizens abroad.

During and after World War I, a small number of Americans such as Walter Reuther and John Reed ventured to the Soviet Union to "help build the world's first Communist state." Government officials sometimes criticized them but rarely interfered. Shortly after World War II, with the advent of "containment" abroad and McCarthyism at home, some citizens who intended to travel to the Soviet Union were denied permission and accused of being Soviet dupes, spies, or worse. Passports were routinely stamped "not valid for travel in the Soviet Union." Those who were able to travel sometimes returned to harrassment by the FBI, inquisitions before the House Un-American Activities Committee, and a blacklisted status that left them unemployed.

After McCarthyism waned, the US government began cautiously promoting citizen exchanges with the Soviet Union. President Eisenhower helped establish People to People International and Sister Cities International, groups that are active today. In 1958, his administration signed an agreement with the Soviet Union on cultural, technical, and educational exchanges. A 1960 agreement added scientific exchanges and a 1962 agreement provided for exchanges in "other fields."

The motivations underlying the US government's interest in exchange programs were complex. According to a 1984 report by Yale Richmond of the Kennan Institute for Advanced Russian Studies, the government sought to remove barriers obstructing the free flow of information and ideas. "Although not publicly stated at the time," Richmond wrote, "it was hoped that opening up the Soviet Union to Western influences would create pressures from within for reforms which might make the Soviet Union more likely to cooperate with, rather than confront, the West." The US government may also have been eager to strip away the secrecy surrounding the Soviet Union for intelligence purposes. Whatever the government's motives, Soviet-American rapprochement was supported by a number of powerful American interest groups. Businessmen saw exchanges as a way of opening Soviet markets, scholars saw them as a way of improving Soviet studies, and travel agents saw a new boon for tourism.

The 1960s were years of experimentation and learning for the governmental exchange programs; both sides established ground rules consistent with their laws and cultural norms. Thousands of Soviets and Americans traveled between the countries both as official participants in exchange programs and as tourists. Yet the governments also remained wary: "The watchwords on both sides," writes Richmond, "were suspicion, control, and strict reciprocity." To deter spying, the US State Department provided escorts for Soviet visitors to the United States and required that they stick to approved itineraries. Most long-term Soviet visitors faced strict travel restrictions and remained under varying de-

15

grees of surveillance. The Soviets applied even tighter restrictions and surveillance to American visitors.

A turning point for Soviet-American people-to-people contacts came during the Nixon-Brezhnev meetings of 1972, 1973, and 1974, when agreements were signed for cultural exchange, trade, maritime cooperation, and joint scientific and technical projects in eleven fields. Détente spurred record levels of tourism, trade, and cooperation. In 1976, 65,864 Americans visited the Soviet Union and 11,960 Soviets visited the United States. Between 1972 and 1979, American exports to the Soviet Union rose from $542 million to $3.6 billion, while imports from the Soviet Union rose from $96 million to $873 million. By the 1978–79 academic year, more than a thousand scientists from each country were spending time studying or working in the other. The docking of Apollo and Soyuz spacecrafts in 1975 was a dramatic symbol of Soviet-American cooperation.

But as the numbers of participants in détente steadily increased, so did opposition to its principles. Believing that détente was not constraining the Soviet arms buildup or its "adventures" abroad, many conservatives repudiated détente, a position reflected in the 1976 platform of the Republican Party. President Jimmy Carter came to office embracing détente, but soon, bowing to pressure not to appear "soft" on defense, he announced a new strategic doctrine for nuclear war fighting and lobbied for the MX and Trident D-5 missiles.

What little was left of détente was torpedoed by the Soviet invasion of Afghanistan in late 1979. President Carter responded with an embargo on grain sales that, within a year, cut American exports to the Soviet Union in half. Tourism also collapsed; whereas 44,166 Americans visited the Soviet Union in 1979, only 12,922 visited in 1980.

When the Reagan administration came to office, it refused to renew the cultural exchange agreement, cut the budgets of many other exchange programs, denied visas to a number of would-be Soviet visitors, and increased restrictions on the movement and activities of the Soviets it allowed to visit. At the same time, the administration accelerated the arms buildup begun by President Carter and began its anti-Soviet "evil empire" rhetoric. But the early Reagan administration's distaste for broad contacts with the Soviet Union was not absolute. Outside of the embargoes on sales of advanced computers and gas pipeline equipment, it still permitted, and sometimes facilitated, other trade with the Soviet Union. It also continued a few exchange programs, particularly those related to technological cooperation, and allowed travel by Americans to the Soviet Union to continue unimpaired.

At times there were wide discrepancies between the Reagan administration's rhetoric and its actions. In June 1984, President Reagan told a private conference on US-Soviet relations: "We should broaden opportunities for American and Soviet citizens to get to know each other better. . . . The way governments can best promote contacts among people is by not standing in the way. Our administration will do all we can to stay out of the way and to persuade the Soviet government to do likewise." Yet less than a year later, Reagan's appointees to the Corporation for Public Broadcasting (CPB), a private nonprofit organization created to channel public funds into the nation's public broadcasting system, refused to provide funds for a delegation of Public Broadcasting Service executives to visit Moscow and discuss arrangements for exchanging television shows. CPB Chair Sonia Landau argued, "I just don't want the CPB name associated with it. Russian TV is not exactly the BBC. We are talking about the same guys who shot down the Korean jetliner."

On November 14, 1985, just prior to the Geneva summit, President Reagan delivered a dramatic televised speech that echoed the same points many citizen diplomats had been making for years:

> Imagine how much good we could accomplish, how much the cause of peace would be served, if more individuals and families from our respective countries could come to know each other in a personal way. . . .
>
> We could look to increase scholarship programs; improve language studies; conduct courses in history, culture, and other subjects; develop new sister-cities; establish libraries and cultural centers; and yes, increase athletic competition. People of both our nations love sports. If we must compete, let it be on the playing field and not the battlefield.

At the summit, President Reagan and Secretary Mikhail Gorbachev agreed to renew a number of exchanges and to resume direct commercial flights between the countries. The President soon created an office at the US Information Agency specifically to oversee and promote private citizen initiatives for exchange with the Soviet Union.

A few weeks after the summit accords on health cooperation had been signed, however, the State Department canceled the American downlinks (closed-circuit broadcasts) of a televised "space bridge" between medical scientists in the United States and the Soviet Union at the last moment.

According to "congressional sources" quoted in the *Los Angeles Times*, "a high State Department official ordered the blackout" because he did not want Dr. Yevgeny Chazov, the controversial cofounder of the Nobel Peace Prize-winning International Physicians for the Prevention of Nuclear War, to receive such "major publicity." And in 1986 the State Department attempted to thwart the Natural Resources Defense Council's agreement with the Soviet Academy of Sciences to monitor nuclear tests by putting restrictive conditions on the visas of visiting Soviet technicians. Assistant Secretary of Defense Richard Perle testified before a House subcommittee in July 1986 that NRDC's attempt at "citizen diplomacy" was "absurd."

President Reagan appears to believe that citizen diplomats embody what is best about America—pluralist thinking, independent initiative, and global responsibility. But he also appears willing to co-opt or limit citizen activities when they begin to encroach upon his policymaking prerogatives. Some have suggested that the President's recent support for citizen diplomacy is mostly rhetoric, shrewdly timed to convince the American people that the administration supports stronger superpower relations even though it refuses to compromise on any concrete arms control measures. Fortunately for the citizen diplomats, however, the new cultural agreement has so far survived a rocky period in US-Soviet relations. And the office of the "President's US-Soviet Exchange Initiative" has become a useful clearinghouse and negotiating service for private initiatives, though so far it has not provided funding for any projects.

In contrast to the American government's relatively laissez-faire attitude toward citizen diplomacy, the Soviet government's response to people-to-people contacts is rooted in a repressive tradition. Rights that Americans take for granted—rights of speech, travel, lobbying, and dissent—have been, at best, occasional privileges for Soviets. The Soviet government's long history of wariness toward foreign contacts has roots in the attitudes of pre-Revolutionary Czarist Russia and reached grotesque extremes under Stalin in the late 1930s, 1940s, and early 1950s. Stalin's paranoia exacerbated and institutionalized existing Russian tendencies toward keeping Western spies and other "corrupting" influences out of the country.

Today, many of the features of the Stalinist state remain. Radio signals are jammed, foreign literature and letters are sometimes confiscated, foreign telephone calls and telex messages are often monitored, delayed, or canceled, and visa applications to visit the Soviet Union can still be capriciously denied. Most significantly, very few Soviet citizens can leave the country, even for business reasons or brief vacations.

After Stalin died in 1953, the Soviet Union slowly and tentatively began opening itself to the West. Some of the Soviet motives for supporting more active relations paralleled those of the American government. The Soviets knew that trade meant economic benefits, that scientific exchanges meant increased access to Western know-how and technology, and that cultural exchanges meant badly needed Western hard currency. The Soviets also may have seen exchanges as a means of getting the United States to recognize it as a superpower with equal prestige. Finally, the Soviets may have supported exchange programs as a promising avenue for establishing "peaceful coexistence" with the United States.

But the Soviet Union was only willing to open itself on its own terms. Governmental exchanges and trade deals were all carefully monitored by the appropriate government committees. American tourists were allowed in, but they generally had to stay at Intourist hotels and be chaperoned by Intourist guides on prearranged tours. The Soviet government wanted Americans to visit, but only if it could control which Soviets they would encounter and how.

Over the years, however, more and more Americans have discovered how easy it is to roam the streets of Soviet cities on their own. The Soviet government has gradually become accustomed to the free movement of foreigners within certain areas of the country. Some seasoned American visitors report that surveillance, overt shadowing by KGB agents, and thorough border searches have all decreased significantly in the past decade; others report never having experienced these controls in the first place.

During the early 1980s, when governmental exchange programs were being curtailed and official dialogue was strained or nonexistent, the Soviet government began communicating its views to American leaders via the "back channels" of citizen diplomacy. "Initially hesitant in 1980," states a 1985 report from the Kennan Institute for Advanced Russian Studies, "the Soviets have responded energetically to the increased interest of private American organizations to engage in cultural exchanges of all types." Although the Soviets tend to prefer organizing exchanges under the auspices of official governmental agreements, in 1983 they acknowledged the special validity of citizen diplomacy by creating a new position at the Soviet embassy in Washington, DC—a "third secretary" specifically assigned to handle the proliferation of projects initiated by American citizens.

Despite all of its "peace and friendship" rhetoric, however, the Soviet government is still a little nervous about the citizen diplomats. Some members of the Soviet government who cling to a Stalinist world view are suspicious that many citizen diplomats are really CIA spies or subversives. In 1984, the Soviet government passed several new repressive laws against foreign contacts—one that punishes any Soviet giving shelter, transportation, or other "services" to a foreigner without official permission, and another making illegal the acceptance of "money or other material value from foreign organizations or persons acting in the interest of those organizations." While enforcement of these laws has been spotty, they are still on the books and can be activated at any moment.

The election of Mikhail Gorbachev as General Secretary of the Communist Party may mark a new era of Soviet openness to the citizen diplomats. There are early indications that Gorbachev and his supporters are eager to invigorate the Soviet economy with foreign capital, technology, and trade, which may in turn expose the Soviet people to more foreign influences. "The new Soviet leaders," writes the noted French international lawyer Samuel Pisar, "know that the choice before them is fateful: either to face up to the challenges of an advanced economy, with the free movement of ideas, people and goods that this presupposes, or to isolate themselves in an armed fortress condemned to obsolescence."

If the March 1986 Soviet Communist Party Congress is any indication, the ideological conflicts between neo-Stalinists and reformists in the Communist Party are far from resolved. Viktor Chebrikov, head of the KGB, announced a new crackdown on video recorders because they were spreading "ideas alien to us, a cult of cruelty and violence and amorality." The previous day Yegor Ligachev, the chief ideologist at the Politburo, announced that "measures have been formulated to start large-scale production of video technology." The tension between competing ideological factions ensures that no matter how much citizen diplomats receive the red carpet today, the Soviet government could in the future attempt drastic curtailment of their activities. The true test of Gorbachev's rhetoric will be the extent to which it translates into actions.

Yet the citizen diplomats may be increasingly beyond the control of either the American or Soviet governments. Global communication and transportation, once affordable only by very few, are now within the reach of millions of Americans. With inflation factored out, the cost of an overseas cable today is now a thousandth of what it was in 1866 and a tenth of what it was in 1970. The cost of an overseas flight is now a sixth of what it was in 1940, and an overseas telephone call costs a sixtieth of what it did in 1935. As more and more Americans attempt to visit and communicate with Soviets, both governments may find flows of people, ideas, and goods slipping beyond their control. Although the Soviet government may always be able to commandeer its telephone and telex lines, the increasing availability of compact, easily transported shortwave radios, tape recorders, video-cassette recorders, personal computers, and satellite transmitters means that in the near future, an increasing number of Soviet citizens may be able to communicate with Americans without either government's interference. Citizen diplomacy may eventually become, for all practical purposes, unstoppable.

In the immediate future, both governments are likely to continue displaying considerable ambivalence toward citizen diplomacy and the citizen diplomats are likely to continue exploiting this ambivalence. Both governments proclaim their interest in greater friendship, understanding, communication, travel, and trade. The citizen diplomats take this kind of rhetoric and run with it. They make citizen diplomacy more real than the governments might really want it to be.

COMMON CRITICISMS

The citizen diplomats are inevitably and unavoidably controversial. Because they spread information contrary to prevailing beliefs and develop relationships with people widely regarded as enemies, citizen diplomats are lightning rods for criticism. To some, they are "naives," "dupes," or even "traitors." Underlying these attacks, however, are three crucial questions: Can the actions of American citizens possibly influence the "totalitarian" government of the Soviet Union? Doesn't cooperation with members of the Soviet Communist Party merely add legitimacy to their amoral activities, especially their violations of human rights? And won't citizen diplomacy simply generate false optimism about ending the Cold War and weaken the free world's resolve to meet the Soviet threat?

Can Citizen Diplomacy Affect the Soviet Union?

Some critics argue that, since the Soviet people have no real influence over their government's foreign policy, expectations that contacts with them will somehow change policy are naive. The common version of this criticism is that this hands-across-the-sea stuff is all very nice, but the Soviet people are not the problem, the Soviet government is. "Our problem with the Soviet Union is not the absence of communication," writes *Christian Science Monitor* columnist John Hughes, "it is the antithetical character of their society to democracy." Neoconservative commentator Irving Kristol goes further: " 'Liberalization' remains a fantasy. . . . The party still rules supreme, its Leninist orthodoxy intact; the Soviet people remain sullen, intimidated and coerced into passivity."

Many citizen diplomats respond by conceding that they do not know for sure whether they can affect policies of either the Soviet Union or the United States, but they feel they must try. Still, there are assumptions hidden in this criticism worth scrutiny. One is that there is a tremendous, uncrossable gulf between the Soviet "people" and the Soviet "government." Yet the closer one looks, the more the distinction blurs. For example, are the seventeen million members of the Soviet Communist Party, approximately 6 percent of the adult population, "people" or "government"?

Also underlying the critics' position is the assumption that working for the government is tantamount to being an unthinking robot. Yet even members of the Politburo, the Council of Ministers, and the Central Committee, while ostensibly unified behind a "party line," have potentially diverse values, interests, and opinions that can change in subtle ways as they meet and cooperate with Americans. George Breslauer, a noted professor of Soviet Studies at the University of California at Berkeley, observes: "When you are trying to run a society with over a quarter of a billion people, over an expanse of land that covers one-sixth of the earth's land surface, there will naturally be differences of temperament— differences that are bound to fuel political struggles." Many of the Soviets with whom the citizen diplomats work are not high-ranking Party members but still have positions that enable them to pull strings for joint Soviet-American projects within their own spheres of influence. For example, a television producer at Gosteleradio, the State Committee on Radio and Television, can have a great deal of influence on whether or not a Soviet-American "space bridge" will happen. Citizen diplomats also keep in mind that the Soviet teenagers with whom they spend an afternoon touring a city, sipping tea, and discussing politics could someday be elected to the Politburo.

Whether Soviet public opinion has any effect on the formation of

Soviet foreign policy is debatable, and the mechanisms by which it might are at best uncertain. But whispers on the assembly line, discussions on buses, and old-fashioned pillow talk all may play some role. The extent to which even an oligarchic dictatorship can afford to ignore the opinions of its own people is limited. Like all leaders, Soviet leaders want public support for their own prestige, and they need it, to some extent, in order to implement their policies successfully. There is evidence to suggest, for example, that growing Soviet public disenchantment over the war in Afghanistan is augmenting the Soviet government's desire to seek a face-saving way out. Even the most diehard skeptic would have to concede that some threshold exists at which Soviet public opinion is translated into policy. If everyone in the Soviet Union except for the Politburo and the Council of Ministers believed that the Soviet Union should stop building nuclear weapons, how long could the oligarchy hold out?

At the very least, the activities of the citizen diplomats may help to build Soviet public pressure for actions by the Soviet government that are consistent with its own "peace rhetoric." Within the power structures of the Soviet Union are "hawks" who believe that Soviet national security should be based primarily on military strength and "doves" who recognize that security in the nuclear age must be achieved primarily through stable relations, negotiations, and compromise with the West. The more Soviets who can learn firsthand about the West, who have American friends, and who become personally committed to preventing a nuclear confrontation, the more strength and backing government members favoring accommodation are likely to have.

The citizen diplomats' ideas and activities may have already begun to exert a subtle influence on Soviet foreign policy. Dusko Doder, Moscow correspondent for the *Washington Post*, observed in January 1985: "Lost in the unfolding East-West propaganda exchanges over the past two years is the extraordinary fact that the question of nuclear weapons has gradually entered Soviet public debate. . . . For a country devoid of real political discourse and given to obsessive secrecy, particularly about military matters, this is a significant turn of events."

In contrast to the tight reins the Politburo holds on foreign policy, its control over many domestic issues is less absolute. On issues that escape Western attention, particularly issues that do not directly challenge Communist ideology such as the quality of consumer goods, medical care, or education, public debate is tolerated and occasionally even encouraged. *Pravda,* for example, includes a "letters to the editor" section covering a number of well-circumscribed but important domestic issues. Occasionally these debates lead to actual changes in government policies. Widespread outrage in the 1960s over the pollution of Lake Baikal, the largest freshwater lake in the world, led to the closure of many industrial facilities operating there.

A few citizen diplomats have attempted to alter Soviet foreign policies by influencing these potentially more flexible Soviet domestic policies. Iowa farmers Roswell Garst and John Chrystal worked with the Soviets to improve their agricultural system because they believed a well-fed bear would be a lesser global menace than a hungry bear. Similarly, in an effort to minimize Soviet incentives to meddle in the Persian Gulf for oil, Frank von Hippel, an energy policy analyst from Princeton University, has worked with Soviet scientists to design and implement energy conservation programs.

American citizen diplomats do not expect their activities to transform the Soviet Union's attitude toward the United States overnight; many complicated, powerful, and contrary forces within the Soviet Union conspire to preserve the adversary context of the Cold War. Yet changes in Soviet policy can sometimes occur with surprising swiftness. In March 1986, former CIA director William Colby remarked: "Five years ago, if someone in the State Department had predicted that in five years the Soviets would stop nuclear testing unilaterally, agree to eliminate British and French arsenals from discussions on intermediate range weapons in Europe, and propose a fifty percent reduction in nuclear weapons stockpiles, we would have thrown them into the loony bin, but that's exactly what the Soviets have done."

Does Citizen Diplomacy Compromise Human Rights?

A second criticism leveled at some citizen diplomats is that working with members of the Soviet Communist Party legitimizes Soviet restrictions on Jewish emigration, repression of dissidents, and harassment of independent peace activists. If citizen diplomats really care about helping people, some critics contend, they should stop toasting to peace and friendship with Party members and instead demand that the Soviet government pull out of Eastern Europe, allow Jews to leave, and stop sending dissidents to labor camps and psychiatric institutions. Involvement with mainstream Soviets, critics add, should be strictly conditioned on concessions for oppressed groups. Dialogue, cooperation, and trade should not just be given away for nothing but rather used as leverage for real concessions.

This criticism is actively promulgated by many Soviet émigrés and supported by many Americans who are concerned with human rights. But it overlooks one fundamental reality: both superpowers have their fingers on a nuclear hair trigger. If the possibility of global incineration did not exist, and human rights were the only salient factor in Soviet-American relations, then conditioning cooperation on the liberalization of the Soviet system might be the only valid approach. In today's world, however, other objectives, including the prevention of nuclear war, have to be reconciled with human rights objectives.

The citizen diplomats do not seek to denigrate or ignore human rights issues, but simply to put them in the context of the possibility of nuclear war. Debating which is more important, human survival or human rights, is pointless; it is enough to admit that *both* are important, and that many different approaches to Soviet-American relations can have validity. While Amnesty International calls attention to Soviet denials of civil liberties, and the National Conference on Soviet Jewry campaigns for fewer barriers to emigration, the majority of citizen diplomats concentrate on the common interest of both superpowers in preventing nuclear war. They are focused on securing the ultimate human right—the right to life itself.

The citizen diplomats are also promoting Soviet human rights by creating innovative channels of dialogue that human rights organizations can use to voice their concerns more effectively. Some citizen diplomats use their relationships with Soviet officials to raise concerns about human rights directly. Such private expressions of concern, repeated often enough within an atmosphere of trust, may in some cases have more impact on Soviet human rights policies than the direct confrontational approach.

History suggests that a choice does not have to be made between working for Soviet human rights and working for global survival. During the era of détente, in the mid-1970s, restrictions on religious worship eased, permission for foreign travel increased, dissidents faced somewhat less persecution, and Jewish emigration figures skyrocketed, with nearly thirty thousand Soviet Jews granted exit visas in 1978 alone. During the renewed Cold War of the early 1980s, Jewish emigration slowed to a trickle, with only 1,085 visas granted in 1985. The Soviet government appears to view increased Jewish emigration as a concession to the West; if the United States seems uninterested in improving relations, the Soviet government will not throw away bargaining chips and get nothing in return.

While there is no guarantee that better relations will improve Soviet civil liberties, there is good reason to expect that they might. Some of the driving forces behind Soviet restrictions on its own citizens are spy-mania and xenophobia, which are grounded in fears that foreigners will once again invade and devastate the Soviet Union. If a permanent trans-formation of the relationship between the superpowers were to reduce this paranoia, it might eliminate some of the Soviet government's ra-tionale for continued repression.

How citizen diplomats should respond to the phenomenon known as the Soviet "independent peace movement" is another vociferously de-bated moral issue. How can citizen diplomats possibly speak with loyal Soviet citizens about peace, critics argue, when the real Soviet peace activists are being exiled or jailed? On June 4, 1982, Sergei Batovrin, a Moscow artist, and several other Soviet citizens announced the for-mation of what they called "The Group to Establish Trust Between the US and the USSR," the expressed purpose of which was to develop "a four-sided dialogue" among the governments and peoples of the United States and the Soviet Union. Nearly a thousand people signed the group's founding appeal, and sister groups sprang up in Leningrad, Odessa, Novosibirsk, and elsewhere.

The Soviet government reacted harshly to the group. The KGB con-fiscated an exhibit of eighty-eight antiwar paintings in Moscow and arrested several of the group's leaders. Batovrin was placed in a Moscow psychiatric hospital, where, he reported later, "They told me that in the Soviet Union only the government can work for peace." When Trust Group members tried to link Soviet and American peace activists by putting a list of US peace organizations in a thousand Moscow mailboxes, the government accused them of being linked to the CIA and told Batovrin to leave the country in a week. The Trust Group still exists, distributes peace buttons, literature, and posters, and welcomes Western visitors, but its members are subjected to regular harassment and interrogation; three leaders of the group were arrested in 1985. Trust Group members insist that they are not dissidents but simply want to magnify the edu-cational efforts of the official Soviet Peace Committee.

Critics argue that repression of the Trust Group proves what the Soviet government's "real" attitude toward peace is. But what it may really reveal is the Soviet government's nearly hysterical antipathy to groups who publicly try to work "outside the system," implicitly challenging the authority of the Communist Party and the State. According to Richard Baggett-Deats, director of the Fellowship of Reconciliation, who has perhaps spent more time with members of the Trust Group than any other Westerner, much of the Trust Group's "peace education" literature is very similar to the Soviet Peace Committee's literature. Batovrin's antiwar paintings were not confiscated because they promoted peace— dozens of crayoned antiwar paintings hang in every Soviet kindergarten—but because they were part of an unofficial exhibition organized by an unofficial movement. It is the Trust Group's method, not its message, that has provoked Soviet wrath.

Some citizen diplomats choose to meet with dissidents, Jewish refuseniks, and Trust Group members. Others believe that their efforts will be most effective if they are directed primarily at the mainstream of Soviet society. The most permanent and influential relationships with Soviets, say many citizen diplomats, are those that take into account the social, cultural, and legal realities of the country—relationships based on an understanding of how the Soviet Union *is* instead of how Americans wish it would be. They are convinced that the relationship between the superpowers will significantly change only when communication is established with people at *all* levels of Soviet society—dissidents and Politburo members, artists and factory workers, party bureaucrats and children.

Will Citizen Diplomacy Endanger National Security?

A final objection critics have raised is that the activities of the citizen diplomats may undermine America's ability to defend the free world. Despite all of their good intentions, the argument goes, citizen diplomats are unwittingly advancing the Soviet Union's foreign policy objectives. By going to the Soviet Union, seeing what the government wants them to see, and coming back to the United States with naive, rosy descriptions of Soviet life, they are perpetrating the dangerous notion that Communism is really not all that bad. And by uncritically reporting Soviet exhortations about its peaceful intentions, they themselves become spokepersons for the Soviet government, eroding our military resolve and strengthening the ability of the Soviet Union to continue—unopposed—its long history of hegemony and expansionism.

The first part of this criticism—that the Soviets have intentionally deceived visiting foreigners to bolster their image—certainly has historic validity and dates to pre-Revolutionary times. In 1787, Grigory Potemkin, Catherine the Great's intimate advisor, decided to impress a group of European visitors taking a cruise down the Crimea River by erecting painted façades and transporting peasants from miles away to create the illusion of real towns. In the 1930s and 1940s, many noted Americans were shown model facilities for health care, education, farming, and criminal rehabilitation, and returned home proclaiming the accomplishments of the Soviet state. In 1944, Henry Wallace, then vice-president of the United States, was given a tour of a Siberian forced labor camp in Magadan and came home comparing it to the Hudson Bay Company. Many years later, former Magadan inmates recalled how, in preparation for Wallace's visit, watch towers were razed, some prisoners were given their first and last holidays, shop windows were suddenly stuffed with goods, and prison secretaries became "prettily dressed swineherd girls at the model farm."

The Soviet government still tries to show its best side to visitors. And a small number of people on the fringe of the citizen diplomacy movement are so anxious to make peace with the Soviet Union that they refuse to confront its problems and defensively compare the Soviet Union's virtues to the United States' vices. These people, however, do not represent the mainstream of citizen diplomacy.

The true citizen diplomats are constantly seeking all sides of the story. They are acutely aware of how others have been duped and tend to distrust official rhetoric. They take advantage of every opportunity to sidestep prearranged tours and, instead, try to interact with Soviet people in the most informal, meaningful, and spontaneous ways possible. They are skilled at setting their own agendas and arranging their own contacts. They make no pretensions of bringing back the whole truth, but simply describe their own experiences and impressions, both good and bad.

Americans have nothing to fear from the citizen diplomats, whose descriptions of Soviet life challenge simplistic depictions of the Soviet Union as either a socialist paradise or an evil empire. As citizens of a democracy based on a "free marketplace of ideas," in which "the truth" is comprised of millions of conflicting views, we should rejoice that a movement has developed to provide inside, nonofficial, and meaningful information about the Soviet Union—information we desperately need to formulate wiser foreign policies. And if we still have doubts about the citizen diplomats' stories, the antidote to our skepticism is even more citizen diplomacy. It is possible to fool some of the people some of the time, but the more Americans who travel, meet, speak, and work with Soviets, the more likely all of us will be able to see behind "party lines" and Potemkin villages.

Citizen diplomacy is not a threat but an opportunity—a chance to transcend our despair that nuclear war may be inevitable and instead work to transform our adversaries, one by one, into our friends and partners. The power to remake Soviet-American relations into an exemplar for an era of enduring global peace is now in our hands. As Albert Einstein wrote at the advent of the nuclear age: "We cannot leave it to generals, Senators, and diplomats to work out a solution over a period of generations. . . . Today lack of interest would be a great danger, for there is much the average man can do."

❧❧❧

CHAPTER ONE

PHYSICIAN TO THE WORLD:

BERNARD LOWN

It could have been a moment of triumph for Dr. Bernard Lown and Dr. Yevgeny Chazov, the cofounders and copresidents of International Physicians for the Prevention of Nuclear War (IPPNW), the recipient of the 1985 Nobel Peace Prize. Instead, the press conference in Oslo, Norway, on the eve of the Nobel ceremony was becoming a mêlée; the international press corps they faced seemed less interested in hearing their "medical prescription" for averting nuclear catastrophe than in cross-examining them on human rights issues. Reporter after reporter asked: "Does Dr. Chazov regret signing a letter denouncing Andrei Sakharov?" Tension built in the stuffy, cramped room as the two physicians defended their organization.

Suddenly a Soviet television reporter slumped over in his chair, convulsing, in cardiac arrest. Lown, Chazov, and other officers of IPPNW raced to the stricken man's side, stripping off their jackets and taking turns thumping his chest and giving mouth-to-mouth resuscitation. Reporters frantically pushed one another to capture the moment on film; the doctors shouted for room to work. Twenty-five long minutes went by before an ambulance arrived, and when it did the Norwegian drivers, believing the man dead, refused to take him to a hospital. The IPPNW doctors insisted there was still a chance. Finally the rescue squad took away the Soviet man, now hooked up to an oxygen mask and an array of heart monitors.

Lown and Chazov, spent and shaken, resumed the press conference. "What you have just seen," said Lown, his voice quivering with emotion, "is a parable of our movement. When a crisis comes, when life is in danger, Soviet and American physicians cooperate. We do not ask the patient if he's communist or capitalist, atheist or believer. We forget ideology, we forget our differences. This individual was a victim of sudden cardiac death, which claims the lives of many many people. But the big issue confronting humankind today is sudden nuclear death."

The reporters listened, momentarily subdued. Headlines the next day read "Nobel-Winning Doctors Join to Save Reporter with Heart Attack in Oslo" instead of "Nobel Prize Goes to Anti-Sakharov Member of Soviet Government." Television and newspaper cameras caught the image of a Soviet doctor and an American doctor bending over the body of a man whose politics and nationality they neither knew nor cared about. Miraculously, the reporter survived and sustained no brain damage.

It was a macabre stroke of luck for IPPNW—so much so that a few suspicious journalists believed at first that the event had been staged by Soviet operatives, until the indisputable evidence of the heart monitors quelled such speculation. Still, as Lown and Chazov staggered from the room in exhaustion, one Western journalist shouted after them, "If that had been Sakharov, would you have saved him?" Another Western journalist turned to his colleague and swore at him in amazed disgust.

When the 1985 Nobel Peace Prize was announced, Dr. Bernard Lown knew that it meant an unprecedented elevation to worldwide prominence for the physicians' group. He also knew that a bitter controversy over the nature of the organization would soon be unleashed. "Before we were nothing to worry about, we were just a little flea," he says. "Now suddenly we were a threat. I did not know where the shoe would fall, but the logic of course was that Chazov would be the fall guy."

Lown was right—the criticism was inevitable. To many, there is something structurally disconcerting about IPPNW. Its existence implies that a high-ranking Soviet physician might be able to place his own politics second to a belief in the necessity of preventing nuclear war. It implies that concerned citizens of East and West can agree on steps toward solving the problems of the arms race and nuclear war while continuing to disagree on human rights and other issues. It implies that the Soviet government is not monolithic or incapable of change. It implies many things that, if widely known, could shake the foundations of the Cold War.

And that is exactly what Bernard Lown hoped IPPNW would do when he first persuaded his friend and medical colleague, Yevgeny Chazov, to join his efforts to prevent nuclear war. "People intuitively feel that if we are to get out of this dreadful impasse, we have to begin a dialogue of people to people, of scientist to scientist," he says. "What we have done is create an ambience, a certain atmosphere in the world in which it is no longer permissible to talk glibly about nuclear war."

A world-renowned cardiologist, the inventor of the direct-current defibrillator, the originator of the modern coronary care unit, Lown could chair any department of cardiology in the world and hardly look at a patient again in his life. He chooses instead to maintain a hectic private group practice, conduct laboratory research, teach at the Harvard School of Public Health, and make the rounds on patients at the Brigham and Women's Hospital in Boston with medical students and cardiology fellows tagging along eager to learn something from his famed bedside manner. "Lown has an inexhaustible pool of energy. He works nights, weekends, all the time," says Tom Graboys, a young cardiologist who works with Lown. "He's a wonderful teacher and an amalgamation of humanist and scientist that is very rare these days." Adds fellow Harvard cardiologist and IPPNW cofounder James Muller: "There's a magical air about him in the way he deals with patients"

Lown is opinionated, visionary, indefatigable, combative, uncompromising, demanding of himself and others, and unafraid to challenge conventional wisdom— qualities that have earned him foes as well as supporters in the medical world. Even as a cardiologist he is known as something of a maverick. He believes that medicine's reliance on technological fixes has gotten out of hand and wages a private battle for the removal of unnecessary pacemakers. He preaches and practices a renewed emphasis on the patient-physician relationship as an essential element in healing His research suggesting that many unnecessary coronary bypass operations are performed in this country has sparked a fierce controversy in the field.

Yet his contribution to medicine has been so profound and his competence so unquestioned that even his controversial leadership in the antinuclear weapons movement has not diminished his prestige as a physician. "Bernie's triumph is that he is such a spectacular scientist that no one has been able to restrain the growth of his career," says H. Jack Gieger, another leader in the physicians' peace movement. Norman Cousins has called Lown "the Albert Schweitzer of our times."

Lown is a slightly rotund man of average height, who has a rounded, animated face and a few locks of brown hair spanning the otherwise bald top of his head. His most striking features are his eyes—hazel, vibrant, full of humor and compassion. An array of smile wrinkles fans from his eyes, and a bent grin often hovers on his face, giving him a quizzical but kindly look. His white coat has "B. LOWN, M.D." embroidered in blue on a pocket. His small, unpretentious office across from Harvard Medical School in Boston is decorated with pictures of his grandchildren and various diplomas. An old-fashioned alarm clock ticks on his desk.

One of the keys to success for the physicians' peace movement has been the doctors' persistent definition of the prevention of nuclear war as a *medical* issue. For Lown, this is not merely convenient imagery designed to attract attention; he takes it quite literally. "As a physician, I feel I have a responsibility to address the major medical catastrophe facing humankind," he says. "Since no effective medical response to nuclear war is possible, physicians have a duty to work for its prevention." He believes that healing a planet threatened by a potentially terminal illness is the greatest medical challenge he has ever faced. And as long as his patient has a heartbeat, no matter how unsteady, he is not going to give up.

"We have been trapped in a catch-22 situation wherein the growing arsenals of genocide stimulate distrust, while the distrust propels the further accumulation of weapons of mass extermination. The climate of fear and distrust leads, in addition, to perceptual distortions, with complex differences between diverse social systems reduced to martial combat between forces of good and evil. The imagined enemy eventually is extruded from the human family and reduced to an inanimate object whose annihilation is devoid of moral dimension. We physicians are duty-bound to reverse these potentially life-threatening tendencies."

Lown speaks slowly, deliberately, with tremendous energy behind each syllable. His first language was Yiddish, and his arguments still carry a trace of the inflections of the Lithuanian shtetl where he was born, an almost Talmudic tendency to pose questions in order to supply answers. His upper-middle-class Jewish family, wary of Hitler, emigrated to Maine in 1935, and Lown learned English as a determined and precocious fourteen-year-old. Years of poring over English dictionaries have made him passionately fond of words, of the feel and texture of language. He is not self-conscious using words like "jeremiad" or "prognostication."

"If we engage in a dialogue with our so-called 'enemy,' meet him face-to-face, and share common endeavors with him, then the myth of the demonic 'other' begins to dissipate," he declares. "Paranoid fantasies of a dehumanized adversary cannot withstand the pressures of reality. We must contribute to the growth of mutual understanding between East and West, for without it nuclear disarmament will not be initiated and, if initiated, will not be sustained. The special role physicians have in our society has enabled our movement to penetrate the psychologic fog of denial and public apathy to help millions of people for the first time confront the unthinkable reality of nuclear war."

Lown traces his initiation into antinuclear activism to another Nobel Peace Prize laureate, Sir Philip John Noel-Baker, the British statesman who won the 1959 award for his disarmament proposals. In 1960 Lown attended a speech by Noel-Baker in Cambridge, Massachusetts, and was deeply moved by his presentation on the consequences of nuclear testing and the threats to humankind posed by the spiraling arms race. Doctors, said Noel-Baker, ought to play a special role in publicizing the dangers of radioactive fallout and the consequences of a nuclear war. Lown and two other physician friends present, Sidney Alexander and Roy Menninger, took his message to heart and decided that night to call together some friends and begin studying the issue. The next week the first meeting of Physicians for Social Responsibility (PSR) took place in Lown's living room.

What they learned, from reading and discussing books and articles, appalled them. "After a year of discussion I was going beserk," recalls Lown. "It was time to take action." He helped persuade his less politically minded colleagues that PSR should draft a series of articles on the medical aspects of nuclear weapons for the prestigious *New England Journal of Medicine*. The first article, entitled "The Physician's Role in the Postattack Period" and written by Victor Sidel, H. Jack Geiger, and Lown, appeared in 1962. More remarkable than Lown's getting the group to write it was his getting the medical journal to publish it. "It was his sheer force of persuasion and his personality that got the article accepted," recalls Sidney Alexander.

The article detailed the effects of a nuclear attack on the city of Boston. "In the Boston area (hit by 10 megatons each on Boston and Cambridge and 8 megatons on Bedford), about 1,000,000 people will be killed on the first day and about 1,250,000 will be injured. Of the injured, approximately 1,000,000 die. . . . Some 4800 physicians would be killed or fatally injured, 1000 would be injured, and only about 650 would remain uninjured. . . . The data . . . yield a ratio of approximately 1700 acutely injured persons to each functioning physician," states the article in a flat, clinical tone. "It follows that most of the fatally injured persons will never see a physician, even for the simple administration of narcotics, before they die."

After discussing the destruction of medical facilities, the nature of injuries, the likelihood of widespread epidemics, and the limitations of civil defense measures, the article concludes that "since it is impossible to prepare adequately for every possible type of nuclear attack the physician's responsibility goes beyond mere disaster planning. Physicians, charged with the responsibility for the lives of their patients and the health of their communities, must also explore a new area of preventive medicine, the prevention of nuclear war."

Other articles soon followed and were collected for a book called *The Fallen Sky* that was influential in the campaign to halt atmospheric nuclear tests. In a nationwide study conducted with several other groups, PSR researchers demonstrated conclusively that strontium 90 from radioactive fallout was moving through the food chain and winding up in children's teeth and bones. In 1963 public pressure persuaded the US Senate to ratify the Limited Test Ban Treaty signed by the United States, the Soviet Union, and the United Kingdom. But after this early success, PSR became dormant as its leaders were swept up in the civil rights movement or anti-Vietnam War efforts. "After the partial test ban victory, it was clear to me that the nuclear war issue would fade into history, because humanity was finally understanding the dangers," remarks Lown ruefully. "The big issue was Vietnam." In 1964, Lown helped organize a medical relief effort to bring Vietnamese children suffering from severe napalm burns to the United States for treatment.

He also turned his attention back to his specialty, sudden cardiac death syndrome, the inexplicable, instantaneous breakdown of the heart's normal rhythm recognized as the United States' leading cause of death, claiming more than four hundred thousand lives a year. In 1959, after staying up three nights with a patient suffering from an arrhythmia (a rapid and irregular heartbeat), Lown plugged in an alternating-current defibrillator, a machine used to give patients whose hearts had stopped a last-ditch electrical shock, and in desperation applied the shock to the patient's chest *before* his heart stopped beating. This had never been done before, and the hospital and its lawyers were not pleased. The patient, however, recovered admirably and left in a few days for a Florida vacation.

Lown refined his technique, discovering a form of direct-current shock that jolted the heart into a normal rhythm without damaging heart tissue. His methods were considered outlandish by some; he had difficulty funding his research and his first paper describing the technique, which he named "cardioversion," was rejected by a peer reviewer. But after Lown began successfully treating life-threatening arrhythmias and resuscitating patients who would otherwise have died, his direct-current defibrillator became a universally used tool in the management of heart disease. Lown also introduced the drug lidocaine for the treatment of arrhythmias, which has reduced mortality by 40 percent among those afflicted by heart attacks, and in 1964 he organized the first modern coronary care unit at the Brigham Hospital in Boston.

Despite these successes, Lown was still frustrated by a lack of research funds and attention. "The medical profession remained insouciant to the issue of sudden cardiac death. It was deemed an act of God, a bolt of lightning, an unpredictable, instantaneous event. This bothered me very deeply, because I felt it was an answerable question." In what he calls a "very calculated, opportunistic move on my part," Lown decided to put the innate competitiveness between the United States and the Soviet Union to good use. "If I get Russian doctors excited about this issue," he reasoned, "then American doctors will immediately find it interesting."

He journeyed to the Soviet Union for the first time in 1968 as a special guest lecturer of the Soviet Academy of Medical Sciences. There he renewed his acquaintance with Dr. Yevgeny Chazov, "a young, bright, rapidly upcoming cardiologist" with dark red hair, a chunky build, and a passion for hard work and hunting wild boar. (They had first met in 1966 at a cardiology conference in New Delhi, India.) While most of the Soviets listening to Lown's 1968 lecture appeared to think that sudden cardiac death was only a large problem in stressful capitalistic countries, Lown and Chazov agreed that if Americans and Soviets were to work together on sudden cardiac death and develop a "Soviet-American method" for treatment, it also might have an impact on the Cold War. "If Russians are saving American lives and Americans are saving Russian lives," Lown told Chazov, "then we cannot hold each other as the ultimate archenemy." Chazov was intrigued by the idea but didn't know quite how to make it happen.

An opportunity came about four years later, with détente and a series of cooperative health agreements between the United States and the Soviet Union. One agreement enabled either country to call in the other's medical experts for a consultation whenever someone in high circles became ill. In 1972, the State Department telephoned Lown and told him to pack his bags for the Soviet Union—a Kremlin big shot needed his ministrations. When Lown arrived, he was astonished to discover that the person had kidney disease, not a heart problem. "I was absolutely surprised that the Russians were so backward that they would call *me* to see a kidney patient," he recalls. The next day, however, the mystery was solved—an official at the Ministry of Health asked him to discuss sudden cardiac death with a number of leading Soviet physicians. The Soviets had now, apparently, decided it was a major health problem, and had used the excuse of a sick official to bring the American expert to the Soviet Union as quickly as possible.

A Soviet-American cooperative study on sudden cardiac death was soon added to the existing agreements. Lown was selected to organize the American side of the study, and Chazov directed the Soviet side. They worked together closely for the next five years.

"I liked Chazov, firstly because he was very hardworking in a society where people tend to have long coffee breaks, come in late, and leave work early," remembers Lown. "He was rounding in hospitals, he was teaching, he was doing research, and he was building this massive new institute, the cardiovascular research center of the Soviet Union. He was an ultrabusy human being, an executive who was driving himself from seven in the morning to the wee hours of the night, seven days a week. And he was moving in very high circles—by the 1970s he was the head physician for the Kremlin group, which means he took care of all the members of the Politburo. But though he was serious-minded, he liked to have fun. He loved to sing and drink and be joyful and show friendship. He loved a good party. He was a very warm-hearted human being, and he was easily moved by emotion, by kind deeds.

"I liked him also," continues Lown, "for his integrity. He was an honest guy, he would tell me the way things were, there was no pretending the way many Soviets would do. He would not go around saying, 'Oh, yes, we have it too,' no matter what you said, which is an attitude that is utterly grating to Americans, who think they must be the top dog in everything."

As their friendship deepened, Lown and Chazov discussed many topics, but only once the possibility of nuclear war. "I predicted in 1978 to Chazov that we are entering a very terrible time, when the Cold War is going to come back again. He absolutely thought I was crazy. He looked at me and said, 'Don't say it, you don't know what you're talking about.' 'The arms race is going to accelerate,' I repeated, like an old and gray prophet disseminating doom."

The nuclear issue began to preoccupy Lown in 1978. Even before the invasion of Afghanistan, detente was showing definite signs of fraying around the edges. "I began to develop great qualms and great uneasiness, because although Carter was talking of peace, he was also building more missiles, and it was clear that we were talking one thing and doing another," recalls Lown. "And the Russians were rapidly catching up, and that was no good, because it would give further spurt to Americans who wanted to 'be ahead.' I saw we were building a massive insecurity system for the world, and this conclusion led me to sleepless nights, to irritability—I became very hard to live with."

Lown thought back to his speeches and writings about the test ban and the arms race in the 1960s. "It became clear to me that it wasn't enough just to talk about the medical consequences of nuclear war. Over and over we heard the same five muddled words: 'We can't trust the Russians.' And since the analogy was that it takes two to tango, then if we do not have a responsive Russian partner, there's nothing we can do. This conclusion reinforced in people a sense of helplessness, evoked massive cynicism, and enhanced the very bad tendency of hating the Russians, *because they make me helpless*. The individual tends to victimize the source of his difficulty.

"It became clear to me that the nidus of the pathology, the very core of it, was a Cold War mentality that built up the image of an enemy. Unless we confronted the Soviet issue, and confronted it in such a way as to bring it into the American living room, into the American consciousness, we would never get off this terrible trajectory of missiles speeding toward the extinction of mankind." He pauses. "I am not trying to be dramatic in my verbiage, but I am very convinced that the present course inexorably leads to war.

"The question was: What could doctors do? And the answer it seemed to me was that we and the Soviets must build an organization that will bring a dialogue to our colleagues in the first place and to our patients in the second place. We are dealing with a complex process and we have to develop a popular constituency of massive magnitude in *both* countries, because Russia has also its military people who are very eager to be on par with the United States and build more nuclear weapons and get the latest technology. We must develop a people's diplomacy and a people's dialogue to negotiate a deeper understanding of one another, thereby diminishing the fear and paranoia, and thereby undermining the process that supplies the petrol for this engine of death riding roughshod over all of our interests."

In the fall of 1978, Lown wrote a letter to Dmitri Venedictov, Deputy Minister of Health in the Soviet Union, suggesting that they meet to discuss arranging a conference of Soviet and American doctors focused on the medical aspects of nuclear war. "I knew Venedictov and Chazov equally well, and in making the choice I assumed that Venedictov was the more important Russian," Lown remembers.

That same year, James Muller, a young cardiology instructor at Harvard Medical School, also began thinking about the need to launch some sort of Soviet-American physicians' organization that would publicize the medical effects of nuclear war. In 1968, as a medical student at Johns Hopkins, Muller attempted to start a medical student exchange program with the Soviet Union and spent six months studying at the First Moscow Medical Institute. A few years later, as an assistant to an administrator in the Public Health Service, he helped draft some of the language of the cooperative health agreements signed by Nixon and Brezhnev in 1972. In 1975, under the terms of one of these agreements, he conducted cardiological research in Moscow for three months, supervising a team of twenty Soviet doctors.

Muller knew the Russian language; Lown had the high-level contacts; both were confident that the Soviets would be interested. They met in late 1978 to discuss possibilities. But Venedictov did not answer Lown's letter. In February 1979 Lown wrote a similar letter to Chazov, but again received no reply.

"I was very perturbed," admits Lown, "but what went through my mind was that I was not going to give up easily, and if I was rebuffed I'd come back for more punishment. I thought Chazov might deem me a nut, but that was a worthwhile price to pay. I figured that if I didn't hear from him, I'd send another letter. And then go to the Soviet Union. If he gave me an equivocating answer I'd come back and back and back—I'd wear him down or else he'd tell me to go to hell."

Five months after he had written to Chazov, Lown serendipitously met a visiting Soviet physician in Boston who happened to work at Chazov's cardiological institute. Lown invited her to his house for Sunday brunch and placed a hastily written second letter in her hands for personal delivery. More months went by with no word.

Finally, in October 1979 Lown received a letter from Chazov endorsing the concept of a Soviet-American physicians' effort to prevent nuclear war. Chazov took Lown's arguments a step further by emphasizing that the current arms race was already exacting a toll on humanity. "Nobody has measured the real losses which are inflicted on mankind," wrote Chazov, "by the uncertainty of the next day, fear of thermonuclear disaster, and encouragement of the most brutish instincts in man by militarism."

Meanwhile, during 1979, the dormant Physicians for Social Responsibility had been rapidly revived by a group of young Boston doctors, chief among them Australian-born pediatrician Helen Caldicott, whose impassioned speeches on the health effects of the nuclear fuel cycle were beginning to rouse thousands. In March 1979 PSR had the odd good fortune to publish a full-page ad in the *New England Journal of Medicine* about the dangers of nuclearism on the same day the Three Mile Island nuclear reactor suffered a loss-of-coolant accident. Hundreds of letters poured in; PSR became a national organization overnight. The doctors benefited from fortuitous timing again when they planned a Cambridge, Massachusetts, symposium on the medical effects of nuclear war for February 1980, just after the invasion of Afghanistan and the collapse of Soviet-American relations. They expected a hundred people to attend; seven hundred showed up, the national media covered the event, and PSR's message leapt into the public consciousness.

Money was collected at the symposium to pay for a full-page open letter in the *New York Times* to Jimmy Carter and Leonid Brezhnev suggesting, among other things, that Soviet and American doctors should work together to publicize the medical effects of nuclear war. A few weeks after the ad appeared, Anatoly Dobrynin, the Soviet ambassador to the United States, responded by telling three PSR leaders—Helen Caldicott, James Muller, and Eric Chivian, a psychiatrist at MIT—that a representative of their group could travel to Moscow and begin making arrangements for a Soviet-American physicians' conference on nuclear war. The PSR leaders said that Lown was in London and could go to Moscow immediately if visas could be arranged. Dobrynin said he would arrange them. At a press conference, PSR announced that Lown was on his way to Moscow. The *Washington Post* ran the story and it was picked up by the *International Herald Tribune* in Europe.

"The first *I* knew about any of this," recalls Lown, "was when I was about to give a cardiology lecture in London and the guy who introduced

me said, 'I hear you're going to Moscow.' They simply volunteered me."
Within two days Lown and his wife Louise had received Soviet visas
and were on their way. Chazov met them at the Moscow airport on a
snowy evening in April 1980.

Although Chazov had given his blessing to the idea of a bilateral
physicians' organization focused on nuclear war, he was reluctant to
become personally involved. "Chazov didn't really know what this was
all about; he didn't know what doctors could do," says Lown. "Chazov's
problem was not that anyone would slap his wrist, but was it worth it
for him to commit his great prestige and his scarce time to an effort that
wouldn't wash historically."

That evening, Lown unleashed all of his powers of persuasion. He
outlined in detail the effects of a nuclear bomb on a city, and remembers
that "Chazov was really shaken up by that. He was a cardiologist, giving
all of his time to his work, and like most American cardiologists he just
knew, 'Yeah, nuclear war is bad and I'm opposed to it.' But the nitty-
gritty of what a nuclear bomb does he did not know too much about. He
hadn't faced up to the fact that there can be no medical response, that
World War II was piddling in comparison, that we would be launching
a World War II every hour for four thousand hours consecutively, that
nothing would be left but rubble.

"Then I talked about the moralistic tradition in medicine, how the
morality of physicians compels us to get involved. There's no way we
can stay out of it. If there was an epidemic threatening to engulf the
Soviet Union and the United States, we would drop everything and plunge
into it like there was no tomorrow.

"And then I talked of Soviet suffering, and how deeply the antiwar
tradition is immersed in their souls, and how if a Russian cannot be
active on this issue then he is not really behaving true to his colors.
Oh, I utilized that, I became very harsh and very provocative." He
pauses. "And whatever swayed him, I do not know."

Chazov has since described telling his daughter Galina that night how
a crazy American physician had said that he wasn't doing enough for
medicine despite his sixteen hours of cardiological work a day, and that
physicians had a responsibility to try to prevent nuclear war. His daughter told him she thought Lown was right. "My whole family told me,"
Chazov says, " 'You should be involved in this. You have a grand-
child.' "

For five hours the next day Chazov listened and took notes while

Lown laid out the group's guiding principles: political neutrality, a single-issue focus, and the eventual goal of inciting such moral outrage against nuclear weapons "that no politician would dare be associated with them." But it was difficult for Chazov to understand how an apolitical group could work on what was clearly a political issue. "I kept saying," remembers Lown, "that we are drawing from a humanistic tradition rather than a political tradition. I kept saying that we cannot favor our respective governments' positions." The enemy, he declared, would not be the United States or the Soviet Union, but the nuclear weapons themselves.

Elated by Chazov's willingness to cooperate, Lown flew home and quickly began organizing details with other PSR leaders. IPPNW was soon incorporated and about twenty prominent American physicians met in July 1980 to lay further plans. Already, however, a difficulty had emerged. Lown had asked Chazov to send a letter addressed to American physicians, signed by top Soviet physicians, expressing their concern about nuclear war. The letter had arrived, but it proved to be nothing they wanted to publicize. "It began with nice genuflections to antinuclearism, but then it says, we know who's responsible," recalls Lown. "It's American imperialism that derives profit from the arms race, blah blah. It was a vituperative political tract. So we buried it."

Lown attributes the letter to continued Soviet incomprehension of how this effort could be apolitical. "Chazov assumed that I wanted to develop a movement that attacked American imperialism. It was *very* difficult for the Soviets to understand that there had to be a certain symmetry, that we were starting a new type of dialogue. It was so un-Marxian, so against Soviet theology, to have a dialogue addressing an enemy that is an inanimate object rather than a person or a class or a society."

After reading this letter, Lown says, "It became clear to me that we had to have it out with the Russians. Really lay it on the table and say that if you're going to pursue this kind of policy, we're never going to have a movement, let's forget it. Let's quit right now and become enemies." Lown and Chazov agreed to hold a planning meeting in Geneva in December 1980. Lown brought James Muller and Eric Chivian, and Chazov brought Dr. Leonid Ilyin, head of the radiological commission in the USSR, and Dr. Mikhail Kuzin, the director of the Vishnevsky Surgery Institute in Moscow. The Americans knew that they would have to discuss American perceptions of the Soviet Union and the dangers of being pigeonholed as a pro-Soviet group. They also hoped to convince the Soviets that any explicit condemnation of either government's foreign or internal policies would be ruinous. But, says Lown, "there was no unanimity among the three of us as to how best to do this."

Muller brought to Geneva articles from *Time* and *Newsweek* criticizing the Soviet Union, and letters from American doctors, with their signatures whited out, dismissing the notion of IPPNW. Said one letter: "The Soviets won't listen to a distinguished scientist like Sakharov, so how will they listen to doctors, whom they hold in low esteem?" When he read one of these letters aloud on the first day, says Muller, "Kuzin got irate. He stood up and started yelling at me, and he drew a map of the Soviet Union and said, 'This is the way we view the situation, please draw for me the American military bases around the Soviet Union.'" Recalls Lown: "Kuzin said 'I didn't come all the way from Moscow to listen to anti-Soviet propaganda, I thought we came here to discuss nuclear war.' And he walked out."

Muller turned pale. Ilyin restively paced the floor. Chazov sat in a chair with an inscrutable look on his face. "I sort of pulled things together at that point," remembers Lown, "and said 'Look, let's forget about it. Our intent was not to red-bait you but to indicate the climate in the United States.'" At dinner that night, Muller apologized to Kuzin but reiterated his earlier points about the need to avoid playing political favorites. "Again Kuzin flared," Muller recalls, "but not as much and finally he said to me, 'We have the same kind of problems, and that's why we have to stick to the medical path.'"

The incident was painful, but it got the point across. "The Soviets decided that we should strictly limit our efforts to the medical issues of nuclear war, which was exactly what we had hoped would happen," says Muller. "The Russians and we," adds Lown, "now understood precisely the boundaries we could not overstep. We all understood that we will not only find it unpalatable to deal with political issues, we will not survive if we do so."

The Soviets describe the meeting in similar terms. Says Chazov: "In Geneva we discussed a large number of topics—Sakharov, Afghanistan, Nicaragua, Chile—but after two days of discussion we understood that the main thing that is really important today for humankind is the right to life." Kuzin says simply: "We pay attention to the problem that unites us, not the problems that divide us."

The incident, says Lown, also "brought to the surface the massiveness of their patriotism, the intensity of their feelings, the fact that they identify strongly with their government, and we were not going to budge them from that. If we had illusions that we were going to create an independent or dissident peace movement, this meeting showed that this was a cultural unreality. We would have to accept the Russians where they were and begin our education in that fashion."

The four founding principles of IPPNW agreed on at Geneva were (1) they would focus exclusively on nuclear war, (2) their work would be part of their professional commitment to protect life and preserve health, (3) they would seek wide publicity of their findings in both countries, and (4) they would not take a position on the specific policies of any government. While the group might make some general recommendations on logical next steps for arms control, it would not criticize, support, or blame specific weapons systems or policies of either side.

Jubilant, the three American doctors flew home, hired a small staff and began fund-raising for their first IPPNW Congress, to be held near Washington, DC, in March 1981, a mere three months away. A Harvard medical student, Jamie Traver, found IPPNW a free office on the second floor of a nearby drugstore, and about twenty of his classmates spent a weekend painting and renovating it. "It was a wonderful grass-roots office," remembers Muller. "To prevent nuclear war you walked through the drugstore past the toothpaste section, then up the back stairs past all the mops and brooms toward this huge picture of Einstein at the top of the stairs."

To attract the American press, Lown suggested to Chazov that they invite Georgy Arbatov, a key Soviet official and director of the Institute for US and Canada Studies, to speak at the congress. Chazov agreed. But even though Arbatov was "balanced" on the program by such eminent American figures as George Kistiakowsky, Harvard professor and science advisor to three American presidents, and Wolfgang Panofsky, the Stanford physicist, Lown later began worrying that Arbatov might overtly criticize United States nuclear policy and ruin IPPNW's fledgling apolitical image. When he met the Soviets at the airport, he took Chazov aside, asking him to please emphasize to Arbatov the importance of talking about the issue rather than who was to blame. Apparently Chazov did so. The political overtones in Arbatov's speech, while present, were restrained, and even skeptical American delegates had to laugh at his quip, "Doctors of the world, unite!"

Although the original concept had been a bilateral Soviet-American group, so many physicians from other countries wanted to join that membership in IPPNW was opened to physicians anywhere in the world.

The first congress attracted seventy-three physicians from twelve countries, who met for three days to discuss such topics as the number of people likely to be killed in a nuclear war, the inadequacy of medicine to mitigate its consequences, and the social, economic, and psychological costs of the arms race. Few speakers were as riveting as Michitu Ichimaru, a Japanese physician who spoke of the effects of nuclear bombs not as a theoretical possibility but as a personal memory. He had been a medical student in Nagasaki when the atomic bomb was dropped in 1945.

Although the meeting in Geneva had created consensus among the Soviet and American leaders, the congress revealed a wide variety of opinions among members of the American delegation concerning how "activist" IPPNW should be. At one extreme were those who envisioned IPPNW as simply a forum for sharing scientific data among physicians. At the other extreme were those who felt that IPPNW should make specific recommendations to superpower leaders about how to reduce the risk of war. During what came to be called "the long night" at the conference, these factions clashed over whether to sign a letter to Brezhnev and Reagan calling for a summit meeting. Several prominent doctors refused to sign, arguing that this was too political a move—given that Brezhnev had already publicly called for a summit and Reagan had already said he wasn't interested. Others refused to sign *any* letter addressed to the heads of state.

But Lown, Muller, and Chivian had already promised the Soviets in Geneva that they would send such a letter. The wrangling went on until past 3 A.M. Chazov went to bed thinking that he had invested his prestige in a movement that was going to fall apart. Lown was in agony with a bleeding gastric ulcer. All of his attempts to hammer out compromise language for the letter had failed. Finally, at 4 A.M., Lown laid down an ultimatum: We are sending the letter, and those who don't feel like signing it can leave the organization. "Here he had negotiated and negotiated, and tried to get a letter everyone liked," recalls Muller, "but when it came right down to it he just made a decision."

The letter to Brezhnev and Reagan stated that nuclear war "would in its very beginning kill tens to hundreds of millions of people. Most of the immediate survivors, suffering from wounds and burns, affected by nuclear radiation, deprived of effective medical care or even water or food, would face the prospect of a slow and excruciating death." Rather than calling for a summit, the doctors recommended "intense collaboration among the nuclear powers" to halt the arms race. The congress was reported widely in both the American and Soviet press. An article in *Pravda*, March 22, 1981, summarized the physicians' conclusions and quoted Lown as saying that "nuclear bombs are not weapons in the traditional understanding of the term, but instruments of genocide."

A second IPPNW congress, held in Cambridge, England, in March 1982, attracted more than 196 participants from thirty-one countries and focused on the effects of a nuclear war on Europe. Chazov was not able to attend this congress for health reasons, and the head of the Soviet delegation, Nikolai Blokhin, who had not attended the Geneva meeting, appeared less aware of the need to steer clear of politics. The Soviets brought boxes of a book called *The Danger of Nuclear War: Soviet Physicians' Viewpoint* to give to the delegates. Although most of the book repeated the scentific data agreed on at the first congress, it also specifically criticized America's neutron bomb, Pershing II missiles, and cruise missiles. Lown was furious; the Soviets insisted this was a Soviet book, not an IPPNW book; the Western doctors worried that the press would be incapable of making such distinctions, and surreptitiously asked some medical students to hide the books until they could be distributed in a low-key fashion at the end of the congress.

A second controversy erupted over civil defense, a topic then much in the news. President Reagan had asked for a huge budget increase for US civil defense programs and his Deputy Undersecretary for Defense, T. K. Jones, had stated in the *Los Angeles Times* that it would only take two to four years for the United States to recover fully from an all-out nuclear war. At the same time, US officials pointed to the Soviet Union's civil defense program as evidence of Soviet preparations to survive a retaliatory strike after launching a first strike against the United States. Up for final approval at the last plenary session of the congress was a "working group" document stating unequivocally that "the belief that a nation possessing nuclear weapons has an effective civil defense program could be seen as provocative to its adversary and is consequently destabilizing. . . . We conclude that there can be no effective civil defense against nuclear war." Signing this statement would imply for the first time that the Soviet physicians explicitly disagreed with some aspect of their government's policy. After some debate, the Soviet physicians approved the document. The delegates also approved a call for a nuclear freeze, a no-first-use policy by the superpowers, and the goal of the eventual elimination of all nuclear weapons.

Western press coverage of the second congress was not as widespread as that of the first, and IPPNW leaders began wondering what they could do to capture world attention again. US diplomats told the physicians privately that they were unimpressed by the Soviets' extensive newspaper coverage of the first two congresses, saying that until they went on television in the Soviet Union they wouldn't have an impact. During a meeting with Dobrynin in the spring of 1982, Lown and Muller launched a "casual balloon" of an idea: Why not have a round-table discussion of Soviet and American physicians talking about the medical aspects of nuclear war broadcast on Soviet television? "Why not?" responded Dobrynin. Arrangements were quickly made with Gosteleradio, the Soviet television station.

On June 24, 1982, six physicians sat at a large round table in a Moscow television studio, ruffling papers and trying to appear calm as photographers and reporters circled them in a vaguely predatory way. The Americans had insisted that the show not be edited, cut, or censored in any way; that it be aired on Soviet prime time without comment; and that the Western press be allowed to witness the taping of the show. Most of the journalists present were convinced that the program would never be aired, or, if it was, it would be tailored to fit Soviet propaganda. Though the doctors had agreed upon a general list of topics, there were no scripts.

"My colleagues and I are privileged and delighted to be able to address the people of the Soviet Union in this completely uncensored and un-rehearsed television broadcast," began Lown. "The multiplying stock-piles of nuclear weapons, with ever-increasing destructiveness, threaten us all with unimaginable catastrophe." Chazov nodded his head and added, "It was our desire to protect life on earth that brought us, people of different nationalities, of different political and religious views, to-gether in this movement."

The program unfolded smoothly. John Pastore, a cardiologist at Tufts University Medical School, recited the exact effects of the bomb on Hiroshima. Soviet radiation expert Leonid Ilyin gave statistics about the probable outcome of a nuclear war in Europe. Mikhail Kuzin detailed the inadequacy of any medical response to such a war. James Muller spoke about the danger of a nuclear war being triggered by misunder-standing or accident.

Through it all, Lown followed the thread of the discussion keenly, jotting notes, often interrupting with questions, and fighting an agonizing internal battle that no one suspected. Should he, or should he not, bring up civil defense? It was not on the agreed-upon list of topics for the show and he knew he risked destroying the entire program. But he wanted the show to intrigue the Western press and he knew "this would really test the waters of the no-censorship rule."

Midway through the show he seized an opportunity. "I want to say a thing that is a little break in our discussion," he declared briskly. "There has been much controversy about civil defense. It's clear that shelter programs in targeted areas will become crematoria with the exhaustion of oxygen from firestorms and the accumulation of noxious gases. So the next policy is, 'let's evacuate populations.' But this is *insane*," he said, his voice warbling into a high register. "It makes an assumption that we know where the bombs are going to fall. It makes an assumption that we know what their size is. It makes an assumption about weather conditions and the wind, which will carry radiation."

As Lown spoke, Chazov took off his glasses and began slowly turning them over in his fingers. He licked his lips a few times. But he did not interrupt or contradict Lown, who was warming to his subject.

"And furthermore, there are negative aspects. It fosters a sense of hope for people, that somehow there is safety in this type of measure. And lastly," said Lown, leaning across the table, wagging his finger, and looking Chazov square in the eye, "it becomes a factor to promote nuclear war. Do you know why?"

It was a direct question. There was the barest hint of a pause. "There can be no winner in a nuclear war. A nuclear war means death to all human beings," Chazov said evenly in Russian, his eyes fixed on Lown.

Lown leaned back to give the final word. "We physicians have concluded that the only remedy is prevention, not civil defense measures, and it's time we said so openly."

The program soon concluded with Muller reading a message to the Soviet people, in Russian, calling for joint efforts to stop the arms race, and Chazov reading a similar message to the American people in English. Lown, sitting quietly, wondered whether he had gone too far. As the physicians left the studio, he said to Chazov, "I hope that you're not upset with me for raising an issue that wasn't on the agenda. I hope that what I said won't affect our friendship." Chazov replied, "No, that's all right, it was very good."

But in the two days between the time of the taping and the scheduled broadcast, Lown became more and more nervous. Most of the Western journalists in Moscow were confidently predicting that the Soviets would never air the show as taped. Would the Soviet government's television station really broadcast the message that the Soviet civil defense program was not only useless but actually increased the risk of war?

At the appointed time, six o'clock in the evening on Saturday, June 26, 1982, Lown and his wife Louise tensely watched the television set in their hotel room. At exactly six o'clock, the station showed only a violinist playing a concert. Lown was sure he had blown it. The minutes ticked by—6:04, 6:05, 6:06. He turned to Louise and said wearily, "I really feel bad that I torpedoed this wonderful program by virtue of this civil defense issue." At 6:07 the program came on. It ran its full sixty-five minutes, including the portion on civil defense.

At least fifty million Soviets (*Time* magazine's estimate) viewed the initial broadcast; numerous Soviet newspaper articles commented on the program; and four days later it was broadcast again. In all, a variety of independent Western observers estimated that between 100 million and 150 million Soviets watched the program. It was a startling breakthrough for IPPNW, causing many in the West to start taking the group seriously for the first time.

As John Pastore later said, "I'm amazed that Bernie Lown could get on there and say, 'We're pleased to be on this uncensored program' before the program was made. We had them in a terrible box. We could have made some nasty comment about Brezhnev, or said some political thing, and then the Soviets would have been in a position where they couldn't do anything right. If they cut it, then they had made liars out of everyone, and if they showed it then they'd share a terrible fate. It took an enormous act of courage and trust on the part of Chazov to make it happen. He deserves all the credit."

Strangely, the physicians had much less success getting the show on American airwaves. After the Thursday night taping, Muller stayed up all night with the Soviet technicians to make the tape compatible with American equipment and to dub in English subtitles. The next morning he flew to New York with what he believed to be the scoop of the decade. Since the show was not to be aired until Saturday, it could conceivably have been shown in the United States *before* it was shown in the Soviet Union. But Muller was stonewalled by all three commercial networks. He was told that, given the show's content, only a network president could make such a decision, and he was unable to get through to that level. "They were not even interested in *looking* at it," says Lown. "They were *afraid* to look at it." Months later, the Public Broadcasting System agreed to air the show late at night, with some cuts, and with two American journalists commenting afterwards that while such a dialogue was "completely unusual," the show covered an "acceptable subject . . . [and] it didn't go into the specifics of Soviet policy."

Others did not take the telecast so lightly. IPPNW held its third congress in the Netherlands in June 1983, and this time received messages of support from Ronald Reagan, Yuri Andropov, UN Secretary-General Javier Perez de Cuellar, and Pope John II. The doctors launched a two-year petition drive for an "international physicians' call for an end to the nuclear arms race," which gained more than one million signatures—nearly 25 percent of all the world's physicians—from doctors in eighty-three countries. Delegates also recommended adding the following language to the traditional Hippocratic Oath: "As a physician of the twentieth century, I recognize that nuclear weapons have presented my profession with a challenge of unprecedented proportions. . . . I will do all in my power to work for the prevention of nuclear war."

In their 1983 letter to the superpower leaders, the physicians added a call for "renewed efforts to achieve a test ban" and, in an oblique reference to both the Soviet SS-20s and the American Pershing II and cruise missiles, stated that "there is no justification for the introduction of any additional nuclear weapons into Europe or any other region." Intriguingly, Chazov joined the Americans in blocking a resolution that specifically condemned the American Euromissiles, a resolution that would have bolstered the Soviet government's official viewpoint but also would have have politicized IPPNW.

The organization was maturing; no longer were all decisions made by a handful of Soviet and American doctors. IPPNW now had a formal constitution, a full-time staff of nine, and an elected International Council that set policy and included one representative from each "national affiliate." PSR, now formally designated as IPPNW's national affiliate for the United States, became under Helen Caldicott's charismatic leadership one of the country's most well-known and effective peace groups. Worldwide, the national affiliates organized numerous speaking campaigns, lobbied elected officials, and distributed books, films, and other media materials. On a local level, physicians delivered hospital lectures on the arms race and nuclear war, designed and introduced courses on the nuclear issue for medical schools, and committed themselves to educating their colleagues and patients. New groups sprang up in Latin America, Oceania, the Near East, and Asia; by 1986 IPPNW was a federation of forty-nine national affiliates representing 150,000 physicians.

Recognition of their efforts steadily increased. UNESCO awarded the group its 1984 Peace Education Prize. Former CBS news anchorman Walter Cronkite endorsed IPPNW and wrote that "against almost insurmountable odds, they [IPPNW] have managed to bridge the boundaries between countries and ideologies to underline the universal horror with which those who know contemplate the aftermath of a modern war." In December 1984 IPPNW received an award from a California-based grass-roots peace group called Beyond War during a simultaneous two-way television "space bridge" between Moscow and San Francisco. The technical wizardry of satellite telecommunications and large video screens brought two audiences, one American and one Soviet, face to face. For many of the people jammed into the two auditoriums, it was their first opportunity to look "the enemy" straight in the eye.

"Through the nearly magical advances of science we are able to traverse a great distance in seconds," Lown told both audiences. "But we must honestly confront the bitter fact that the misapplication of science and technology has brought us microseconds away from unparalleled disaster. The dismantling of nuclear weapons will not succeed unless we can excite moral outrage among the intended victims, which includes all of us. We and the Soviet people have a linked human destiny. We will either live together or die together, there is no other alternative."

Chazov stepped to the microphone in Moscow. "I, like Dr. Lown, am a cardiologist, and every day we listen to the beating of the hearts of our countrymen. This is the sound of the heart of a healthy Russian," he announced as a recording of the familiar lub-dub was broadcast to both audiences. "And this is the sound of a healthy American heart." The lub-dubbing continued unchanged. "You can hear their desire for love, for well-being, for happiness. All of this can only occur, however, when on our planet we have peace, and this is why we physicians are called upon to protect the life and health of our patients. Either we will live together on our beautiful planet, or we will die together in the flames of nuclear war."

In the emotional atmosphere of the space bridge, it all seemed so easy and effortless. Tears flowed on both sides as audience members sang with folksingers and a children's chorus before waving good-bye.

More than a few gulped as the screens went black and the vision disappeared.

But Lown knew they could not afford to rest on their laurels. He pushed, impatiently, persuasively, for IPPNW to sharpen its message. "While physician activity has helped rouse thousands to the common nuclear peril, the world is not safer as a result," he warned IPPNW members at their fourth congress in Helsinki, Finland, in June 1984. "On the contrary, the drift to nuclear war has become a gallop. I believe we shall not succeed unless we forge ahead beyond the description of the horrors of nuclear war. The physician's responsibility to the sick extends beyond correct diagnosis. The aim is to find an effective remedy. Need we cast ourselves only in the role of modern-day Cassandras intoning warnings of the threats to the health and survival of our communities? Or should we advocate and lobby for policies that will reduce the likelihood of nuclear war?"

He minced no words regarding the inadequate remedies now being applied. "Twenty-five years of negotiations—seven thousand or more sessions between the US and the Soviet Union—have not led to the dismantling of a single major weapons system. Why should we say more of the same? I believe that when we say 'negotiations' without a critical analysis of why negotiations have failed, we are not doing a service to humanity." More promising, he said, is "a process of reciprocating initiatives set in motion by world public opinion. The moment one side takes a measure then enormous public opinion concentrates on the other side to compel them to do the same. And the world is kept in suspense wondering what the next step will be—suddenly you have public involvement. Negotiations then occur to formalize the agreements. You bring in the experts, who obfuscate the matter like medieval scholars with their trivial esoterica, at the end, not the beginning."

Lown believes this treatment has already been given a successful clinical trial—when President Kennedy's unilateral moratorium on atmospheric tests in June 1963 set in motion a chain of events that culminated in the signing of the Limited Test Ban Treaty just a few months later. In June 1984 Lown suggested that IPPNW define a "medical prescription" to end the arms race—a call for either superpower to suspend unilaterally all nuclear tests and invite the other country to do likewise. Such a moratorium could be a first step toward the signing of a comprehensive test ban treaty. Negotiations for a comprehensive test ban treaty had been actively supported by American presidents Kennedy,

Johnson, Nixon, Ford, and Carter, and were in a final stage of completion in 1979, when the Soviet invasion of Afghanistan dampened US enthusiasm for the treaty. The Reagan administration formally called off the negotiations in June 1982.

But the Soviet physicians balked at such a prescription. For nearly a year, Lown and others showered Chazov and the other Soviets with arguments and data in favor of the unilateral test moratorium. In January 1985, at an IPPNW executive committee meeting in London, the Soviets were still resisting the test moratorium call. Finally, in February 1985, they acquiesced. On July 1, 1985, at the conclusion of the 1985 congress in Budapest, Hungary, attended by more than one thousand physicians, IPPNW's forty-one member International Council approved a letter to President Reagan and Secretary Gorbachev stating: "The time has come for deeds to support words, for deeds to impel other deeds. As a first step, we recommend a moratorium on all nuclear explosions."

For exactly one month the call went unanswered, and the Soviet physicians were on record officially urging their government to do something it was not then doing. Then, on July 28, 1985, Gorbachev announced that the Soviet Union would unilaterally halt nuclear testing until January 1, 1986, and would continue the moratorium indefinitely if the United States would do the same. The same day, the Reagan administration termed Gorbachev's action "propaganda" and claimed that further nuclear tests were necessary for US national security.

During the fall, IPPNW physicians continued to try to mobilize public opinion behind the test moratorium. Then suddenly, on October 11, 1985, the Nobel Peace Prize Committee decided to give the doctors some extra publicity.

Lown was tipped off, the night before, by a Norwegian journalist. "We've been right 98 percent of the time," she told him. Lown went to bed feeling that 2 percent could be a very large number indeed. Coincidentally, he and Chazov happened to be in Geneva for a World Health Organization meeting, and had decided to call a press conference to alert the media that IPPNW had been in existence for five years. When, just before the press conference was about to start, an unfamiliar man with a Norwegian name asked Lown if he could make a short announcement, Lown felt his heart thump. "Is it good news or bad news?" he managed to ask. "It isn't bad news," replied Gunnar Staalsett, a Nobel Committee member. A few minutes later Staalsett announced that

IPPNW had won the prize for rendering "a considerable service to mankind by spreading authoritative information and by creating an awareness of the catastrophic consequences of atomic warfare."

"Suddenly correspondents seemed to multiply like *amoebas*. From the ceilings, from the chandeliers, they emerged," remembers Lown. "And then it became mad." With tears in their eyes, Chazov and Lown hugged one another as the television cameras whirred.

"If this prize has any message," declared Egil Aarvik, the Nobel Committee's chairman, "it is to say to the American and Soviet negotiators in Geneva that it is very important that they come up with a successful result." The committee had chosen IPPNW from a nominated list of sixty individuals and thirty-nine organizations. A source close to the committee told the *New York Times* when the prize was announced that the choice was "a safe one. You don't get too much criticism for choosing a group, there is no personality you can argue about."

He was wrong. Western journalists who had never heard of IPPNW did a double-take when they learned that its Soviet cofounder and co-president has been a full member of the Communist Party's Central Committee since 1982, is a deputy member of the Supreme Soviet, has won two Orders of Lenin and a Hero of Socialist Labor award for his medical work, and is the personal physician of the Kremlin leadership. Not only is Chazov not considered a dissident by the Soviet government, he is, to some extent, a *member* of the Soviet government. For many, that fact alone was sufficient grounds for indignant protestations that the Nobel Committee had given the prize to Soviet propaganda.

The ensuing controversy over the nature of IPPNW and the ad hominem attacks on Chazov by Western editorialists in the following weeks was a "sobering and frightening experience that made me grow up, in a way," says Lown. "I realized how immense are the forces working to sustain the edifice of the Cold War, which is a way of life for many, the only life they know, and they're not going to give it up even if it causes a nuclear war."

IPPNW had been subject to criticism before, of course—as early as 1981, Stephen Rosenfeld had commented in the *Washington Post* that the American doctors "should never have accepted the Soviet doctors as 'non-political' soulmates. This invites all the shameless fraud of which the Soviets are capable. . . . Let us have no more of this nonsense about physicians dedicating themselves to life without regard to political boundaries. If the group wishes to be taken seriously, let it throw the

Soviets out." But after the Nobel Prize announcement, the intermittent grumblings suddenly turned into a chorus.

Many critics pointed out that IPPNW's formal policy positions in favor of the nuclear freeze, the no-first-use policy, and the nuclear test moratorium are all currently supported by the Soviet government. The *New Republic* commented acidly that "there is an elaborate pretense that the Soviet bloc doctors are, like the Western doctors, an independent group for influencing public opinion and pressuring government at home. The Western doctors do not seem to notice, or perhaps to care, that their Eastern bloc colleagues never take a position contrary to the current Soviet line." But the *New Republic* did not seem to notice that IPPNW adopted each of these positions well before the Soviet government did. The question, says Lown, is: "Who's following whom?"

"We've always had the problem that if the Russians say the sun is shining, and we say the sun is shining, then we are accused of fitting the Soviet position," James Muller told reporters at a 1985 press conference. "When we formed, people told us we would have little influence within the Soviet Union. To my surprise, and I think to everyone's surprise, the record shows that we and other Western groups may have had enormous influence on Soviet policy. We've had three proposals— the nuclear freeze, the no-first-use-policy, and the testing moratorium— which arose from a medical analysis of the nuclear arms race. We Americans came up with each of these proposals and showed them to the Russian doctors, and they resisted and rejected them. And we argued and argued with them, for months, until finally we convinced them, and they went back to the Kremlin, and these ideas floated in what I would call a *pre-policy phase*, in a policy void. The Soviet leaders then said, 'Is this an idea that is good for us or bad for us?' And in the case of these three proposals they decided it was good for them, and these proposals became part of Soviet policy.

"Now at this point there are two ways of looking at it," Muller continued. "If you're looking at this with Cold War glasses, you say, 'Aha! The Soviet government likes this, therefore it's bad for us.' And that's a very effective way of dismissing *anything* they do. The other interpretation is to say that the Soviets have heard an idea on how to stop the arms race, which is draining huge amounts of money away from their consumer economy, and they decide this idea is in their interest. What people miss is that something that's good for the Soviets might also be good for us, that these proposals are in the interest of both countries."

IPPNW leaders maintain that arms control proposals should be judged on the basis of merit, not who happens to endorse them. Accusations that the comprehensive test ban is a purely Soviet idea are baseless, they say, given the twenty years of support for test ban negotiations by American presidents and the Congressional resolutions supporting such negotiations passed by the US Senate (1983) and the US House of Representatives (1986). The heads of state of Argentina, Mexico, Greece, Sweden, India, and Tanzania recommended a worldwide nuclear test ban in 1985 as part of their "Five-Continent Peace Initiative."

The Soviet Union is also not the only country that has been influenced by IPPNW and other peace groups, say IPPNW leaders. IPPNW and PSR's firm exposés of the futility of nuclear civil defense planning, in conjunction with the efforts of hundreds of other groups and local citizens, have helped dramatically reduce US funding for such programs in recent years. One of President Reagan's first uses of the phrase, "A nuclear war cannot be won and must never be fought," was in a message of greeting to IPPNW. American rhetoric about "winning" or fighting "limited" nuclear wars has vanished. Polls show that as many as 80 percent of Americans support a nuclear freeze, and a call for a nuclear freeze was an official plank of the 1984 Democratic Party platform.

A second line of attack by IPPNW's critics was that the group's message has not been disseminated to the Soviet public, and therefore the fear of nuclear war "weakens the resolve" of the West but has no similar restraining influence on the East. The *Wall Street Journal* claimed on October 14, 1985, that "activity inside the USSR has been the barest possible window dressing. . . . [The] one joint panel discussion on Soviet television [was] unadvertised and shown in the daytime when viewing is low." (It was in fact shown twice, the first time at 6 P.M. Moscow time on a Saturday evening.) Soviet émigré Sergei Batovrin, an exiled leader of the independent Soviet peace group called The Group to Establish Trust Between the US and USSR, claimed in the *New York Times* that the Soviet wing of IPPNW was a "government-run propaganda arm" that distributed no information to the Soviet public, held no public seminars, and generated no news articles, and as a result "few Soviet citizens can imagine the consequences of nuclear destruction in any vivid or personal way."

IPPNW leaders cite abundant evidence to the contrary. Their Boston office has a stack of several hundred clippings from leading Soviet newspapers, magazines, and medical journals with articles by and about

Soviet IPPNW leaders detailing the medical effects of nuclear war, the possibility of "nuclear winter," and other conclusions of the IPPNW congresses. Chazov has appeared several times on the nation's most watched news program, *Vremya*, presenting IPPNW's data and conclusions; Soviet and American physicians, singly and together, have appeared at least twelve times on Soviet national television since the 1982 joint broadcast. Every IPPNW congress since 1982 has been the subject of a major Soviet documentary. American physicians have joined their Soviet colleagues for major speaking tours through Moscow, Leningrad, Kiev, Tashkent, and Tbilisi, and have received extensive radio, newspaper, and television coverage. According to Lown, "We have far more problems gaining access to the American media on this issue than we have in gaining access to the Soviet media."

All of this may be catalyzing discernible changes in Soviet public attitudes. In 1983 American psychiatrists Eric Chivian, John Mack, and Jerry Waletsky interviewed sixty Soviet teenagers whom they chose randomly from among thousands at two Pioneer camps. Nearly 80 percent of the teenagers said that the United States and the Soviet Union would not survive a nuclear war; more than 80 percent said that they and their families would not survive. Several said that they learned about the effects of nuclear war from television and the newspapers. "I watch the television show, *Vremya*," said one twelve-year-old, "and they constantly show how there shouldn't be any nuclear weapons."

Since the 1982 television broadcast, when Lown called nuclear civil defense an illusion, the Soviet government has displayed ambivalence toward its own civil defense programs. On one hand, Chazov and others make frequent and unequivocal statements in the Soviet press that civil defense will do little to mitigate the consequences of nuclear war, including the climatic changes of a "nuclear winter." On the other hand, the Soviet Union continues to keep its civil defense programs alive under the justification of preparedness for conventional attack. Civil defense against nuclear war, however, is a butt for satirical jokes among the Soviet people, and the Soviet teenagers interviewed in the Harvard study certainly had no illusions about it. "You couldn't survive a nuclear strike," said a thirteen-year-old. "The nuclear radioactivity remains for a very long time. And even if a person goes underground, no matter how much he wants to live, he wouldn't."

Other critics attacked IPPNW's effectiveness from another angle, saying that since Chazov and the other Soviet physicians are not "independent" of their government and do not publicly contradict Soviet policy, they have no influence within their country. On December 7, 1985, the US State Department issued a statement saying that it shared the "overall goal" of the physicians' group and admitting that Lown and other Westerners were engaged in a "sincere effort to grapple with difficult issues." But it added that "the same cannot be said for Dr. Chazov, who is an official of the USSR and cannot take public positions not sanctioned by his government."

From this point of view, only when the Soviet group begins openly calling for changes in its government's policy can it be taken seriously by Westerners. "When we begin to see Dr. Chazov, in the Soviet media, express doubts, however slight, about the deployment of so many Soviet SS-20s aimed at Western Europe," wrote American psychiatrist Walter Reich in the *New York Times*, "then we will know that something new has happened."

Without doubt, the Soviet group is quite different from its American counterpart, which takes public positions in opposition to the status quo and overtly lobbies for changes in government policies. But concluding on this basis that Soviet IPPNW physicians therefore have no influence "betrays a real lack of understanding of the Soviet political system," writes Jerry F. Hough, a noted Sovietologist, professor of political science at Duke University, and staff member of the Brookings Institution. "The role of the men and women in this movement is far more complex than we in the West usually recognize."

Chazov appears to be shrewdly using his position to educate both the top echelons of government and the Soviet public at large about the medical consequences of nuclear war. Wrote Hough in the *Los Angeles Times* in December 1985: "The [Soviet] peace movement's role has been to get [Soviet] political and military leaders to understand that nuclear war would be different from World War II. To a large extent they have won on this point."

According to Hough, rhetoric about winning a nuclear war and launching preemptive nuclear strikes was part of official Soviet military doctrine in the 1960s and 1970s. Such statements have trickled to a halt in the 1980s. In 1983 a high-ranking Soviet official privately told Muller that "prior to Chazov's work the Soviet military talked about winning a nuclear war, but now that cannot be done." The Soviet physicians, said Hough, are writing in the Soviet press "things which are deeply disturbing to powerful military and conservative elements in the establishment."

Indeed, one testament to the Soviet physicians' effectiveness is that they appear to have aroused an opposition within their own country. There is significant evidence that some members of the Soviet military-industrial establishment consider IPPNW too Western-dominated and grumble about the widespread media coverage given a group that advocates accommodation with the West. A few years ago a Soviet military magazine accused Chazov of "demoralizing the Soviet people at a time of great danger." Says Lown: "I have been told privately in Moscow that Chazov has been very courageous. He has been on television stating that nuclear war will bring no victory, only defeat, that civilization will be a shambles and nothing will survive. Surely, this is not the way to mobilize people for war, but this Chazov has done."

Soviet Marshal Nikolai Orgakov, before he was removed as the chief of the general staff, hinted at the need for a counteroffensive against IPPNW's efforts and wrote, "It is necessary to bring the truth about the existing threat of a military danger to the Soviet people in a deeper and more well-argued manner." Like the United States, like all countries in the world, say IPPNW leaders, the Soviet Union contains its hawks and doves—and the Soviet branch of IPPNW is a highly visible collection of the doves.

Perhaps the most vocal and damaging criticism of IPPNW centered around Andrei Sakharov, the dissident Soviet physicist and human rights campaigner who won the 1975 Nobel Peace Prize. Sakharov was not allowed by Soviet authorities to go to Oslo to collect the prize, and in 1980 was sent into internal exile in Gorky. Chancellor Helmut Kohl of West Germany and nine other leaders of Christian Democrat parties in Europe signed a letter asking the Nobel Committee to rescind IPPNW's prize after it was publicized that Chazov had, in 1973, joined twenty-three other members of the Academy of Medical Sciences in signing a letter that denounced Sakharov for his public statements criticizing Soviet foreign policy and supporting an American military buildup. The letter, published in *Izvestia*, claimed that Sakharov had "lost touch with his own people."

Efrem Yankelevich, Sakharov's son-in-law who now lives in Newton, Massachusetts, wrote in the *Boston Globe* that IPPNW officials had been indifferent to Sakharov's plight and had refused to see members of his family, who traveled to the Helsinki Congress in 1984 to lobby IPPNW to take up Sakharov's cause publicly. Yankelevich and others, such as Edward Lozansky, the executive director of the Andrei Sakharov Institute in Washington, DC, maintain that a resolution of disputes over human rights in the Soviet Union is a necessary precondition to progress in stopping the arms race. "There's a fundamental link between preservation of world peace and human rights," says Lozansky. "Only when Soviet people like Dr. Sakharov have the opportunity to speak free can we talk about trust, about stopping the arms race, about nuclear disarmament."

IPPNW is founded on a different assumption, which is that citizens of East and West can work together to stop the arms race while continuing to disagree on "human rights" and a host of other issues. IPPNW concentrates on the issue of nuclear war because broadening its agenda would ruin the delicate consensus so far achieved by the doctors, which has enabled their message to be spread all over the world. "To be effective in today's world is to be focused," says Lown, who points out that few criticize Amnesty International, the human rights organization that won the 1977 Nobel Peace Prize, for failing to address the nuclear issue.

Several prominent American human rights activists agree. Alan Dershowitz, a professor at Harvard Law School who once represented the Soviet dissident Anatoly Shcharansky in Soviet courts, wrote in his syndicated column in December 1985 that IPPNW "has received more television and print coverage in the Soviet Union than any other non-party-controlled group" and that "the physicians' group can't achieve an effective dialogue about both nuclear war and human rights issues. . . . I hope that, as an organization, it will continue to focus its attention on the single most critical issue in the world today—human survival."

Even Sakharov's "letter from exile" of May 4, 1980, seems to suggest that such prioritization is necessary. "Despite all that has happened, I feel that the questions of war and peace and disarmament are so crucial that they must be given absolute priority even in the most difficult circumstances," wrote Sakharov. "It is imperative that all possible means be used to solve these questions and to lay the groundwork for further progress. Most urgent of all are steps to avert a nuclear war, which is the greatest peril confronting the modern world."

When the Sakharov family visited Helsinki in 1984 and asked for a meeting with Lown and Chazov to discuss Sakharov and his wife's condition, they were turned down because IPPNW leaders felt that the two copresidents were too closely identified with the organization to be able to meet with the Sakharov family as private individuals. Instead, James Muller, who was not then an officer in the group, and several other

IPPNW members met with Yankelevich and his wife in Helsinki in an unofficial capacity. They reviewed the electrocardiograms of Mrs. Yelena Bonner, Sakharov's wife, and passed on two confidential medical requests to their Soviet physician colleagues; these requests were subsequently fulfilled and Muller communicated the results back to the Sakharov family.

The Sakharov issue is a painful one for Lown. "I have tremendous respect for Sakharov, not for his point of view on the nuclear issue, which I don't agree with, but for his courage in speaking out when the whole state apparatus was against him. Believe me, the worst thing in any country is to be deemed a traitor." There is an edge of bitterness in Lown's voice—he speaks from experience. During the McCarthy era he was called up under the doctors' draft to serve in the Korean war and asked to mark on the "attorney general's list," created by the Walter-McCarran Act, whether he had ever been a member of the four hundred listed organizations deemed subversive. Among them were some of the student groups to which Lown had belonged in medical school, "which at the time were considered left-wing because they called for the admission of more blacks, women, and Jews to medicine." (While a student at Johns Hopkins Medical School, Lown had decided it was idiotic to label blood banks separately as "colored" or "white," and, when "one kind" ran short, simply took blood of the "other kind"—an act that got him temporarily expelled from medical school.)

Lown knew that if he signed the attorney general's list he would be required to "name names" of others in those groups, some of whom had lied about their past affiliations and would consequently have gone to jail. Lown refused to sign the list and pleaded the Fifth Amendment. He was discharged from the Army as a captain and promptly drafted as a private. After boot camp, he was sent to a military hospital in Tacoma, Washington, where he spent a humiliating year sweeping up cigarette butts on a hospital floor in the morning and doctoring in the afternoon. Afterwards, no civilian hospital would hire him, until finally one of his old mentors managed to land him a position at Harvard. "It ruined my life for a year and slowed down my career for a decade," says Lown, "but it made me a better doctor. I went from being top man on the totem pole to being a nobody. Here I was a bright young guy, I was moving ahead very rapidly in my career, patients were incidental, and suddenly I was bounced out of medicine and I didn't know what was going to happen. It made me say, what are the issues? What does being alive mean? It was rich and complex and painful."

But Lown does not let his empathy for Soviet dissidents deter him from his main mission of preventing nuclear war. "We have found a small area of common interest with the Soviets and we pursue it with obsessive intensity," he told reporters who insisted that he and Chazov comment on Sakharov. "We and the Soviets, very early, said, 'Look, if we're going to bring in other issues, it will be very hard to define boundaries for them, and the moment it is unbounded then our group will not exist.' " Added Chazov: "Is there an appeal being made here to disrupt this dialogue? Of course we could leave each other, go our different ways, and instill hatred in each other, but what would be the result? Do you know that every day ten more atomic warheads appear on the earth? If we deal only with hatred and confrontation, that would be the path to war."

IPPNW members, many of whom are members of Amnesty International and other human rights groups, frequently bring up their concerns about human rights to their Soviet colleagues in unofficial ways. Says John Pastore, IPPNW's current secretary: "The evidence we have to date is that an improvement in the climate between the superpowers is going to have a greater effect on human rights than the direct confrontational approach. The Soviets listen. They don't necessarily agree verbally all the time. But they hear the message. And when they see doctors who are deeply concerned about the nuclear arms race also questioning, in private, many of the other things that are going on in the Soviet Union, I think it has an effect on them."

The *Wall Street Journal*, among others, contrasted the repression of some members of the "independent" Soviet peace group, The Group to Establish Trust, with the "pampered" status of IPPNW's Soviet members. The exile of Trust group leaders and a three-year labor camp term for Dr. Vladimir Brodsky, a Trust group founder and intensive care specialist who was arrested on charges of "malicious hooliganism" for distributing Trust group literature, clearly revealed, according to these critics, the Soviet Union's real attitude toward peace. They declared that IPPNW, which is allowed to exist by the government, was therefore nothing but a front. Some even claimed that Chazov bore direct responsibility for the crackdowns on the dissident peace group members. "Chazov represents a regime and a medical establishment . . . that have for years been dispatching members of the one small, independent Soviet peace group to psychiatric hospitals and labor camps," wrote Andrew Nagorski, a former *Newsweek* reporter, in the *New York Times*. Senator Bob Dole, in a letter to President Reagan accompanying a US Senate resolution condemning the awarding of the prize to Chazov, remarked that "Chazov is not only unworthy of the award, his selection is an affront to the very principles which the peace prize is supposed to represent."

These critics assume that a large majority of Soviet citizens would not, if given a chance, freely support the policies of the Communist Party or the Soviet Union, and that therefore Chazov does not really represent the majority of Soviet physicians. "You are an independent group, and you should work with independent groups in the Soviet Union," Edward Lozansky of the Andrei Sakharov Institute told Dr. Robert Jay Lifton, an IPPNW representative, during a public television debate in December 1985. "Dr. Chazov and Dr. Vartanyan [a prominent Soviet psychiatrist] don't speak for Soviet people. They speak for party and KGB."

But Lown disagrees that this would be the most effective way of influencing Soviet behavior. "Chazov represents the overwhelming mass of Soviet physicians," he says. "Most Soviet physicians are supportive of their government whether we like it or not. Who Brodsky represents, I do not know. If he represents a hundred dissident physicians, which some Moscow correspondent said he did, I'd be surprised. But we have to deal with the mainstream of Soviet physicians. Why? Supposing Chazov decided to organize a movement that dealt with the Communist Party physicians in the United States, of which there are maybe—I'm guessing— a hundred. We'd regard him as an idiot! Yet we aren't able to reverse the argument and look at it objectively. I don't mean to pass value judgments against Brodsky and what he's trying to do. I feel the treatment Brodsky got is outrageous, and I have no doubts on that. But if we want to influence Soviet public opinion, do we reach the Russian public through Chazov or through Brodsky? Which? Or is our aim to reach the Western media and show them how righteous we are?"

Intriguingly, Brodsky himself appears to support the kind of dialogue IPPNW members engage in. In a 1983 interview with Canadian journalist Andrew Orkin in a Moscow park, published in the *Canadian Medical Association Journal* on February 14, 1984, Brodsky and his colleague Dr. Igor Subkov, also a Trust group member, said that "one must not think of these doctors [Soviet members of IPPNW] as merely sympathetic with the government. They are the government." But according to Orkin, "This is as close as these physicians will come to criticism [of the Soviet branch of IPPNW]." "Should Western physicians continue meeting with their colleagues of the Soviet Committee?" asked Orkin. "Of course," replied Brodsky, "as often as they can. We have a very dangerous (nuclear weapons) situation and these people are close to the people in power. It is most important that all opportunities to meet with them be pursued." "In the context of their persecution," a somewhat thunderstruck Orkin reports, "this is a most unexpected reply."

Lown believes that Chazov has been absolutely essential to IPPNW's success. "He is an enormous facilitator. Our movement is in the very corridors of power. I do not know of anybody else whom I've met who has his connections, his savvy, and his courage to do the things that are necessary for our movement." He and Chazov often have vigorous disagreements on many issues, "but the differences are such that we resolve and compromise. Because the things that pull us together are much more important than the things we dissent on."

The controversy over the Nobel Prize has brought them closer together. "Chazov says, 'You're my brother. You're as close to me as my brother.' He says it in the way that Russians will embody enormous feelings in certain phrases. If we had separated a little bit during this controversy. . . ." he trails off. "Chazov said to me many years ago, 'Look, Bernard, as long as you and I remain friends and are consistently committed to our principles, we are invincible. But the moment a fissure, a crack develops between us, that's the end of the movement. Remember that.' "

Lown has no doubts that the overall effect of the Nobel Prize will be overwhelmingly constructive. "Even the controversy is very positive," he declares. "Because fundamentally what it does is bring us to the attention of people, and I have great confidence that people will sort out the facts." IPPNW's new prestige earned for Lown and Chazov a three-hour private meeting with Mikhail Gorbachev on December 18, 1985. Lown argued relentlessly that Gorbachev should extend his test moratorium. "It was a very charged meeting," remarks Lown. "Friendly— but not without its moments of controversy." According to Lown, Gorbachev asked him, "What is the value of our engaging in unilateral activity when the Americans are not going to honor it? Unilateral action like that after all endangers our security." Lown tried to persuade him otherwise. Less than a month after this meeting, Gorbachev announced a three-month extension of the Soviet test moratorium.

Lown hopes that President Reagan will also agree to meet with the IPPNW leadership. "I am by nature an optimist," he says, "and I believe it must be some neurochemical derangement in my brain, because when you look at the world objectively you see little basis for optimism. But optimism springs from activity," he adds with a grin, "and no patient has ever faulted me for being unduly optimistic." IPPNW, he hopes, will someday disband for lack of subject matter.

When that day comes, Lown will not be idle. He claims he has enough interests and passions for several lifetimes. He speaks longingly of the books he would like to read, the extra time he wishes he could spend with his wife, children, and grandchildren. On his home bookshelves are forty large, leatherbound, meticulous scrapbooks, each representing one year, that Lown assembles during his annual two-week vacation in a little cabin in Maine. Color snapshots of grandchildren playing on a beach are juxtaposed with yellowed clippings from the *New York Times* diagramming increases in military spending. There are pictures of his son-in-law windsurfing on a lake, portraits of actors from a Shakespeare festival, labels of fine wines, photographs of IPPNW meetings, concert programs from London. The pages represent hours of work. They are his attempt to create a reasonable and harmonious record of his diverse and complicated life.

Most of all, if IPPNW became unnecessary, Lown would spend more time practicing medicine. Despite his hectic schedule, he has never considered giving up clinical practice. "There's no drama that can compare with the drama of watching patients and participating in their lives," he says with relish. "If there were any justice, the doctor would pay the patient for the privilege of participating in this drama." Direct, immediate interaction with human patients is a welcome relief from the abstraction and enormity of trying to save his most intractable patient.

Watching him visit patients in the hospital, it is tempting to wonder who is drawing more strength from whom. Lown brings a sense of humor into the sterile hospital environment—one of his favorite quotes is from the seventeenth-century physician Thomas Sydenham, who said, "The arrival of a good clown has more beneficial effect on the health of a town than twenty asses laden with drugs." Lown infects his patients with his own indomitable passion for life. He cajoles them into playing a role in their own cure. He feels that spending twenty minutes with a patient listening to his or her problems can often do more good than all of his clinical expertise. He is not afraid to touch his patients, look them straight in the eyes, and say, "I want you to heal."

One patient he visits is convinced that his heart condition means he will die soon. He is too depressed to get out of bed and stares at Lown with blank, desperate, uncomprehending eyes. Lown places both hands on his chest and makes eye contact. "You do not need this pacemaker, so we will see about getting it removed," he tells him in a calm, sonorous voice. "You are getting better all the time. You are strong enough to walk now, and I want you to walk around the nurses' station, as many laps as you feel that you can, but at least five, twice a day. I want you to say hello to the nurses. I want you to feel better."

Lown and his entourage of white-coated medical students and cardiology fellows soon move on. Ten minutes later, as Lown is discoursing about another case in the hall, the depressed patient, dressed in a bathrobe, shuffles past. Lown interrupts himself and remarks casually, "I'm glad to see you walking. You walk with purpose." The patient does not look up. A few minutes later, he circles past again. On his third lap, the patient calls out something incoherent to Lown. Lown breaks away from his group and grasps the patient's shoulder firmly. The fellows and students hold their breath. Lown and the patient lock eyes again, until the sheer force of persuasion in Lown's eyes kindles something new in the patient's face. "I know I can do it, doctor," the patient says. "I know I can make myself well."

CHAPTER TWO

A SUMMIT MEETING:

CYNTHIA LAZAROFF

Cynthia Lazaroff concentrated on taking one step at a time. The sun had just topped the ragged crest of the Caucasus Mountains, bringing little warmth, but transforming the icy, rounded shoulders of Mt. Elbrus, the highest peak in Europe, into a painfully brilliant expanse of white. Each effort to place one foot ahead of the other seemed to go against all instinct and reason. Each breath required an uncanny deliberateness. And she still had more than two thousand feet to climb.

Behind and ahead of her were the anonymous figures of the Soviet and American teenagers she had led to this point, their shapes obscured by gaudy padded jackets, their faces covered by balaclavas and glacier glasses, their noses pure white with protective cream. By her side was the head Soviet guide, Slava Volkov, who gauged his pace so that at every moment his body sheltered Lazaroff from the wind.

Her mind, she realized groggily, was numb. She had imagined, planned, and worked for this day for nearly five years, and now that it was here she found herself curiously emotionless, almost bored by the unending vista of ice, the necessity of sinking her crampons into the snow again and again. From below, each pile of rocks or slightly rounded hump looked cruelly like the summit, sparking irrational hopes that they were nearly there. Each time a minor crest was gained, a new horizon of implacable ice stretched before them.

Then, ahead of her, Cynthia Lararoff saw a Soviet girl and an American girl link arms, put their heads down against the wind, and move up the mountain with their steps in perfect unison. She remembered, through the haziness of oxygen deprivation at sixteen thousand feet, why she had taken so many steps already, and why she would take many more.

*   *   *

Cynthia Lazaroff is a slim, petite woman with blue eyes, curly blond ringlets, and dark eyebrows that hint at her Slavic ancestry. The office of the US-USSR Youth Exchange Program, which she founded and directs, occupies the ground floor of a gray stucco house in a quiet neighborhood of San Francisco. She wears a blue sweater, a string of pearls, and a plum-colored down vest; her favorite colors are lavender, pink, and blue. There is a refreshing, unassuming femininity to her office and her materials, revealed in small ways, such as her powder-blue stationery with its calligraphied letterhead, the doodled designs of flowers on her brochures, and the Russian *matrioshka* dolls tucked between videotapes and books on her shelves.

Lazaroff cannot count the times American experts in Soviet affairs patted her on the head patronizingly when she first told them her plans for the US-USSR Youth Exchange Program. Most said, "Nice idea, honey, but it will never happen." Their pessimism, she thinks, had something to do with her own youth (she is now twenty-nine), her height (five foot one) and her sex. "People say I look like a cute little girl, and it's hard to be taken seriously in this field as a woman," she says in a firm, musical voice, her large delicate earrings catching the light as she nods her head for emphasis.

Although she often hires men as consultants, her office is staffed entirely by women. A woman gave her program its first major grant. Almost half of her advisory board members are women, a significant number in view of the preponderance of men in foreign affairs in general and Soviet-American relations in particular. It is almost too predictable that women should run a program that focuses on children and education. But Lazaroff negotiates, fund-raises, administers, and organizes within a world of men. She often works with officials of the Soviet Sports Committee, an organization with little predisposition to things feminine.

When Cynthia Lazaroff was seven years old, she saw a picture of St. Basil's Cathedral in Moscow, with its fantastical, swirling domes, on the cover of a *National Geographic* student bulletin. She announced to her parents that someday she would go to the Soviet Union and see it for herself. "It was so mysterious and magnificent," she recalls. Her parents smiled and patted her on the head, but they didn't tell her it was impossible.

Lazaroff was exposed to the Slavic tradition at a young age by her father's parents, who emigrated from a tiny peasant village in Macedonia, in what is now Yugoslavia. "I went with them to their church, I did a lot of Macedonian folk-dancing, and I developed a feel for their language, which is similar to Russian," she says. When she was a senior in high school, she overheard a friend of her family, a history professor, remark that the two most important languages to learn in the twentieth century are Russian and Chinese. Lazaroff decided that she would learn both. The summer before leaving for Mt. Holyoke College, she bought a Berlitz book and started studying Russian on her own.

During her freshman year at Mt. Holyoke, Lazaroff took several political science courses from an inspiring professor, Ruth Lawson, who encouraged her to make Soviet-American relations her field. But Lazaroff soon tired of commuting to another college to take Russian language courses, and Professor Lawson was retiring that year. Intrigued by Princeton professor Richard Falk's studies of world order and international affairs, she decided to transfer to Princeton University, which had excellent departments of political science and Russian.

It was a big step for a little girl from Pittsburgh, she recalls. "I came from a high school where my guidance counselor said, 'Who do you think you are?' when I said I was applying to Mt. Holyoke." Princeton's application deadline had already passed, and an admissions officer told her she had no chance of being accepted. "But there are times when you just know something is right for you," she remembers. "I pushed and pushed. And finally they agreed to look at my application if I sent it Federal Express." She got in.

Lazaroff studied Russian and international affairs intensively at Princeton for more than a year. (She now says that studying Chinese will be her "after-age-forty" project.) In autumn 1978 she went to the Soviet Union for the first time to study for four months at Leningrad University as part of a student exchange program.

Her semester did not begin auspiciously. Her dorm room, which she shared with three other Americans and a Soviet, was located in a pre-revolutionary brothel. The food was abysmal, and Lazaroff, a vegetarian, had to subsist on potatoes and overcooked cabbage. It was the coldest winter since 1941, with temperatures dropping to forty below zero. The winter sun rose at 11 A.M. and set at 3:30 P.M. And her Soviet roommate was the Komsomol (Young Communist League) leader for the entire university, a young woman wary of foreigners, one of whose responsibilities was to write a weekly report on Lazaroff's activities. "The relationship between her and my American roommates and me basically consisted of her saying every time we left, 'Where are you going?' and every time we came back, 'Where have you been?' We got into a standard routine where we would always say, 'I got so drunk last night I can't remember,' and as long as she asked the question and as long as we gave her that answer, she had done her job and we had done ours!"

But some of the drawbacks to dormitory living turned into opportunities. Since the showers worked only sporadically, Lazaroff and her friends began going to the *banya* (public baths) to get clean. The *banya*, a time-honored Russian tradition, was the center of a lively social scene. Dozens of women of all ages, including ancient babushkas and young girls, crowded into the steamy saunas of the women's *banya*. In dimly lit wooden rooms, the women traded stories and jokes while occasionally someone took a long stick with a pail on the end and poured water on the coals in a wall stove. For a few kopeks, Lazaroff and the other women could buy freshly cut birch branches and use them to swat one another playfully to improve blood circulation. Once thoroughly steamed, the women jumped into a cold shower or pool. Naked elderly women often handed Lazaroff stiff sponges and asked her to wash their backs. The good-humored, relaxed, celebratory atmosphere of the *banya* showed her a side of Soviet life very different from her uptight roommate and drab dorm room.

Before leaving the United States, Lazaroff had collected addresses of Soviet people from friends and decided that "the least important aspect" of her time there was her classes. "I wanted to try to really find out what life was like for Russians," she recalls. She visited numerous homes, made several friends, and started getting invited to parties where she was the only American present. Once, some Soviet students cajoled her into going to a party in a log cabin in a wooded area outside of the thirty-mile limit for foreigners. They dressed her in Soviet clothes and forbade her to say a word, even in Russian, in case her accent gave her away. "All I was allowed to say in public was *da* and *nyet*," she remembers. "We ate *bliny* and drank Georgian moonshine in front of the fire and stayed up partying and playing in the snow. But then the next day in a grocery store some big husky guy came up to me and started talking, and I had to pretend that I was deaf and didn't understand."

One day a Soviet friend took her to the apartment of a young couple in their twenties, both artists, who lived with their baby son and a grandmother. Lazaroff remembers feeling as if she had walked into a comfortable Soho flat in New York City—Simon and Garfunkel's "Scarborough Fair" was playing on a stereo and smells of delicious vegetarian cooking wafted through the apartment, which contained a hand-built loft. Beautiful, somber oil portraits and country landscapes hung on every wall of the room, which had a marble fireplace and large windows overlooking a park. Pre-Revolutionary sculptures adorned two ceiling corners; what had once been a nobleman's receiving room had been divided into five apartments.

Irina and Lev, the young artists, offered her tea and *zakuski* (Russian hors d'oeuvres). They talked animatedly about art, poetry, vegetarianism, and philosophies of living. An hour later, Irina expressed what they all felt—that it seemed as if they had always known each other. Before Lazaroff left, Irina asked her whether she would allow her to paint her portrait; she had always wanted to paint a portrait of an American, she explained. Lazaroff knew that it meant sitting perfectly still at their house for several hours a day for many weeks. She agreed.

By the time the portrait was finished, Lazaroff had become a member of the family. She often helped put their baby to bed, accompanied the grandmother on visits to the doctor, and assisted with the shopping and cooking. Potatoes, cheese, and a special kind of dark "health bread" were their staple dinner foods. On "good" nights, when the shopping went well, they had salads of chopped carrots, cabbage, raw garlic cloves, tomatoes, eggs, and parsley. On "bad" nights their salads were just cabbage. Lazaroff learned how to shop like a Soviet; once she spotted oranges for sale and stood in line for five hours.

She and Irina often went to the *banya* together and talked about literature and philosophy. The family took long walks on warmer days, and Lazaroff met their circle of friends. Soon she began sleeping in their warm loft instead of going back to her cold dorm room; she told her Soviet roommate that she had met a "wonderful Marine at the American consulate." When she went out to do the shopping or some other errand for the family, she wore their fur coats, army pants, and peasant felt boots so that everyone she met would think she was Soviet.

Lazaroff's Russian went from good to fluent—neither Irina nor Lev spoke any English—and she gained a deep, insider's understanding of everyday Soviet life. But her relationship with her "family" meant far more to her than simply an opportunity to learn about the Soviet Union. "They were so giving, so willing to give me everything they had, even though they had comparatively little materially," she says, struggling to put words to what she several times refers to as her "spiritual" connection with Irina and Lev. "The Soviets put such a higher priority on friendship than we do; friends always come first."

The hesitation in her voice shows that she has not told this story often, and the responsibility of disguising her friends still weighs heavily on her. "I had invaded their lives, and completely made myself at home in their apartment, and I wanted so much for them to come here and share, even for a day, in my life in America," she says after a pause. "And I realized that was out of the question. Yet they were completely accepting of that. They would tell me, 'We have come to accept our position here and we love our country very much.' I would bring them treats that I had brought from the United States, like peanuts and fresh raisins, and I worried that it wasn't fair for me to be doing this, because they would never be able to have these things again. And they said, 'Cindy, it's not important to us that you bring us these things. It's fun, but we don't need them, and our relationship isn't built on this stuff.' "

The semester ended and Lazaroff had to leave Leningrad. On the plane home, she decided that she had to figure out a way to see her friends again. "Irina and Lev really introduced me to the Russian soul, to the poetry of life there, and nurtured my love for that country," she says. "If I hadn't met them I probably wouldn't be doing what I'm doing today."

Lazaroff returned to the US and finished her year off from Princeton by working in a Pittsburgh art gallery specializing in Russian and Soviet art. At night she wrote a thesis on Leo Tolstoy's and Mohandas Gandhi's perspectives on nonviolence. Back at Princeton, she applied for a scholarship to spend the year after graduation studying in Leningrad. But the timing could not have been worse; the week before she was scheduled to defend her proposal before a panel of Princeton professors and alumni, the Soviets invaded Afghanistan. "The panel baited me," she says with a grimace. "They said, 'Why do you want to go to a country whose sole purpose is to impose misery and suffering on the rest of the world?' " Lazaroff didn't get the scholarship.

But she was still determined to go back to the Soviet Union. She graduated from Princeton with a magna cum laude degree in Politics and Russian studies, then heard about the American Field Service's teacher exchange program, which sends a handful of American teachers each year to teach special classes on American culture in Soviet schools for ten weeks. She applied even though she wasn't a teacher. At first the program directors gave her little encouragement, but Lazaroff insisted that she could teach about America, and she did speak Russian. The program, like many others, was endangered by the serious crash in Soviet-American relations after the invasion of Afghanistan, but at the last minute Lazaroff was told she could go. In autumn 1980 she and her three hundred pounds of luggage, including two hundred books and an assortment of maps, magazines, postcards, advertisements, bumper stickers, Hallmark cards, rock 'n' roll albums, and four pounds of popcorn, left to spend six weeks in Moscow and four weeks in Leningrad.

In Moscow she was assigned to School ;45, which specializes in English language instruction; in addition to the regular curriculum, students begin learning English at the age of six or seven. Moscow has more than 100 such language schools, most of which teach English, French, or German. Admittance is by entrance exam and the English language schools are considered the cream of the crop. Most, though not all, of the students are children of the well-educated and the Party elite. About eight hundred Soviet children, aged six to seventeen, attend Moscow School ;45.

When they met on her first day, Lazaroff was amazed at the flexibility and openness of the principal and the other teachers, especially Alexander Zakharovich Bessmertny, the head of the English department, a kindly, stout man with a quick sense of humor and an obvious fondness for his students. Lazaroff and Bessmertny agreed that Lazaroff should spend as much class time with the children as possible. "In our socialist society, we're going to exploit you," he said with a twinkle in his eye. "That's all right," replied Lazaroff, keeping a straight face. "I'm from a capitalist society, so I'm used to it." He suggested some possible subjects for lectures, then asked her what *she* would like to teach. After Lazaroff told him, Bessmertny broke into a broad grin. "You know the Beatles?" he began. "Well—we can work it out!"

On her first day, Lazaroff hung a map of Pittsburgh in the classroom and started telling her students about her hometown. She was so nervous that she lost her voice, and Bessmertny solicitously rescued her with cups of hot tea. But by the second day all of her jitters were gone. She began teaching about the Freedom of Information Act and the system of "checks and balances" in the American government. She hung an American flag in the classroom and explained the meaning of the stars and stripes. She described the differences between shopping in Moscow and New York City. She revealed the mysteries of slang like "I dig it" and "Wow!"

Some days she taught six fifty-minute lessons plus an extra seminar after school for the teachers. "There were days when I would lecture from seven forty-five or eight in the morning until four in the afternoon with no breaks, because during every supposed break one of the teachers would find me and say, 'Could you just give us a short lecture on fashion?' And I'd pull out a *Vogue* magazine. Or, 'Can you just tell us about meditation?' Every free second they wanted to learn more.

"Initially both the teachers and the students really wanted to know if they could trust me. They could tell that I loved the United States and I loved being an American. But it made all the difference in the world that I was willing to be critical of some American policies. They asked me about Harlem, and I said that the first time I went to Harlem I cried, which is true. When they asked, I said I was embarrassed about Vietnam and Watergate. It was *such* a revelation for the kids. The teachers told me that some of the kids came to them and said, 'Won't Cindy get in trouble for what she said?' They were worried that the United States government might punish me."

Her honesty not only helped the students realize that Americans can speak their minds freely, but also heightened her credibility. "I knew one American teacher who would go into Soviet classrooms and say, 'In America, we have *everything*. It's the greatest, most wonderful, most beautiful country on earth.' And she had no credibility with the teachers or the kids at all. It's when they can see your love *and* your criticism of your own country, and when they feel that you respect *them,* that you have an impact."

Both teachers and students were overwhelmingly appreciative and eager to become close. Bessmertny, who loved to tease, made up a doggerel in English for her benefit:

> Little Cindy Lazaroff,
> Passed on to me her nasty cough.
> I hate to think of this affair,
> As a case of biological warfare.

The students discovered she was a vegetarian and began bringing peanuts, cauliflower, pickled beets, cans of peas, jars of "eggplant caviar," and other presents of food from their parents. The windowsill of the hotel room where she lived was soon stacked with cans and jars. Every day the students argued over who would have the privilege of taking her that night to see a movie or a play.

One fifteen-year-old girl found out that Lazaroff admired Boris Pasternak, and took her to meet some of Pasternak's family at his home, located in a beautiful wooded area outside of Moscow called Peredelkino where many writers maintain country retreats. Afterwards, Lazaroff and several of her young friends visited Pasternak's snow-covered grave, placed flowers on it, and recited some of his works by candlelight.

Other students figured out ways to sneak Lazaroff into performances at the Taganka Theater, Moscow's most avant-garde and intellectual theater at the time. Tickets were often difficult to obtain, but these students knew a stagehand and wangled free passes. Once, between performances, they took her backstage where only stagehands and performers were supposed to be. A guard came along, and in a panic Lazaroff's friends shoved her into a nearby closet, whispered to her to be silent, and left. Alone in the dark, Lazaroff had plenty of time to visualize the headlines announcing this new international incident: "American Teacher Found Hiding Out in Moscow Theater." But the guard left, her friends returned, and they escaped to their seats just before the curtain went up.

A framed collage that her students gave her shows a black-and-white photo of Lazaroff with her hands raised and her face ignited with enthusiasm; above the photo are the words: "It's great!" Between scribbled comments in Russian are some of the children's other favorite Americanisms: "Hi! Wow! Three branches, H.E.W., Hamburger, Halloween, I (heart) New York, Prom, I dig it, Congress, X-mas." At the bottom is a "Thank you very much." On her last day of teaching in Moscow, the school had to hire two taxis and ask four boys to leave class in order to carry away all of her gifts.

Lazaroff then arrived at her Leningrad school, where the principal handed her a detailed schedule listing the topics she was to teach—a list that conspicuously avoided contemporary American culture. Cynthia was polite but firm, and she succeeded in substituting "Twas the Night Before Christmas" for *Pinocchio* and Andrew Wyeth for Michelangelo. But she taught only three or four classes a day, and it took much longer for her to develop close relationships with the students and teachers.

"The difference between the schools was vast, absolutely vast," she says. "I began to see that there were individuals in that country who could have an impact on their immediate environments. The schools reflected the personalities of the people who were running them. The *collectiv*, the group of people who are teaching there, can create an environment that's really favorable for learning, exploration, and free kinds of inquiry, or they can create an environment that's more closed and controlled.

"Teaching," she adds, "completely changed my whole perception of the Soviet Union. After being a student there, I felt a connection with individuals and not with the society at large. I thought unofficial contacts were the only worthwhile contacts. I thought that anybody who was a Party member was connected with something that was wrong. But when I went back and taught, I worked and lived in an environment where I was with Party members every day. And I realized that Party members are human beings, too."

As soon as she got to Leningrad she went to see her "family." In the two intervening years, they had frequently written and occasionally spoken on the phone, but Lazaroff, worried that their conversations were being bugged, decided not to mention that she was coming to Leningrad. Her heart pounded as she climbed the once-familiar stairs to Irina and Lev's apartment. "I had dreams that I would go to their house and that they wouldn't be there, that they would disappear. I was so scared that they had taken too much of a risk with me."

The night before Lazaroff showed up on their doorstep, Irina dreamed that they were once again together in the *banya*. "Cindy, you're here," she muttered in her dream. When Irina awoke, she told her husband about the dream. A few hours later, the doorbell rang, and Irina opened the door and began screaming near-hysterically, "Cindy's here!" Lev was sure she was still dreaming.

The three of them talked until four in the morning. Irina and Lev's son, Misha, was now three years old, and there had been other changes in their lives. The previous spring, Irina had been seriously ill, and only recently had recovered her health. She was painting the portrait of a dying poet and had to rush to finish it before he died; it was such a wrenching experience that Irina, whom Lazaroff says "internalizes the people she paints," started manifesting the poet's symptoms.

Before leaving the Soviet Union, Lazaroff returned to Moscow and to School ;45 to say good-bye to the students and teachers. In a last free-for-all question-and-answer session, the students asked her whether she believed in God, what she had learned by being in their country, and many more questions. "We think of the American students our own age as our friends," one student said. "Do American students think of us as their friends?"

Lazaroff paused, then decided to be candid. She explained that many American students believe that Soviet young people are automatons who have no individuality or free choice. A silence filled the room. Lazaroff wondered whether she had been too honest when she looked at their hurt and confused faces. "That's only because they don't have a chance to learn about who you are," she added hastily. "Many of them would really like to get to know you better, but they don't know how."

While flying home, she realized that she owed it to her Soviet students to help give American students that chance.

She moved to New York City, worked odd jobs to pay the rent, and began an all-out search for a job in the Soviet-American citizen exchange field. During the next six months she wrote letters to nearly two hundred individuals and groups offering her services or asking for advice on starting her own exchange program. She rose at 6 A.M. and went to bed at midnight every day, single-mindedly pursuing every lead she could find. She contacted exchange groups, trade groups, peace groups, publishing companies, television networks. She thought about teaching English to Soviet émigrés. She considered becoming a nanny in Leningrad. She spent nearly two months researching Armand Hammer, the chairman of Occidental Petroleum and granddaddy of Soviet-American trade, and plotted attention-grabbing ways of contacting him personally. She even sent Hammer a colorful "balloon-in-a-box" birthday greeting that explained her interest in expanding Soviet-American exchanges and mentioned that her Soviet students all admired him.

But one by one, all of her trails went cold. In early 1981 the political climate for starting new exchanges with the Soviet Union could not have been worse; a full-throttled revival of the Cold War was under way. Existing Soviet-American exchange groups were pruning their staffs as various programs withered or were cut. For a time, Lazaroff appeared to be making progress in negotiating a teacher's exchange under the aegis of the Citizen Exchange Council, but a Soviet official in the Ministry of Education turned her proposal down. She took a job teaching Russian émigré children, but it turned out to be nightmarish—"They were little devils. They couldn't handle their newfound freedom." In the meantime, her family dropped hints about "When are you going to go out and get a real job?"

The stress of her fruitless search began weighing on her; she almost began believing that what she wanted to do was, indeed, impossible. Then in July 1981 her body intervened. While running on a beach she felt a sharp pain in her abdomen, and although she had just received a clean bill of health from a routine checkup, she went to see a gynecologist. As soon as the doctor began examining her she screamed in pain. Ultrasound tests showed an ovarian tumor the size of a grapefruit.

She went into surgery not knowing whether the tumor was malignant, or whether the operation would mean that she would never be able to have children. She was lucky; the tumor was benign, and was skillfully removed, leaving her ovaries and uterus intact. But the hospital stay gave her a chance to think over her life. She decided that she had to give up her dream of working in Soviet-American affairs for now and concentrate on getting well. When she came home from the hospital, she found a form letter from the personnel office at Occidental Petroleum saying that "no positions were available." It seemed a sign.

Lazaroff moved to San Francisco, took a tedious job as a paralegal to pay the rent, and focused on healing her body. She tried to forget about her search, sure that California was a complete wasteland so far as exchange projects with the Soviet Union were concerned. Then a friend mentioned that he had heard that the Esalen Institute in Big Sur had a Soviet-American exchange program. Lazaroff didn't believe him at first. But eventually she called, and went to see Anya Kucharev, a translator for the Esalen program. "Someday," said Kucharev, "you are going to have to meet Jim Hickman."

Nearly eight months went by before Lazaroff and Hickman met ("which isn't surprising," Lazaroff remarks, "knowing Jim and his schedule"), but in the meantime things began looking up. Her health regained, Lazaroff landed a job in early 1982 at the International Center at Stanford University, advising students who wanted to study abroad. The Citizen Exchange Council, the group through which she had unsuccessfully tried to organize a teacher's exchange the previous year, asked her to lead a group of forty-five high school students to the Soviet Union in spring 1982. When she and Jim Hickman, the director of Esalen's Soviet-American program, finally met at a Chinese restaurant in San Francisco, they discovered that they would be in the Soviet Union at the same time and arranged to get together in Moscow.

Hickman accompanied Lazaroff on a visit to Moscow School #45 and was impressed both by the school and the easy rapport Lazaroff seemed to have with the staff and the students. He encouraged Lazaroff to focus her talents on youth exchanges. On this trip, Lazaroff took along a tape recorder and interviewed dozens of Soviet students at Moscow School #45, asking them to describe their lives, their hopes and fears, and their feelings about war and peace. When she returned, the tapes were broadcast on a local public radio show that was nationally syndicated, and she started getting calls from people interested in making contact with Soviet children.

In December 1982 Joan Steffy, a staff member at the Esalen program, called Lazaroff to tell her that children in an Oakland elementary school wanted to send New Year's Greetings to children at a school in Oakland's Soviet sister city, Nakhodka. Lazaroff agreed to help and mentioned in passing, "Wouldn't it be wonderful if the Oakland children already knew something about the Soviet Union, so that their greetings could have more substance?" Lazaroff and Steffy, who has a background in writing school curricula for McGraw-Hill and designing educational simulation games, began talking about creating a Soviet studies curriculum for American students. They met for a weekend in January 1983 to brainstorm. "We got up at 8 A.M. on the first day and said, 'Let's work a little before breakfast,' " recalls Lazaroff. "Then about 2 P.M. we looked at each other and said, 'I wonder what time it is? Maybe we should eat breakfast.' That's how excited we were about working together."

At first both thought that this project could be moonlighted, but it soon became clear that the task was huge and would require a full-time commitment. In spring 1983, Steffy, Lazaroff, and Terry Killam-Wilber, a filmmaker and educator, created a nonprofit group called the US-USSR Youth Exchange Program. In addition to designing the curriculum, they hoped to launch pen pal and art exchanges, lead numerous trips of American young people to the Soviet Union, and eventually bring Soviet young people on tours to the United States.

In early 1983, American interest in Soviet-American citizen diplomacy was on an upswing, and Lazaroff had offers to lead three groups of educators and high school students to the Soviet Union. She decided to risk quitting her secure job at Stanford in order to direct her new program, although she did not know where her salary would come from. One of the financial supporters of the Esalen program had offered to donate office space, but the Youth Exchange Program had no money, and Lazaroff personally had "not a penny to my name," she says. "The night after I turned in my keys at Stanford I was in tears thinking— What am I doing? How am I going to live?"

Fortunately, encouragement came quickly. The next day, at lunch, a friend promised five hundred dollars. Two hours later a woman philanthropist on the East Coast who had heard about the Soviet studies curriculum called and, after a twenty-minute conversation, promised five thousand dollars. Using this as seed money, Lazaroff and her colleagues managed to raise enough from foundations and individuals to start financing their plans.

Lazaroff spent half of the next year in the Soviet Union, guiding nearly two hundred American high school students and adults on trips. Her wide array of Soviet friends enabled her to take her Americans to many Soviet homes, schools, and other places not normally included on an Intourist tour. Her teen-agers danced rock 'n' roll, competed in talent shows, and played soccer games with Soviet teenagers; many came home with a desire to study Russian.

Consistently, she found, the Americans passed through a stage of euphoric shock best expressed by the phrase, "The Soviets are people, too." But she also had to guide her students through a second, more disconcerting stage of coming to terms with the differences between American and Soviet societies. "If people don't get beyond realizing 'The Soviets are human beings' and start asking, 'Yeah, okay, they *are* just like us, but why do we have these problems?', it can become a dead-end stage," she says. "Our trips are intended to whet people's appetites and inspire them to learn about the complexities."

Meeting Americans has just as important an impact on Soviets as meeting Soviets has on Americans, Lazaroff believes. Many Soviets are very curious about American life and will stop foreigners on the street to ask questions such as, "Why does Reagan want to go to war?" Many, "especially the old proletarians who generally believe what the Soviet government says," shift their preconceptions of the United States when they meet Americans working to improve relations between the countries.

Once a close woman friend, Nina, the daughter of a middle-level government official, invited Lazaroff to her home to meet her parents. Lazaroff asked Nina what her parents thought of Americans. "My mother, she will like you very very much," Nina replied. "My father—he probably will not talk to you." Lazaroff began trying to engage the father in conversation as soon as she arrived. At first, he responded to her overtures as minimally as possible without being openly rude. But as the night went on, as the cognac and wine flowed and the food was consumed, and as Lazaroff continued to tell him about herself and her work, a change came over the government official. He began participating in the conversation with genuine interest. He volunteered some of his own opinions. By the end of the evening, he and Lazaroff were robustly singing every Russian song they knew in common.

Now Nina's father is one of Lazaroff's closest Soviet friends, and their relationship has transformed his feelings about the United States. "Soon after we met, he told me that he had gone to his weekly Party meeting where everyone kept talking about the imperialist Americans. And all he could think of, as he sat there, was his new American friend, and the discrepancy between the Party line and reality. That kind of impact, extrapolated over the whole country, is not something that's necessarily quantifiable, but it can't be discounted."

Even a conversation with a cab driver can feel like a breakthrough. One of Lazaroff's friends from Princeton was aboard the Korean airliner shot down over Soviet airspace on September 1, 1983. Lazaroff went to the Soviet Union a week later "still harboring a lot of personal grief." During a twenty-minute cab drive in Moscow, the driver, a burly fellow with blond hair, pleasantly asked her where she was from. The United States, she replied. The cab driver stiffened and was silent. After a long minute, he asked her abruptly, "What makes you think you can just go flying over our territory and violating our borders like that?"

"Wait a minute," Lazaroff said evenly. "I think of the world as one world, as a global community. What right do we have to create boundaries in the air, when the astronauts and the cosmonauts have seen one world from outer space? Isn't it absurd that we're going to kill each other over these artificial boundaries?" She described how the Korean airliner incident seemed to her a kind of signal from above, an attempt by higher powers in the universe to dramatize for humankind the fiery tragedy that might take place on a global scale if concepts like "boundaries" were not soon transcended.

After she finished, the cab driver was silent again. Finally he said, in a quiet voice, "I never thought of the world that way, but that's really interesting." When they arrived at her destination, he shook her hand warmly and wished her luck with her work.

Between the end of one tour and the beginning of the next, Lazaroff often stayed in the Soviet Union to lay the groundwork for future projects. She went "fishing" for sympathetic contacts in various Soviet organizations that deal with children and youth—the Ministry of Education, Sputnik (the youth travel agency), Pioneer Palaces, children's theaters, and many, many schools. Lazaroff estimates that she has personally visited about fifty Soviet schools. To help pay her expenses, she also worked as a consultant and negotiator for a half dozen American youth groups, theater groups, artists, and schools interested in organizing exchanges.

Always, she found, the intangibles of human relationships had a profound impact on the outcome of such negotiations. "There's always someone to whom I feel closest on the Soviet side of every negotiation. And if we reach an impasse, over money, or permission for something, often this particular individual will come up later and say, 'You know, if you were to present it in a different way, and offer this—but please don't let anyone know where this came from—then you'd get what you want.' There's always someone who's willing to go the extra mile. These are people who could lose their jobs if others knew that they were doing this.

"Individuals *can* make a difference in that country," she adds, "if they believe in something and have the personality and drive and determination. It's important to seek out the people who are open, and who are in positions of influence over there, and encourage them to take risks and get involved in exchanges."

Meanwhile, Lazaroff had to unlist her home phone number because strangers started calling her at midnight and six in the morning, pleading with her to help them start an exchange program with the Soviet Union. Not everyone filled with enthusiasm for citizen diplomacy, she discovered, was equally enthusiastic about putting in the long hours and hard work that creating new private exchanges requires. "A lot of American organizations come up with an idea, say, 'Let's do it,' don't talk to the Soviets, start it on this end, and get everybody excited here," Lazaroff says. "Then it falls through and it's a disaster, because people get disillusioned and start believing, 'See, you can't do anything with the Soviet Union.' "

Lazaroff is concerned that some of the Americans now involved in Soviet-American citizen diplomacy are following a fad, and that if it were to become more fashionable to do something else, like help airlift supplies to Ethiopia, many would drop their Soviet efforts. "That doesn't mean," she adds, "that what they're doing isn't worthwhile. Even if it is just a fad for someone, or they only go on one trip, that person will come home and share his or her experience and get people thinking."

But Lazaroff can also happily point to spectacular examples of people who *have* been willing to do the dirty work, cope with the inevitable frustrations and disappointments, and successfully launch their own exchange programs with her help. One of her protégés, Paula DeCosse of Minneapolis, Minnesota, now directs the Consortium on New Educational and Cultural Ties with the Soviet Union (CONNECT), which has brought art by Soviet children to the United States and sent paintings to the Soviet Union by American children from forty states. With Lazaroff's help, David Woollcombe, the director of the Peace Child Foundation, successfully staged his play *Peace Child* in Moscow in July 1985 with a cast of both Soviet and American children, and created a live two-way satellite television linkup between children in Minneapolis and Moscow that was dedicated to the late Samantha Smith—feats that required his making no fewer than eleven trips to Moscow within a period of eighteen months.

Sharon Tennison, a San Francisco nurse and cofounder of the Center for US-USSR Initiatives, is another example of someone whose dedication has allowed her to accomplish extraordinary things in a short period of time, according to Lazaroff. At the end of Tennison's first Soviet trip, in September 1983, her group crowded into a hotel room in Leningrad and began, one by one, to talk about how the experience had changed them and how they intended to communicate what they had learned upon returning home. Lazaroff, their guide and interpreter, sat cross-legged on the floor and listened, remembering how two years ago it had seemed as though she was the only person in the world interested in citizen diplomacy. When it was her turn to speak, she started crying. "I can't tell you how much it means to me to see what this trip has done to you," she said. "I can't tell you how it feels to know I'm not alone anymore."

Lazaroff is now confident that the inroads citizen diplomacy has made are irreversible. "The fabric of US-Soviet relations will never be the same," she declares. "It's been blown so far out of the water by our wacky ideas. I don't think that it can ever go back to being the way it was, purely government-to-government, because of the initiatives that individuals have taken. People will not let it go that way—in either country. An interest has been sparked and it will never be the same."

The personal relationships that have been created between Americans and Soviets will not fade easily, she believes. Lazaroff has about five intimate Soviet friends who "have shared everything, inside and out, with me." She counts an additional two dozen Soviets as close friends, and she has visited more than a hundred Soviet private homes. How far Soviets will go in opening up their private lives, she has found, is very much an individual matter. "There are some people with whom I've shared incredible experiences, with whom I've become very close in many ways, yet who to this day, when it comes to certain questions, still just put up a barrier," she says. "Will not answer. Will not tell me if they're in the Party, for example. There's a barrier of fear, and I realize that they're just not going to break through it easily. But we can keep chipping away at it. I have official contacts who last year wouldn't tell me home numbers, who wouldn't see me outside of officially arranged meetings, and who now are willing to do that secretly. It's a challenge to get inside someone's apartment, to know that they trust you so much that they're willing to let you into their private lives."

It is also a trust that has to be handled carefully. Once, while staying with a Moscow friend, Dmitri, she asked if she could use his phone to call official Soviet contacts, such as the Soviet Peace Committee and Gosteleradio. Dmitri shrugged and said, fine. Lazaroff made calls for several days, until one day when Dmitri happened to come into the room just as she was dialing and casually asked her, "Who are you calling?" The American embassy, Lazaroff answered. Dmitri grabbed the phone and threw down the receiver. "You can't do that," he whispered, white-faced. "If you call the American embassy, or call an American journalist from someone's home, they could be accused of working for the CIA." Lazaroff shakes her head at the memory. If he hadn't walked in at that exact moment, she might have caused his whole family to be interrogated.

"Xenophobia predates the revolution, it carried over after the revolution, and it probably reached its most alarming and outrageous proportions under Stalin," she says. "Many people who had foreign friends at that time were suspected of being spies, and simply disappeared. Members of their families have not forgotten that, and they never will. That's why the younger generation is so important, because they did not directly experience Stalin. They don't have the same level of fear that their parents grew up with. It's another reason why my energy has gone toward young people." As the memory of Stalin fades, and as more Soviets have a chance to meet Westerners, more Soviets, she says, "want to have the opportunity to travel, to go abroad for vacations. And that's not something that can be withheld from them forever. In every exchange we have, the Soviet kids say, 'We hope someday to travel to your country.' The parents don't say that, but the kids do."

Lazaroff knows that the day when young Soviets and young Americans can in large numbers freely travel between the countries is still years in the future, but she hopes her programs will hasten that day. In the meantime, her Soviet studies curriculum is designed to give American students an experience that is the next best thing to a trip to the Soviet Union. If young people in both countries can learn more about each other, Lazaroff believes, "maybe they can negotiate with each other and learn how to share the planet more successfully than their parents and grandparents have. The fear and ignorance that exist in this country about the Soviet Union has been building up over decades, and it's bred into us at a very young age." Recently Lazaroff discovered an old sixth-grade textbook in the attic of her Pittsburgh home that said little about the Soviet Union other than "the evil Communists are out to rule the world."

During 1983 Lazaroff gathered textbooks, photographs, maps, and suggestions from Soviet teachers for her curriculum. By March 1984 she, Joan Steffy, and several dozen volunteers and consultants were ready to field-test a seven-part curriculum designed for the seventh through twelfth grades called "Step One: Getting to Know the Soviet Union and Its People." Using videotapes, slides, maps, games, skits, and reading assignments, the lessons introduce students to the geography, history, culture, and everyday life of people in the Soviet Union.

"At the beginning the kids usually realize they don't know anything," Lazaroff says. "We ask, how many of you have ever seen a picture of the sun shining in the Soviet Union? They shake their heads. Nobody. What colors come to mind? Black, red, gray, blood it's interesting they say 'blood' when we ask about colors. Then we show them one of our videotapes, and they start thinking—wait a minute, why haven't I ever seen this before?"

One of the videotapes, called *What Soviet Children Are Saying about Nuclear War*, is a selection of interviews with sixty Soviet children chosen randomly at two Soviet Pioneer camps. Lazaroff served as a consultant for the film, made in July 1983 and supervised by American psychiatrists Eric Chivian, John Mack, and Jerry Walctsky of the International Physicians for the Prevention of Nuclear War and the Harvard Nuclear Psychology Program. The Soviet children, aged ten to fifteen, grow subdued when asked about nuclear war and express their fears that "the entire earth will become a wasteland."

Evaluation forms filled out by American students who have seen the video reveal surprise. "Soviet children aren't miniature terrorists . . . they are just like me," wrote one American student. Another student said that the video made him believe "that some of the Soviets, if not all, in time, could be our friends, and we, theirs." One child wrote that she had learned that "the Soviet Union isn't just a bunch of beasts—they are caring people."

Perhaps the most unusual lesson in the curriculum centers on J. D. Salinger's novel *The Catcher in the Rye*, which is often studied in high school American literature courses in both the Soviet Union and the United States. In 1983, Lazaroff asked one of the Soviet teachers at Moscow School #45 for something written by Soviet students that they could share with American students. The teacher asked her twelve- and thirteen-year-old students, who all knew and trusted Lazaroff, to write out their impressions of *The Catcher in the Rye,* one of their favorite American novels. Two days later, her friend handed her a dozen essays in English. "I haven't had a chance to correct them," the teacher apologized, "some of the grammar's wrong, but I think there's some wonderful stuff here. Use what you can."

Lazaroff still has the original essays, written on lined composition paper with words misspelled and crossed out. "They weren't pre-prepared or glossed over, and the teacher didn't change them. They were really what the kids had to say," Lazaroff remarks. "It was an example of the importance of personal relationships to this kind of work. A journalist, or someone they didn't know, could never have gone into that school and gotten something like that."

Nearly all the Soviet children seemed very moved by the book and wrote intensely personal, often poetic expressions of their feelings about it. Some interpreted the novel, the story of a rebellious teenager in a high-class preparatory school, as an accurate portrait of contemporary America; one wrote that it depicted "the real life of the American society with all its problems and difficulties," and another said that "after reading this book I understand how hard it is to live in the world where everything is sold and bought." Yet most of the students identified strongly with Holden Caulfield, the protagonist, and when they speak of his struggle to maintain principle, his loneliness, and the tragedy of others misunderstanding him, their rhetorical tone shifts and they seem to be speaking about their own lives. "Holden fights (tries somehow) for his principles, but fails. Everywhere wins stupid strength," wrote one girl. The lesson encourages American teachers to ask their students to write their own essays about *The Catcher in the Rye* before showing them the Soviet students' essays.

Other lessons teach Soviet geography through a game called "Trans-Siberian Odyssey," introduce the works of Russian and Soviet authors such as Chekhov and Akhmatova, and explain "how the Soviet political system influences the lives of its young people." A final lesson encourages students to consider studying Russian, writing to a Soviet pen pal, or participating in art, essay, or poster exchanges with Soviet schools.

"It's a menu of possible exchanges that kids can participate in, so that every kid, no matter what he or she's interested in—stamp collecting, hockey, art, the outdoors—can see there's a way to get involved," Lazaroff explains. Several of the lessons are currently distributed through Social Studies School Service, the largest distributor of supplemental social studies materials in the country; Lazaroff estimates that one hundred thousand students in thirty states have been exposed to at least one lesson.

Lazaroff's curriculum is upbeat but not pro-Soviet; it clearly states, for example, that "Soviet citizens marching with a banner voicing opposition to their government would almost certainly be immediately arrested and interrogated by the KGB." And: "A good Komsomol [Young Communist League] record is generally considered highly advantageous, if not essential, for career advancement and admission into prestigious institutions of higher learning."

What do her Soviet friends think of lines like these? "The people who have seen it, some of whom are in the Party and some of whom are not, have mixed reactions," she admits. "Some kind of laugh at those parts, others are a little embarrassed, others are shy, and a few argue. But they all know I know the system too well for them to convince me that these things aren't true. And since my Soviet friends appreciate the overall idea and purpose of the curriculum, they've been very supportive. Those who understand America understand why I have to include critical things.

"I feel that we don't try to paint a *good* picture of the Soviet Union," continues Lazaroff. "We try to paint a *realistic* picture, and try to help people here come to terms with the differences between our countries. We don't say the Soviet Union is a wonderful place to be. We don't try to hide some of the very horrible things, very tragic things, that have happened there during the last century. It's important that people know about these things and have a context for them beyond the usual stereotypes."

During their brainstorming session in January 1983, Joan Steffy asked Lazaroff what else she wanted to do in addition to writing the curriculum and leading high school trips. Lazaroff remembered that while teaching in Moscow in 1980 she had shown her Soviet students an Outward Bound film, borrowed from the American embassy, and they had loved it. Wouldn't it be wonderful, she had thought, if half of the wilderness trekkers in the film were Soviet and half were American? An expedition where survival would be dependent on mutual cooperation and inter-dependence seemed a perfect metaphor for the task before the two governments. She proposed the idea to various exchange professionals when she returned to the United States in 1981. Everyone told her it was impossible. Everyone, that is, except Jim Hickman, who thought it was a terrific idea.

When Lazaroff told Steffy in 1983 that she wanted to organize Soviet-American youth wilderness expeditions, Steffy replied immediately, "Great. We'll take groups of American kids and Soviet kids hiking in the Caucasus Mountains of the Soviet Union." The trek lingered in the idea stage for several months until one of the advisors of the Youth Exchange Program put Lazaroff in touch with Dick McGowan, an American representative of the Soviet Sports Committee, who organizes climbing expeditions for adult mountaineers in the Caucasus Mountains through a company called Mountain Travel.

Of course you can take American kids to the Caucasus, McGowan told Lazaroff. Could they hike with Soviet kids? Well—that was something else. Nothing like it had ever been done. McGowan offered to introduce her to the appropriate people in the Sports Committee, but she would have to do the negotiations. Encouraged, Lazaroff telephoned Ken Mack, a twenty-one-year-old rock drummer and freshman at Hampshire College who had organized and co-led one of Lazaroff's 1983 high school tours, and Mack agreed to start assembling the American delegation.

Lazaroff spent spring 1984 taking additional American groups on tours and "literally knocking on the Sports Committee's door in Moscow every few days for four months and begging them to let us have Soviet kids." At first the director of the Sports Committee's division of international mountaineering camps, Mikhail Monastyrski, received her politely but told her that it would be "very, very difficult." Because his division of the Sports Committee only handled accommodations for foreign visitors to the Caucasus—Soviet visitors fell under a different heading—his first reaction was that Lazaroff was suggesting a bureaucratic nightmare.

But Lazaroff kept dropping by his office and nicely, but firmly, explaining her vision for this trip. As Monastyrski began getting to know her better, his manner grew less formal and he started offering her tea, chocolates, and cookies when she arrived. He began hinting that getting Soviet kids on her trip might be possible after all. Then the Soviet Union announced its boycott of the 1984 Summer Olympics in Los Angeles, and although he never referred to the Olympics directly, Monastyrski again told Lazaroff that arranging for Soviet teenagers to participate would be extremely difficult and that he could make no promises.

Lazaroff decided to bring the American kids anyway, although she canceled plans to film the trek. When she, Ken Mack, and her eight American teenagers arrived in Moscow in July 1984, she took them to meet Monastyrski. That apparently made a difference. The night before the group flew to the Caucasus, Monastyrski told her, "I can't guarantee anything, but I'll come to the mountains with you and help you look for some Soviet kids to hike with."

The mountains themselves, however, proved nearly as challenging as conquering the Soviet bureaucracy. Lazaroff had no prior high-altitude experience and had been too busy leading tours to get in shape. The night before she left for the Caucasus, a Soviet friend asked with some concern, "Cindy—are you a mountaineer?" "No," Lazaroff replied nervously, "but I'm about to become one!"

On their itinerary was a rigorous seven-day trek into a remote region of the Caucasus called Svanetia and a four-day ascent of 18,481-foot-high Mt. Elbrus, the highest peak in Europe. The challenging but technically uncomplicated climb of this ancient volcano in the isthmus between the Black Sea and the Caspian Sea quickly became the symbolic focus of the trip. According to Greek myth, when Jason and the Argonauts caught sight of the snow-covered double peaks of Mt. Elbrus they believed they had reached the end of the earth. A traditional Georgian legend says that a magical bird, named "Simurg," has its nest atop Mt. Elbrus and sees the past with one eye and the future with the other. "When the bird Simurg rises in the air," the legend goes, "the ground shakes from the beating of its wings, the storms howl, the sea grows rough, and all the sleeping powers of the deep wake to life."

But it was quickly apparent that few of the American hikers were in sufficient physical condition to attempt Mt. Elbrus. Their first training hike, at eight thousand feet, left Lazaroff and many of the others exhausted. One calamity after another winnowed out all but the most hale. Ken Mack became ill on a three-day training hike over a glacier. Lazaroff sprained her ankle in the snow and had to be supported between two Soviet guides during a ten-hour hike back to the base camp. One American hiker had asthma and couldn't handle the altitude; another suddenly manifested a fear of heights.

Fifteen-year-old Paul Brunell, whose fair-skinned complexion made him particularly vulnerable to high-altitude glare, did not put on his protective dark goggles in time during one glacier climb and became snow-blind. The Soviet doctor with the group, Boris Donnikov, wrapped Paul's head in bandages and led him by hand down the glacier. The rest of the group followed them, subdued, worried that Paul might have permanently damaged his eyes but also moved by this living demonstration of Soviet-American trust. Two hours later, they were off the snow. After a brief rest, Donnikov continued to lead Paul, who was in excruciating pain, by the hand and to carry him over icy streams for another five hours of hiking back to the base camp.

The Soviet guides soon leveled with Lazaroff and Mack—the group would never survive the Svanetia trek. But the guides cheerfully offered to take them on simpler hikes that were more in keeping with their abilities. And a week after they had arrived, Monastyrski announced that he had worked out a way for the American trekkers to team up for several hikes with a group of young Soviets who were spending a month and a half in a nearby mountaineering training camp.

A few days later, the remaining healthy Americans set off with no less than seventy Soviet youths on a three-day trek through lush meadows carpeted by wildflowers and ringed by imposing snow-covered massifs. Despite the language barrier, the Americans quickly made friends with some of the less shy Soviets. Mark Lawrence, a freshman at Stanford, wrote on his return that "in the mountains, I found all people—Russians, Americans, and the people of other nationalities we met—are reduced to just that—people. Not only are the basic necessities of mountaineering contingent upon teamwork, but when a group of people is ten miles and a twelve-thousand-foot-high pass away from the nearest civilization, the indomitable human need for companionship, for comfort in the wilderness, comes through loud and clear."

During one lunch break in the brilliant high-altitude sunshine, Lazaroff's friend Andrei Orlov, a Soviet free-lance journalist, brought together a group of about two dozen Soviets and Americans and started asking them questions about the future of their two countries. "We'd never seen Americans before except through the windows of tour buses," one young Soviet said as he spoke about how the hike had changed his perceptions. Remembers Ken Mack: "The Soviets would say, 'I think there should be peace between Americans and the Soviet Union, and I'm committed to that,' and the Americans would agree. And then Andrei said, 'When your parents were young they might have said the same thing. But as they got older, they lost their commitment to peace. What is it that will keep you from losing your commitment?' They were very good questions."

The Soviet hikers invited the Americans to their "graduating" party marking the end of the Soviets' training session. In elaborate mock rituals, the Soviets dressed up in wild costumes and pantomimed placations to the mountain gods; the Americans joined in the skits, singing, dancing, and general high jinks. "I remember there seemed to be people in togas everywhere—on top of the buildings, in the trees, on the ground," Ken Mack says. The Soviets were pinned with badges signifying the completion of the alpine training program. "They pinned us too," Lazaroff recalls, "even though we hadn't earned it."

Only two members of the American group, Mark Lawrence and Amy Bayer (who later wrote about the trip for *Seventeen* magazine) were capable of attempting the Elbrus climb, which requires a grueling seven-hour final ascent over snowfields and glaciers. But they were thwarted by the weather, which even in July can turn from sunny and calm to an opaque blizzard in minutes. The morning they planned to make their final ascent was overcast, and the Soviet guides said it was too dangerous to try.

"On the horizon lurks the peak of Elbrus reminding me how close we came to what would have been an incredible accomplishment for us inexperienced Americans," Mark Lawrence wrote in his journal. "Yet also on the horizon lurks a more elusive and spectacular summit, that of world peace and understanding. Our expedition perhaps nudged the world ever so slightly up that mountain, but a very long way remains unscaled."

At the end of the trip, Lazaroff told Monastyrski and the Soviet guides that she would bring another group of American kids next year to the Caucasus along with a film crew; they would be "in absolutely tip-top physical shape," she hastily added. Monastyrski agreed to arrange for ten young Soviet hikers to accompany the ten Americans for the full three weeks. "The Soviets were willing to give us kids for the entire time and let them be with us day, night, in tents, sharing everything—things we couldn't have dreamed of the year before," says Lazaroff. "They had caught the vision. That is the most exciting part of all of this for me—getting Soviets who really couldn't have cared less about any of this to the point where they are absolutely thrilled about it, proud of it, and brainstorming how to make it bigger and better."

During much of the next year Lazaroff and film producer Lynne Joiner fund-raised and negotiated with the Sports Committee and Sovinfilm, the Soviet agency that handles foreign filmmaking, for an American film crew of six to accompany the hikers. Through *The Challenge of the Caucasus*, an hour-long documentary narrated by Leonard Nimoy to be shown on the Turner Broadcasting System, and a shorter film clip for the MacNeil-Lehrer Report on national public television, they hoped to bring the image of Soviet-American cooperation to an audience of millions.

By spring 1985 the trek had become an all-consuming task, and as she fell behind schedule in her other projects Lazaroff at times wondered whether the trek was worth it. But she knew that an important precedent would be set if Soviet and American young people were allowed to mingle so unconventionally in the wilderness. She hoped it would help make some of her other long-range visions come true—bringing Soviet kids to the United States for wilderness expeditions, expanding the mountain treks to include teenagers from China and other countries, and getting young people from East and West to go to Third World countries for cooperative work projects and wilderness trips.

Lazaroff and Mack chose the American participants, all between the ages of seventeen and twenty-one, from over a hundred applicants on the basis of their physical condition and their commitment to working to improve Soviet-American relations, and selected a geographically, ethnically, and socioeconomically diverse group. Some were enrolled in Ivy League colleages; some were not college-bound. Some came from privileged backgrounds, while others needed full or partial scholarships from various sources to pay their way.

In Moscow, Monastyrski found a group of ten teenagers who belong to a mountaineering sports club and who were already planning to spend the summer in the Caucasus Mountains. Although this meant that the Soviet group was not as diverse, Lazaroff did not blame Monastyrski for resorting to the simplest solution. "He normally doesn't deal with any Soviets, just foreigners, so this was a tremendous amount of work for him," she says. "He told me once, in good-humored exasperation, that he could organize fifteen trips of American adults to the Caucasus in the time it took him to organize our trip."

In July 1985, ten young Americans stepped out of a bus in the Caucasus village of Cheget and shyly shook hands with ten young Soviets. Within minutes the Soviets were helping unload the Americans' gear and carrying it into the unpretentious hotel that would be their base camp for day hikes. At the end of the valley loomed Mt. Elbrus, blanketed in snow, mysterious, awesome.

A few days later, Lazaroff, the young hikers, a half-dozen Soviet mountain guides, and an American film crew lugging several hundred pounds of equipment set off with backpacks through the beautiful poplar, beech, birch, and rhododendron forests of the Caucasus Mountains, crossing wildflower-filled meadows to snowfields where they could practice their snow-climbing and ice-ax techniques. Lazaroff knew within hours that this trip would be nothing like the previous year's ordeal; this time, she had been in physical training for months. "We did a very rigorous hike, and I didn't even feel it," she says. "It was an invigorating reminder of the individual potential we all have, if we choose to work at it and develop it—and an indication of what's possible on a larger scale."

The hikers soon confronted the language barrier. Only two of the Soviet teenagers spoke any English, and only two of the American teenagers spoke any Russian. Impromptu language lessons began springing up next to rock piles and rivers, but communication often became frustrating. "Verbal communication hasn't been the ice breaking element in our relationships with the Soviets," noted Harvard undergraduate Jay Winthrop after a few days of crossed signals.

The intricacies of a modern American dome tent perplexed the Soviet young people who tried earnestly to help the Americans put up their tents one night as darkness approached and a freezing wind came up. "The long poles were going in the short slots and the short poles were going in the long slots, and the tent looked like a square when it was supposed to be a dome," recalls eighteen-year-old Beth Ewing of Washington, DC. "We kept saying 'pull,' and they didn't understand 'pull.' It was so frustrating, we all felt like killing each other." After their efforts resulted in something that resembled a crumpled hang glider, they started over again—and succeeded.

Another source of frustration was food, and the hikers' differences in taste. Food was complicated enough among members of the American group, which was half vegetarian, but even the nonvegetarians had trouble getting used to the regular fare of boiled goat meat. "Each night you'd have twenty-five kids sitting around a campfire, who don't speak the same language and don't eat the same food, trying to cook a dinner for twenty-five people," says Jay Winthrop. And after surviving dinner, there was breakfast to contend with. The Americans gagged on the Soviet hot cereal, which to them seemed to consist entirely of milk and sugar with a few cereal grains mixed in, but eventually they discovered a compromise concoction.

Soon the hikers were ready for their first major trek, a six-day journey across the 11,500-foot-high Betcho Pass to Svanetia, a region in the Soviet republic of Georgia. The weather was mild when they hiked to a camp several thousand feet below the pass. The next morning, however, a stiff wind came up and snow swirled around them as they struggled against the wind for five hours to gain the pass. Although everyone made it, Betcho Pass "intimidated a lot of people," Lazaroff says. "It was supposed to be a checkout test to see if we were ready for Elbrus. But a lot of people started wondering 'If this is so hard, how will I ever make it up Elbrus, which is seven thousand feet higher?' "

At the pass, which is part of an ancient route connecting Russia and Georgia, the hikers could fully appreciate the feat memorialized by several plaques; during World War II, a handful of Soviet mountaineers made more than twenty trips across Betcho Pass to lead hundreds of children, women, and old people out of Nazi-occupied territory to safety. But the hikers could not rest long—they still had a five-hour descent to the valley below. A mile from their campsite, twenty-one-year-old Maureen Eich twisted her ankle on a loose rock. Soviet physician Boris Donnikov, who had gone with Lazaroff's group the previous year, piggybacked her to the camp.

Although the ancient Greeks knew Svanetia well, and Alexander the Great's armies visited there in 300 B.C., the area is known to few travelers today. Villagers run sheep and goats on mountain pastures in a way of life that has changed little over the centuries. Medieval fortress towers that once protected families during invasions still stand. Georgians are famous for their exuberant hospitality toward guests, and when the hikers arrived in the village of Mestia they were welcomed by men with daggers tucked in their belts and women in long sky-blue dresses leading a ceremony that included a lamb-slaughtering and traditional music and dancing in a meadow. It was a scene as foreign to the hikers from Moscow as it was to the Americans, but soon the Svanetians had pulled everyone into the circle and had them dancing as well.

Delighted by these unusual guests, one of the older dancers spontaneously invited the entire group to his daughter's wedding feast the next evening. "We are all here as his family," Lazaroff announced at the feast, translating a toast by the proud father, and the rest of the night was spent in singing, dancing, and general merriment. "The group really came together," says Lazaroff. "It was the high point of the trip so far."

Lazaroff and Mack noticed that some of the Soviet guides who had been diffident the previous year were now eager to talk with them, over tea brewed with freshly gathered mountain herbs, about possibilities for other joint wilderness trips. "That's what's really exciting to me," says Lazaroff, "getting them so enlisted in the process, so invested in the idea, that they start suggesting things. 'We could take you on a canoe trip through a historical part of Old Russia,' they said, or 'We could take you cross-country skiing, or white-water rafting.' "

Closer friendships also began developing between the young Soviet and American hikers. The Soviets threw a surprise seventeenth birthday party for Kari Anderson, one of the Americans. The Americans persuaded their base camp hotel to let them play their rock 'n' roll tapes, a language the Soviets had no trouble understanding when everyone hit the dance floor. There was much giggling in tents and singing around campfires, and almost anything, from seeing a new wildflower to attempting to cook a meal, became a pretext for a language lesson.

Inevitably, a few conversations turned to politics and different ways of looking at the world. Once one of the Soviet boys whispered to Lazaroff over breakfast that "I had an incredible conversation late last night with Jay [one of the Americans]." Lazaroff could tell from his voice that he had "just gone through something monumental. He had seen the world through an American's eyes."

But to the American hikers' surprise, the Soviets did not devour their ideas about individual rights and free enterprise. It was difficult for the Americans to accept that while the Soviets loved rock 'n' roll, enjoyed wearing blue jeans, and were curious about life in America, they were not anxious to become just like Americans. "I thought by this time we'd be winning them over," said one puzzled American halfway through the trip. A few suspected that the Soviets had been screened for ideological purity; they couldn't believe that random Soviet teenagers would react lukewarmly to descriptions of the American political system and democratic principles. Lazaroff reports, however, that "the Soviet kids did not strike me, based on my experience, as Party-line, one-sided kids— they were more curious and open, but very shy."

The Soviet group was closely knit, but the American group was so diverse that Lazaroff had to do nearly as much diplomacy within her own group as she did with the Soviets. "We tried so hard to get kids that were *so* self-sufficient and strong that we went a little overboard," admits Lazaroff. And this collection of individualists had to grapple with the differences between a society that emphasizes individual values and one that emphasizes communal values. "When Americans are out in the wilderness, they want to prove that they can be strong and self-sufficient," says Lazaroff. "The Soviets, on the other hand, feel that the group has to share the burden for everybody, and that if someone isn't as strong as someone else, the stronger person carries the weaker person's stuff."

One American who was determined to carry her own heavy pack got furious when some Soviets insisted on lightening her load. She couldn't understand why they wouldn't leave her alone, and they couldn't understand why she wouldn't let them help her. Another time, this same young woman was trailing the rest of the group, and one of the Soviet guides asked, "Where are your friends?" She explained they were up ahead, that they moved at a different pace. "I don't understand," said the Soviet. "Are they really your friends? In our country we would never make someone walk alone."

Once the headstrong individualism of the Americans got them into trouble. At an icy river crossing, the Soviet guides directed the group to the best fords. But some of the Americans ignored their warnings, tried their own route, and promptly fell in the river. A Soviet guide helping to pull them out also slid in the current. "When the water is freezing, and you have twelve more hours to hike," muses Lazaroff, "that kind of thing makes a real impression."

Meanwhile, tension built about the Elbrus climb. While the group was hiking up another snowfield a call came over the walkie-talkie of the head Soviet guide, Slava Volkov, reporting that a Czechoslovakian woman climber, who had attempted to climb Elbrus without a guide, was missing in a blizzard. Two days later, they learned that the woman had been found frozen to death near the summit. It brought the number of people who had frozen on the mountain to ten that year.

Nervousness about whether the group would make it to the top led to small disputes even as the group came closer together. The Soviet guides found the American hikers' tendency to wear Sony Walkmans on dangerous stretches of glacier exasperating. The Americans grumbled about the food and their lack of showers. The hikers were scared, says Lazaroff, and they "were taking it out on each other, complaining about little nitpicky things that had nothing to do with what they were really afraid of. We said that getting to the top of Elbrus wasn't the most important thing, and the kids knew that, but it was another thing to really feel it."

It was a relief, everyone felt, when they finally began climbing toward the Priutt Refuge, a metal bunkhouse on the slopes of Mt. Elbrus located at nearly fourteen thousand feet. They spent a day acclimatizing to the altitude and doing a last "checkout" climb to an overlook at fifteen thousand feet. Most of the climbers made it. One who didn't was Joel Mahnke of Telluride, Colorado, who had missed the Svanetia trek because of altitude sickness and had difficulty breathing once again. "Elbrus isn't what we're here for," he said that night, lying on his back in pain and fighting back tears while the movie cameras and microphones hovered over him. "I did my best, and I feel I've gotten a lot of things out of this trip, but Elbrus isn't one of the things I'm going to get."

That night, Slava Volkov gave the climbers longer odds than they had expected: if the weather held he thought they had a fifty-fifty chance. Many of the hikers had chronic headaches, diarrhea, and shortness of breath. The group was split in two so that the stronger climbers would have a better chance of making it. At 3 A.M. on August 3, 1985, the Soviet and American hikers rose and ate breakfast. No one said much. Led by Slava Volkov and Cynthia Lazaroff, the first group set off in the below-zero darkness.

The mountain—majestic, looming, seemingly so near—glowed in the moonlight. Stars shone. Though it was windy, it was unusually clear. Later the hikers would recall the extraordinary beauty of that dawn: the pink alpenglow striking faraway peaks, the sun creeping brilliantly over the Caucasus range. But at the time they kept their thoughts to themselves while they concentrated on breathing, on one step at a time.

It took five hours for the lead group to trudge to the eighteen-thousand-foot mark called "the saddle" and plop on the snow, now blazing in the midmorning sun, for a rest. At this altitude even opening a water bottle took concentrated mental and physical effort. In the thirty-five-mile-per-hour wind, many had lost all feeling in their hands or feet. Several considered turning back. Maureen Eich had already turned back, reluctantly, realizing that if she continued she might permanently damage her injured ankle.

Far below the saddle, twenty-year-old Karen Bortolazzo fought dizziness, a fever, and extreme fatigue with the help of Soviet guide Victor Goryach. She wavered on her feet, her crampons and ice ax sinking heavily in the snow. Every few hundred yards, she collapsed. Every time she collapsed, Victor Goryach held her in his arms and let her cry out of frustration and exhaustion. Every time, he asked her, "Down?" meaning: "Do you want to turn back?" "*Nyet!*" replied Karen Bortolazzo. "Up!" He would then coax her into standing up and walking a little farther before collapsing again. "Down?" "*Nyet!* Up!" Slowly, excruciatingly, the young American woman and the young Soviet man inched toward the summit.

Also below the saddle was Ken Mack, the coleader of the trek, who had had a year to brood about not making it to the summit last time. He was ill again, but he tried not to panic and paced himself. "You know, Kenny is going to have to turn back," Slava Volkov told Lazaroff at the saddle, after conferring with the other guides by walkie-talkie. Lazaroff knew how hard Ken Mack had worked for this trip, how much it meant to him to make it this year. But she had to put it out of her mind and concentrate on getting her own reluctant body up the mountain. Although she didn't know it, Ken Mack persuaded the guide with him to let him continue a little longer.

The climbers couldn't rest at the saddle long. The last five hundred feet of elevation gain, they knew, would be the toughest of all. An hour after they began hiking again, Lazaroff saw a red American jacket splayed on the snow ahead of her, a few feet off the trail. She couldn't see who was in it at first. "Cindy!" she heard a voice call out weakly. It was Jay Winthrop, one of the strongest and most self-confident of the American climbers. Lazaroff and Volkov went over to him. "I need water," he moaned. "I don't think I'm going to make it." Lazaroff's voice grew determined. "Jay. You're so close. You *have* to get up. You can do it."

A little ahead of them, seventeen-year-old Troy Shortell, of Solvang, California, was following the bootsteps of Alexei Khokhlov, his Soviet tent partner. Alexei paused and hunched over, needing to catch his breath. Troy decided to keep going. Kick, test, up. Kick, test, up. He was almost there. The rounded curve of ice ahead of him gave way to an arch of blue. Alexei was at his side. Kick, test, up. They were there.

Troy took a tiny forty-eight-star American flag out of his pack, a family heirloom passed down from his grandfather, and tied it to his ice ax. Alexei did the same with a tiny handmade Soviet flag. Smiling behind the faceless masks of their balaclavas, they joined hands, planted their ice axes on the summit, and watched the flags whip in the brilliant sunshine.

"It was the meaning of the trip for me," Troy said later. "I was standing there with my hand in the hand of a human being who has been called my enemy for so many years. I felt a real triumph both personally and for the whole world—the youth of two countries coming together, really trusting one another and respecting one another and cooperating and serving as a model for the world to follow. Standing there with one common bond and one common goal, I knew that we *can* have peace and live together and respect each other as human beings."

One by one, others joined them. It had taken them an average of two hours to climb the last five hundred feet. Lazaroff, Slava Volkov, Jay Winthrop, and the other Soviets and Americans in the lead group stood on the summit and hugged each other in a circle around the flags. Many were crying.

Over the next few hours, the rest of the climbers, including Ken Mack, including Karen Bortolazzo and Victor Goryach, staggered to the summit.

And how did Cynthia Lazaroff, her five-foot-one frame buried beneath the bulky padded arms of two Soviets hugging her in that summit circle, feel now that her dream of five years had come true?

I couldn't believe it. I had no sense of reality, partly because at that altitude reality becomes very elusive," she recalls. "It was a numb feeling—it was so exciting, so wonderful, so unbelievable. Seeing the flags planted there brought tears to my eyes.

"But I also had the sense it was only the beginning. It wasn't the climax—it was only a step. Even when people say that something isn't possible, if you really try, and if you envision it and give that vision life, and if enough people believe in it, then you can do it. That's what I felt at the top. That it is possible. That it can be done."

CHAPTER THREE

THE IOWA CONNECTION: JOHN CHRYSTAL

Bankers in Iowa these days are about as popular as temperance ladies in saloons. In a state rapidly moving from severe agricultural recession to outright depression, where dozens of farming communities have already turned into ghosttowns and dozens more will in the next few years, farmers and bankers are eyeing each other with bewilderment and fear across a chasm of debt that no one knows how to cross.

The Soviet Union is also not especially popular among the proud, straight-backed individualists of the Iowa plains. All of which makes the enormous popularity of John Chrystal, a former farmer, the current president of one of Iowa's largest banks, and a consummate citizen diplomat who has for nearly thirty years maintained active relationships with agricultural officials in the Soviet Union—including, most recently, Mikhail Gorbachev—a bit astonishing. Many Iowans say he should run for senator or governor. Many say he would win.

In 1958 John Chrystal took off his farming coveralls and put on a suit to work for an ailing bank owned by relatives in his hometown of Coon Rapids, Iowa (population 1,300). He soon became president of the bank, a job he held for twenty-six years, and he served terms as Iowa's superintendent of banking and as the president of the Iowa Bankers Association. In 1984, at the age of fifty-eight, he left Coon Rapids to become president of Bankers Trust at a time when it, like most other Iowa banks, was facing severe losses. He now appears comfortably settled in the executive offices of a rust-tinted skyscraper, the tallest in Des Moines, affectionately known by locals as "In Rust We Trust."

With his paisley bow tie, wire-rimmed glasses, and gray tweed jacket bridging his ample belly with a single button, John Chrystal looks more like an Ivy League professor than an Iowa farmer, businessman, and banker. But his voice—deep, jovial, and unhurried—gives him away as a Midwesterner. His manner is casual and no-nonsense; little time is wasted on formalities or superfluous words. Etched on his pinkish face are fine craggy lines left by years of squinting in the sun. At six foot two he towers over most people, and perhaps from many years of peering down at the world his shoulders have elevated in relation to the rest of him, giving him the appearance of a plump and kindly eagle.

For years a six-foot-high poster of Lenin hung in his office, a souvenir of one of his Soviet journeys, because, he says waggishly, he "liked the pose." His impeccable capitalist credentials allow him to get away with such sport. He likes to startle people, rattle their preconceptions a bit, and then deliver, with a touch of mischief in his pale blue eyes, one of his long-considered opinions about the Soviet Union, American agriculture, or whatever else happens to be on his mind. He proudly calls himself a "supertypical Iowan." His roots go deep into prairie soil.

Since 1960, John Chrystal has been traveling to outlying farming areas of the Soviet Union and returning to Moscow to consult with top Soviet agricultural officials on how to improve their food production. He has also brought innumerable delegations of agricultural officials from the Soviet Union and Eastern Europe to Iowa. He is a one-man exchange program, acting outside the scope of any governmental agreement or private exchange organization, and both the United States and the Soviet governments appreciate his activities and advice.

Chrystal also frequently speaks to Midwestern audiences about his experiences, attempting to convince his listeners that arms control, better Soviet-American relations, and increased trade are not only essential for preventing nuclear war but also for staving off further economic catastrophe in the Midwest farm industry. It's a message he takes to local Chambers of Commerce, Rotary Clubs, banking associations, farming conventions, church groups, universities, and women's clubs. And he is finding more and more willing ears.

"We must understand that US arms expenditures and the agricultural depression are first cousins," he declares. "The arms race directly affects agriculture through the restraint of available capital for investment. The US has a guns-and-butter debt economy, and our budget deficit affects our real interest rate and our balance of payments. In a capital intensive industry such as agriculture, the result is devastating.

"We are now spending more real dollars on the military than we spent during the Korean war, without a war. We've just borrowed that money because we've always been unwilling to pay for what we were spending, and even though we're an enormously rich country, we've now used up quite a lot of the fat. We spend such an amount on defense that we are destroying what we wish to save. It's hit first in agriculture, because it's a low-return business that only returns 3 to 5 percent on investment. When that interest rate got very substantially higher than that return rate, suddenly the nonfarm investor disappeared from the farm real estate market. And the emperor had no clothes. Inflation was gone, and the real interest rate was the highest it's ever been in the history of the United States, and —" he lets out a long, ominous sigh.

His farming and banking audiences do not have to be convinced that something is amiss. Farmers have been hit with falling exports, prices, and equity at the same time they have been hit with rising surpluses, debts, and interest rates. Small-town bankers have been hurt by bad agricultural loans and dropping collateral values; eleven Iowa banks collapsed in 1985. A 1985 US Department of Agriculture survey indicated that 31 percent of all commercial farmers in the country were "economically threatened," meaning that they either could not then or soon would not be able to pay their bills, a level approaching that of the Great Depression.

Suicides in farming areas are at record levels as well; in late 1985, one desperate Iowa farmer shot his banker, his wife, and his neighbor before shooting himself. John Chrystal knew the banker, "a decent, compassionate man. But what's happening to these farmers is a terrible, wrenching thing, and some just can't handle it and flip out. They don't know what they did wrong. They were farming land that had been in their families for 125 years. If a farm family goes broke it isn't like a hardware dealer going broke, where he can lose the store, but he's still got the house. On a farm, they're one and the same. And suddenly, zingo. What is the farmer going to do? He has no experience working for other people, and obviously he's going to have to, because he has no capital to start his own business. Plus the shame of it—you're not supposed to go broke, unless you're wasteful or a gambler."

Chrystal worries that if dramatic steps to ease this situation are not forthcoming, there will be irrevocable changes in the economic and social fabric of the Midwest that will rival, or even surpass, the upheavals of the Great Depression. "If we in Iowa don't come up with an alternative for the people being forced out of rural America,"he warns, "they're all going to the Sun Belt. And this will be South Dakota, with more rain." One step in the right direction, he believes, would be halting the arms race, cutting back on military expenditures, and therefore reducing the budget deficit. "I do not for a moment believe that successful arms control negotiations are impossible," he says, "but I have come to the conclusion that there will be no mutually benefical agreement reached until something is done to reduce the dangerous level of fear and distrust between the two nations. What is needed is a nationwide effort by the citizens, institutions, and governments of both countries to learn about one another's culture, history, individual aspirations and way of life. When we have an adversary or competitor and do not appraise that opponent correctly, we injure ourselves. If we can't stop that arms race, if we can't find some accord with the Soviets—who need an accord something terrible because of their own economic problems—then we're heading for a real economic disaster."

Head down Highway 141 west and north of Des Moines, on a road so straight that each turn is an event, skirting towns like Perry and Dawson with their clusters of dark trees and grain elevators visible to the north, and one will eventually arrive in Coon Rapids, Iowa. The town is not attractive or quaint in any usual sense. The low-slung buildings are rather drab, the storefronts unadorned, the signs functional and to-the-point.

But Coon Rapids has a plainspoken, prarie-faced beauty. It is far enough away from highways and cities to have been spared neon outbreaks and creeping suburbia. It is far enough away from shopping malls to have retained the self-sufficiency of a small Midwestern town, and has a clothing store, two hardware stores, a half-dozen beauty shops, two banks, three coffee shops, a supermarket, a pharmacy, a dental clinic, a newspaper, a high school, a post office, five churches, and two bars. There are no traffic lights. Scattered behind the downtown area are modest white frame houses with big yards.

Corn is the lifeblood of Coon Rapids. The buildings and yellow-and-orange logo of the Garst Seed Company, the largest single-facility seed corn plant in the world, are everywhere. There are Garst Seed Company calendars in every gas station, coffee shop, and hardware store. There are Garst clocks, Garst doormats, Garst jackets, Garst hats, and, most prominent of all from the highway, the Garst Seed Company's "Welcome to Coon Rapids" sign, which features a perpetually spinning, ten-foot-high ear of yellow corn.

Roswell Garst, who started the seed corn plant in the 1930s with his partner Charley Thomas, left a more subtle legacy to Coon Rapids as well. Inhabitants of this otherwise completely normal Midwestern community think nothing of seeing gentlemen with European fedoras and tiny red Lenin pins on their lapels, escorted by a member of the Garst family, stroll into Arlene's Café for lunch. John Chrystal inherited his connection to the Soviet Union from his uncle, Roswell Garst, one of the more colorful characters to enliven the Iowa plains in this century.

Roswell Garst was a flamboyant, blunt, and visionary farmer, agricultural salesman, and businessman, who for most of his life publicized and marketed the then avant-garde techniques of planting hybrid corn, using chemical fertilizer, and feeding protein-enriched cellulose to beef cattle. As each new method emerged from research laboratories, Garst launched an energetic campaign to convince farmers of its virtues. He was outgoing and opportunistic, blustery and dynamic, and he knew how to persuade. "His body had a shape rather like that of Alfred Hitchcock, larger in frame but marked by a sway-backed posture to balance a stomach that made him look like a man who had just swallowed a watermelon," says his son-in-law and biographer Harold Lee. The writer John Dos Passos, who interviewed Garst for a lengthy *Life* magazine piece on American agriculture in 1948, wrote that his weatherbeaten face, with its large hooked nose and firm jaw, "comes at you like the prow of a ship."

Garst considered himself a teacher as well as a salesman; his life passion was, as he put it, "teaching people to grow more food with less labor" in whatever country they happened to live. Always intrigued by international affairs and politics, he was greatly influenced by his friend Henry Wallace, one of the architects of the New Deal, a pioneering agriculturist, and vice-president of the United States from 1941–46. Wallace's controversial 1946 speech advocating that the United States find some way to live and cooperate with the Soviet Union made a deep impression on Garst.

In the early 1950s, Garst became increasingly disturbed about the schism between the Soviet Union and the United States. And as the techniques he had helped sell started to create enormous crop surpluses, he knew that American farmers needed to find substantial foreign markets for their agricultural products. Both problems could be eased, he decided, if the United States began selling some of its excess food to Eastern Europe and the Soviet Union. Garst came up with an idea he called "full-belly diplomacy," which was that "if people had enough to eat, and some standard of living they wanted to protect, they would be less likely to want to risk that by starting a war." Feed the Russian bear, he said, and it will be less likely to claw the United States.

Garst began lobbying acquaintances in the US Departments of State and Agriculture and suggesting that the United States sell agricultural products to the Soviet Union and Eastern Europe. Despite his efforts, the 1954 law establishing the "Food for Peace" program stipulated that food surpluses should only be sold or given away to "friendly nations." Garst persisted, however, winning influential supporters such as Hubert Humphrey and John Kenneth Galbraith to his cause. "I keep reading in the press," Garst explained, "that one great difficulty in Russia is food. I think in food we have a potent weapon to use for peace."

In a major speech in early February 1955, Soviet leader Nikita Khrushchev announced that the Soviet Union should emulate the agricultural successes of the United States and suggested that agricultural cooperation might be a basis for better relations between the countries. A few days later, Lauren Soth, an editorial writer for the *Des Moines Register*, called for an exchange of agricultural officials between the countries: "We hereby extend an invitation to any delegation Khrushchev wants to select to come to Iowa. . . . We promise to hide none of our 'secrets.' " Soth also suggested that a delegation of Iowa farmers, agronomists, and livestock specialists go to the Soviet Union.

A few weeks later, the *Des Moines Register*'s Washington reporter asked President Eisenhower at a news conference whether he would support such an exchange. Eisenhower said he would and spoke about its possibilities enthusiastically. Soviet diplomats quickly responded that they were interested, and officials at the Departments of State and Agriculture began cautiously negotiating the details with the Soviets.

A few months later, in June 1955, a delegation of American farmers, agricultural officials, and journalists toured collective farms in the Soviet Union, and in July 1955 a Soviet delegation of farming officials came to Iowa. Emotions ran high about the visit. McCarthyism and virulent anti-Communism had left a vivid impression on many Midwestern farmers, and while everyone resolved to be polite, the State Department was so worried about appearing unduly receptive to the Soviets that it asked agricultural journalist John Strohm, a private citizen, to escort the group rather than a government official.

Khrushchev had proposed creating an "Iowa corn belt" in the Soviet Union, and while the visiting Soviets were apparently extremely interested in learning what they could about American farming techniques, their American hosts were more interested in displaying to the Soviets the individualistic values and traditions of small family farms. No farm of more than 640 acres was included on the Soviets' itinerary, and small 160-acre farms predominated. Roswell Garst's 2,600-acre farm in Coon Rapids, already well known as a hotbed of advanced cattle-feeding and hybridization techniques, was not to be visited.

But fate deemed otherwise. Three members of the Soviet delegation stayed the night at the home of Roswell Garst's cousins, Warren and Eleanor Garst, in the nearby town of Jefferson. Roswell's son and daughter-in-law, Steve and Mary Garst, who dropped by to have breakfast with the Soviets, asked whether they would like a quick tour of Roswell's farm. The three Soviets eagerly replied yes. Roswell Garst showed them his beef-feeding operations and fields, and the Soviets were delighted; here at last was something on a large enough scale to be relevant to their own huge collective and state farms.

That night, Roswell Garst attended a cocktail party for the Soviets in Ames, Iowa, and met the head of the delegation, Vladimir Matskevitch. Matskevitch told Garst that after hearing a report from his three colleagues about Garst's farm, he believed that "the Americans are only showing us what they want us to see." Would Matskevitch like to visit his farm? asked Garst. Very much so, he said, but it is impossible. The itinerary will not allow it. Garst gave him a shrewd look. "If you raise hell, you can come. Can you do that?" Matskevitch cracked a grin. They shook hands.

The next morning, despite Matskevitch's request, the delegation's cars began heading north, away from Coon Rapids. Matskevitch asked his driver to stop and then got out and stood with his arms folded, refusing to budge until he was given a fast car, a fast driver, and a chance to go to Coon Rapids. A few hours later Garst was again giving the grand tour of his farm and his hybrid seed corn plant. When they shook hands and said good-bye this time, Matskevitch invited him to come to the Soviet Union.

Garst wanted to bring his order book and persuade the Soviets to buy some of his seed corn and agricultural machinery. Although skeptical of his chances for success, the US State Department eventually agreed to issue an export license if he did manage to arrange a deal; the July 1955 summit meeting between Khrushchev and Eisenhower had created a "spirit of Geneva" that suggested such trade would have high-level approval. Garst also decided to visit Rumania and Hungary, since some reading had convinced him that these areas were more climatically suited for corn than the dry Russian steppes. Officials at the State Department dutifully stamped his passport to enable him to enter these countries, but they assured him that Rumania and Hungary would never let him in.

In September 1955 Garst visited the Soviet Union for the first time and presented lectures to the Ministry of Agriculture on hybrid corn genetics and production, drought-resistant strains of corn and grain sorghum, chemical fertilizer, livestock feeding techniques, and agricultural equipment. He then toured promising corn-growing areas, primarily in the Ukraine. Matskevitch, now Minister of Agriculture, asked Garst not only to inspect what was currently being done but also to recommend a comprehensive plan for corn and livestock production in the area. On a typical day, Garst was taken to one collective farm, tractor station, or experimental institute in the morning and another in the afternoon. Farm chairmen, technicians, scientists, managers, and workers crowded into cavernous offices to hear his speeches, which began with what Garst called his "preface"—a tactful acknowledgement of how World War I, the civil war, and World War II had hampered Soviet efforts to modernize their farms. Such a preface, Garst believed, would enable the Soviets to listen to his pointed critiques without becoming partriotically defensive.

It seemed to work. Everywhere he went, people avidly wrote down his every word. News of his willingness to share his knowledge and his inventive ideas spread rapidly. While staying on a collective farm near the Black Sea, Garst was interrupted in the middle of a morning speech, taken into the hall, and told that Khrushchev wished to speak with him. Soon he was on a plane to Yalta, where he was picked up in a black sedan and driven along the Black Sea Coast to an old summer Czarist residence.

The two men immediately hit it off. As journalist Harrison Salisbury has written, they had much in common: "Each was expansive, earthy, verbal, given to broad gestures, and passionately interested in land, soil, crops, animals, and food." Garst talked at length about the benefits of East-West trade, and found Khrushchev, Minister of Trade Anastas Mikoyan, and Minister of Agriculture Matskevitch all extremely interested in expanding commerce with the United States. Garst stayed the night, and the next morning met with Khrushchev to haggle the details of a hybrid seed corn deal. Several hours later, Khrushchev ordered five thousand tons of hybrid seed corn and agreed to send a Soviet delegation to Coon Rapids the following month.

Garst continued on to Rumania and Hungary, where, contrary to State Department predictions, he was not only let in but also given enthusiastic receptions by high-ranking officials. He continued to dispense advice and collect orders for seed and farm machinery, and invited agricultural delegations from both countries to visit him in Iowa. In Rumania, during a meeting with the full Rumanian cabinet, he suggested that they buy $500,000 worth of hybrid seed corn and agricultural machinery. A minister replied that they very much wanted to buy these things, but the money was simply not available. Garst eyed the cabinet speculatively and pulled a cigarette from his pocket. He waved it in front of them and announced that in the United States such a cigarette would cost three cents. "There are seventeen million Rumanians, and seventeen million times three cents is $510,000. I don't want anybody in this cabinet to tell me that they can't afford to spend the price of one cigarette per person to learn how to raise crops with less labor." The Rumanians agreed to the deal.

In rapid succession Garst entertained Soviet, Rumanian, and Hungarian delegations in Coon Rapids before the winter snows arrived. He was invited back to the Soviet Union for the autumn of 1956, and he sent his sons Steve and David, both young farmers, to train and supervise their new customers in Rumania for the 1956 planting, growing, and harvest season. Harold Smouse of the Grettenberg Implement Company in Coon Rapids, who stayed in Rumania from April to November training workers and doing repairs on the new machinery, became famous in Coon Rapids for his panicky telegram that summer: "Not for my sake, but for God's sake, send more pliers!"

All this activity produced more than a few grumbles and raised eyebrows at home. "At that time," remembers Steve Garst, "you were considered a Communist if you were hardly caught speaking with one." Scathing editorials in several newspapers complained that opportunistic Americans were bolstering the economic base of Communism, and Roswell Garst began receiving uncomplimentary mail (although positive letters, he said, always outnumbered critical ones by at least four to one). None of this criticism stopped, or even slowed, his activity. "We cannot afford to have one-third of the world possess the atomic bomb and be hungry," he told his critics.

111

On a second Soviet tour the following year, Garst again freely shared his opinions and his "Peace through corn" toasts. Managers of collective farms eagerly showed him the results of their following his advice, including fields planted with his five thousand tons of hybrid seed corn. Garst and his wife, Elizabeth, also went to Rumania to inspect the corn that their sons had helped raise, then to Hungary.

But here their triumphal march collapsed into sudden ignominy. On October 23, 1956, the Hungarian revolt erupted in Budapest. The Garsts, isolated in their hotel on an island in the Danube, were wakened by machine-gun fire in the middle of the night. Unable to leave for ten days, they played bridge with other trapped foreigners and waited. Finally they escaped up the Danube to Czechoslovakia on a grimy Polish coal boat that ran out of coal, forcing them to travel overland to Prague. Thoroughly disenchanted with Russian-style diplomacy, Garst refused to return to Moscow to sign another corn deal.

Although a few delegations from Poland and Czechoslovakia came to Coon Rapids in the spring of 1957, all contact between the Garsts and the Soviet Union was cut off for more than a year. But Roswell eventually decided that if he could not talk to the Soviets, he had little chance of influencing their behavior. In January 1958 he began exploring the possibility of another Soviet seed corn deal. Matskevitch, meanwhile, offered to send two Soviet "field workers"—young sturdy agriculturalists with a future in farm management—to Garst's farm in Iowa to learn the latest American farming techniques firsthand, by driving tractors and helping with the harvests. Garst agreed, and the two Soviets, Alexander Gitalov and Vassily Shuydko, accompanied by an interpreter and a Soviet agricultural geneticist, arrived in June 1958 for a five-month stay. Garst arranged for the four of them to live and work on his nephew John Chrystal's farm just north of Coon Rapids.

Chrystal was then thirty-three and had been farming in partnership with his younger brother Tom for about nine years. Although Garst was Chrystal's uncle, the relationship between them resembled that of father and son. Chrystal's mother had died of heart trouble when he was nine and Garst had promised his sister that he would look after her children. After graduating from Iowa State University with a degree in economics, Chrystal had chosen to go back to a life of corn, soybeans, cattle, and hogs.

Chrystal remembers that summer with a kind of golden nostalgia. The Soviets were "thrilled" by the conveniences on his farm, such as running water and electricity, and by the yields of the crops, the young butchering age of the cattle, and the numbers of eggs the chickens laid. "It was just like going to agricultural heaven for these people," says Chrystal. Side by side, they planted grain sorghum, cultivated crops, chopped hay, and fed cattle. He and the four Soviets also traveled to many agricultural colleges in the Midwest for meetings, tours, and speeches. Their reception was generally cordial, and Chrystal's neighbors accepted the presence of his unusual "field workers" without fuss.

In January 1959 Garst wrote to Khrushchev explaining that he wished to see him again, both about putting some of his agricultural recommendations into effect and "getting this armaments race stopped." Garst bluntly told the Soviet leader that he was "extremely disappointed" that some aspects of his advice had yet to be carried out. Khrushchev promptly invited Garst back to his Black Sea dacha. Although Elizabeth Garst was still shaken and outraged by the Hungarian episode, Roswell managed to persuade her to go back to the Soviet Union—"like a reluctant bride," she now says.

Ninety-year-old Elizabeth Garst still lives in a graceful white farmhouse shaded by trees and situated on a knoll just outside the town limits of Coon Rapids. The Garst "home farm," as other Garst family members call it, is a bucolic and prosperous-looking homestead, with a stream in front and horses grazing in the pasture below the knoll. Inside, a painting of Elizabeth as a dark-haired young woman hangs over the piano, which is laden with photographs of her five children, sixteen grandchildren, and six great-grandchildren.

Spry and talkative, Elizabeth Garst loves to tell stories about the past, and with little prompting recounts some of her favorites—such as the time Bulgarian women field workers paused in their planting of tomatoes to pick a bouquet of wild daffodils for her. "I was married to a very unusual man," she says as if she were confiding a great secret, pulling out a red leather guest book and spinning tales about many of the entries. A glance through the book turns up names from Bulgaria, Tanzania, Indonesia, Brazil, Ceylon, the Soviet Union, Yugoslavia, South Africa, Japan, New Zealand, and Venezuela.

Elizabeth Garst's description of the 1959 meeting with Khrushchev is succinct. "All morning long," she says, "the discussion went on about corn." Thanks to Roswell Garst's help, the Soviet corn harvest for 1958 was 600 million bushels, more than double the 1957 harvest and well over the previous high in 1956. The relaxed visit, filled with leisurely discussions of agriculture on a veranda in the warm afternoon sun, had only one real moment of tension. Khrushchev bristled when Garst advised him to "quit the arms race" and divert money from the military to agriculture. "How would you like to be surrounded by air bases?" Khrushchev replied angrily, ticking off the names and locations of US military bases in Western Europe and Turkey. Nor was he mollified when Garst told him he should "laugh at those bases" because the United States was not interested in war. The conversation soon drifted back to agriculture.

As they were walking down the tree-lined driveway toward the gate, Elizabeth Garst thanked Khrushchev for his hospitality and invited him to come to Coon Rapids if he should ever visit the United States. Khrushchev warmly replied that he would. She now chuckles about her innocent offer: "Little did I know I'd eat those words!"

When word came in August 1959 that Khrushchev had accepted Eisenhower's invitation to come to the United States, John Chrystal and Roswell Garst were having breakfast at the South Side Café in Coon Rapids. "You'd better call Aunt Elizabeth and tell her to change the sheets," Chrystal remembers telling Garst, "because Khrushchev's coming to Coon Rapids." The phone didn't stop ringing at the Garst farm for the next month as the press flooded them with requests for interviews—"for a month," says Elizabeth, "I couldn't go downstairs with my slip showing." Huge television towers and wires rigged on the hill behind the Garsts' house caused nearly as much stir in Coon Rapids as the thought of the premier's presence. As James Reston reported in the *New York Times*, everything but the hogs was wired for sound.

But the editorial staff of the *Coon Rapids Enterprise*, "Official Newspaper for Both Country and Town," apparently took the news of Khrushchev's impending arrival coolly. The front page article on August 27, 1959, announcing the visit is miniscule compared to the story accompanying the banner headline, "$1,500 Subscription Drive Announced." "All the world, save Coon Rapids, seems to be excited over Soviet Premier Khrushchev's coming visit to the Roswell Garst home here," remarks an editorial. "While we should greet Soviet Premier Nikita Khrushchev respectfully during his visit here, . . . we should not forget that the Soviet leader is a confirmed and dedicated Communist with the goal of world communism ever in mind. Let's beware of the Russian tranquilizer and always be alert and ready to defend the free world and free people."

Nevertheless, stories about the visit inexorably began dominating the

Enterprise's pages. The reactions of all of the local church pastors were sought and printed. (They cautiously approved.) Two weeks before the visit, Garst submitted to the *Enterprise* a thorough history of his relationship with Khrushchev. In another article, on September 17, a somewhat appalled Garst reported that nearly five hundred press people were expected to descend on them and urged his townsfellows "to stay away from Coon Rapids for a day."

The big day, September 23, 1959, turned out to be, if not exactly a disappointment, not quite a glowing triumph either. Elizabeth Garst says that at first it was "awful." Roswell Garst became outraged at the hordes of press people trampling on his silage, obstructing views of livestock, and interfering with his demonstrations of machinery. At one point he launched a counterblitzkreig with handfuls of silage thrown at some hapless reporters—a moment caught in the most widely reproduced of the photographs of the day. Chrystal, who was assigned to look after Adlai Stevenson, remembers it as "simply a big public relations event."

But it was not a total fiasco. In one of Elizabeth Garst's photo albums is a picture of a wriggly-looking six-year-old granddaughter and namesake, Liz Garst, sitting on Mrs. Khrushchev's knee in the Garst living room. "We had arranged to take Mrs. Khrushchev to town, to show her the store, the school, the library, but she wouldn't go," explains Elizabeth. "She said that in the East the press was so awful when they went into a store that reporters tipped over shelves of produce. So we stayed in the house and had a very nice time." During the picnic under a huge tent in the backyard, Khrushchev, Roswell Garst, Adlai Stevenson, and Henry Cabot Lodge sat together and talked at length about trade, world health, economics, and arms treaties.

Whatever else Khrushchev's farm visit accomplished, it certainly signaled to Soviet agricultural planners that they could adopt American farming methods into their master plans. Khrushchev later reported at a Communist Party Congress: "Mr. Garst is a sensible man. He is a capitalist, but he is for competition with us on an honest foundation. We should utilize his experience in the growing of corn and learn from him."

A gallstone operation in autumn 1959 left Garst fatigued, so when the Soviets again invited him to tour and inspect Soviet agricultural areas in 1960, he decided to send his nephew instead. John Chrystal was thrilled, although the prospect of taking his uncle's place was rather daunting—especially since he'd never been east of Chicago.

Chrystal arrived in Moscow expecting to begin immediately touring farms, as Garst had always done, but bureaucratic delays kept him fidgeting in the city for ten days. Finally he told his guide that if he wasn't taken to a farm the next day, he would go home. "I told him I was not taking up permanent residence here," he says. "I was amazed at my own bravery." He learned early that speaking his mind to Soviets got results. The next day he was taken to a farm.

For nearly two months Chrystal visited everything from hog pens to plum orchards to fox houses to wheat farms to cornfields. He was taken to at least two farms or agricultural plants each day; the schedule began at 6:30 or 7 A.M. and lasted through long evening banquets. At one farm, he was led past a mile of hog pens, with a female attendant standing primly at every fourth pen; he estimated later that he had personally inspected two thousand hogs and five hundred attendants.

In general, the agriculture he saw impressed him as being "almost Third World," with, in his opinion, inadequate use of fertilizers, hybridization, irrigation, pesticides, herbicides, and machinery. But the enthusiasm he encountered on the farms had an almost childlike quality. One farm chairman, who had visited Coon Rapids in 1955 and seen Roswell Garst's swimming pool, was bursting with pride about his plans to build a swimming pool for his workers.

On another farm, a young zootechnician reported on the gains that had been made in the past year, and "you could just tell she was almost out of her mind, she was so proud of herself." At a dance at the farm that night, the elderly, illiterate parents of the zootechnician shyly came up to him and asked what he thought of their daughter and her report. "When I said I thought their daughter was wonderful, they just beamed," he recalls. "In those early days, you'd see people everywhere reading books, trying to make themselves better. The elevator operator would be sitting there struggling with a book. It was thrilling—*thrilling*—to see these people raising themselves up."

Chrystal's cheerful outlook, well-placed criticism, and stamina won him admirers, and after a final jaunt through Eastern Europe, he returned to Iowa with his reputation as a sensible capitalist farmer almost as firmly established as Garst's. But Soviet-American relations, which had warmed noticeably in 1958 and 1959, took a turn for the worse that summer; the downing of an American U-2 espionage plane over Soviet territory on May 1, 1960, led to the collapse of the Eisenhower-Khrushchev summit in Paris. Saddened by what he conidered the overreaction of both sides, Garst stuck by his beliefs about the arms race: "It is global insanity—and nothing else—for the world to spend a hundred billion dollars a year preparing for a war that no one wants—no one expects— a war that no one would survive." But in September 1961, during the face-off in Berlin, Garst described himself to friends as "rather worried" about the possibility of war and in "deep confusion" about Soviet-American relations.

In spring 1962 Garst heard that Khrushchev wanted to talk to him again about agriculture. Hoping that Khrushchev's confidence in his agricultural opinions might make the Soviet leader similarly receptive to his views on the arms race, Garst wrote a letter offering to come. He was immediately invited for autumn 1962, but in October 1962 a small malignancy was found on Garst's larynx and it had to be removed. In spring 1963, with a mechanical voice box in hand, Garst set off for the Soviet Union "to make one more hard attempt," he told Phil Maguire, an Agriculture Department official, "to get Chairman Khrushchev to be more flexible and cooperative in doing away with further nuclear test- ing—and in getting a *lowering* of the arms burden on both of our two countries."

This time he took Chrystal with him. "Traveling with Uncle Bob [Roswell] through Eastern Europe is what I imagine it is like to travel with the Queen of England in the outlying parts of her Empire," Chrystal later remarked. They met with Khrushchev in his Kremlin office on May 10, 1963, and talked, sometimes argued, on a variety of subjects, in- cluding exit visas for Jews, the economic burden of the arms race, and inspection of nuclear testing facilities, an issue that was holding up progress on nuclear test ban treaty negotiations. They then went to his dacha, located in the midst of apple orchards near the Moscow River, for dinner with his family. Mrs. Khrushchev had prepared roast wild duck, and Khrushchev asked them to guess who had shot the duck. "Castro," he answered for them, bursting into laughter at his guests' befuddled faces. He wasn't kidding—Fidel Castro had visited him just a week before. Garst asked him what he thought of Castro. "A nice young man," responded Khrushchev, "who is still a little wet behind the ears."

What were Chrystal's impressions of Khrushchev? "Um, Sam Ray- burn." He pauses to let the image sink in. "Physically looked like him, and they were alike in other ways. Kind of wily. Not very well educated. Quite a little bluster. Pretty smart. Came on pretty strong. Attached to his family." The relationship between his uncle and Khrushchev, he said, "was more than just a simple friendship. There was a kind of electricity between them."

Following their meeting with Khrushchev, Garst and Chrystal traveled through the Ukraine on another agricultural inspection tour. Despite Chrystal's solo run in 1960, "I was the aide-de-camp. There was no question who the star was," says Chrystal with a grin. Roswell Garst's message after he saw the agricultural progress that had been made in the last eight years: "You don't need me anymore."

When the news came in October 1964 that Khrushchev had been deposed, Garst tried to get a message of gratitude and appreciation through to Khrushchev by way of Anastas Mikoyan, a surviving Politburo member, but he never knew whether it was received. The family never heard from Khrushchev again and thought their Soviet connection had ended for good. "The Russians used to come flying through Coon Rapids just like it was a way station on the Underground Railroad," says Chrystal, "but that all stopped." Roswell Garst turned his attention to building up his company and developing agricultural programs and aid for El Salvador and other Latin American countries.

Then in 1970 Leonid Brezhnev reappointed their old friend Matskevitch as Minister of Agriculture. Garst invited him to the United States in 1971, and Matskevitch went home with ten bags of grain sorghum seed. Soon the Soviets began negotiating purchases of grain sorghum, cattle, and equipment from the Garst family's businesses. Chrystal estimates that most of their business transactions with the Soviets have barely broken even. Sending lawyers and representatives to Moscow to haggle the deal isn't cheap, and after getting through Soviet red tape they sometimes faced US export license delays of several years while committees scrutinized farm machinery for any conceivable defense applications. "We weren't exporters, mainly, so it was partly our fault, but *boy* they're tough folks to do business with. Once you have the agreement, though, they're very good about keeping it."

In 1972 Garst and Chrystal once again traveled through agricultural areas of the Soviet Union to offer their opinions; another joint visit followed in 1974. Garst found that Khrushchev's fall from favor had no effect on his own stature in the Soviet Union. "I believe that they would plant corn upside down if he told them they could do it," remarked Chrystal after the 1974 visit. "People would literally crowd around him, just to catch a glimpse of him. And he loved it. He was just like the visiting emperor—pulling away from the crowds with a wave."

Roswell Garst died of a heart attack in 1977. But by this time, citizen diplomacy had become a Garst family institution, and other family members took on the task of hosting visitors from the Soviet Union and numerous other countries—putting them up in their homes, giving them tours of the farms and the seed corn plant, and feeding them in local cafés. Even American visitors who drop by the Garst Seed Company office on Main Street are likely to be offered coffee, a Garst company hat, and a tour of the seed corn plant, in that order. Back in the promotional products room, where a choice of a glow-in-the-dark orange or a gray hat is available, Roswell's granddaughter Liz Garst deadpans, "Why don't farmers wear tennis shoes? Because seed companies don't give them away."

Liz Garst, the current business manager of the Garst Seed Company, recalls chatting with a high-ranking Soviet official at a table in Arlene's Café while, one table over, John Chrystal's brother Tom entertained a Chinese delegation interested in buying seed corn. "The Chinese were just so culturally out of it that I don't think they even picked up there was another foreigner in the room," says Liz Garst. "But all of a sudden this Russian guy got a funny look on his face and started asking, 'Who are *they?* What are *they* doing here?' He was just amazed. We explained but didn't try to introduce them." She laughs. "An international incident right there in Arlene's Café."

While the rest of the Garst family helps host the steady stream of international visitors, John Chrystal continues to make extensive agricultural tours of the Soviet Union every two years and give public talks around the Midwest. He disarms his audiences with his silver-haired dignity mixed with a homespun wit and an independence of mind that Midwesterners appreciate. Completely at ease at a podium, he puts his listeners at ease, making the Soviet Union sound as down-home and familiar as corn on the cob.

"Soviet agriculture is not a failure when compared to its own past, instead of compared to US agriculture," he tells his audiences. "Soviet agriculture has produced more food of higher quality with fewer workers each year. By any standard, that is success. Soviets do not go to bed hungry, but after having eaten too many potatoes, cabbage, and bread, and not enough luxury food—mostly meaning meat. They don't need more food—they have a demand for a more luxurious diet.

"I have always told the Russians that American agriculture is far, far ahead of theirs. Not because we are smarter or better, but because we have not had wars on our farms, because we have had 125 years of universal education, and because we have had 50 percent more rain." Considering their climate, history, and bureaucracy, and keeping in mind that tens of thousands of people died in famines under the czars and in the early days of Communism, current Soviet agriculture, he says, "is really an enormous success."

Why, then, do most American newspaper accounts present Soviet agriculture as a dismal failure? someone in the audience asks. "I don't know," he replies. "We both like to think that we're the best, and when we think we can get the goods on the other guy in something, we do, whether it's justifiable or not. I mean, in some ways it *is* disastrous—a terrible drought year once every three years is a big problem. But you don't hear anything about half of the rural population moving to the cities, and yields increasing astronomically, and the production of chickens now being three-fourths that of the United States, from almost *nothing*."

Chrystal likes to think that his family's full-belly diplomacy is partly responsible. He rattles off a list of recommendations that were eventually carried out: "Better road system. Hybridized grain sorghum. Meat cattle. Cross-breeding instead of hybridization. Protein for animal feed—we had a very big argument on that, but they bought it. Now who's to know that they wouldn't have done all that without me?" he adds. "Those are not exactly my inventions."

The single most important, and most expensive, improvement their food production system now needs he sums up in one word: *infrastructure*. "The Soviets lose 15 percent to 20 percent of their agricultural produce between the farm and the table. We lose less than 5 percent. If they could match our minimal loss, it would tremendously increase production, but to do that they have to have more all-weather roads, on-farm storage for the harvest, supply depots for feed, machinery parts, quality and packaging control, more transportation, especially refrigerated transportation, and more responsible management. Can you imagine how much those things cost if you don't have them?"

In contrast, the US has an enormous capital investment in its food production system. "Here a supermarket's inventory is turned every ten days, perishable items every three days. Can you conceive of the timing necessary by the producer, processor, broker, and retailer, to make a supply of food of high quality unquestioned by the customer? We have been building our modern infrastructure since 1930. And we did not start from scratch."

Building a food infrastructure takes money, and lots of it: scarce money that presently is fed into the Soviet military, he says. "They know what they need to do, and their agriculture is really on the brink of sophistication. But it needs capital to become sophisticated." Management also continues to be a major problem. "There needs to be a right of refusal—if I buy my seed corn, or fertilizer, or whatever, from you, and you do a lousy job, the next time up I ought to be able to say, 'Baloney. Cut the price, or I'm going to buy from Mikhail.'" This ill is of course not confined to the agricultural sector. "I have told Russian friends that the last radical act of their government was the revolution itself. Too much is decided by committees. Committees never decide in the extreme, but by consensus, so that no chances are taken, responsibility is diffused, and change is hard."

Although he recognizes its considerable shortcomings, Chrystal does not give the standard doom-and-gloom description of the Soviet economy offered by most Western analysts. "The Soviet standard of living is below ours, but their progress has been successful when compared to themselves. They were a largely illiterate, backward nation, and in sixty years, in three generations, here they are, a technological superpower. That's amazing. With two wars in the interim. They've done it through universal education, the denial of luxuries to the population, and forced investment. And it hasn't been an economic failure—it's just not as successful as it might have been."

Among the biggest changes he's seen in the last twenty-five years: "Fashions. Resorts. The things that people are interested in for their homes. I have a friend, who isn't loaded, who bought a chandelier for his living room. Cost him a lot of bucks. The quality of their buildings has improved—those first apartment houses, my God, I thought they would fall down then. The road system. A lot of the changes have come just in the last seven or eight years. For instance, semi trucks are now just beginning to appear. Airplanes. When I first flew in the Soviet Union, it was sometimes on old military transport planes, C-47s, and I rode by the windows facing the freight! Now they have quite a good passenger airplane.

"Dogs and cats. Because now they can afford to feed them. The dachas. *Lots* of people got those dachas. Cars. A little bit of frozen food, pre-prepared. Electrical appliances. Health fads. The Russians are very into health, and always have been, but god Almighty, now they just are *crazy* on the subject. If you eat this you won't have liver trouble, and how many glasses of water to drink in the morning, and—we've got millons of people like that here in America, but I almost think it's worse over there. And that's a *luxury*. People in Pakistan, I tell you, aren't drinking three-and-a-half glasses of water that are seventy-two degrees instead of seventy-three degrees every morning.

"Enormous changes," he continues after a pause. "But still enormous needs. Fifteen percent of the people still share kitchens. They need more living space, more recreation. Life's too tough. They still don't have in my opinion enough education, or high enough quality education, above high school.

"There's no comparison in the standard of living from when I first started going. But also gone is a little of that old-time religion. A little of that—'Boy, we're all going to get together and we're going to make it a better country, a better world, a better everything.' " Parents of farm technicians no longer come up to him at parties and ask him about their daughters with unconcealed pride, he says; "It's a generation later." Some of his Soviet friends still have that kind of idealism, "but I don't think it's as universal today as it was twenty-five years ago. Communism has lost some of its mystique. A little of the magic is gone."

In 1981, Chrystal was taken to see the newly appointed Minister of Agriculture, a young, relatively unknown member of the Politburo. An old friend and high-ranking Soviet official told him beforehand that this minister "was going to be a very important man in the Soviet Union someday." "I didn't know how you could go up from being a member of the Politburo," Chrystal later remarked, "unless you become the General Secretary." The minister's name was Mikhail Gorbachev.

Right away, Chrystal sensed that something was different. In contrast to most Kremlin offices, which Chrystal describes as uniformly having dark wainscoating, dark tables, red curtains, bowls of fruit and mineral water, and large somber portraits of Lenin and Marx, Gorbachev's office was light and airy, decorated with blond wooden Scandinavian furniture, and contained no portraits other than a small framed photograph of Brezhnev on his desk.

After he greeted Chrystal, Gorbachev began to talk about the world situation, including "the usual jazz about how intractable the United States is on arms control, and how the Soviets are for peace, and so on," recalls Chrystal. After listening for about ten minutes, Chrystal said quietly, "Well, in the United States we have an old saying that it takes two to tango. The Soviet Union is not entirely innocent in the matter. But I came here to talk about agriculture." Chrystal slaps his broad hands together with a loud *smack*. "And boy, bingo, we're all done. He immediately stopped the litany and we went straight to substance."

Chrystal found Gorbachev "strange" compared to other Soviet officials, in that "he was more of a listener than a talker. A questioner, who was obviously learning. Intelligent. Overvalued as a farmer. He graduated from an agricultural institute, but his real role was a political one. I don't mean he was a dumb agriculturist, but I don't think he'd milked a helluva lot of cows."

Chrystal became convinced that a "kind of campaign" among reformist groups in the Soviet Union was being mobilized to move Gorbachev into the General Secretary position. After his 1981 trip, he called the State Department and offered to tell them about whom he guessed the next General Secretary would be. The State Department politely replied: "Don't call us, we'll call you." After his second visit with Gorbachev, in 1983, Chrystal came back still more convinced that he had spoken with the future Soviet leader, but again the State Department was uninterested. Then suddenly, when Yuri Andropov became ill, the phone started ringing in Coon Rapids, Iowa, and Chrystal was flown to Washington to brief officials, who thought Gorbachev might succeed Andropov. Konstantin Chernenko got the job that time, but Gorbachev was installed just three days after Chernenko's death in March 1985.

In a briefing at the State Department for President Reagan and other top Administration officials before the November 1985 Geneva summit, Chrystal offered his observations: "The difference I would make between Gorbachev and other Soviet leaders I have met is that the others lacked the education that he has, and I think they suffered from an inferiority complex. They knew they had won World War II mostly with human bodies as opposed to a good economy or good manufacturing, and that the history of Russia is not generally considered a great success. So I think they operated on bravado—they barked louder than they could bite, and they knew it.

"Gorbachev is different. I think he has absolute self-confidence, and is brave enough in that utterly fixed culture to operate differently from his peers. He is perfectly willing to hear criticism of his country. He is perfectly willing to criticize it in a way not having to do with politics. He's a smart man, not as charismatic as the media would make him, but interested in the people he talks to, anxious to learn, not nearly so attacking as his predecessors, who I think attacked out of a lack of feeling of equality."

Standing in the way of many of the reforms Gorbachev appears to want to apply to agriculture and other sectors of the Soviet economy, says Chrystal, is the infamous Soviet bureaucreacy. "Their government guarantees a job, guarantees a home, guarantees a minimum level of existence, and that's a wonderful thing. But there has to be a system of rewards and punishments above that minimum level. Boy, if you don't show up for work, then you don't get to go to Sochi for your vacation. If I'm supposed to deliver the goods to you every Thursday, and I don't do it, what happens to me? Nothing, or almost nothing. I think Gorbachev intends to change that. And I hope he is successful."

Replacing management and rehauling the way goods and services are handled is a long-term, politically treacherous job, but "if Gorbachev can't do it, then he's just another Brezhnev and Chernenko. I don't suppose it would put him out of office, but it would certainly be a terrible disappointment to the Soviet people. They're expecting more. He was so looked forward to, and they were so discouraged with the long period of old, ill leaders, who were not a part of the modern world, that I think he'll have quite a long honeymoon. He's *enormously* popular."

But Gorbachev faces a quandary. The economic machinery of the Soviet Union needs tremendous capital investment and managerial revamping to meet the rising expectations of the average Soviet consumer. At the same time, the need to "keep up with the West" is so deeply ingrained that Chrystal believes Gorbachev is obliged to respond tit-for-tat to whatever new weapons systems the United States decides to build. "He'd be thrown out of office," he asserts, "if people thought he wasn't protecting them. If they have to make a choice, defense is going to win, simply because of their culture and background. Sixty Soviets died for every American killed in World War II. The citizens of the Soviet Union will give popular support to any military expenditures so long as they perceive those expenditures to be defensive. They will spend any amount of money, pay any price, not to let it happen again."

Following Chrystal's 1983 visit, Gorbachev hinted that he would like to receive an invitation to visit Iowa. Chrystal swiftly made arrangements to host him in 1985, but after Gorbachev was made Party Secretary, Chrystal knew such a visit would be impossible. Instead, he went back to the Soviet Union in 1985 for another inspection tour, fully expecting to see Gorbachev at its conclusion. To his chagrin, he did not. Gorbachev sent numerous apologies, saying he was "terrifically busy." Chrystal did not hesitate to let Gorbachev know that he was mad at being stood up, and Gorbachev invited him to come back in 1986 instead of 1987, "which was his way, I suppose," says Chrystal, "of saying he was sorry." In several letters, Chrystal repeated his invitation for Gorbachev to come to Coon Rapids if a summit meeting brought him to the United States.

Would it be 1959 revisited? Chrystal thinks not—times have changed, and the appearance of the Soviet leader would not be nearly the novelty it once was to the American people. "They've seen more Russians," he says. Still, a visit would once again put Coon Rapids on the map. And this time the *Coon Rapids Enterprise* might run it as their lead story.

Iowans are not prone to putting people on pedestals, even favorite sons, and the citizens of Coon Rapids seem to take Chrystal's statewide celebrityhood and appearances on national news programs in stride. Chrystal, for his part, is known for not putting on airs. "I don't think *position* of other people means a whole lot to John," says Bill Hess, who replaced him as the president of the Iowa State Savings Bank in Coon Rapids. "He's comfortable talking to Armand Hammer, he's comfortable talking to my kids. We don't think about how big-time he's gone—he's just John to us, who comes through the Garst Store to see us and grabs a couple of pieces of candy on the way."

Bill Hess is one of many Iowans who would like to see John Chrystal turn his popularity into a run for governor or senator. Chrystal terms himself both a congenital and an ideological Democrat. "My father was a real honest-to-God liberal," he says, and one can tell he means it as a high compliment. While still a farmer, he bought his first television set in order to whisk in from the fields and watch the McCarthy hearings. "It was wonderful," he says, his voice warming, like a boxing fan recalling a favorite match. "It was good versus evil." And it kindled a lifelong interest in civil liberties—Chrystal was once president of the Iowa American Civil Liberties Union and is still active in the group.

But would he consider a run for office? It's clear he has considered it—and rejected it, at least for now. He mentions his responsibilities to Bankers Trust; he mentions the difficulty and expense of campaigning. Finally the real reasons come out. "I just don't *want* to enough," he admits, "and I think you have to have a real honest-to-God desire. Besides," he says with a wink, "I couldn't stand being beat."

Coon Rapids, like most small towns, has a resident sage. Eddie Reid, a retired cattleman in his eighties, maintains an office across the street from the P & S Coffeeshop so that folks who feel like getting an opinion on grain or cattle futures can drop by. Many do. He sits in a faded and cracked vinyl chair near a TV monitor perpetually flashing the latest market reports from Chicago. Delighted to have a visitor, Eddie Reid begins talking about his friends Roswell Garst and John Chrystal. Every few minutes he discreetly turns his head to peek at the numbers on the monitor. He wears a Garst hat.

"Dedicated diplomats, both of them, and also dedicated Americans," Eddie Reid terms Garst and Chrystal with an air of authority. He pauses and grins. "That last about 'dedicated Americans' doesn't need to be said—it makes it sound like there was some doubt about it." Was there ever some doubt about it in Coon Rapids? "Oh, well, when it first started there were some haters in the community who said things like that, but that's all faded now, because everybody knew it wasn't true. And today everybody knows that John Chrystal is a fine citizen." From the way he utters these last two words, it is clear that being a "fine citizen" is the highest title of honor a resident of Coon Rapids can bestow.

Eddie Reid has developed some distinct impressions of Soviet people after years of having lunch with them at the South Side Café. "I think they're eager to learn, they're friendly people, they always act appreciative. All the Russians I've met have been decent, compassionate, open-like people, willing to discuss agriculture in great detail. It also goes without saying that they are dedicated to *their* own country, or they wouldn't be on a visiting delegation!" Does Eddie Reid think there should be more exchanges and contacts with people in the Soviet Union? He looks incredulous, as if one had to be simple-minded to ask such a question. "Oh my *yes*, it ought to be expanded as much as possible. God knows that if there's anything that's needed, it's that. That's where it's got to start—with the people."

"I suppose I have seen as much of the Soviet Union as any American," observes Chrystal. There are still two Soviet republics—Byelorussia and Kazakhstan—that he has yet to visit, and one of these days he wants to go fishing on Lake Baikal. "The first time I met with Gorbachev he made some reference to Leningrad," he recalls, "and I said I'd never been there. You would have thought I'd said I put a bomb in the Kremlin. He couldn't believe I hadn't been to the most beautiful city in the world. So the next trip, boy, there I am in Leningrad—in November." Even after all these years, Chrystal can still surprise his Soviet hosts. Once a farm manager stopped in front of a horse chestnut (buckeye) tree and said, "Some of our silly superstitious peasants believe that carrying these chestnuts around can cure arthritis and bring good luck." Chrystal pulled a buckeye from his pocket. "Some of us silly US peasants believe the same thing."

His rapport with the Soviets, he says, gets better with every visit. "They have a great interest in people whom they have known for a long time who haven't done something bad to them. I've been going to the Soviet Union for so long that I have watched babies of my friends become parents." Has he ever wondered whether he's only been taken to their top-of-the-line agricultural places? "Oh, sure. I do the same thing to them, too—you don't show off your worst. But if we're driving along and I want to stop and look at something, that's perfectly all right, even though it can screw up the schedule."

After twenty-five years, the Soviets have grown to trust him, and his being a bona fide capitalist has not seemed to have gotten in the way. "I've never pretended to them that I was sympathetic to Communism as an economic idea. Because I'm not, at all. I think there are things wrong with our country, but I do think an economy in which people can go broke, in which people get to take a substantial chance, has a lot going for it. I'm a strong capitalist who can be pretty critical of capitalism."

Asked whether his primary goal in his trips is to help the Soviets with their agriculture, or talk to them about arms control and better relations, Chrystal replies unhesitatingly that agriculture is his top issue. "But the other is there, of course," he says. "The United States is turning into the military-industrial nation Eisenhower warned about, and that's a terrible thing. I think our attitude leaves a lot to be desired, and so does theirs. You've got two superpowers who want to have the most political and economic friends they can have in the world. The Soviets will be difficult adversaries for the United States, forever, as long as both of us remain superpowers.

"The Soviets don't have a monopoly on military action; we have a scruffy past ourselves. But I do think this—that the Russians are so inward-turned that they will never send soldiers where they can't walk home. I do not think they would send substantial numbers of troops to Central America, or to Africa, or anywhere that was not a contiguous country. And I think again that's part of their culture. They are just *balmy* about that country. They feel some kind of actual physical identification with the Kremlin, and the birch trees, and the soil, and the rivers. Maybe it's because they're the descendants of the people who *didn't* emigrate."

Westerners, he believes, generally fail to appreciate the history and culture that have indelibly marked the Soviet system, and facile comparisons with Western countries can be misleading. "I would ask you to name a country today that practices censorship, hinders emigration out of the country, banishes people within its own boundaries, requires internal passports, has a political police in a society that is, itself, secretive, and is autocratic and bureaucratic. Your answer would be, of course, the Soviet Union. In fact, it is also a description of Czarist Russia. Some of what we see as so objectionable is part of a thousand-year-old culture. That doesn't make these attributes more attractive—but it does make them more understandable.

"I think it's a lot freer in private discussions and in the private arguments in those Communist meetings than we think it is. Now once they've got the line, the show's over. But there's plenty of argument beneath that. We have our arguments in public, and that's one of the really wonderful things about this country—the ability to dissent. But what I find disappointing in the last fifteen years about our political system is that we have these awful arguments about arms control—and then nothing happens, we don't accomplish anything, we just go on."

Since the Soviets run their economy largely on a cash basis, and have only a very small national debt, the diversion of capital from the consumer economy into the military affects the lives of their citizens today, he says, while in the United States the burden for paying for the military buildup is postponed by running up the national debt. "As soon as the Soviets build a little fat they take it out for defense. They're really *denying* their population stuff, whereas we're just borrowing the money and putting it on the next generation." Thus the Soviets, he believes, are looking for a way out of the arms race more urgently than Americans are.

Even with the strain of a huge defense budget, Chrystal believes the Soviet economy will continue to creakily improve, and that this will create economic opportunities for American farmers and businessmen. "I don't think the Soviets will ever be able to produce, if their agriculture is successful as hell, the amount of grain and thus of meat that their citizens will desire, simply because of their climate. As they get richer, they're going to want to eat less potatoes and cabbage and soup and bread, and eat more meat. I think we have more to sell than they do, and I think we can make money by dealing with them, and there's nothing wrong with that. And forgetting the money, trade is one of the things that builds friendship." On the other hand, "If their economy falters, it will not be good for us. Very few people or nations look in the mirror when they seek those responsible for their own failure."

The problem in the United States, he says, is that the military-industrial establishment so thoroughly riddles the American economy that cutting too big a chunk of the defense budget at once would throw so many people out of jobs, if provisions were not made to employ them elsewhere, that it might touch off a depression. "We can't just declare peace," he says. "We have to become friends by stages. But if you admit that we can't do it, then we must be committed to war, mustn't we?" He throws up his hands. "If we *must* manufacture arms in order to maintain a strong economy, then it seems to me that you have right there said that we are committed to a war."

How hopeful is he that the arms race can be brought to a halt? "Not very," he responds at first, a touch wearily. "Because I think what is going to end the arms race is an economic debacle, which is a pretty high price to pay. And if there is an economic debacle, then that makes the possibility of war greater." What would such a debacle look like? "A *real* depression in the United States. Then we'd start to cut back. Until then I don't think our high-minded civilization is going to be equal to the task of stopping the arms race."

He doesn't seem very happy about this conclusion, nor does it seem to fit with his sustained efforts to educate Iowans and others about the Soviet Union and the arms race. As he keeps talking, he softens it a bit. "I *hope* that as the economy gets worse, then our efforts become more important, and we can stop short of what I call a real depression. Otherwise we're just wasting our time. And maybe we are anyway, but it's in a just cause. But maybe we can get this all under control just *before* we have a real debacle.

"I guess we shouldn't underestimate the power of an aroused American public," he continues after a pause. "You can't tell how countries make up their minds about things. But the American public stopped that war in Vietnam. The American public finally forced civil rights. The American public drove Lyndon Johnson and Richard Nixon from office. Those were really public decisions. And I don't know how we arrived at them, but we did, by some osmosis. It wasn't necessarily the politicians. It was kind of a consensus." His tone is now firm and strong again. "I haven't given up hope that that kind of consensus will arise again."

❧❧❧

CHAPTER FOUR

AN ORDINARY AMERICAN MOTHER:

SHARON TENNISON

At 7:30 A.M. on a gray, dreary morning, Sharon Tennison and three other Americans left their Intourist hotel in the Soviet city of Minsk and began walking toward a cluster of high-rise apartment buildings a mile away. The road soon narrowed and dwindled to a cobblestoned path lined with weathered, gingerbread-trimmed wooden houses and tiny gardens. A few Soviets hurried past them on their way to work, taking no notice of them, but otherwise the neighborhood seemed deserted. Tennison began wondering whether they had been sent on a wild-goose chase.

When she and her American group had arrived at their Minsk hotel late the previous evening, the first thing she checked was their schedule for the next day. Prior to the trip, she had asked Intourist, the Soviet travel agency, to arrange for the group to visit a local school on September 1, 1984, their first day in Minsk. She had read and heard from others that this was the opening day of school and was observed throughout the Soviet Union as a time to commemorate the suffering of World War II and teach the children that war must never happen again.

Tennison's experience had been that requests like these were routinely granted. But no visits to schools appeared on the schedule the Intourist service bureau handed her. She argued and pleaded with the hotel staff, but it was clear that no one wanted to take responsibility for meddling with a decision already made. It was too late, they all said. All of the principals of the schools had gone home. Nothing could be done. One hotel receptionist remarked unhelpfully, "Come back next year and we'll arrange it."

Finally, a woman behind the hotel desk threw up her hands and looked her straight in the eye. "Listen, if you want to visit a school tomorrow, this is what you do. Get up early, go back behind the hotel, and follow one of the roads leading to the apartment complexes. When you see a child, follow that child. He or she will take you to a school."

Tennison and several other Americans decided to follow her advice. But after walking for a half hour without seeing a single child, they paused at an intersection and wondered whether they should turn back. Just then they spotted a towheaded boy of about seven, dressed in the blue blazer of his school uniform, resolutely walking down a street with a huge bunch of red gladioli in his arms. Ten paces behind him walked a young man and woman, who appeared to be his parents. The Americans traded looks, paused discreetly until the threesome was nearly out of sight, then followed them toward the labyrinth of apartment buildings.

The boy led them to the outdoor basketball court of an old school, "one to which I know Intourist would never have taken us," Tennison says, "because it was small and rather run-down. The backboards for the basketball hoops had been repaired many times with baling wire." The school yard was already full of students, parents, and teachers, and all of the students were dressed in their first-day-of-school finery—new pinafores and crisp white chiffon hair bows for the girls, new blue blazers for the boys, bright red scarfs for both. Some of the older girls ran up to the teachers they had not seen in three months and hugged them, while the younger boys shyly held hands with each other and waited for the ceremony to begin. In all of the commotion, few seemed to notice the Americans in the crowd.

Eventually the people arranged themselves into neat rows ringing the basketball court, with the youngest children in front, the older ones behind them, and the parents behind them. An elderly man managing a creaky phonograph player attempted to locate a song on an old 45-rpm record while everyone waited patiently. Snatches of music reverberated in the air; at last the right song was found and the ceremony began. A color guard marched forward to present the school flag, local dignitaries and students made short speeches, and finally a stout, bent, worn-looking older woman, her ample black dress covered with war medals, went into the center of the basketball court and began to speak in a powerful voice.

She had been a guerrilla during World War II, a member of the underground resistance who had taken to the forest at age twenty and done everything from disrupting Nazi communication lines to helping evacuate children and Jews from the area. The entire area around Minsk was Nazi-occupied; five death camps for Soviet people had been set up in the Minsk area alone. The woman told the children how frightened she had been when the Nazis came. She told them that weapons were now so dangerous that if any kind of war began, the human race would be destroyed. She told them that they *must* work for peace. When she finished, the youngest children, their faces beaming, ran up to her and gave her the flowers they had been carrying.

Sharon Tennison watched from the sidelines, her eyes filling with tears. "So these are the children of the enemy," she recalls thinking. "This is what they teach the children of the enemy. This is what the enemy does with their children when they're not on display, when they don't know that people are looking at them. That experience," she adds, "was so powerful because I *knew* it hadn't been planned for American consumption."

In the fall of 1983, Sharon Tennison gathered a group of twenty-one other "ordinary mainstream Americans," as she calls them, to travel to the Soviet Union and see "the enemy" for themselves. She never expected to go to the Soviet Union again. Instead, this softspoken, serene-looking mother of four and grandmother of two has become the center of a maelstrom of grass-roots diplomacy in the last three years. She has led sixteen trips to the Soviet Union; many veterans of her trips have organized and led *their* own trips; and some who have gone on a trip led by one of Tennison's veterans have now organized and led *their* own trips. "It's not any one person," she says in reference to the snowballing of interest in citizen diplomacy throughout middle America that her efforts have helped generate. "It's the vision that's catching."

Although she once avoided traveling and was afraid of airplanes, Sharon Tennison now spends the months she is not in the Soviet Union journeying through the South and Midwest of the United States, presenting slides and stories about her experiences in the Soviet Union to civic clubs, businessmen's associations, church groups, universities, and high schools. She speaks about her friendships with "black-market" teenagers, Communist Party members, Jewish refuseniks, intellectuals, Christian believers, bureaucrats, college students, and the people with whom she finds the most empathy: "average, ordinary people who were simply born in the USSR and are making the best of their lives there." She relays to her American audiences how the Soviets she has met see their country and the rest of the world. "I am not an 'expert,' " she says, "but simply share what I am hearing and learning around Soviet kitchen tables, in their small friendly living rooms, and during chance meetings in parks, ice cream shops, and churches. I am not attempting to present *the* truth—God alone knows what the truth is—but rather to look at how differently We and They look at the same situations. We think we know the truth—they think they know the truth. It reminds me of listening to a friend talk about her husband, her marriage, and her reasons for divorce—it all sounded so completely truthful and logical. Then I spent several hours with the husband. He was equally believable and logical. And I wondered, was I even hearing about the same relationship—the same people? I find myself in the same place in relation to our two countries."

Sharon Tennison is a trim, attractive woman of fifty with brown-black eyes, a smooth, tranquil face, and expressive hands. She speaks decisively in the soft drawl of her native Kentucky and Texas, and emanates the self-assurance of a mature woman who has tried many things in life and is now doing exactly what she finds most meaningful. She is at once motherly and youthful, and has a dry, self-deprecating sense of humor. Simply dressed in a blouse and slacks, with her dark hair neatly coiffed, she appears poised to take off at any moment in her clean white tennis shoes.

A registered nurse who specializes in intensive care, she prefers action to talk. She abhors insincerity, and says she would much rather spend eight hours working in an intensive care unit, where people are straightforward and honest with each other, than an hour at a cocktail party. She values efficiency and order, two qualities missing from her present life with its constant traveling, phone calls, organizational brush fires, interruptions. The phone seems to ring every few minutes. First, an interview with a Tucson newspaper reporter. Then a detail concerning an Alcoholics Anonymous group she is taking to the Soviet Union. Then something about a citizen diplomacy workshop in Alaska. Then a request to speak in Chicago.

Becoming a citizen diplomat has had costs—she has had to put her small business, the manufacture of nursing uniforms, literally into mothballs. Her life, once tidy and organized, is now neither. But her dedication to what she calls "the work" is complete. "I'm in this," she says, smiling whimsically at the enormity of her goal, "for as long as it takes to bring understanding between the American and Soviet peoples."

In 1980 she was working in an intensive care unit of a hospital in

San Jose, California, when a physician friend told her that the then-fledgling Physicians for Social Responsibility (PSR) needed help. Tennison replied that she wasn't a doctor. "That doesn't matter," her friend said. "You can talk about taking care of burns and trauma—that's your business—and that's what we're talking about when we talk about the medical consequences of nuclear war." Tennison joined the South Bay Chapter of PSR and began speaking to audiences about the effects of blast, fire, and radiation, the ineffectiveness of civil defense, and the unsurvivability of nuclear war. Few people, she recalls, argued with her data. But the question "What about the Russians?" surfaced again and again.

"In every audience these *immediate* fears of the Soviets would come out. 'Well, but we have to build nuclear weapons,' they would say. 'Look at these Russians, they're all barbarians, we can't trust them, we have to be strong.' And I never knew what to say in response. So it occurred to me that I needed to go and see for myself what 'the enemy' was like." Her own images of the Soviet Union at that time: "Bleak. Controlled. Desperate. Desolate. Robot-type people, who never smiled, who had no emotions, who were totally subservient to an evil government." She pauses. "Pretty typical!"

For a few months she and some friends fantasized about the possibility of arranging a citizens' trip to the Soviet Union. Then—she doesn't know why—something inside her told her that she had to organize this trip as soon as possible. But first she needed to find out if there was any chance the Soviets would permit the kind of spontaneous, people-to-people journey she envisioned. She looked up the number of the Soviet Consulate in the San Francisco phone book and made an appointment. Her nerve almost failed her, however, when she parked her car and looked at the imposing building with its iron spiked fence. Suddenly she felt like she had stumbled into a bad spy movie. "On that beautiful bright sunny day there was not a single person, not even a dog or cat, in sight on that entire street," she says. "And for a fleeting moment I thought, what if I go in there and disappear?" She was further discomfited when both the iron gate and the front door swung open to admit her before she had seen any sign of human life.

But once inside, she was startled to find herself in an office with a vice-consul, "the first real Russian I'd ever seen," whom she describes as a "tall, handsome young man with black hair and a kind face, wearing a wool tweed jacket with suede patches on the sleeves. I had fully expected to see a paunchy and bald-headed old man. And I just stared at him and thought: 'You don't look like a Russian!' " Recovering her composure, Tennison explained that she was very concerned about the nuclear situation, that she had been speaking for PSR, and that it had become obvious to her that nuclear weapons were symptomatic of a deep hostility between their countries. "Will you allow me to go to your country, walk out of the hotel, wander the streets, nose in your shops, go to your parks and ride your metro?" she asked him. "Is there any chance I can do this? Because if I have to go on a regular tour, I don't want to go."

The vice-consul said yes, it was possible, although all visiting American groups are assigned an Intourist guide—that was simply Soviet law. But he also told her that "you can excuse your guide for the day, tell her you're not going to do the program. Just leave. Get yourself a map, learn some Russian words, and go." Tennison listened and was encouraged, although "part of me was so heavily invested in my own stereotypes that I thought, he's probably telling me a lie. But I decided I would go ahead and take the risk and see for myself."

Soon after her visit, a friend told her that everyone who sets foot in the Soviet consulate is automatically checked out by the FBI. Confident that she had nothing to hide, Tennison again went to the phone book, found their number, and paid a visit to the local FBI office to explain what she was doing. They were somewhat surprised, friendly, but skeptical that she could pull off her plans for spontaneous interactions with ordinary Soviet people. "You will not go anywhere that was not previously planned," an agent told her. "You will not meet anyone who was not previously contacted."

Another friend told her about a Seattle travel agent who arranged Soviet tours. Tennison spent hundreds of dollars on long-distance phone calls to Seattle, unaware until much later that many San Francisco travel agencies could have handled the trip. Meanwhile, people began hearing about her journey through friends of friends and called up wanting to go. Nearly all were middle-class Americans from a variety of professions, including a fire fighter, a city planner, an airline flight attendant, a textile worker, and several teachers, nurses, businessmen, and housewives. Tennison felt that if their stories were to be believed on their return, they had to represent a cross-section of mainstream America. "I wanted people who were respected in their own communities," she says. "Cub Scout leaders, businessmen, Sunday-school teachers, and the like."

After nine months of preparation, everything seemed set. But two weeks before their departure in September 1983, the Korean Air Lines jumbo jet was shot down by a Soviet fighter plane over Soviet territory. Soviet-American relations went into a tailspin and Tennison's flights to the Soviet Union were canceled. Two members of the trip backed out. But the rest felt it was even more important in times of crisis for citizens of the two countries to be talking with each other. Tennison managed to patch together new flight connections via Yugoslavia that were finalized only hours before their departure.

Tennison's citizen diplomacy began even before she landed in Moscow. Soon after their plane took off from Belgrade on a midnight flight, a Soviet woman in her midforties, with red hair and a gold tooth, tapped Tennison on the shoulder. *"Amerikanka?" "Da!"* Tennison replied. The woman's face lit up. Although she knew almost no English, and Tennison at that time knew almost no Russian, they enthusiastically conversed with gestures and started trading small pins and buttons. Three rows back, other Americans were having an animated conversation with two English-speaking Moscow teenagers. Several rows behind them, still more Americans and Soviets had discovered one another's nationality, and the Soviets were passing out food—*piroshki,* dried fish, even some caviar. A full-fledged party soon erupted, complete with singing, that lasted through the night. Even the copilot and the navigator wandered back into the cabin to join in. As the plane descended to Moscow in the early dawn light, the passengers broke into a sentimental, multilingual rendition of "Moscow Nights."

Within hours after being settled in a hotel, the Americans had scattered across the city on the subways, "splitting in ten different directions," says Tennison. "If anyone was trying to follow us they would have had a very hard time." They struck up conversations with people in parks, strolled through shops, wandered into cafés and schools, jogged early in the morning and met Soviets walking their dogs, and passed out their "friendship buttons" to everyone they met. During the next two weeks, they also visited museums and tourist sights, but such excursions were almost respites from the intensity of their "apartment experiences" with Soviets. Some of these were arranged by their American guide and interpreter, Cynthia Lazaroff, while others grew out of chance encounters on the streets, in stores, and in parks.

The Korean airliner tragedy seemed to hover in the background of every conversation. "The Soviets were very aware of it, very tense, scared that maybe this would start off a major nuclear exchange," Tennison recalls. "People would say—well, I heard what Voice of America says, and I heard what BBC says, we've had some news from Tokyo, and of course we read *Pravda*, but what do *you* know?"

Tennison remembers the trip as a rollercoaster, a blur—there was so much to try to put together, so many different points of view to absorb. One day the group met in the morning with members of the official Soviet Peace Committee, "who ran us through the paces of how many initiatives for peace the Soviets have had since nineteen-whatever, and how the United States is all to blame. And I just blew up at one point. I felt like they were badmouthing my country and they weren't taking responsibility for their own actions in the world, and I stood up and told them that." That afternoon, Tennison and several others went to have tea with a woman whom Tennison describes as an "independent, cooperative member of that society." Members of this class, whom she believes are in the majority, do not belong to the Party, admit there is much room for improvement in the Soviet Union, but generally support the system and are uninterested in radical changes. Then, in the evening, they visited a Jewish refusenik family who had applied to emigrate to Israel and been turned down. The family welcomed them warmly into their home, then startled them by intoning praises of the current American military buildup and warning them about the nefarious global ambitions of the Soviet government.

"Here we are at the end of the day," Tennison says, "sitting in our hotel rooms trying to sort out these three totally different points of view." Into every situation, she discovered, she carried deeply ingrained suspicions. For example, she had arranged, through Intourist, for the entire group to visit the main Baptist Church in Moscow. They were astonished to find the church packed to the rafters for a weekday evening service, with five hundred people sitting and another six hundred standing. The ministers invited Tennison to make a speech from the pulpit, and she explained that they had come for peace and friendship. As she left the podium and walked down the center aisle, "men and women started reaching out and kissing my hands, and some of the babushkas pulled me over to kiss my face. I was probably touched by a hundred and fifty or so people." Moving as this experience was, it was tarnished by the knowledge that their visit had been prearranged. "It was a situation that easily could have been rigged; I thought, well, did they call all of their people and pay them a ruble to be here?"

Chance, spontaneous interactions that they knew couldn't possibly have been planned were the most meaningful. One afternoon Tennison and several other women literally stumbled into a lively wedding party and feast after investigating music they heard from the street. The American women reached into their purses and pulled out perfume and lipstick to give to the bride; the next thing they knew, "the mother of the bride had invited us all inside, and we're all drinking champagne, and this young Russian kid, about twenty-two, has got me out on the dance floor."

At first the Americans, convinced that their hotel rooms were bugged, contrived elaborate arrangements for group meetings so their conversations would not be overheard and carried "magic-write" pads in case they needed to communicate quickly—and impermanently. "We played out all of our paranoias," Tennison remarks dryly, "but eventually we got to the point where we realized that if anyone was listening, from either side, they probably needed to hear what we were saying."

By the end of the trip, "We had really seen some of the bitter and some of the sweet of the Soviet Union. We'd seen the things that are working and the things that aren't working; we'd talked with people who liked the system and people who didn't like the system and people who just lived there and made the best of their lives. The variety of our experiences demolished for us the idea that this is a monolithic country with standardized people and a government that controls it all."

Tennison came home "passionately interested in learning more about that country, probably because I had met people there whom I'd come to love and respect, which I certainly had not expected." She came home "confused and disturbed" about the very different concepts attached to words like "control" and "freedom" that she had encountered in the Soviet Union. She also came home angry. "I felt I had been deceived all my life by this tale that continues to be told in my country, that blackballs, almost unconsciously, a whole piece of humanity. No one stops to examine it or to factor in new information."

Her confusion was amplified when she picked up the *San Francisco Chronicle* a week after her return and read a front-page article reporting that news of the Korean airliner tragedy was just beginning to trickle down to ordinary Soviet people. "I read this funny two-column article and I thought, where do they get this information? Did they make this up? We had been padding the streets over there, and *everybody* we talked with knew all about it and was concerned."

Soon after this, she spoke about the trip to a Houston conference of

139

business and professional people, sharing her jumbled impressions and her confusion, anger, and hope. To her surprise, a number of people told her after her speech that they wanted to go to the Soviet Union. Could she take them? Within weeks thirty people, mostly from Texas and other parts of the South, were signed up and ready to go.

During this second trip, in May 1984, Tennison resolved to avoid any situation that might be artificially arranged. For example, she showed up at the Moscow Baptist Church unannounced and discovered just as many people as before, with no other foreigners in sight. Returning to the United States, she gave more slide shows, "and wherever I went, people wanted to go." Says Annie Head, a recreation therapist from Palo Alto: "After hearing Sharon speak, I knew I wanted to go to the Soviet Union, and I knew I wanted to go with this woman and no one else."

Overwhelmed by requests to give presentations and lead trips, Tennison decided to quit nursing for one year and work full time on citizen diplomacy. "That first trip did U-turns to everybody," she remarks. "None of us had intended to go back." Bob Sturdivant, a city planner from San Jose, took three groups of planners and architects to the Soviet Union. Sarah Seybold, a professor of nursing at the University of San Francisco, quit her job to become a full-time peace educator and citizen diplomat. Ray Gatchalian, the captain of the Oakland Fire Department and an ex-Green Beret, won a peace education fellowship from the Kellogg Foundation with a grant called "What One Ordinary Person Can Do." Two Bay area teachers, Barbara O'Reilly and Artemis Yaffe, each led several trips of educators and students; another teacher took a job instructing American children in Moscow. The list goes on.

"*No* one on that first trip has stopped spreading the word," Tennison says. "It's amazing how many of them have become *resource* people in their own communities. Soviet-American work seems to turn into passion with them; they drop almost everything and just do this. Part of the joy in my work has been watching these other people take off and do things that just astound me. One man who's become very active told me recently, 'I was a very fine apathetic American businessman until I met this little grandmother in tennis shoes!' "

Tennison has found plunging into "the work" a satisfying release of years of pent-up energy. "For much of my life I was in a position where I had to keep my mouth shut about my concerns, because they weren't acceptable in the world I was living in—that of a corporate wife, for instance, or a suburban mother," she says. "However, now it seems like almost everybody I meet has the same concerns I have! And that feels *so good* after going through thirty-five years of always wondering why I was the one who couldn't fit in, who couldn't be satisfied with the status quo."

When she was a little girl growing up in Owensboro, Kentucky, the word "segregation" was unknown; it was just a fact of life that blacks handled the dirty work, served as maids in homes, and had scrawny, ill-clothed children who went to separate schools if they went to school at all. Tennison lived on a street that divided the white neighborhood and "Colored Town," and as she looked out her bedroom window and watched these mysterious "other" people going about their lives, it occurred to her that something was wrong. "I started asking questions as a very small child, questions nobody around me was asking. 'Why should this be?' 'Because they're dumb, they're just niggers, they can't learn,' the answers came back. But when I got a little older I asked, 'How do we know they can't learn if we don't send them to school?' I wrote papers about this in high school, and I always had a very deep sense that there was a better way for people to live with each other. And I don't know where it came from—certainly not from my family, or from any school-teachers I can remember."

Tennison married soon after entering college, moved with her husband to Dallas, Texas, started having children, and lived "an average, comfortable life. My husband did well, my children went to good schools." But her questioning continued. While raising her four children, she took courses in political science, psychology, philosophy, geology, and art history from a local college as part of a search for answers.

Once, in 1964, she took action. She was living in a small town just north of Dallas when a desegregation ruling made it possible for black parents to sign up to have their children placed in a white school. Tennison visited the local black high school and found two dozen books in the entire library; she discovered that the boys had to take four years of wood shop and the girls four years of home economics because there were not enough other classes to fill the day. Working with a local minister, Tennison organized meetings with black parents, mostly women, in the community. Many expressed fears that their children would not be able to keep up academically in the white school, so Tennison arranged for retired white teachers to tutor the black children if they needed help. "It was simply work that needed to be done, and I was in the right time and place," she says. To protect her family, she did it quietly, almost covertly; the intimidation from disgruntled whites, on the other hand, was overt. Tennison was warned that her car had been "marked." As soon as the black parents signed up saying they wished their children to attend the white school, a number of them lost their jobs. But a few months later, black children were attending the white school.

Although she continued to be an "ordinary corporate housewife and mother," Tennison felt something was missing. She became disillusioned with politics after the deaths of John F. Kennedy, Robert Kennedy, and Martin Luther King, Jr. She stopped reading newspapers and became introspective, searching religious and philosophical books for answers, wondering how she could fit her concerns about world poverty, global ecology, and nuclear war into her personal life. In the early 1970s, she learned about Mother Teresa, the saintlike nun who works with Calcutta's most hopeless and dispossessed. "I saw her as a woman who had been able to shuck all the claptrap of modern society and find meaning in life," says Tennison. "At that point her example was desperately important to me." She decided to enter nursing school, intending to work as a nurse in a Third World country after her children were grown.

It was not an easy time—along with this questioning came the dissolution of her second marriage—but Tennison credits those years of reading and contemplation with giving her the personal security and spiritual grounding that have made "the work" possible. Although she was raised a Baptist and had attended a Congregational Church most of her adult life, she had to struggle to integrate her spiritual beliefs with a sense of purpose in her life. "I went through a real dark night of the soul, and emerged out of that agony with a belief in something universal, something that transcended the human condition," she says. "It meant dropping out of the political and social worlds for a time, but it eventually gave me the confidence that there existed without a shadow of a doubt some sort of perennial wisdom, some energy in the universe that I could give myself to."

Although she always felt she was alone in her soul-searching, she now meets many people in her age group—forty to fifty-five—"who are coming out of very similar convolutions, who asked a lot of uncomfortable questions for years and couldn't find any answers. And now it seems like our time has come, and people who were not involved before but who always had this real yearning to do something meaningful are becoming active. I've been amazed to find these people everywhere, even in small towns. It's not just a flaky California phenomenon."

Tennison never advertised her trips to the Soviet Union. She never knew whether the next one would be the last. But people kept calling and wanting to go. Many simply read about her in a newspaper, or caught a few words on a radio show, and then found her number through San Francisco directory assistance. She keeps her number listed deliberately; she feels it's her responsibility to remain accessible. "People see me as an average, ordinary American woman, so they're comfortable about calling me," she explains. "Who would have the nerve to call someone like Bernie Lown or Norman Cousins on the phone and say they wanted to do citizen diplomacy?"

Tennison sees each trip as an ongoing process rather than an isolated three-week experience. She sends out recommended book lists several months before departure, and her other pretrip materials pass along tips, such as bringing along buttons, postcards and other small gifts for Soviets, as well as helpful hints about Soviet etiquette (how to get off at the right stop on a crowded bus when four babushkas and their shopping bags are blocking the door, for example). She encourages people to learn as much Russian as possible (she herself has taken an intensive month-long language course in Leningrad) and to be ready to take advantage of every opportunity for impromptu interactions.

During her pretrip seminars in Helsinki, Finland, held the day before the group enters the Soviet Union, she prepares travelers to "take off their American spectacles for three weeks and really try to learn, without immediately judging or being critical, how another part of humanity looks at the world." There are techniques and skills to being a good citizen diplomat, she explains; simply being a tourist will not suffice. Many tourists to the Soviet Union become intimidated by their Intourist guides, never strike out on their own, discuss only the quality of toilet paper and food, notice that people on the streets do not seem to smile much, and come home with their stereotypes largely intact. A single trip, she cautions her travelers, is really only a peephole into a vast and complicated country. Real friendship and understanding do not happen overnight; they require the accumulation of hundreds of small memories and interactions with Soviets. Building trust takes time and tact.

One Soviet friend, a Party member whom she originally met through one of the official peace committees, told her on her third visit: "You made a big mistake on your first visit. You told us that you were going to go home and do public education, and that really scared us. We didn't know what you were going to say about us." This woman has slowly grown to trust Tennison enough to invite her into her home and her friends' homes. "She's opened up a whole world of people to me," Tennison says, "but it didn't happen right away. I was the first American whom she allowed into her private life. She came to realize that even though I was a person who doesn't necessarily see everything the way she does, I would never do anything to compromise her. We've had a lot of complicated conversations on difficult political issues, but we don't talk about things in terms of 'I'm right and you're wrong.' And that has built a trust between us."

Tennison has found that once that trust is gained, Soviets will open up their lives in extraordinary ways. "They seem to experience life at a level of emotional depth that we seldom do here," she muses. "I think it may be because there are so many options in our society. It's easier for us to avoid the harsh realities of life. We can skip out on things we don't like—go to another city, get another job, leave our families, leave our marriages, leave our children and our old people, or at least plant them in places so that they don't interfere with our beautiful mobile lives. That's not possible in the Soviet Union. People have to work out conflicts with each other. The only way they've been able to survive is by sticking together—parents helping the children after they're married, babushkas caring for the young, everyone pulling together."

Once, while she walked with a Soviet friend through an old residential section of Kiev, a man dressed in a jogging suit, carrying a baby in his arms and holding a nine-year-old boy by the hand, spotted Tennison's American clothes and stopped her with an urgent question. "Is it really true that Samantha Smith was killed?" he asked, his blue eyes troubled. "How could that happen?" When Tennison explained, he shook his head and relayed the news to his son. Then he offered condolences to Tennison and to all Americans, shook her hand warmly, and was gone. For a moment Tennison remembered, and winced at, her former images of the Soviet Union: "Robotlike people, who never smiled, who had no emotions . . ."

Shattering these images can be exhilarating but also disconcerting: "Going there really forces you to question all kinds of things in your own life that normally you don't question." She recalls sitting at a kitchen table with one Soviet woman about her age, an anthropologist named Masha, and asking her what it was like to be under the "control" of the state. Masha had difficulty understanding her question. When Tennison described "the maze of perceived controls I had in my mind," Masha said, a little exasperated, "Do you have controls? Do you have to be at work by a certain hour in the morning? Do you have to do a certain amount of work to get paid? Do you obey the law? Do you follow certain rules in your society?"

One of Tennison's Moscow friends has a point of view on the two countries seldom heard in the United States. Paula Garb is an American citizen who has lived most of her adult life in the Soviet Union. She fell in love with a Soviet tour guide while visiting the Soviet Union as a teenager, married him, and began living in the Soviet Union. Five years and two children later the marriage dissolved, and Paula returned to the United States with her sons. But two years of being a single parent, trying to go to college and provide for her family at the same time, left her in debt and exhausted. She decided to return to the Soviet Union, where she knew she would find free day care, cheap rent, and a stipend to support her while she finished her degree. Her sons Andre and Greg are now eighteen and fourteen, have dual Soviet and American citizenship, and will choose between the countries when they reach twenty-one. Paula has no regrets about her decision: "She sees the problems in the Soviet system, but she has a deep loyalty to it because it took her in when she was desperate," says Tennison. "She's told me that she doesn't think she would have had the strength to raise children in a Western society with all of the drugs and commercialism."

Still another point of view is offered by members of the dissident and refusenik communities, who often will welcome Americans enthusiastically into their homes, tell them their stories, but disagree with what Tennison and other citizen diplomats are trying to do. "Through their lenses, anyone who wants to make any kind of accommodation with the Soviet Union, for any reason, is a traitor to their cause," she says. "But at the same time they very much want to have Westerners visit them. So they receive us with mixed emotions. They think we're very naive, but they're still willing to talk with us, and I think it's important that Americans understand that slice of the pie, too. Because they have a point; there's no doubt the refuseniks are disenfranchised and discriminated against.

"It's a chicken and egg situation. For instance, the fact that a number of well-educated Jewish people have applied to emigrate makes the Soviets leery about educating Jewish children. The assumption is that they'll educate them and then they'll leave. And since there aren't that many places at the universities, they would rather admit a good Russian kid or Uzbek kid, whom they know is going to stay. So you begin to see how this craziness reinforces itself, and the situation just gets worse and worse.

"The average Soviet person doesn't understand why the Jews want to leave the country. Once they apply to emigrate, they are seen as traitors to the system that has housed, fed, educated, and provided work for them, because they are not staying to continue to help build the society. It reminds me of families I knew when I was growing up in the south, who felt that the sons were obligated to stay and help with the family business. It was almost unthinkable if a son wanted to break away." Tennison once asked two non-Jewish Soviet teenagers to come with her to services in a Leningrad synagogue and translate for her. After a few minutes the teenagers became uncomfortable and wanted to leave. "We don't like Jews," they told her simply. "They think they are better than the rest of us. They meet in secret and plan ways to leave our country."

Tennison compares talking to dissidents and refuseniks about the Soviet Union with talking to black activist Angela Davis about the United States. "She is so concentrated, so focused, on the evils going on against blacks in this country that she doesn't see a lot of other things," Tennison says. "It's almost as though people on the cutting edge of change have to be *consumed* by their vision of the evils in order to be able to break some of the existing structures open. When people stand on that edge of change they develop a certain brand of craziness and interpret things through a skewed set of lenses."

She pauses. "You know, it would take chapters to talk about the psychology of the dissidents and refuseniks," she adds. "I think they're a necessary part of that society. But the agents of change pay prices. The old structures give way slowly, and the dissidents and refuseniks are moving too fast for most of Soviet society. Yet I'd be willing to bet that the borders will be essentially open to Jews in five years—maybe even three years—and it will be because some of them stood on that line and were willing to take the consequences. Just like the schools in this country were eventually opened because some blacks were willing to stand on that line and take the consequences."

Tennison cautions visitors from getting too stuck on categories like "dissidents" and "Party members"—there is much more crossover and mingling than Westerners tend to assume. One Soviet woman acquaintance, Olga, a Party member, recently took her to the apartment of one of her best friends, Tanya, who is a devout Russian Orthodox believer. There Tennison also met Tanya's boyfriend, a Jewish man who wants to emigrate, and Olga's boyfriend, an older married man who is an alcoholic. "Suddenly around this table we had everything from Party to dissident," Tennison says, "and they're all great friends."

Absorbing their Soviet experiences is "emotionally exhausting for everyone," she says. "We begin questioning the entrenched rights and wrongs that we've lived with all our lives, and we start doing flip-flops. One day we're all thrilled by something positive that we see them doing with kindergarten education, for example, and then we turn around and are hit in the face with the control on dissent. And our minds get rototilled."

She tries to find an opportunity each day to pull the group together and let everyone hash through their experiences and feelings. "It's a constant process. It's so hard for us to take off our American spectacles. And how do we pick up their spectacles and see how it looks through their eyes? How has their society developed? How are we bound by different customs, geography, history, circumstance? How would I feel if my father had gone to the gulag under Stalin? Or my mother had survived the war on her own?"

Tennison also has to cope with the emotional reactions of Americans traveling with her—usually one or two every trip—who find the entire experience extremely disturbing. "They look around and say, 'My God, why have I wasted my money to come here? The food is rotten, I don't get good service, I can't get a decent cup of coffee, there are too many people in uniform on the street'—and all this bottled-up fear and prejudice starts coming out. It's grueling to try to keep everyone in balance, especially when we get hit with Party people in meetings and they start bad-mouthing the Reagan administration and talking about how hard the Soviet Union is trying to make peace in the world, and we're sitting there thinking about Poland and Afghanistan."

Her most difficult case was a retired American army colonel. "That trip pushed every button that man had," she says ruefully. "He had so much personal investment in the Soviet Union being the enemy that it almost cracked him, I think. The whole trip he was angry, attacking the Party people, just unable to keep quiet for a moment. One day our Intourist guide got fed up and challenged him on our own human rights problems, which he had never faced. He went home and separated from his wife and took off in a van, and a year later I received a hundred pages of his journal in the mail telling me how that trip had unwound him, and where he was now.

"There's a constant balance between our urge to be critical with our need to just learn. There are things in Soviet society that I wouldn't want to live with. There are things in our society that I wouldn't want to live with either, but I do, and I'm a patriot of my country, I love it, I wouldn't want to live anywhere else. I'm a capitalist—I own my own business, for goodness sake. But I also want to keep my mind open to understanding other ways of living that other people have come up with that look fairly normal to them."

After going through this "mind-scrambling" experience, most are eager to communicate what they've learned to their friends and colleagues. Tennison asks that those traveling on her trips spend at least six months doing public education after they return. The techniques she recommends include: giving slide shows; speaking to schools, colleges, and civic associations; appearing on radio and television; writing newspaper articles and letters to the editor; writing articles for professional journals; writing to members of Congress and the President; starting personal newsletters; sending journals of their experiences to everyone on their Christmas lists; starting local lecture series and educational workshops; initiating sister-city projects; and, of course, leading new trips.

Tennison gives most of her slide presentations in the heartland of the country—Texas, Oklahoma, Arkansas, Illinois, Kentucky—and she attempts to speak to audiences not self-selected for prior interest in peace work or citizen diplomacy. Her average listener, she says, is a middle-aged American businessman with moderate to conservative political tendencies. She talks frankly about the parts of the Soviet system that "aren't working"—the stifling centralized bureaucracy, the alcoholism, the small apartments and shoddy construction, the living conditions that, though improving, are still far below Western standards. But she is equally frank in describing the parts of the Soviet system which she believes *are* working—for example, the low crime rate and safe streets.

Her slide show addresses aspects of Soviet society little understood in the United States, such as religion. American scholars estimate that between 25 and 30 percent of the Soviet population is made up of practicing believers. There are numerous churches registered with the government that have active congregations; the Russian Orthodox Church is by far the largest, with approximately seven thousand "working" churches and some fifty million faithful. Baptist, Pentecostal, Evangelical Christian, and Mennonite Churches together total approximately one million members. There are also Jewish synagogues, Islamic mosques, and churches that are closely linked to ethnicity, such as the Lithuanian Catholic Church, Georgian Orthodox Church, and the Armenian Apostolic Church. In addition, there are a small number of "unregistered churches," Christians who meet in homes and "who are still experiencing intimidation and persecution," says Tennison. "They have only one loyalty, that being Christ, and they feel that to register with a Godless state would compromise that loyalty. They are a spunky and determined group who will go to prison to 'witness to their faith.' Although they are a minute fraction of the people worshiping in the Soviet Union today, they are frequently the only ones we hear about in the West."

The Soviet government has been generally hostile toward religion over the years; the early Bolsheviks vehemently opposed organized religion because the Czar and the Church were synonymous. Stalin persecuted religious believers and decimated churches, although he allowed a revival of religious practices during World War II to boost morale. But Tennison believes that the conditions for religious worship have been steadily improving in the last ten years. "The people at the churches uniformly tell us that 1975 was the year when things started relaxing," she says. "Now you find young Russian men in blue jeans in Orthodox churches kneeling down and kissing icons and lighting candles. I am under the impression that one didn't see that ten years ago. That the state itself is going to be celebrating the one-thousand-year anniversary of the Russian Orthodox church in 1987 is a sign that things are changing."

Another topic her slide presentation covers is human rights. "Once in an official meeting we were talking about human rights, and finally I was confronted by a Soviet who said, 'How can Americans say anything about human rights when Leonard Peltier is in prison?' " Tennison had never heard of Leonard Peltier. The Soviet explained that he was a Native American from South Dakota, a leader of a small spiritual community of traditional Indians on the Pine Ridge Reservation who opposed the selling of Indian sacred land to the US government for energy development. Peltier, alleged the Soviet, was framed for murder and tried on the basis of false testimony bought by FBI agents, and he has spent ten years in prison under two life sentences. Tennison listened and thought, "This is probably propaganda he's making up." But a few weeks after she returned to the United States, she read a similar description of Leonard Peltier in the *Christian Science Monitor*. A few weeks later, she read an article in the *Los Angeles Times* by Elizabeth DiLauro, coordinator for the Human Rights Office of the Cathedral of St. John the Divine in New York City, saying that Peltier's case, which is now being appealed, raises "the very real issues of genocide, government oppression and suppression of religion" in the United States.

Two wrongs don't make a right, and the unjust imprisonment of Leonard Peltier doesn't excuse the unjust imprisonment of Andrei Sakharov. "But it helps me to understand how the Soviets can overlook their Jewish situation, for instance, when I find it so easy to overlook my Native American situation, or the black situation right here in my own city. I had to go to the Soviet Union to find out about Leonard Peltier, a human rights problem in my own country. What we grow up with we get immune to. We don't see our human rights violations, and they really don't see theirs. We wear strange lenses to protect ourselves from our own discrepancies, which allow us to see only the discrepancies of others."

An additional complicating factor, says Tennison, is the emphasis on different values in the two societies, leading to quite different definitions of what "rights" are. The United States, a nation largely composed of immigrants seeking religious, economic, and personal freedom from authorities in the "old country," has developed into a society that cherishes *personal freedom* above all other values. The Soviet Union, a country that has suffered repeated invasions during the past thousand years by conquering armies of Mongols, Poles, Lithuanians, and Swedes, has developed into a society that cherishes *collective security* above all other values. Americans, protected by two oceans, the one major war fought on their territory—the Civil War—all but forgotten, have never developed the obsession with defending the homeland that the Soviets have; Soviets, living in a land where serfdom was a way of life until little more than a century ago, largely isolated from the intellectual revolution of the Enlightenment in the late eighteenth century, have never developed the preoccupation with individual rights that Americans have.

Thus the two countries have come to look at concepts such as "human rights" in very different ways. "Soviets perceive that their rights are to housing, education, medical care, food, and safe streets, not to freedom of speech, assembly, or religion," Tennison says. The difference is the relative importance that Americans and Soviets tend to assign to collective and individual values. An American in Moscow, while admiring the safe and efficient subways, asks: "But why can't you let your artist exhibit whatever they want to paint?" A Soviet in New York City, while breathless in his admiration of the art galleries, asks: "But why can't you regulate handguns when so many people die from handgun wounds every year?"

"All of us," Tennison observes, "seem to grow up accepting the craziness in our own societies. The Soviets are much more accustomed to the notion that there are some things you can do, and some things you can't do. I've noticed it in the school classrooms I've visited—there is a tendency to accept authority. So most of them—and of course there are many exceptions, like the black marketeers, who are sick and tired of being told what to do—but the majority of Soviets don't seem to have the same flashpoint we do when it comes to being told what they can and cannot do. In the United States, people tend to respond, 'Don't you dare tell me what to do, I'll do whatever I please,' when a bureaucracy tries to encroach on some of our personal freedom.

"Once a Soviet friend asked me, 'What is it like to not be able to walk in your parks at night?' I live next to Golden Gate Park, and I wouldn't be caught dead there at night. I just said, 'Well, that is a problem, but I can't do anything about it, that's just the way it is, so I choose to do other things.' And I don't get worked up about it. But my friend couldn't imagine what it would be like to not be able to sit on the park benches and talk and smoke and catch a metro home late at night. I have some émigré friends, who didn't like the Soviet Union and left it, but who just get *incensed* at the fact that they can't walk around parts of San Francisco at night. They're incensed that they have to pay forty dollars to go to a ballet they went to the ballet or opera every week when they lived in the Soviet Union. We all have different reactions to different restrictions, depending on what we are used to."

Tennison doesn't attempt to talk about arms control or nuclear weapons in her presentations, although she answers questions on those topics if they come up. Instead she expresses her concern, as a mother and grandmother, that her children and grandchildren may not have a future, and that with fifty thousand nuclear weapons in a world riddled with hostility and ignorance, "it's folly to think they will never be used. But I have to be careful about overload. If I break into these people's stereotypes about the Soviet Union, that's about as much as I can do in one sitting and get away with. My slide presentation is not a powder-puff piece. It raises the hackles in a lot of places, but in such a way that people can ask questions without making me a target. The slides are key—one picture will filter into levels of the mind where words will never go. I've heard conservative Southern men say afterwards to each other, 'She handled such hard issues in such a soft way. I came here expecting to resist everything she was saying, and I didn't.' "

Her Southern accent has also been an advantage. "People don't see me as an outsider. I come to them in my wool suits and silk blouses looking like everybody's wife, mother, or daughter." And being a woman, she thinks, has helped as well. "I think men, especially men in my generation, have an easier time accepting being emotionally *moved* by a woman than by a man. Men have to be guarded around men, but it's acceptable to listen to a woman speak from her heart. And I've been amazed at what happens when I speak. I think there's a pervading suspicion, even among right-wingers, that we are not being told the whole truth about the Soviet Union."

As much as she enjoys traveling to the Soviet Union, Tennison deliberately spends at least half of the year speaking in the United States, "because the real work, I feel, has to be done here. Many Soviets have told me, 'Of all the people in the world we admire, it's Americans,' and the need to resolve the tension between our countries seems to be in the forefront of their minds. It's the first thing they start talking about. Even some of my dissident friends have begun changing their minds about this in the last few years. Whereas here, when I speak in some little town in western Kentucky, people don't arrive with this issue in the forefront of their minds, but then the slide show does something, and very similar feelings come to the surface.

"A number of us who started to do citizen diplomacy back when this was a cold issue have connections and a level of trust with people in the Soviet Union that new people just don't have. None of us can afford to back out now. Sometimes I feel that we're all just moving out on a limb, and *going for it*, without having any idea whether or not it's going to work. But if nobody does anything, it's obvious what's going to happen to us. I know that if I could stick any American into my back pocket, and take them along with me—including President Reagan and Cap Weinberger—they would be changed human beings, with changed international policies, by the time we were finished."

Tennison is now writing a book, a collection of vignettes and stories about her Soviet experiences, and she sends a quarterly newsletter to two thousand people across the country. In 1985 she and several other citizen diplomats created a nonprofit group called The Center for US-USSR Initiatives. The Center sponsors monthly educational programs on Soviet affairs in San Francisco, runs workshops on successful citizen diplomacy techniques, provides a speakers bureau, distributes educational materials (including a thirty-seven minute videotape of Tennison's first trip), and serves as a clearinghouse for information on grass-roots Soviet-American initiatives.

At present the Center's funding comes from private donations, but Tennison and two associates are resurrecting her nursing uniform business, renaming it "Dove Professional Apparel," and hoping that the profits will underwrite their educational programs. When Tennison first began practicing nursing, she was appalled by the impracticality of available uniforms, and in her characteristic way took action. She designed and made a garment with large sectioned pockets, then found that every nurse in the hospital wanted one. She had to hire profesional seamstresses to keep up with the demand and soon was producing and distributing a line of medical wear. Now Tennison and her colleages intend to mix capitalism and idealism by inserting fliers into the uniform packages that describe ways to get involved in planetary as well as local health issues, such as going on a trip to the Soviet Union. "We're combining global education and selling medical garments," says Tennison matter-of-factly. "There's a growing market out there for both things."

In late 1986 the Center began cosponsoring a bilateral citizens' exchange with the Soviet Peace Committee. In a marked break with the past, the Soviets have stayed exclusively in private American homes, and the Peace Committee has allowed Tennison to request names of Soviets whom she wants to come to the United States—including several Soviet friends who are not members of the Party and whom she originally met in a variety of circuitous and chance ways. "I've no doubt they will look these people over carefully," she says, "but I've told them why I want them to come, and why these people are more likely to make an impact on Americans than Party people or scientists or professors."

One Soviet whom she is eager to bring to the United States is Sonya, a thirty-five-year-old Jewish woman who teaches English at a night school in Leningrad. A petite woman with dark eyes and black hair, married with a ten-year-old daughter, Sonya has never had anything to do with the official peace committees or friendship societies. Tennison met her through friends of friends; originally Sonya was mainly interested in meeting Americans so that she could practice her English and hone her American accent (which is considered very chic in the Soviet Union).

When she found out what Tennison was trying to do, however, she was at first intrigued, then moved. "Meeting Americans affected her so profoundly," say Tennison, "that she now feels she has to help break down the misunderstandings between our countries."

Sonya has arranged a number of unusual interactions between ordinary Soviets and members of Tennison's groups. Recently she gave Tennison a handwritten letter addressed to the American people expressing a desire for peace and friendship, signed by about three hundred of her students at the night school. Once she took Tennison into her daughter's classroom; on the spot, the Soviet children gave her artwork to give to American children. Although Sonya has several friends who have left the country or want to leave, she tells Tennison that she herself loves her country, is happy with her job and her family, and would never want to leave.

Another Soviet friend Tennison would like to bring to the United States is Yuri, her twenty-five-year-old "adopted son" from Odessa. "Our Intourist guide didn't want us associating with him because she thought he was black-market, even though he isn't; he's just this average kid who's thinking about joining the Party but isn't sure whether he should. He came to meet us outside our hotel one day, and our guide took him aside and started telling him in Russian that it was wrong for him to be associating with us, that he was probably telling us bad things about their country. And he just looked at her and said firmly in English, 'Get off my back. I'll get my Soviet Constitution out and show you what my rights are.' Then he waved his arm to us and said, 'Come on, let's go,' and off we went.

"He took us to a bar where we stayed until midnight talking about politics and religion. He may join the Party because he's an idealist. He really believes in taking care of everybody and trying to build the Great Society. But then he started asking me if I believe in God. I told him how I feel when I'm out alone walking under the stars at night, and his face lighted up and he whispered—*I know what you mean! I've felt that! I'm not sure I can be a good Communist and still believe there's something out there. . . . '* We went on like this for hours."

When "the work" becomes discouraging or difficult, Tennison savors memories of her Soviet friends. She recently visited the fifth-floor studio of an avant-garde artist named Sergei and his wife Anna, whom she first met at a large public exhibition of eight hundred works of "unofficial art," one of the first allowed by Soviet authorities. Sergei has a job designing book and record covers, but spends most of his time on his own art, which Tennison describes as "very abstract and symbolic." He works in the gray area between the mainstream and the fringe of Soviet artistic life—some of his shows are sanctioned, others not.

One painting that particularly moved her, of which she includes a photograph in her slide show, depicts a thorny metallic tangle, resembling both a barbed-wire fence and a rosebush, looming in front of a deep blue background. A circle of light is breaking through the blue, like the sun breaking through an overcast sky, and touching the metallic latticework with a fiery glow. "This is our country," Sergei told Tennison simply. "You see the briars, the pain, the hardship. But you also see beauty—things are beginning to clear, the light is coming through."

Sergei, Anna, and Tennison sat on the couch, drinking home-brewed espresso, talking about art. Then Anna, a woman about Tennison's age, "who is totally absorbed in her husband's work, and normally very quiet," suddenly looked at her and asked, very seriously, "You have been to our country many times. What do you think of us? What do you think of our country?" Tennison could tell, from the slightly scared, slightly defiant look on her face, that Anna expected her to tell the truth.

A charged, vulnerable silence filled the room. Tennison took a deep breath and began speaking about what she had discovered in the Soviet people. "It seems to me," she said, "that you are a people who have been born in a very harsh historical time, in a very harsh climate. You've had to deal with tragedy on a scale that few other peoples have known, and you've had to survive and go on and become productive. And your suffering has produced a quality, a spiritual depth, an ability to create human connections, that touches me very deeply." Tennison kept talking, absorbed in articulating what was in her heart, oblivious to the effect her words were having on Anna.

When she stopped another powerful silence filled the room. Anna's brown eyes glistened; her face was streaked with tears she had not bothered to wipe. "You have seen into our heart," she whispered. "How have you done that, when so many have come and not understood? You have seen into the soul of who we are."

CHAPTER FIVE

PROVING THE EXPERTS WRONG:

NORMAN COUSINS

On October 22, 1962, a dozen Americans and a dozen Soviets gathered around a television set in the lounge of a New England preparatory school. Some stood quietly, their arms folded; some sat; some paced back and forth. Everyone's face wore the same expression of somber concern. The shopping sprees in New York City, the visit to a restored colonial village, and the high-spirited jokes and first steps toward friendship during their ride to Andover were forgotten. All that mattered at that moment was President Kennedy's announcement that he had ordered the United States Navy to block all Soviet military shipments to Cuba in order to force the Soviet Union to remove nuclear missiles from Cuban soil.

The Americans and Soviets in the room — government advisors, journalists, diplomatic scholars, and influential private citizens—did not need to be told that nuclear war was now an imminent possibility. Events that were out of their control, that indeed seemed to be out of even President Kennedy's and Chairman Khrushchev's control, could at any moment convert their congenial conference into a divided camp of official enemies. Never had the terrifying absurdity of the enmity they had gathered to address seemed so painfully clear. Never had the importance of what they were trying to do become so poignantly vivid.

After President Kennedy's address concluded, the chairman of the Soviet delegation, scientist Yevgeny Fedorov, rose slowly from his chair and asked the chairman of the American delegation, Norman Cousins, if he would excuse the Soviet group for a few minutes. Cousins agreed, mindful that the Cuban ultimatum had placed the visiting Soviets in a bizarre position. If war were to break out, the Soviets would probably be imprisoned—if, that is, the war lasted long enough to make this an issue. Cousins decided that if the Soviets wished to call off the conference and head for home while they could, the Americans would support them. But he hoped that the Soviets would stay. As the only group of private citizens from the two countries meeting during the crisis, perhaps they could contribute to its resolution.

A half hour later, Fedorov returned with the worried-looking Soviets. He had called the Soviet embassy in Washington, DC, he said, and received encouragement to continue. "Gentlemen, we are in your hands," he said, extending his arms. "If you wish to proceed with the conference, we will stay. If not, we will leave."

Norman Cousins turned to the American delegates and asked for a show of hands of those who wished to continue. Every hand went up. "Very well," said Fedorov, "we will stay." He asked Cousins for the floor. For the next thirty minutes Fedorov meticulously defended the Soviet emplacement of missiles in Cuba, arguing that they were necessary to deter a United States military invasion of Cuba. The Americans asked questions and expressed their own views no less candidly. The discussion became heated but never acrimonious—everyone understood that the stakes were too high for mere point scoring. Everyone struggled to see the other's point of view. Everyone realized that resolution was needed, not a hollow "victory" in debate.

For the rest of the week, the conference delegates attempted to address some of the issues on their original agenda—disarmament, a strengthened United Nations, a cessation of nuclear weapons tests, and increased cultural and scientific exchange. But the discussion kept straying back to Cuba. Much of what they said was rapidly relayed to government officials on both sides.

Cousins remembers that even as the crisis deepened and the ideological gulf between the delegates widened, the personal rapport between the Soviets and Americans grew stronger. The conference was no longer a polite, gentlemanly interchange on long-term problems; it was a round-the-clock attempt to grapple with immediate life and death issues. "The effect was not one of intensified hostility; quite the contrary, a mood of heightened awareness and responsibility predominated," wrote Cousins afterwards. By the end of the week, "it was possible to be forthright without being caustic, impassioned without being abusive, severe without being cutting." The Andover conference was a dramatic confirmation of Cousins's belief that private citizens, working in off-the-record settings, might be able to resolve some of the issues that persistently become stymied in official diplomatic negotiations.

The conference had ended and the Soviet and American delegates were on their way to Cousins's house in New Canaan, Connecticut, for a farewell dinner, when someone heard a radio report. Chairman Nikita Khrushchev had announced that President Kennedy had assured him that the United States would not invade Cuba, and he was therefore ordering the Cuban missiles removed. The Soviets and Americans shared their relief with boisterous cheers and toasts. At the same time, the delegates knew that much needed to be done to ensure such a crisis would never occur again.

For most of his adult life, Norman Cousins, author, editor, lecturer, activist, and private ambassador for two US presidents, has been advocating by word and deed an enlarged role for citizens in foreign affairs. In 1960 he initiated a series of private, off-the-record talks between prominent Soviet and American citizens known as the Dartmouth conferences. Among American participants have been influential leaders in the business, academic, diplomatic, scientific, and artistic fields, including George Kennan, Donald Kendall, James Michener, Patricia Harris, David Rockefeller, Paul Dudley White, John Kenneth Galbraith, Zbigniew Brzezinski, Margaret Mead, and Paul Warnke.

Although assessing the impact of off-the-record events is inherently tricky, the Dartmouth conferences, according to Cousins, have "scouted the ground" for agreements on cultural exchanges, direct air connections, trade deals, a copyright agreement, and certain arms control treaties. But perhaps their most important accomplishment is that they have been held at all. When official negotiations have broken down or degenerated into shouting matches, the Dartmouth conferences have kept a "back channel" alive for Americans and Soviets to explore the reasoning behind the other's position, avoid the miscalculations that lead to crises, and seek common ground.

As the editor of the magazine *Saturday Review* for thirty-five years, Cousins wrote hundreds of editorials and essays calling for a strengthened United Nations and the creation of international laws, norms, and institutions that would allow nations to resolve their disputes without war. His message has been updated, rephrased and refined, but it has not really changed in nearly forty years. Through his writings comes a crisp, strong, yet moderated and reasonable voice, pitched in a consistent tone of rationality and compassion. He never shouts. He never whispers.

In recent years Norman Cousins has also become a prophet for a different kind of citizens' movement. In 1964 he was stricken with a serious collagen disease, a form of rheumatoid arthritis, that left him bedridden and in great pain. Medical experts said his chances of recovery were only about one in five hundred. Cousins accepted the diagnosis but rejected the verdict. In partnership with his physician, who was willing to try innovative approaches, Cousins began a self-treatment plan that included massive intravenous injections of vitamin C and a steady diet of Marx Brothers movies and Candid Camera episodes. "I made the astounding discovery," he relates, "that ten solid minutes of belly laughter gave me two hours of pain-free sleep."

Cousins recovered completely, and more than a decade later wrote about his experiences in a best-seller, *Anatomy of an Illness,* which established Cousins as a familiar figure on the talk-show and lecture circuit. In 1981 he again managed to recover from a serious disease, a severe heart attack, and he refined his principles of healing in a second popular book, *The Healing Heart.* "I take note of the fact that I have written a dozen or so books over the years on the ills of nations," he noted recently. "All of them combined did not get the response that the account of a personal bout with illness received."

Norman Cousins left the *Saturday Review* in 1978 to become an adjunct professor of medical humanities at the medical school of the University of California at Los Angeles, a post that allows him to lecture widely, write, and cooperate with UCLA scientists in attempting to establish a scientific basis for the theory that positive emotions—laughter, determination, hope—create physiological changes in the body that aid in the healing process. His present office is on the fifth floor of a huge, sterile building in the modern UCLA medical complex in Westwood. Forty-five minutes after the appointed interview time, Cousins opens the door, grinning apologetically. "You've come to talk with me. I'm *so* sorry I've kept you waiting." His handshake is firm; his face very, very kind.

It's apparent that everything is behind schedule this morning. His secretary beseeches him to send a telegram to Soviet Ambassador Anatoly Dobrynin about some urgent matter regarding the next Dartmouth conference, the fifteenth in the series. Jet-lagged from a speaking tour on the East Coast, Cousins is moving slowly and tiredly. His voice is gravelly and there are long pauses between his words; some are so soft and indistinct that the tape recorder does not pick them up. His eyes are red and he rubs them often. The conversation lasts for perhaps forty minutes before another appointment calls him away; it will be necessary to meet again later.

The next day he is scheduled to lead a day-long seminar called "Health Is How We Live Our Lives" at the nearby Veterans Administration Hospital. "Now don't you snitch on me," he confides as he leaves his office, "but I'm taking off between sessions to play tennis. I don't see any point in sitting *indoors* all day through a workshop on healthy living." As he leaves a disturbing thought appears: How will this obviously weak seventy-year-old man survive a grueling all-day seminar, much less hit a tennis ball?

But the next day he has metamorphosed. The sprightly man who takes the podium does not seem to be the same person of the day before. He leads off with several jokes that send his thousand-member audience into giggles, and then launches, without any notes, into an emphatic, superbly organized hour-and-a-half discourse on how patients can contribute to their own recoveries. His voice has changed timbre, lost all of its roughness, and at times becomes forceful, almost thundering. Someone in the audience whispers disbelievingly: "He's *seventy?*" There is no longer any doubt that he will play five sets of tennis between this session and the next one, and that he will probably win.

An anecdote he tells about a visit to the cellist Pablo Casals sheds some light on his own transformation. He describes how the nearly ninety-year-old Casals first entered his living room, bent, stiff, wheezing, with his fingers pitifully twisted in clawlike shapes due to severe arthritis. When he reached the piano, Casals paused, sat down at the keyboard, and his deformed hands slowly "opened like beautiful morning glories." Soon Casals was playing a Brahms concerto with nuance and skill. When he finished he looked up at Cousins, who is himself an accomplished pianist and organist. Casals smiled and said, "Brahms for exercise; now Bach for the spirit," and launched into the Toccata and Fugue in D Minor. Then Casals stood up straight, walked gracefully to the breakfast table, and for several hours seemed to be completely free of infirmities.

What playing a Bach fugue did for Casals, interacting with a thousand people does for Cousins. For several hours he holds the audience's rapt attention, his hands making precise, confident gestures to underscore his words. He describes volunteering himself as a guinea pig for a pilot experiment to see if mental attitudes could affect the population of various blood cells that are important parts of the immune system. After the first blood sample was taken, he says, he spent five minutes "attempting to put myself in a mood of joyous determination, purposeful excitement, and robust anticipation. I did this by trying to imagine what a wonderful world we would have if the United States and the Soviet Union had rational foreign policies." The audience interrupts with applause and laughter.

"I tried to imagine all of the changes that could be brought about on our planet, and how it could be made safe and fit for human habitation, if we could just use a fraction of the 750 billion dollars a year that are now going to make the planet unsafe and unfit, release those resources for human good, and try to create a situation for genuine peace in the world—" he pauses and cracks a cherubic grin. "That was a very heady thought!" The doctors took a second blood sample, and the measurements showed that there was an average increase of 53 percent in the population of five categories of immune cells during those five minutes. "Now this has no standing in medical research, it's just a single case," Cousins went on, "but I don't come from Mars."

The vision that quickened his blood so effectively has been energizing him for most of his life. When, as a twenty-nine-year-old magazine editor, he first heard about the atomic bomb dropped on Hiroshima, he "couldn't have been hit harder than if a report had just been flashed that an interstellar collision involving the earth was possible and likely." That night he began working on one of the most famous essays of the postatomic age, published in the *Saturday Review* a week later under the title "Modern Man Is Obsolete." Long before most had caught on, Cousins realized that the atomic bomb signified "the violent death of one age and the birth of another. . . . Man stumbles fitfully into a new age of atomic energy for which he is as ill equipped to accept its potential blessings as he is to counteract or control its present dangers."

His predictions are eerie to read in retrospect, considering that in August 1945 the overwhelming majority of Americans believed that the atomic bomb was the technological savior that would not only end the current war but all wars. "Far from banishing war, the atomic bomb will in itself constitute a cause of war," Cousins warned. "In the absence of world control as part of world government, it will create universal fear and suspicion. Each nation will live nervously from one moment to the next, not knowing whether the designs or ambitions of other nations might prompt them to attempt a lightning blow of obliteration. . . . Since the science of warfare will no longer be dependent upon armies but will be waged by push-buttons, . . . the slightest suspicion may start all the push-buttons going."

Cousins concluded that modern man would be obsolete only if he refused to recognize that "the greatest obsolescence of all in the Atomic Age is national sovereignty. The world is a geographic entity. This is not only the basic requisite for world government but the basic reason behind the need." Whereas before nations might have had the luxury of gradually creating a world government, atomic bombs had made the necessity of some sort of orderly substitute for international anarchy immediate and urgent.

His essay was widely reprinted, anthologized, and expanded into a book, *Modern Man Is Obsolete* (1945), which appeared briefly on the best-seller list. Cousins began speaking all over the country to try to galvanize a citizens' movement in favor of world federalism. Nations would retain the right to maintain their own cultures and political institutions, he said, but the United Nations would have authority in matters related to world security. In the heady atmosphere of the immediate postwar period, such a plan seemed possible and desirable to many. By mid-1946, seven US senators and nearly a hundred House members openly supported some form of world government, and many others expressed support in private. A 1946 Gallup poll revealed that 52 percent of Americans supported the liquidation of national armed forces and the creation of an international police force with responsibility for keeping the peace; only 24 percent were opposed, with 22 percent undecided.

In 1947 Cousins helped found an organization called the United World Federalists, which has consistently lobbied to turn the United Nations into a strong federation. In his first book, *The Good Inheritance* (1942), Cousins argued for world federalism on the strength of two historical examples—ancient Greece and the drafting of the American Constitution. Although the independent Greek city-states were able to unite successfully to fight the common enemy of Persia, they were unsuccessful in their attempts to create a united federation because the strongest states, Athens and Sparta, refused to relinquish any of their sovereignty or power. The result was the Peloponnesian War and the crumbling of Greek civilization. According to Cousins, this example was not lost on the creators of the American Constitution, who constantly referred in *The Federalist* to ancient Greece in their own argument for federalism.

But the Cold War inexorably eroded public support for world federalism. In a 1946 commentary on Winston Churchill's famous "iron curtain speech," Cousins decried the temptation to lay all the blame for world tensions at the door of Communist nations alone. There have been wars long before Communism existed, said Cousins, and there would be wars even if the Soviet Union were to disappear from the face of the earth, as long as competitive national sovereignties accepted no higher political authority for arbitrating disputes. But the world federalists were placed on the defensive by Senator Joseph McCarthy and his supporters, who termed "subversive" any plan that included the cooperation of Communist nations.

Cousins's pleas to avoid "deep-freezing the peace" went unheeded, and membership in the United World Federalists plummeted between 1951 and 1956. The opportunity that had once seemed within grasp slipped way. In 1952 Cousins lamented, "Seven years ago, when world law was mentioned, people said it was too soon. Now when it is mentioned, they say it is too late." Criticizing the spy mania, blacklists, and textbook censorship that McCarthyism produced, Cousins noted in 1953 that "Communism is a real danger in America, not because of the size of its membership, which is small enough to put into a single baseball park, but because the very groups which profess to hate it the most are helping to fashion it day by day with such exquisite perfection."

In essay after essay, with little apparent fear of repeating himself, Cousins hammered his main points home. He argued that simply abhorring war was not an effective way of preventing war, pointing out that the pacifist movement in the 1930s, with its earnest declarations and ads proclaiming the horrors of war, had done little to stop World War II. Nor was it enough to simply destroy the weapons and disarm. "The answer, if there is an answer," he wrote, "must lie in the direction of establishing an authority which takes away from nations, summarily and completely, not only the machinery of battle that can wage war, but the machinery of decision that can start a war."

The actions of ordinary individual citizens, he believed, were the main hope. In a pointed 1957 essay called "Checklist of Enemies," Cousins wrote: "The enemy is a man who not only believes in his own helplessness but actually worships it. His main article of faith is that there are mammoth forces at work which the individual cannot possibly comprehend, much less alter or direct. . . . The enemy is a man who has a total willingness to delegate his worries about the world to officialdom. He assumes that only the people in authority are in a position to know and act."

In his essays, Cousins managed to be erudite without being stuffy, sophisticated without being pompous. He never allowed his urbane style to mask his impassioned calls for public action and moral leadership, and he never deigned to lose respect for anyone, remaining courteous and dignified in the midst of heated debates. His rhetorical power lay in expanding articulately on the "whys"; the nuts-and-bolts of the "hows" he left to others. Yet his evenhanded approach to world problems, never averting his eyes for a moment from less-than-altruistic Soviet intentions and the potential abuses of government power, led several generations of *Saturday Review* readers to trust him.

Cousins always acted in as well as wrote about the international scene. He reported to *Saturday Review* readers from a plane during the 1948 Berlin airlift, from Kashmir during a 1954 border dispute, from the Israeli-occupied Gaza strip in 1956, and from Laos in 1961. He visited Hiroshima in 1949, initiated a "moral adoption" program for some four hundred Hiroshima orphans, and brought two dozen young women who had been disfigured by atomic burns and radiation, known as the "Hiroshima Maidens," to the United States for plastic surgery and rehabilitation, all with funds supplied by *Saturday Review* readers. Several years later he organized a similar project to bring thirty-five Polish women who had been subjected to grotesque medical experiments by Nazi scientists, the "Ravensbrueck Lapins," to the United States for treatment. For these and other humanitarian activities he was nominated by Vatican officials, a mayor of Hiroshima, and Red Cross officials for the Nobel Peace Prize.

In 1956 Cousins was first shown data on the health effects of radioactive fallout by scientists at Washington University in St. Louis. He soon launched a campaign for a halt to nuclear testing in the pages of the *Saturday Review*, and went to the West African jungle clinic of Dr. Albert Schweitzer, the Nobel Peace Prize winner and revered humanitarian, to persuade him to speak out on the testing issue. Several months later, on April 24, 1957, Schweitzer issued his historic "Declaration of Conscience" calling on the nuclear powers to cease atmospheric nuclear testing.

The American media paid little attention to Schweitzer's call and it might have sunk quickly from public view if a member of the US Atomic Energy Commission, Dr. William Libby, had not decided to refute the famous physician, stating that any health risks posed by atmospheric testing were greatly outweighed by the risks to national security from a cessation of tests. A vigorous public debate soon erupted on the health hazards of weapons tests, and Cousins and others seized the moment to found a new organization called the National Committee for a Sane Nuclear Policy.

"The danger facing us is unlike any danger that has ever existed," Cousins wrote in November 1957. "In our possession and in the possession of the Russians are more than enough nuclear explosives to put an end to the life of man on earth. Our approach to the danger is unequal to the danger. . . . If what nations are doing has the effect of upsetting the delicate balances on which life depends, fouling the air, devitalizing the foods, and tampering with the genetic integrity of man himself— then it becomes necessary for people to restrain and tame the nations."

In 1958 the Soviet Union began an informal, nonbinding moratorium on nuclear weapons tests, and the United States followed suit. Negotiatons for a comprehensive test ban treaty were soon under way. But Cousins was impatient with the slow progress of the negotiations. He insisted: "There is no point in talking about the possibility of war breaking out. The war is already being fought. It is being waged by national sovereignties against human life. . . . What the world needs today are two billion angry men who will make it clear to their national leaders that the earth does not exist for the purpose of being a stage for the total destruction of man. . . . Our security depends on the control of force rather than on the pursuit of force. It is not enough for the governments to recognize this. The citizen must recognize it, give it priority over his personal affairs, and create the kind of mandate that can give leadership to leaders."

In 1958 President Dwight Eisenhower, who had just signed a cultural exchange agreement with Chairman Khrushchev, wondered aloud to Cousins whether "people-to-people" contacts could have a direct impact on negotiations at the government level. (Cousins and Eisenhower first became acquainted when Eisenhower wrote some supportive letters in response to Cousins's editorials on world government in the late 1940s; their relationship deepened while Eisenhower served as president of Columbia University, Cousins's alma mater, and continued after Eisenhower was elected President.)

Eisenhower was all too aware of how easy it was for official negotiations to become blocked over trivial details because of the tendency for each side to view any retreat from an initial position as a sign of weakness. This was clearly happening with the nuclear test ban negotiations. Would it be possible, Cousins and Eisenhower mused, for a small group of private citizens—who had the confidence and ear of their respective governments and yet could freely explore areas for agreement without commitment or publicity—to succeed where the official diplomats were failing?

As it happened, Cousins had been asked by the State Department to lecture in the Soviet Union in 1959 under the terms of the new exchange agreement. Cousins informed the Soviet government that he was only interested in coming if he could speak his mind and that they ought to know that he had actively protested the Soviet suppression of the Hungarian revolt in 1956 and been a loud spokesman for "distinguishing between a true campaign for peace and propagandist activities designed to advance the interests of the Soviet Union." He also specified that he be allowed to speak about the problems in Soviet-American relations and the concept of the "natural rights of man" as reflected in the US Constitution. The Soviets replied that the invitation still stood. Cousins went on a five-week tour and in July 1959, with Eisenhower's unofficial blessings, proposed to the Soviet Peace Committee in Moscow the notion of holding a small citizens' conference to "see whether, on a non-political basis, we might indicate some approaches to meaningful agreement."

Cousins told the Peace Committee that a few days earlier, a Moscow traffic policeman, discovering that he was an American, had given him a warm bear hug on the street. "This incident made a strong impression on me," he remarked. "I have been in many countries of the world, but never before have I been embraced, affectionately or otherwise, by a policeman." The policeman had been one of the Soviet soldiers who had met the American soldiers at the Elbe River at the end of World War II, and Cousins became, as he put it, "the beneficiary of his warm recollections."

Cousins related his surprise at many seemingly non-Communistic aspects of Soviet society, such as savings accounts, private produce markets, and well-attended churches. Most of all, he told the committee, he was impressed by the genuine friendliness and desire for peace he encountered among the Soviet people he had met. He asked them to believe that the same goodwill and yearning for peace existed in the United States. Yet, he said, "This has not been enough to create peace. Why?"

Cousins then candidly told the Peace Committee why the American people are fearful and suspicious of the Soviet government, asking that they not "necessarily agree that those feelings are correct, but merely consider that those feelings exist, and what are the reasons and causes behind them." He detailed the activities of the American Communist Party, which he called a "party without honor" because it was clearly more interested in furthering the foreign policy objectives of a nation six thousand miles away than bettering the lives of people in the United States. He reminded them, politely but pointedly, of Soviet actions in Czechoslovakia, Poland, Berlin, and Hungary.

He also spoke optimistically of the recent liberalizing trends within the Soviet Union and the apparent willingness of current Soviet leaders to seek coexistence with the West. "The obvious thing to do," Cousins concluded, "is to create a great design for survival and for the making of a genuine peace—a design to rescue the world from its present anarchy, a design for effective law and justice among nations. . . . It is doubtful whether the national governments can do the job by themselves. Indeed, the peace of the world is much too important to be left to governments. If the peace is to be real, people everywhere will have to speak up."

The Soviets' response to his idea of a private citizens' conference was polite but muted—perhaps because they were still a little in shock from his candor. Several months went by. Then in November 1959, two leaders of the Soviet Peace Committee, author Nikolai Tikhonov and journalist Mikhail Kotov, sent him a three-page letter that is marked in Cousins's files with a red star. "The ice of the Cold War is melting," wrote the Soviets, who mentioned Khrushchev's American visit in the fall of 1959, the Camp David talks, and the impending visit of Eisenhower to the Soviet Union. "Direct friendly contacts should be established between public representatives of our countries in the interest of rapprochement between the USA and the Soviet Union, in the interest of universal peace. . . . Aware of your prestige and the influence you enjoy in the US public circles we would like to make a counter-proposal: Why not arrange a Soviet-American meeting as soon as possible?" Cousins, elated, scribbled two exclamation points in red pencil next to the question.

While the Soviet Peace Committee originally envisioned a meeting between their members and the directors of American peace organizations, Cousins successfully persuaded them that the conference would have more impact if organizational ties were deemphasized and the individual stature of the participants highlighted instead. Within a few months Cousins had put together a blue-ribbon collection of eminent American businessmen, lawyers, artists, and former diplomats, including choreographer and dancer Agnes de Mille; Arthur Larsen, a former advisor to President Eisenhower; Grenville Clark, a prominent lawyer and advocate of world federalism; Philip Mosely of the Council on Foreign Relations; former US Senator William Benton; William Loos, director of the Church Peace Union; writer Stuart Chase; and George Kennan, former US Ambassador to the Soviet Union. The Soviets responded with a similar collection of "who's who," including playwright Alexander Kornietchuk, known to be a confidant of Khrushchev, who headed the delegation; economist Modest Rubenstein; writer Boris Polevoi; Baptist clergyman Alexander Karev; radiologist Zoya Lagunova; and cinema producer Sergei Yutkevich.

The president of Dartmouth College, John Dickey, offered his campus as a secluded, quiet environment where the delegates could avoid publicity and reporters. Plans for this "Dartmouth conference" had progressed sufficiently by the spring that the downing of a US espionage plane over Soviet territory on May 1, 1960, which precipitated a sudden downturn in Soviet-American relations, led to a postponement rather than a cancellation of the conference. The delegates gathered at Dartmouth on October 29, 1960.

Forty years of nearly complete isolation between Soviets and Americans and fifteen years of the Cold War had taken their toll; it took several days, Cousins wrote later, for the "strangeness" to wear off and for the participants to look at each other as human beings rather than stereotypes. "Inadvertently, almost instinctively, the participants found themselves arranged in two 'lineups' confronting each other across a chasm of xenophobia and ideological estrangement." On the agenda were five general areas of discussion: the economic development of emerging nations, the psychological texture of peace, the problems of world arms control, the structuring of global peace, and the role of citizens in developing responsible foreign policy.

Cousins later characterized the meetings as nonaccusative and nonpolemical, and there were surprisingly broad areas of consensus about what should be done to ease tensions—nuclear tests should be halted, cultural exchange and trade expanded, and the United Nations strengthened. But sparks flew on definitions of ideological terms like "democracy" and "censorship." At one of these moments, when tempers appeared in danger of being lost for the sake of national prestige, Grenville Clark stood up and declared that the Americans admired the Soviets for their courageous struggle against the Germans in World War II. This simple statement had a remarkable effect—it appeared to reassure the Soviets that the Americans understood their history and respected their country. From then on, the tone of the discussions became markedly more intimate and adventuresome. "This human relations breakthrough," Cousins says succinctly, "was freighted with vast political implications."

Although the proceedings were off the record, the American and Soviet delegations told a *New York Times* reporter their general impressions, leading to an editorial several days later that praised the Dartmouth conference as a "small—but potentially important—gleam of light" and commented: "It is a measure of the straits we are in that a mere civilized discussion of the issues dividing our nations must be counted an appreciable advance." Apparently Cousins's strategy of including only American participants with unimpeachable credibility worked; the *New York Times* scoffed at the idea that such an experienced American panel was in any danger of being "hoodwinked."

George Kennan remarked that in two decades of diplomatic service he had not had as many frank, freewheeling discussions with intelligent and well-informed Soviet citizens as he had during those few days at Dartmouth. "Major positions were not altered—there were no expectations in that direction," wrote Cousins, "but human relationships were established. Each position had the name of a man attached to it—someone who would sit next to you at the breakfast table and enjoy a stroll with you on the campus." Both sides agreed to continue this unique dialogue, and the Soviet delegation invited the Americans to come to the Crimea the following spring.

The Soviets and Americans sat next to each other at the Crimean conference, which tackled issues in a greater depth. Cousins thought he noticed a change in Soviet attitudes toward the United States since his visit two years before. "Five years ago or less, a sense of elemental discovery seemed to be involved in even the most cursory meeting between Americans and Russians. . . . Each tended to observe the other as though making a massive effort to penetrate a biological riddle. All this is no more. The staring phase of American-Soviet relations is ended. The serious dialogue phase now begins."

Cousins recorded some of his thoughts during the Crimean conference in a faded blue notebook: "Nations want the benefits of law without being willing to create the machinery of law. . . . No technical differences about test ban—aboveground or underground. . . . Soviet delegates did not lecture to us about our national characteristics, etc., although more than a few Americans took the rostrum. . . . The ease with which an unimportant position hardens. Just in the act of reacting negatively to a proposal, a hardening process begins. . . . If on a matter as simple as this, we take a" (the words "tough stand" are crossed out) "pigheaded stand, what hope is there? . . . Two organized systems of self-right-eousness. Each compares its best with the other's worst."

When Cousins returned, American skeptics frequently asked whether the conferences had revealed anything about the Soviet Union that was not already well known. One change he had detected, he replied, was that the realities of nuclear war were beginning to reshape traditional Marxist theory that war with capitalist nations was inevitable. The Soviets were starting to realize that they, too, would perish in a nuclear war, and that coexistence was therefore a practical necessity. Cousins noted that Communist China had not gone along with this change in dogma, and that Chinese leaders bragged that they could lose two or three hundred million people in a nuclear confrontation and still win.

Cousins said he was also "pleasantly startled to hear a Soviet econ-omist make a most persuasive case for . . . the fact that American cap-italism was not dependent on military spending. This was a far cry from the traditional Marxist view with its emphasis on the inevitability of depression because of capitalism's inability to produce for peace as it produces for war." The Soviets, however, still believed that socialism would ultimately triumph in the world, not because the Soviet military would force it upon the developing nations, but because the West was not offering a relevant social or economic philosophy to the Third World.

The Soviets listened with interest to Cousins's arguments for world federalism, but were not enthused. "There was a general resistance to the idea of a 'structured peace,' " Cousins admitted in the *Saturday Review*, "the feeling being that if the Soviet Union and the United States could agree on the day-to-day questions, then no world authority was necessary. And if they couldn't agree on the day-to-day questions, then no world authority could make them agree." He noted that similar ar-guments were used by opponents to world federalism in the United States. "The basic problem is with the term 'national security,' " Cousins in-sisted. "The term has a built-in contradiction. In the atomic age, no *national* security is possible. Either there is a workable *world* security system or there is nothing."

A third Dartmouth conference was soon scheduled, but official Soviet-American relations impinged on their plans. Negotiations for a test ban treaty seemed hopelessly stymied over the issue of "inspections," and in the summer of 1961 a new crisis arose in Berlin over the stationing of American troops. In August 1961 the Soviet Union announced that threats to its national security were forcing it to break the informal joint testing moratorium. Cousins immediately sent a strongly worded cable to his friend Alexander Korneitchuk, the cochairman of the conferences, urging him "to dissuade the Soviet government from this dangerous course which is filled with hazard for all mankind."

Korneitchuk replied a few days later that the Berlin crisis had "compelled our government to take measures to strengthen security. . . . I firmly believe that in this exceedingly tense atmosphere the world's peaceloving forces will find a way out of the created dangerous situation." Korneitchuk added that he was "disappointed" by Cousins's declaration in the *Saturday Review* that the people of the world should mount a huge protest campaign against the Soviet action. Cousins's reply was swift and pointed. "I can conceive of no circumstances that could justify the unilateral resumption of nuclear testing. We have taken this position consistently about the United States. We would have done everything in our power to persuade the United States to reverse its decision if it had announced unilateral plans for further tests, whatever its reason might have been. Our hope is that advocates of peace inside the Soviet Union are prepared to do the same."

But the downward spiral was already in motion; a week later, the United States announced that it, too, would resume its nuclear testing. The third Dartmouth conference was postponed from April 1962 because the Soviet delegates would have arrived in the United States just as the first American nuclear test was held. As it turned out, the week chosen instead—October 21–27, 1962, the week of the Cuban missile crisis— made the awkwardness of the April date pale in comparison. But the success of the third conference at Andover proved the resiliency of the Dartmouth concept.

Soon after the Andover conference, Cousins became swept up in a dizzying series of private international diplomatic missions, which are lucidly recorded in his book *The Improbable Triumvirate*. Through an odd combination of circumstances, he found himself shuttling messages between President John F. Kennedy, Pope John XXIII, and Chairman Nikita Khrushchev during a six-month period. It began like this: in March 1962, a representative from the Vatican, Father Felix Morlion, asked Cousins if he could unofficially attend the Andover conference and speak to Soviet delegations privately about creating better relations between the Vatican and the Soviet Union. Pope John XXIII, Morlion said, was keenly interested in encouraging the recent liberalizing trends within the Soviet Union and helping reduce the risk of nuclear war. Cousins let him come to Andover, and Morlion's consultations with the Soviet and American delegates directly influenced the wording of Pope John XXIII's dramatic call for restraint addressed to the superpower leaders during the Cuban missile crisis. Several months later, the Soviets indicated that one of Morlion's original proposals, that a single, unattached individual meet with Chairman Khrushchev to discuss religious matters within the Soviet Union, had been approved.

Cousins agreed to take on the highly secret mission. Before leaving for Rome and Moscow in December 1962, he met with President Kennedy at the White House to find out if he wished to communicate anything to Chairman Khrushchev. According to Cousins, after they had discussed the current impasse in test ban negotiations, Kennedy stood up, went to the window, and seemed lost in thought for a few minutes. "Khrushchev will probably say something about his desire to reduce tensions, but will make it appear there's no reciprocal interest by the United States," Kennedy said. "It is important that he be corrected on this score. I'm not sure Khrushchev knows this, but I don't think there's any man in American politics who's more eager than I am to put Cold War animosities behind us and get down to the hard business of building friendly relations."

Cousins flew to Rome on December 1, 1961, and was briefed by Vatican officials, who recommended that he discuss steps the Soviets could take to improve conditions for religious worship within the country. They also suggested that the Soviets could demonstrate goodwill toward the Vatican by releasing Archbishop Josef Slipyi, who had been imprisoned for seventeen years under charges of cooperating with the Nazis in the Ukraine. Cousins then flew to Moscow and met privately with Khrushchev for more than three hours.

They spoke of the pressures Khrushchev was under within the Communist world for appearing to have "appeased the paper tiger" of the West by pulling Soviet missiles out of Cuba. Cousins noticed that Khrushchev's eyes glazed over when he referred to that terrible week. "The Chinese say I was scared. Of course I was scared," Khrushchev told Cousins. "It would have been insane not to have been scared. I was frightened about what could happen to my country—or your country and all the other countries that would be devastated by a nuclear war. If being frightened meant that I helped avert such insanity then I'm glad I was frightened. One of the problems in the world today is that not enough people are sufficiently frightened by the danger of nuclear war."

He had been grateful, said Khrushchev, for Pope John's appeal during the crisis—"It was a real ray of light." Khrushchev asked Cousins what he could do to express his gratitude to Pope John. Cousins suggested the release of Archbishop Slipyi. Khrushchev stiffened and launched into a detailed history of the Ukrainian Church's behavior during the Nazi occupation. Cousins replied that there was no need to reargue the merits of the original case—the release would simply be on humanitarian grounds, so that the archbishop could live out his few remaining years peacefully in a seminary.

Khrushchev said that he wanted to improve relations with the Vatican, but this was not the way to do it. The release would be exploited for propaganda purposes in the West, he said; headlines would scream: "BISHOP REVEALS RED TORTURE" or something similar. Cousins assured him that the Vatican intended to keep the matter quiet. After listing more reasons why it was impossible, Khrushchev asked Cousins in some exasperation, "Why should I release this man?" Cousins leaned forward and said quietly, "I think it's the right thing to do." Pause. Khrushchev leaned back and said, in a bemused voice, something to the effect of "Oh, I see."

Cousins then changed the subject to peace. He told Khrushchev that, in his opinion, President Kennedy was sincerely interested in improving relations with the Soviet Union and agreeing on a nuclear test ban treaty. At that time, Khrushchev was on the defensive within the Communist world to prove his assumption that the Americans were interested in coexistence. Failure to achieve a test ban treaty would be gleefully interpreted by some Politburo members and Chinese leaders as failure of Khrushchev's entire policy toward the United States. Khrushchev told Cousins to assure the President that he, too, genuinely wanted a nuclear test ban treaty and that there was "no reason why it shouldn't be possible for both our countries to agree on the kind of inspection that will satisfy you that we're not cheating and that will satisfy us that you're not spying." Before Cousins left, Khrushchev wrote Christmas greetings to both Pope John and President Kennedy on Kremlin stationery and gave them to Cousins to deliver.

Cousins flew to Rome and reported the details of his meeting directly to Pope John, who gave him his personal medallion as a token of his appreciation. Several weeks later, the Soviet Union released Archbishop Slipyi. But the story leaked, and headlines reading "BISHOP TELLS OF RED TORTURE" appeared in the United States and other countries. Although Cousins assured the Soviets that there had been no breach of faith on the part of the Vatican and the Vatican issued a disclaimer stating that the newspaper stories were false, the Soviets were understandably annoyed.

Meanwhile, the mood of optimism following the Cuban crisis was waning. Test ban negotiations were deadlocked. The United States insisted on a minimum of eight annual on-site inspections. The Soviet Union insisted on no more than three. To make matters worse, a misunderstanding between the negotiators at Geneva had left the Soviets with the impression that the United States had offered three inspections and then reneged on their offer when the Soviets agreed to three inspections. Those within the Soviet Union and other Communist countries who opposed the test ban seized upon this as evidence that the United States was not negotiating in good faith.

The Vatican asked Cousins to meet with Khrushchev a second time and request the release of Archbishop Josyf Beran of Prague. President Kennedy asked Cousins to tell Khrushchev that he felt the impasse in the Geneva negotiations was the result of an honest misunderstanding and that he wished to make a fresh start. On April 12, 1963, Cousins flew to Sochi and was driven to Khrushchev's country retreat in Gagra on the Black Sea.

Their remarkable seven-hour meeting began after a gourmet luncheon well lubricated with vodka, a tour of the Chairman's indoor swimming pool, and an energetic game of badminton. Cousins thanked Khrushchev for releasing Archbishop Slipyi, apologized for the news leak, and said that Pope John was also concerned about the health of Archbishop Beran in Prague. Khrushchev said that he was unfamiliar with Archbishop Beran's case and that his release would be up to the Czechoslovakian government, but after Cousins pressed the matter he agreed to look into it. (Archbishop Beran was released several weeks later.)

Cousins then brought up the test ban treaty, saying that President Kennedy had asked him to clarify the American position and reiterate Kennedy's desire to reach an agreement. Khrushchev told Cousins that after the Cuban missile crisis, based on what he had heard from his ambassador at the Geneva negotiations, he had gone before his Council of Ministers and told them that a test ban treaty could be achieved if the Soviet Union would agree to three on-site inspections. Recognizing that President Kennedy would not be able to get a treaty with no inspections ratified by the US Senate, Khrushchev said, he had argued that the Soviets should accommodate the President and give him three inspections. "The Council asked me if I was certain that we could have a treaty if we agreed to three inspections, and I told them yes. Finally, I persuaded them."

Now it appeared to the Soviets that the United States had backed down from its previous offer, and Khrushchev believed that he had been made to look foolish in the eyes of his Council of Ministers. "People in the United States seem to think I am a dictator who can put into practice any policy I wish," Khrushchev told Cousins. "Not so. I've got to persuade before I can govern. I cannot go back to the Council. It is now up to the United States. Frankly, we feel we were misled." He then told Cousins that his generals and nuclear scientists were clamoring to be allowed to test some new devices they had designed. Given the current deadlock, he was tempted to tell them to go ahead.

Cousins insisted that this would only damage both Soviet and American security. He repeated his request from President Kennedy that the misunderstandings be set aside and a new approach taken. "Very well," said Khrushchev testily. "Let us forget everything that happened before. The Soviet Union now proposes to the United States a treaty to outlaw nuclear testing—underground, overground, in water, in space, every place. And we will give you something you don't really need. We will give you inspections inside our country to convince you we aren't really cheating."

Khrushchev did not say how many inspections. Cousins repeated that President Kennedy believed he could not get the Senate to accept a treaty that contained only three inspections. "I cannot and will not go back to the Council of Ministers and ask them to change our position in order to accommodate the United States again," Khrushchev repeated.

Then Khrushchev sighed and leaned back in his chair. He said nothing for a moment. "You can tell the President that I accept his explanation of an honest misunderstanding, and I suggest that we get moving," he said at last to Cousins. "But the next move is up to him."

Changing the subject, Cousins asked him to explain his shoe-banging statement at the United Nations: "We will bury you." Khrushchev replied that the Soviet Union would not force socialism upon the United States;

rather, it would be demanded internally by American workers as capitalism collapses on its own accord. "What I meant was, not that I will bury you but that history will bury you," he told Cousins. "Don't blame me if your capitalist system is doomed. I am not going to kill you. I have no intention of murdering two hundred million Americans. In fact, I will not even take part in the burial. The workers in your society will bury the system." When Cousins suggested that perhaps Karl Marx could not have foreseen the development of the United States, Khrushchev cheerily answered that he had a tremendous admiration for the American people and that "when they become a socialist society, they will have the finest socialist society in the world."

Cousins asked Khrushchev what he thought his principal achievement in office had been. "Telling the people the truth about Stalin," he replied. "There was a chance, I thought, that if we understood what really happened, it might not happen again. Anyway, we could not go forward as a nation unless we got the poison of Stalin out of our system. He did some good things, to be sure, and I have acknowledged them. But he was an insane tyrant and he held back our country for many years. . . . One of Stalin's great mistakes was to isolate the Soviet Union from the rest of the world. We need friends. We have mutual interests with the United States. These two great countries would be very stupid if they ignored these mutual interests. They also have serious differences. But no one need worry that these differences will be glossed over. There are people in each country who make a career out of the differences. But someone has to speak also of the serious mutual interests. I have tried to talk about them."

On April 22, 1963, Cousins met with President Kennedy and presented his report. Kennedy shook his head when he heard of Khrushchev's difficulty in persuading his Council and his generals of the United States' sincerity. "He would like to prevent a nuclear war but is under severe pressure from his hard-line crowd, which interprets every move in that direction as appeasement," Kennedy told Cousins. "I've got similar problems. Meanwhile, the lack of progress in reaching agreements between our two countries gives strength to the hard-line boys in both, with the result that the hard-liners in the Soviet Union and the United States feed on one another, each using the actions of the other to justify its own position."

Cousins then suggested that what was needed was a startling new move on the part of the United States. Such a move might include a fresh approach to the test ban treaty within the context of a general call for replacing the Cold War with an era of global cooperation. The timing was crucial, said Cousins, because the Chinese were hoping to exploit the failure of the Soviet Union and the United States to reach a test ban treaty as a reinforcement of their own position that accommodation with the capitalist world was hopeless. Anticipating such a failure, the Chinese were sending a high-level delegation to Moscow in June 1960 in hopes of strengthening Moscow-Peking ties. If no progress had been made by then, Cousins argued, Khrushchev might be forced to acknowledge that the Chinese were right and back away from his policy of coexistence. The result would be a reinvigorated Soviet arms race, the diversion of resources within the Soviet Union away from the consumer economy, and a general hardening of the Communist position toward the rest of the world.

Kennedy said he would think about it and asked Cousins to write a memorandum and to meet with several of his advisors.

Six weeks later, in a June 10, 1963, commencement speech at the American University in Washington, Kennedy outlined a step-by-step program for ending the Cold War and declared that the United States would not conduct nuclear tests in the atmosphere "so long as other states do not do so. We will not be the first to resume." Khrushchev immediately responded favorably to President Kennedy's speech, and soon announced that the Soviet Union, too, would halt atmospheric tests.

In the meantime, several US senators had proposed a partial test ban treaty, outlawing all tests except for those underground, as a way of getting around the inspection question. Once this major agreement had been reached, they felt, it might be easier to find accord on underground testing. Ambassador Averell Harriman traveled to Moscow and, less than two weeks later, a partial test ban treaty was initialed on July 25, 1963. But the real battle had only begun. Sixty-seven Senate votes were needed for ratification, the President thought he had perhaps fifty, and Congressional mail on the test ban was running against ratification by about a fifteen-to-one margin.

On August 7, 1963, President Kennedy and his advisors met with Cousins and other leaders in the Citizens' Committee for a Nuclear Test Ban Treaty to plot a strategy for mobilizing public opinion behind the treaty. Prominent leaders in the business, academic, scientific, labor, farming, and religious communities were galvanized. Anti-test-ban forces, led by the nuclear physicist Dr. Edward Teller, also moved into action, claiming that the dangers of radioactive fallout were miniscule and that all types of testing were needed to develop a new generation of nuclear weapons necessary for US national security. Cousins debated Teller on television several times. Slowly, the ratio of supporting to opposing letters in the congressional mailbag shifted, and public opinion polls showed increasing support for the treaty. On September 24, 1963, the treaty was ratified by the Senate by a vote of eighty to nineteen.

During the summer and fall, President Kennedy began laying the groundwork for further agreements with the Soviet Union on nuclear nonproliferation, step-by-step disarmament, enlarged cultural exchange, security arrangements for Southeast Asia and Berlin, and a more robust United Nations. But within a year, "the improbable triumvirate" was no more. John F. Kennedy was assassinated, Nikita Khrushchev was deposed, and Pope John died of cancer.

Although the delegates at the fourth Dartmouth conference, held in Leningrad in June 1964, could celebrate the partial test ban treaty, the "hot line" between the Kremlin and the White House, and the agreement banning nuclear weapons from space, there were ominous signs that the upturn in relations would be short-lived. Their joint communiqué expressed concern that "there remain areas in the world, specifically Central Europe and South-East Asia, where the lack of political settlements constitutes a potential threat to world peace."

Soviet-American relations collapsed several months later as the United States deepened its involvement in Vietnam. Twice a year for the next three years, Cousins issued invitations to the Soviets to attend a fifth Dartmouth conference. He received no official response, but Korneitchuk indicated privately that the Soviets could see no hope of holding fruitful talks as long as the United States was bombing North Vietnam. Cousins replied that the Soviet Union was supplying arms to North Vietnam, and that it was precisely at times like these that the Dartmouth meetings could have their greatest value.

Finally, in 1968, with the Paris peace talks on Vietnam getting under way, the Soviets agreed to attend a fifth conference, convened in Rye, New York, in January 1969. The Rye conference marked the beginning of a new generation of Dartmouth conferences; according to Cousins, their meetings became "less concerned with broadening the official dialogue than with exploring ways of resolving specific issues." The reconstituted Dartmouth conferences reflected some structural changes as well. The Ford Foundation, which had originally sponsored the conferences, transfered fiscal and administrative responsibility to the Kettering Foundation, where it has remained ever since. On the Soviet side, specialists from research academies associated with the Soviet Academy of Sciences, such as the Institute of US and Canada Studies and the Institute of International Relations and the World Economy, came to dominate the Soviet delegations.

During the early 1970s, the conferences developed proposals for increased Soviet-American cooperation in trade, science, and environmental protection. Dartmouth VI, held in Kiev in July 1971, helped establish the International Institute of Applied Systems Analysis to study changes in the global environment, and contributed to shaping the government agreements on scientific cooperation signed in 1972. At Dartmouth VII, a task force on economic issues, chaired by David Rockefeller of the Chase Manhattan Bank and a high-ranking Soviet official in the Ministry of Trade, helped formulate the principles of the 1974 trade agreement between the countries and assisted in the creation of the US-USSR Trade and Economic Council.

In 1973 the Soviet Union apparently considered joining a variety of major international economic institutions, including the International Monetary Fund, the World Bank, and the General Agreement on Tariffs and Trade. Soviet delegates at Dartmouth VII even spoke seriously about making their currency convertible on the world market. Less than two years later, however, a deterioration in relations between the Soviet Union and the United States once again made these possibilities seem remote. At Dartmouth IX, held in June 1975, the Soviets complained that the Ocober 1974 Jackson-Vanik amendment to the Soviet-American trade bill, which tied the granting of most-favored-nation status to the Soviet Union to the number of emigration visas approved for Soviet Jews, was an attempt to interfere with the Soviet Union's domestic affairs. Compounding Soviet disillusionment was the Stevenson amendment of December 1974, which effectively cut the USSR off from US government Export-Import Bank credits. The Soviet Union therefore rejected the proposed trade agreement in January 1975. By this time, the Soviets had also been made nervous by the enormous impact on the US domestic economy of the Iranian oil embargo, and were not anxious to similarly subject their own economy to the unpredictable behavior of other nations. By Dartmouth X, in April 1976, the Soviets were so opposed to joining international economic institutions that the topic was dropped from the agenda of future Dartmouth conferences.

In the mid 1970s, the Dartmouth conferences explored new approaches to resolving tensions in the Middle East. At Dartmouth VIII there was agreement that the chances for a durable peace in the region depended on the United States and the Soviet Union acting jointly to maintain stability in the area. Following the 1973 war, both Israeli and Arab officials seemed interested in a negotiated settlement, and the United Nations' decision that the superpowers should cochair the Geneva peace conference on the Middle East gave the Dartmouth conferees much to discuss. In December 1975 a special Dartmouth interim task force hammered out three basic principles for an overall settlement in the Middle East: (1) a comprehensive peace that guaranteed the right of existence and security for all states in the area including Israel; (2) withdrawal by Israel from territories occupied in the war of 1967 and the establishment of permanent boundaries; (3) acceptance of the right of Palestinian Arabs to full self-determination. On October 1, 1977, an official joint Soviet-American statement on the Middle East was issued that was clearly influenced by the positions worked out at the Dartmouth conferences.

But the delicate consensus built over three years soon evaporated. The US Jewish community was immediately critical of the Soviet-American statement and it was shelved only four days after it was announced. Egyptian President Anwar el-Sadat's spectacular visit to Jerusalum in November 1977 caused many to lose interest in a Soviet-American plan for the region. At Dartmouth XII, in May 1979, the Soviets complained that they were being systematically excluded from Middle East negotiations and the Egyptian-Israeli treaty process. Soviet officials who had urged Soviet-American cooperation in the Middle East lost credibility in their own country, and the topic faded from the Dartmouth conferences.

When détente began running into trouble, the Dartmouth conferences were filled with lively discussions of who was to blame. The Americans protested that a continued Soviet military buildup was undermining the American public's support for détente. The Soviets replied that they were simply "catching up" to achieve parity with the United States so that arms control agreements would be made on a fair basis. The Americans pointed out that Soviet support for Cuban intervention in Angola put American supporters of détente on the defensive. The Soviets answered that they could not abandon liberation movements in Third World countries. The Americans argued that Soviet behavior had a tremendous impact on American public opinion and that Soviet actions greatly affected the climate within which American leaders could afford to act. The Soviets replied that, as far as they could tell, American public opinion was simply manipulated by major American media in collusion with the American government and had no independent impact on the shaping of American foreign policy. The Soviets worried that editorials in American newspapers calling détente a "snare" or an "illusion" reflected doubts about détente's workability among American government leaders. The Americans insisted that public opinion was a real and independent force in the United States.

During Dartmouth IX, an American delegate drew attention to an article written by a Soviet scholar and published in an internal journal that justified détente in Marxist terms by saying that it would cause the West to lower its guard and lead to a hastening of world revolution. This sort of statement, said the American, made many uneasy about Soviet intentions regarding détente. The Soviets said they had not read the article or heard of the author, but they assured the American delegates that it did *not* represent the mainstream of Soviet thinking. Rather, the Soviets said tactfully, it should be seen as a manifestation of an internal struggle in the Communist world to define détente in a way that does not leave the Soviet Union open to accusations of having abandoned the ideals of the socialist revolution.

The Soviets then pointed to declarations by Defense Secretary James Schlesinger saying that détente did not mean that the United States would hesitate to use tactical nuclear weapons first in a conflict, nor was it an excuse for cutting back the military budget. How, asked the Soviets, were these remarks consistent with the principles of détente? How, asked the Americans, was the accelerated pace of a Soviet military buildup consistent with détente? "The real issue isn't what your leaders say or how your people feel," an American delegate told the Soviets, "it is the capabilities you are acquiring and building up." While in general the Soviets tended to emphasize stated principles and rhetoric, the Americans preferred to talk about the actual behavior of the two countries.

The commitment to resolving these difficulties was strong on both sides, yet disagreements, rooted in fundamentally different interpretations of world events, remained. For example, the Soviets believed that President Carter's statements about the importance of human rights were intended to undermine détente and create a hostile climate in the United

States toward the Soviet Union. Carter's public statements about Soviet dissidents, said the Soviet delegates at Dartmouth, actually lessened the chances of the Soviet government releasing them, since Leonid Brezhnev was unlikely to want to appear to be "giving in" to American pressure. Cousins and others tried to explain to the Soviets that concern about human rights was not a convenient political strategy but a deeply held core of American traditions and values and that Carter's pronouncements, which were overwhelmingly supported by the American people, were statements of principle rather than diplomatic jabs.

"It was apparent at Jurmala [Dartmouth XI, in July 1977] that both countries tend to be chained to mirror images," wrote Cousins. "Almost identical charges and responses characterize the stance of each country toward the other." Also clear, he said, is "the existence in each nation of powerful forces that have a stake in the failure of détente." While the Soviets initially felt that the breakdown of détente was entirely the fault of the United States, a few eventually admitted—hesitantly—that Soviet actions in the military sphere, the Third World, Poland, and Afghanistan might have influenced US behavior and opinion.

In 1977 Cousins launched an offshoot to the Dartmouth conferences, a series of similarly informal, off-the-record, private gatherings of prominent Soviet and American writers. The first meeting was sponsored by the US State Department and took place at the headquarters of the Union of Soviet Writers in Moscow. The American delegation included the playwright Edward Albee, the poet Robert Lowell, and the novelist William Styron. Both sides had laundry lists of complaints and questions, which were expressed, Cousins notes dryly, with "the extravagance of language that writers get paid for producing."

The Soviet writers, Cousins recalls, emphasized two themes: the wide availability of books by American writers in the Soviet Union, and the contrasting absence of current Soviet writing in the United States. Translated editions of classical American authors (Mark Twain, Walt Whitman, Edgar Allan Poe, Nathaniel Hawthorne), early twentieth century American writers (Ernest Hemingway, F. Scott Fitzgerald, John Steinbeck, William Faulkner, Sinclair Lewis) and contemporary American writers (Saul Bellow, John Cheever, John Updike, Kurt Vonnegut, Joyce Carol Oates, Joseph Heller) are published in huge printings (averaging eighty-five thousand copies) and are generally sold out within a few days. Yet few contemporary Soviet writers are published in the United States, complained the Soviets, unless they are dissidents.

Cousins agreed that it was a problem, but added that progress had been made since his first visit to the Writers' Union in 1959, when similar complaints had been voiced. (Cousins's purpose at that time was to try to persuade the Soviets to sign a copyright convention and stop reprinting American authors' works without permission or royalties. Over the next dozen years Cousins was instrumental in behind-the-scenes negotiations for the Soviet Union's acceptance of the Universal Copyright Convention in 1973.) But Cousins also pointed out that this problem was not confined to Soviet books—writers in nearly every country, whether Brazil, Japan, Ethiopia, Indonesia, Italy, or even Canada, frequently grumble that while American writers are well known in their countries, few non-American writers are published in the United States. "American readers as a whole," admitted Cousins, "have a lot of catching up to do in their knowledge of contemporary world literature."

The Soviets were also appalled by what they saw as a profusion of pornography and violence in American literature and television. "It seemed to us," remarked Cousins, "that they had taken an unattractive fraction and were substituting it for the whole." Cousins answered that both violence on television and pornography were heatedly debated within the United States, but that in general the cure—approval and possibly censorship by some government agency—was felt to be worse than the disease. "Words and ideas, unlike meat and drugs," maintained Cousins, "cannot be inspected for public consumption." The Americans had their own concerns, mostly about the treatment of dissident writers in the Soviet Union. "The Soviet writers tended to believe," Cousins later wrote, "that their own government is wise and conscientious and can be trusted to protect its people in every respect. [The American writers believe] that governments by their very nature are collectors and misusers of power and therefore have to be monitored and restrained."

Seven such writers' meetings have now been held, and they have "mellowed," says Cousins, to include more discussion of literary issues and less of political concerns. The Americans have noted a distinct lack of "Party line" unity among the Soviet writers and a sense of fresh experimentation in current Soviet literature. "It is no longer accurate to say that Soviet writers can be divided into only two categories—the out-and-out dissidents and the hard-line party members. There is a wide octave between the two."

Both the writers' conferences and the regular Dartmouth meetings have taught Cousins that Soviets have great difficulty understanding some basic attributes of American culture that are absent from their own society. They are often bewildered at what seem to them to be mercurial and unpredictable shifts in American policy and American public opinion. And the existence of open dissent, he says, seems to puzzle even many well-educated Soviets. Few know how to interpret American newspapers, which has at times led to dangerous miscalculations—for example, the assumption that numerous American editorials calling for an invasion of Cuba in 1962 meant that the American government was really going to invade. "When they read criticisms of the Soviet Union in articles or editorials that they regard as objectionable and volatile," he says, "it is very difficult for them to understand that this doesn't necessarily reflect American policy."

What the leaders of both nations continue to resist understanding, Cousins believes, "is that even the way in which they go about trying to *improve* their relations with one another is basically fallacious. These two countries don't have the right to carve up the world or put their interests ahead of the interests of the majority. We're going to enter a safety zone only as both of these countries are willing to accept obligations to the community outside themselves, as well as to create specific instruments of world order in which other nations play a full part."

Slight improvements in official Soviet-American relations can temporarily mitigate the dangers, but do not create lasting solutions, he believes, because bilateral summit meetings and arms control negotiations have inherent limitations. "Of course, it's always good to reduce the fever," he adds. "You can reduce the fever with aspirin, but you're not getting at the underlying problem. Still, if the fever gets too high, the patient can die. Therefore, the attempt to reduce tensions is certainly essential and welcome. But at some point we've got to address ourselves to the basic problems involved in structuring a genuine peace. Otherwise, the tensions that are inherent in a given situation are bound to recur and erupt."

Likening the world situation to a human illness is more than a metaphor to Cousins. He believes that lessons learned from the way humans individually combat disease can apply to the way humans must collectively combat nuclear catastrophe. "I've learned that you've got to have a healthy disrespect for experts," he remarks, "and that you always want to seek out their advice, but never abandon the need to make your own decisions, even if it goes against the experts. In both international affairs and medicine, expertise can be fallible. The human body biologically tends to move in a path of its expectations; fear tends to be self-fulfilling and self-justifying. Nothing is more characteristic of serious illness than feelings of helplessness, the fact that one's losing control, and the consequent panic.

"In dealings among nations, you can always justify your pessimism. You may not always be able to create a level of rapport, but nothing is easier than to create tension, because you can do that unilaterally. The equivalent of panic among nations is represented by the readiness to believe the worst and the ease with which the worst can be portrayed and an appeal made to the collective sense of insecurity.

"There *are* people who benefit from panic, in both countries. After Nixon was able to come up with a very wide set of agreements with the Russians, the military and the private defense contractors in the United States were profoundly disturbed. They felt that it had gone too far in the direction of warming up relationships, and they had a stake in the Cold War, no doubt because it helped create an environment where it was possible to get military budgets through.

"One of the big dangers is that we've had tensions for such a long time that the tensions may become combustible. Almost anything can happen when people get tired, fretful, panicked. They reach out for easy solutions. And people who tend to shoot from the hip in ordinary matters can't be trusted to be intelligent and restrained in extraordinary matters."

He pauses, and a look of weariness crosses his face. It would seem that Cousins has every reason to feel discouraged when he thinks back on the events of the last four decades. Thirty-five years ago, he watched the Cold War chill the possibility of creating a peaceful transition to an orderly system of world federalism. Thirty years ago, he helped galvanize an enormous citizens' movement for nuclear sanity, only to have other world events divert public attention. Twenty-five years ago, he helped launch a hopeful series of agreements between the superpower leaders, only to have one leader assassinated and the other deposed before the ink on those first agreements was barely dry. Even the Dartmouth conferences have not been the panacea that he perhaps once hoped they would be. Bringing together influential private citizens for amiable discussions has created a number of modest accomplishments, but the scale of what still needs to be done is staggering.

"It's not easy to be friendly in this world. There are always people who will declare you're being naive or subversive," he continues quietly. "But I've learned from my experiences with illness that there's a very large area of possibility that opens up with the use of human ingenuity, imagination, and courage. And there are resources that you can count on that exist inside yourself, but they have to be put to work.

"We can take what we know and feed this into the channels of public opinion. I've always been troubled by the disparity between the evidence of what I've seen and believe to be true, and the situation as stated, unofficially or officially, to the public. While no individual can dictate policy, no individual should exempt himself from the attempt to do so. And that attempt repeated often enough is what public opinion is."

Even his belief that laughter, fun, and play can be mobilized as healing forces has relevance to the world situation, he says, reminiscing about his freewheeling badminton game with Nikita Khrushchev by the Black Sea. "That helped to create a nice mood. And we told stories to each other. I try not to run too far behind others in the telling of stories. So we had a good time, and that created a stage where all sorts of things were possible. In dealing with Khrushchev, one would suppose that you're dealing with these large, impersonal, implacable forces, many of them the legacy of churnings going on in history itself. But I found it was possible to cut through all that.

"It's so easy to become solemn, especially in diplomacy, if we take ourselves too seriously, and there's nothing like a sense of fun to loosen people up," he adds, his eyes brightening as he recounts some of the jokes that have started Dartmouth conferences off with a laugh. And as he begins talking about what gives him fun in life, what nourishes and sustains his more sobering activities, his face, despite the wrinkles and the thinning hair and the mild jowl, begins looking almost boyish.

"I enjoy hitting a golf ball so that it screams for mercy. I enjoy the company of lovely women. It seems to me that any species that can produce anything as wonderful as my wife has a great deal to be said for it. I enjoy playing a good game of tennis. I enjoy running to get shots that seem to be impossible, and converting those shots into winners. I enjoy the sensation, which I find exquisite, of not being in a hospital bed. And not for one moment," he adds meaningfully, "am I not mindful of the difference.

"I enjoy the challenge of taking something that's beyond my reach on the piano or the organ, such as Chopin's Opus 84, and saying to myself that I'm going to play it, and to try to do it very well. And then I go through anguish when I actually try to meet that challenge and see how far beyond me it is. But I keep working at it and working at it. I get up in the middle of the night to practice. And then, if I am lucky, it will finally begin taking shape."

Cousins accepts the diagnosis of a world threatened by nuclear catastrophe, but he rejects a verdict of hopelessness. "No one," he likes to say, "really knows enough to be a pessimist." Instead, he continues to urge humanity to believe in its own powers of transformation, its own capacity for change. "All things are possible once enough human beings realize that the whole of the human future is at stake," he wrote in his book *Human Options*. "The biggest task of humanity in the next fifty years will be to prove the experts wrong."

Sharon Tennison, a San Francisco registered nurse and self-described "ordinary American mother," has spoken about her experiences in the Soviet Union to hundreds of American audiences (*Chapter Four*). (Photograph by Chris Stewart, *The San Francisco Chronicle*)

John Chrystal in front of the Iowa State Savings Bank in Coon Rapids, Iowa. A former farmer and the current president of Bankers Trust, one of Iowa's largest banks, Chrystal has been traveling to the Soviet Union and offering advice on agricultural policy since 1960 (*Chapter Three*). (Photograph by Charles Nixon, *The Coon Rapids Enterprise*)

Dr. Bernard Lown and Dr. Yevgeny Chazov, the cofounders and copresidents of the Nobel Peace Prize-winning International Physicians for the Prevention of Nuclear War (IPPNW), in a moment of communication during the fifth IPPNW Congress held in Budapest, Hungary, June 1985 (*Chapter One*). (Photograph by Ted Polumbaum)

Norman Cousins, author and private diplomat for two US presidents, at the fourth Dartmouth Conference on Soviet-American Relations held in Leningrad in 1964. Second from left is Alexander Korneitchuk, Soviet playwright and co-chairman of the conference; third from left is Cousins (*Chapter Five*). (Photograph courtesy of Norman Cousins)

Cynthia Lazaroff, the director of the US-USSR Youth Exchange Program (left), and Soviet mountain guide Slava Volkov (right) on the slopes of Mount Elbrus in the Caucasus Mountains of the Soviet Union. Lazaroff has arranged for American teenagers to hike with Soviet teenagers in the Caucasus Mountains since 1984 (*Chapter Two*). (Photograph by Roy H. Bonney, © 1986 Tides Foundation/US-USSR Youth Exchange Program. All rights reserved)

Jim Hickman, director of the Esalen Soviet-American Exchange Program (center) confers with former astronaut Rusty Schweickart (right) and interpreter Harris Coulter (left) prior to the first conference of the Association of Space Explorers held in October 1985 in Cernay, France (*Chapter Six*). (Photograph by J. Michael Kanouff, courtesy of the Association of Space Explorers—USA)

Armand Hammer, chairman of Occidental Petroleum, shaking hands with Soviet Chairman Leonid Brezhnev in Moscow (*Chapter Seven*). (Photograph courtesy of Occidental Petroleum)

Samantha Smith in her home in Manchester, Maine, holding the English translation of the letter she received from Soviet Chairman Yuri Andropov on April 26, 1983 (*Chapter Nine*). (Photograph by SYGMA, courtesy of Jane G. Smith)

Christopher Senie and his Soviet partner Vladimir Semenets, 1972 Olympic gold medalist in the tandem sprint, push off for another day's ride on the tandem bicycle they pedaled from Moscow to Washington, DC in 1983 (*Chapter Eight*). (Photograph courtesy of Teamworks, Inc.)

CHAPTER SIX

NEW AGE DIPLOMACY:

JIM HICKMAN

Dawn was just beginning to lighten the sky above Moscow when Jim Hickman walked out of his hotel on September 4, 1982. A few hours earlier, he had left the main television studio of the State Committee on Television and Radio (Gosteleradio) to grab some much-needed sleep. He did not know what he would find on his return. Still rubbing his eyes, he remembered the studio as he had last left it: an enormous room, heavy with quiet anticipation, containing nothing but a yellow rug on the floor. When he remembered what was supposed to begin happening at 5 A.M. that morning, he began having fresh doubts. Was he about to participate in an unprecedented breakthrough for Soviet-American communications—or a fiasco?

The guards at Gosteleradio's door recognized Hickman and his American colleague Richard Lukens and waved them past. They climbed the stairs to the appointed studio and opened the door—and caught their breath.

Spirited rock 'n' roll was blaring from two Soviet rock bands and the huge yellow rug was covered by three hundred bopping young Soviets in their late teens and early twenties, dressed in blue jeans and sports shirts. A third band was setting up equipment on another stage. Someone had supplied a dozen colorful beach balls and the Soviets were tossing them, with giggles and shrieks, from one side of the room to another. Six television cameras panned the dancing crowd and the bands as lights were adjusted.

Hickman sidled through the crowd to the middle of the room. He turned around in circles, trying to believe what he was seeing. Later he would call it "one of the most extraordinary moments in my life."

But there was little time for reflection. Immediately he and Lukens began consulting with the cameramen, telephoning California, and checking technical details for the live, two-way satellite linkup of American and Soviet rock performances about to take place. Seven thousand miles away, darkness had already fallen on a huge outdoor amphitheater in the San Bernadino Mountains, the site of an ambitious rock 'n' roll bonanza called the US Festival put together by Steve Wozniak, the thirty-three-year-old millionaire founder of Apple Computers, to promote the notion that sophisticated global communications technology can help create an era of world harmony among peoples. Rock star Eddie Money was warming up on stage to the exuberant cheers of a hundred thousand fans.

Six weeks earlier, two organizers of the US Festival, Peter Ellis and Richard Lukens, had conceived during a late-night brainstorming session what seemed a preposterous yet appropriate idea: including Soviets in the rock festival via a live satellite television linkup. Such a demon-stration of the universal appeal of music would fit perfectly with the festival's theme. Lukens had heard of the Esalen Soviet-American Ex-change Program's success in arranging unusual bilateral exchanges, and a few days later proposed the idea to Jim Hickman, the program's executive director.

Though he knew it was a long shot, Hickman agreed to suggest it to officials at Gosteleradio on his next trip to Moscow. As it happened, former astronaut Rusty Schweickart was also along on this trip to lecture about energy technology at the Soviet Academy of Sciences. Well aware that many Soviets view cosmonauts—and thus astronauts—with some-thing close to undiluted hero-worship, Hickman decided to bring Schweickart with him into the Gosteleradio offices. One of Hickman's Soviet colleagues, writer and film producer Joseph Goldin, swiftly made them an appointment. Since it was early August and many of the top officials at Gosteleradio were on vacation, they met with a deputy minister who normally would have been third or fourth in the decision-making hierarchy.

Hickman, Schweickart, and Goldin shrewdly emphasized that the festival was occurring on Labor Day, a workers' celebration, and that the exchange would be purely musical and nonpolitical. They mentioned, but did not emphasize, that the concert would be rock 'n' roll—a musical style often officially branded as a symbol of Western decadence, which nonetheless has a huge and devoted following in the Soviet Union. They spoke about the powerful emotional impact the satellite exchange might have.

When they finished, there was silence. The Gosteleradio official spread his hands on his desk and closed his eyes. Thirty long seconds later, he opened them. "In three days I am to leave for my vacation," he said. "But this project is—very interesting. I will postpone my vacation and see what I can do to make this happen." The Americans tried not to look stunned as the official began making phone calls and barking orders to assistants rushing in and out of the office.

But many hurdles remained. Despite this "agreement in principle" to proceed from Gosteleradio, hundreds of tiny and not-so-tiny details concerning cost, format, content, and other logistics needed to be negotiated. Coordinating the technical aspects of the linkup alone was a mammoth task. Before leaving for the United States, Hickman asked Gosteleradio to help expedite the visas needed to allow him and Richard Lukens to return to Moscow five days before the festival and continue working out the details.

Five days before the festival, however, there had been no word from Gosteleradio and no visas had been approved. Hickman's messages did not seem to be getting through. Lukens and other US Festival officials continued to make the technical and travel arrangements necessary for the linkup, but the outlook was bleak. Hickman made alternative plans for Labor Day weekend—a family fishing trip.

Then a call came from Moscow; the visas had been approved. Hickman and Lukens immediately flew to Moscow, only to find that miscommunication and red tape still threatened disaster. Somehow the idea that this was an event signifying world worker solidarity had taken root in the bureaucracy, and Gosteleradio was prepared for solemn speech trading between Party officials and the heads of American labor unions. Hickman hastily straightened them out. He told them they needed to find several hundred young people who knew how to dance. He specified that the young people wear jeans and other casual clothing. He explained that they should invite Soviet rock bands to play for the American audience.

The day before the telecast, the leaders of three well-known—and so far as some Communist Party officials are concerned, notorious—rock bands in Moscow were visited by a Gosteleradio messenger and told that they and their instruments and equipment would be picked up at midnight that night. The messenger, however, failed to tell the bands where they would be taken or why. The band members, thinking that they were going to be arrested, nervously got on the phone to the American embassy. Within hours the rumor was flying through the Moscow diplomatic community: a crackdown on Soviet rock bands was under way. The American attachés at the embassy were unimpressed by Hickman's reassurances that the bands were going to participate in the first satellite rock concert between the Soviet Union and the United States. Since that's completely impossible, they said, what's *really* going on?

The rock band members allowed themselves to be picked up. But even as they jammed for the young Soviets in the studio, many of them still could not believe that in a few hours they would be broadcasting to California. Even the Soviet cameramen and technicians scurrying around the studio, who had worked twenty hours a day for the previous four days to set up the transmission, did not really believe it was going to happen. Hickman was standing next to one of the head technicians when the first signal came in from Califorina. The technician stared at the thousands of dancing, cheering, waving young Americans who suddenly appeared on his monitor. He turned to Hickman, wide-eyed, and whispered in English: "Jesus Christ!"

When the transmission from the Soviet side began, Hickman, Lukens, and the Soviet young people threw their beach balls into the air and with space-age elan shouted, in English, "LIVE! FROM MOSCOW! IT'S SATURDAY NIGHT!" A ten-foot-high video screen erected in the Moscow studio allowed the Soviets to see the amphitheater, the rock bands, and the fans in California; a sixty-foot "Diamond Vision" screen above the Californian stage broadcast a picture of the Moscow studio to the Americans.

For the next half hour, the Soviets and Americans danced to Eddie Money's latest hit and to several tunes from the Soviet bands. "There was a point when we saw each other seeing each other, back and forth," Hickman recalls. "It was a powerful, wonderful thing. The Russians were crying, screaming, hollering; it was one of the most moving experiences they had ever had. Afterward some of them told me that for the first and probably the only time in their lives, they had lived history."

The young Soviets' later comments revealed both elation and awe: "It's amazing, we saw the Americans, and they're the same as us . . ." "I am shaken to the core, something has changed inside me . . ." "I feel a spiritual uplift . . ." "I was overwhelmed by the recognition that we are all inhabitants of the same small planet . . ." "Music is a language through which we can understand and communicate with each other— we with the Americans and they with us."

Later that day, Hickman went to the American embassy and told them that Gosteleradio would be featuring the linkup that night on *Vremya*, the national news program with an average audience of about 150 million Soviets. An American cultural attaché told him that was impossible—the Soviets might have allowed the broadcast to happen in order to "humor" him, but it was definitely not something they would let their own people know about. Hickman offered to take him to a Soviet friend's house where they could watch the news together. On the way there, the attaché began saying, "Well, they might mention it, but they'll show the two hundred thousand American kids and say it was a demonstration against President Reagan, and never mention rock 'n' roll." Hickman, his Soviet friends, and the attaché watched *Vremya*'s three-and-a-half minute feature on the linkup that, to the attaché's befuddlement, showed both the Americans and Soviets dancing wildly to the rock 'n' roll music and reported the event accurately. The next day, the Soviet newspaper *Literaturnaya Gazeta* extolled the satellite exchange: "It became clear to everyone once more that we are the crew of a very small ship, the 'Earth,' and its survival in the cosmic ocean depends on us."

The first "space bridge" had successfully taken place before anyone had time to come up with a reason why it should not. It was an example of how citizen diplomats can stretch the limits of what is possible by adhering to the unofficial Soviet maxim: "Anything that is not strictly prohibited is permitted." And it was a precedent that would have far-reaching implications: less than three years later, eleven other Soviet-American satellite linkups had taken place, focusing on subjects as diverse as the scientific data on nuclear winter, children's films, Soviet and American journalism, the awarding of the Beyond War Award to the International Physicians for the Prevention of Nuclear War, and a "dialogue of ordinary citizens" for the *Phil Donahue Show*.

"When I began working on the first satellite exchange, people on the US National Security Council told me, 'It's impossible, you cannot do that with the Russians, they will not allow it,' " recalls Hickman. "To me, that mindset means *they're* not about to try something like that. They're afraid of what that sort of communication might mean. But it's not important to get agreement beforehand on whether these kinds of innovative things can happen. What's important is to *avoid resistance* so that you can do what needs to be done, and then it just becomes a new fact in the relationship."

It is not easy to pin Jim Hickman down. Talk to almost anyone in the Soviet-American citizen diplomacy field, and his name will invariably appear. Try to explain to almost anyone outside of the field what exactly it is that he does, and the explanation comes hard. Some simply call him "the most effective of the citizen diplomats." Others refer to his "art of network building" aided by his "shrewdly focused sense of humility." Says James Garrison, who took over the directorship of the Esalen Soviet-American Exchange Program from Hickman in 1986: "He's a master. While other people are grandstanding about the wonderful things they're going to do with the Soviets, Jim is working behind the scenes to actually do them. And when the agreement comes through, his name isn't on it, but he's the one who made it happen."

Even his closest friends and colleagues say they are not sure they know everything he has done or is doing. For three years he flew to Moscow an average of six times a year, coordinated strategy with his San Francisco office by electronic computer mail, and took off his pointy cowboys boots to grab sleep whenever and wherever he could. He catalyzed dozens of exchanges of Soviet and American scientists, musicians, psychologists, and anthropologists during a time when government-sponsored exchanges had been allowed to expire. His efforts have directly or indirectly spawned a half dozen other citizen diplomacy groups in such varied fields as literature, space exploration, veterinary science, and computers.

Yet Hickman himself is something of an enigma. A stocky, slightly barrel-chested man of average height, with a balding, squarish head, thin lips, and piercing blue eyes, he looks more like a middle-aged banker than a New Age psychologist. Although he claims that one of his secrets is that he has nothing to hide, ferreting detailed information out of him is a challenge. One moment he is cool, precise, reserved, speaking in a somewhat nasal monotone about his work with dispassion, almost detachment; the next he is rubbing his hands with glee as he recalls some favorite incident, his eyes as merry as a child's. He says that he "just slipped into" this work long before he had any vivid concerns about nuclear war, yet his main focus now, he admits, is "creating a world that survives for awhile."

Jim Hickman lives on a houseboat in Sausalito. On his porch, he rocks from one foot to the other to demonstrate his floating existence; the water smacks the boards under his feet. Hickman likes it that way: moored, but afloat; flexible; able to be rocked. His kayak is tied to the porch. The San Francisco Bay is his front yard, and he paddles through his neighborhood of marinas, yachts, and shorelines the way other people take walks around the block. The houseboat fits a certain restlessness. Even though it could never really disattach and head for the sea, the possibility is deliciously inherent nonetheless. He is still not quite land-bound.   .

The houseboat is riddled with whale paraphernalia. A silk Chinese kite of an orca (killer whale) hangs from the ceiling; on the tables are whale books and whale carvings: by his bed is a stuffed toy orca and in the bathroom a green rubber whale that squeaks. Jim Hickman and his animal totem are a good match: both are intelligent, smooth-surfaced, fully in control, inscrutable.

Few things seem to ruffle him. He leans back in a chair, kicks off a shoe, and wriggles a foot while he speaks. When the phone rings, as it often does, Hickman lets it ring, unperturbed, until he has finished his train of thought. "The main interest of my life," he states, "is the range of human potentials that are there for us to develop, and that I feel are essential to solving the problems of the world today. How do we access the deeper realms of the human spirit and manifest them in the world in a way that moves us toward a reorganization in relationship between people and communities and nations?"

Hickman's down-to-earth, almost phlegmatic manner contrasts oddly, but pleasingly, with his esoteric philosophy. "I believe that we're now in a time when the earth as an entity is beginning to take a more active role in its own survival," he says. "Now that human beings threaten all life, the collective unconscious as a force has become very important in moving us toward the next steps. We have an opportunity to listen to a kind of guidance that comes from this greater consciousness, and that is trying to order the relationship between the superpowers in a way that will create opportunities for us to reduce the threat to all life."

Through a series of chance (or, as Hickman might argue, not so chance) events, Hickman and his Esalen colleagues have managed to infiltrate the lively, shadowy world of the Soviet Union's version of 1960s counterculture. Call it a search for new values to replace some of the lost mystique of Communism, call it a flowering of activities that in the Western world are loosely grouped under the rubric of "New Age," call it the manifestations of a bored Soviet intelligentsia with time on its hands and an urge to try something new, call it a "human potential movement"—whatever the name and whatever the explanation, such a phenomenon exists in the Soviet Union. Growing numbers of Soviets are experimenting with and avidly pursuing interests in meditation, yoga, vegetarianism, exercise, massage, encounter groups, gestalt groups, est, underwater birthings, crystals, psychic healing, clairvoyance, telepathy, aikido, and transformationalism.

All the things, that is, that the Esalen Institute of Big Sur, California, became famous for pioneering in the United States in the early 1960s through seminars, conferences, and sheer experimentation. In 1976 the *New Yorker* called Esalen an "extremely influential center of the human-potential movement—a somewhat amorphous but rapidly growing effort to tap unsuspected resources of energy or perception or sensory awareness in all of us." But Esalen leaders claim they didn't transport these ideas to the Soviet Union. They were already there when they first arrived—mysteriously, separately germinating in Soviet culture, building upon Russian and other indigenous ethnic groups' cultural and spiritual foundations, with devotees eagerly seizing upon concepts from the West, India, China, and the Middle East when they drifted their way.

Michael Murphy, the charismatic, energetic cofounder of the Esalen Institute, learned in the early 1970s that some of the leading research on certain parapsychological phenomena was being conducted in Czechoslovakia and the Soviet Union. Following a hunch and not much more, Murphy set out with two Esalen colleagues on an expedition to Eastern Europe and the Soviet Union in May 1971, hoping to make contact with scientists there of like mind. Sukie Miller, one of Murphy's colleagues, later described the experience as alternately "bizarre," "confusing," "dangerous," "wonderful," "stressful," "wonderful," "jarring," and "like living through the McCarthy Era five times over." They carried out many of their discussions in public parks, to avoid surveillance, and found that some people to whom they had been introduced in the morning during unofficial meetings would, when encountered in the afternoon in an official setting, pretend they had never met. In Czechoslovakia, after many frustrated attempts, they finally met a group of scientists willing to talk about their research on psychic phenomena. Discussions were in full swing until Miller incautiously exclaimed, "The spirit in this room is wonderful!" One of the Czechs jumped to his feet and burst out passionately, "This is no spirit! This is not a question of spirit! This is *science!*" Still, Murphy managed to meet with a few scientists at the Soviet Academy of Sciences and came away convinced that fruitful collaboration might be possible in the future.

Although Hickman and Murphy would not meet until 1975, they had similar goals for their early travels to the Soviet Union. In 1972 Hickman made his first trip there as an invited speaker at a scientific conference in Moscow titled "International Meeting on the Problem of Bio-Energy and Related Areas." The conference looked at the biological aspects of "exceptional performance" in humans, particularly athletes and individuals who seemed to be imbued wth parapsychological powers. Hickman, who has a masters degree in psychology from Sonoma State College, had worked at the Menninger Dream Laboratory in Brooklyn, New York, researching the use of sensory deprivation and sensory bombardment to induce states of altered consciousness. He went to Moscow "purely as a scientist," he says, hoping to contact Soviet colleagues working on similar subjects.

"The Soviets have explored certain ideas and philosophies in the human development field in a different way than we have," Hickman says. "Many Soviet scientists have looked at unusual types of phenomena that verge on what traditionally we would call the spiritual dimension of the human being. They attempt to explain these phenomena within a materialist, scientific framework, but their materialist framework begins to expand beyond what ours has ever been, because they're trying to explain things that we separate from science and put in the realm of religion. Now they tend to oversimplify, from my point of view, the nature of these phenomena because of their need to bring them within a Marxist or Leninist framework. But it still has given them permission, in a sense, to explore ideas that are not taken so seriously by American scientists."

An example of this, he says, is Kirlian photography, also known as "high-voltage photography," a technique invented by Soviet and Czech oslovakian scientists to record "auras" around living things. "They really take much more seriously than we do the idea that there are fields around the human system that carry with them information about the way the system is organized, that extend beyond what we ordinarily think are the physical limits of the system." Using Czechoslovakian designs, Hickman had built a similar high-voltage-photography device in the United States, about which he spoke at the 1972 Soviet conference.

Hickman and Murphy met in 1975, discovered their many mutual interests, and together set up an ongoing research project under Esalen's wing called "The Transformation Archives," which now has ten thousand articles and is kept up to date by a weekly computer cross-check of some seven thousand scientific journals—including many in the Soviet Union—for references to "the ways and means by which mind and body interact to extend greater human capacities." Among the key words used in the literature search are fire walking, galvanic skin response, love, meditation, mysticism, placebo, schizophrenia, sorcery, sports, and stress.

In 1979 Hickman was again invited to speak in the Soviet Union, this time at a scientific conference on the subject of the "unconscious." In a society where Freudian theory is still anathema, the conference was something of a breakthrough and represented the first time, according to Hickman, that Soviet scientists "had been given permission to engage with scientists from all over the world in a exploration of what that term means."

Hickman and an Esalen colleague, Mary Payne, planned to travel after the conference for six weeks through Soviet Central Asia and Siberia looking for evidence of the "rebirth in consciousness" that many Western devotees of New Age philosophy believed was taking place around the world. At the time, Michael Murphy was in the midst of writing a novel, *An End to Ordinary History*, whose central character, a top KGB agent, studied as a young man in secret Sufi orders in Central Asia and in the novel tries to use his abilities and position to move the Soviet Union toward a more peaceful and enlightened existence. With Murphy's help, Hickman and Payne designed an itinerary that might allow them to discover whether the fiction had any basis in fact.

To their astonishment, they found it did. "We met a number of people who in a sense fit into the scheme Michael had perceived, people who were on spiritual quests," says Hickman. "It seemed to us that there was something going on there that was reminiscent of the early sixties in America." At the Tbilisi conference, Hickman met the editor of a leading Soviet popular science magazine—"sort of like *Omni*, but for a younger audience"—who, at a dinner where the vodka and wine flowed bountifully, suddenly embarked on a clairvoyant reading of Hickman, expounding on Hickman's early life, his parents, and his parent's early lives. Hickman was impressed. "He was really quite accurate at what he had said," he recalls, "and then he made this cryptic reference to the number seven, and assigned it to me." Later, in Moscow, the editor came to his hotel room, sat down on the floor, "and drew a picture that was his scheme of the universe, in which he said that consciousness was the principal force, and that from the begining of the universe there had been a relationship between the evolution of consciousness and the evolution of form," says Hickman. "It was a composite of the Cabala and Sufi teachings and some Buddhist teachings and some esoteric Christianity, and it was clearly a major influence in his life."

In Bukhara, a small city in Uzbekistan, Hickman met a young woman who was well acquainted with parapsychological research and knew about Uri Geller, the Israeli psychic. Her grandmother, she said, was a shaman, and both her grandmother and her mother were well known as healers. She also told Hickman about a nearby sacred mountain where barren women climb, wailing and chanting, to purify themselves, after which a high proportion become fertile.

Hickman and Payne also discovered several "health and fitness clubs" in Soviet cities where members gather to practice yoga, often renamed "rhythmic breathing exercise" because the word "yoga" has a foreign, semi-religious taint and suggests a kind of self-centeredness—a focusing on the individual—that runs against the nap of Marxism-Leninism. One such club in Tbilisi has more than three hundred active members who meet once a week for jogging, yoga, meditation, and what can only be called "rap sessions."

When Hickman and Payne returned to the United States and reported their observations to Michael Murphy and his wife Dulce, the four of them decided that Esalen should initiate a program to try to bring individuals from the two nations together "who are really exploring the greater nature of the human being and society," says Hickman. "For a number of years, the US-Soviet relationship has been involved in an interaction that is on a lower order of creativity. Yet there is also significant exploration going on in the two cultures into the higher nature of the human being and the role spirit plays in matter. We wanted to launch an endeavor where the Soviet Union and the United States could take the high road together."

Such a project was made possible thanks to the creative energy and courage of forty-four-year-old Soviet writer and film producer Joseph Goldin, whom Hickman met at the 1979 Tbilisi conference. Goldin, by all accounts, is a temperamental, visionary genius who has little patience for authority, has occasionally been detained by authorities because he does not hold a regular job, tends to infuriate conventional Soviet officials whose turf he invades, yet manages to live an avant-garde "free-lance" life through sheer mad brilliance. According to Hickman, so many people value Goldin for his irrepressible creativity, including people "in influential places," that so far he has managed to stay out of real trouble. In 1979 Goldin started a commission in the Soviet Academy of Sciences to study "hidden human reserves," the Soviet equivalent for the phrase "human potentials." Goldin knew everyone who was anyone in the Soviet counterculture, and he began introducing them to Hickman and his Esalen colleagues.

"Meeting friends of Joseph is like going down into the subway," says Harriett Crosby, a Jungian psychologist who has studied at Esalen and is the current president of the Washington-based Institute for Soviet-American Relations. "Suddenly you're into whole networks of people. You can't tell where it's going to lead, but if you just trust the process it will take you where you want to go. If you want to meet healers, or people interested in Jungian archetypal studies, you'll find them." In a short time the Esalen program had a galaxy of unusual Soviet contacts and friends, including Djuna Davitashvili, the faith healer who is rumored to have practiced her art on no less a personage than Leonid Brezhnev; Victor Krivorotov, a sports psychologist and artist who, with his wife Iza, leads a meditation group in Tbilisi; and Igor Charkovsky, a pioneer in "underwater birthings."

Michael Murphy was so excited by Hickman and Payne's news that Hickman feared he had perhaps overstated the scale of the Soviet human potential movement as he, Payne, and Michael and Dulce Murphy prepared to spend another six weeks in the Soviet Union in summer 1980 as guests of the Soviet Sports Committee. But after they attended an international conference on "Sports and Modern Society" and met with scientists, journalists, artists, athletes, and political analysts who had a personal interest in "human potential" ideas, their enthusiasm was redoubled.

"Everywhere we went we found people who were interested in the same things we were," Murphy later told *New Age* magazine. "We found encounter groups, meditation circles, Gurdjieff groups, parapsychology clubs, and similar communities of allied interests. Thousands of Soviet citizens are reading books by Fritz Perls, Carlos Castaneda, John Lilly, and Abraham Maslow. Literature on yoga, Sufism, Buddhism, Vedanta, Cabala, the lost knowledge of ancient civilizations, and other esoteric subjects is available and finds a wide audience. . . . Soviets who travel bring these books back, and visitors also bring them in. The average Russian has more freedom to explore such subjects than he or she did when Jim and I made our first trips to the Soviet Union in the early seventies, and we know for certain that many top officials are involved in these activities themselves."

From the beginning, the Esalen leaders agreed that the only way to establish a valid, long-term Soviet program was to do it completely above-board, "without violating their laws, their cultural values, or the personal boundaries they observe." During the next several years, with little public fanfare, a dozen Soviet scientists, economists, and political scholars with either personal or professional interests in "New Age" ideas came to Esalen and various American universities for low-key, private discussions and seminars. Among them were economist Dr. Georgy Skorov, Deputy Director of the Institute for US and Canada Studies, and Dr. Vlail Kaznacheyev, former president of the Siberian Academy of Medical Sciences, who met with scientists at Princeton, the University of California at Davis, and the National Academy of Sciences to discuss his controversial research suggesting that cells can "communicate" with one another through the transmission of photons.

In a return exchange, Dr. David Deamer, a molecular biologist from the University of California at Davis, met in Moscow with Soviet colleagues for ten days of private talks about possible future collaboration. Other Americans sponsored by Esalen to go to the Soviet Union included "biofeedback" researchers Dr. Elmer and Alyce Green, who lectured at Moscow research institutes and conducted training programs in stress management; Dr. Robert Solso, chairman of the Department of Psychology at the University of Idaho; John Burton, a conflict resolution specialist and vice-president of the International Studies Association; and Richard Baker-roshi, a well-known American Zen Buddhist who spoke about philosophy and religion with members of the Soviet Academy of Sciences and the Russian Orthodox Church.

Esalen decided to avoid publicity for the individual exchanges; since the mainstream press often treats "human potential" work as wacky, Soviet-American cooperation on human potential was likely to be misunderstood. But word started getting out. In January 1983, *Newsweek* ran an article about the Esalen program which half-derisively, half-wonderingly labeled their efforts "hot-tub diplomacy" and "détente California style." The article began with a description of a "middle-aged economist" who seemed "right at home in laid-back Marin County," but went on to brand Dr. Georgy Skorov a "Soviet doctrinaire." The article also insinuated that "some US officials believe the Kremlin might have special uses for the human potential movement. . . . The Kremlin would like to discover new techniques of behavior modification—or mind control."

Hickman and Murphy dismiss the possibility that their work could have sinister applications. "We're not in that league," Murphy says.

"The Soviets have their gulag methods—they don't need this newfangled stuff." Hickman adds, however, that anyone working with the Soviet Union in a sustained way has to be aware "that we're only dealing with *one* part of the society there, the people who want a relationship with us and who see that the nature of peaceful coexistence is for these two countries to have a web of relations that is so interwoven that it can never be torn apart. And there are many people in the Soviet Union, including people in influential places, who understand that this is essential for survival. But there's a whole other part to that society that is the absolute opposite—that does not want a relationship, is isolationist, is Stalinistic, is very authoritarian, and will try to use this other part, that *is* interested in relationship, to their advantage to subvert as much of our country as they can."

The *Newsweek* article, which concluded that the Esalen program merely "generated some good vibrations," created problems for three years, according to Hickman. "One of the Soviets mentioned in that article, with whom we had a very deep relationship, will never be able to work with us again. He was interested in meditation, in running, in his own development, but then he gets quoted in *Newsweek* in an article about some flaky human potential stuff, and his boss said, 'What are you doing with these people? Don't ever talk to them again.' "

Hickman sees himself as the midwife rather than the father of the Esalen exchanges; the set designer rather than the director. If there seemed, to some outside observers, few patterns in who was invited and who was sent, it was because Esalen's method was designed to skirt conventional patterns. Rather than boxing itself into a formal agenda with explicit short-term goals, Hickman explains, the Esalen program seeks to put the right people together at the right time and trust that personal chemistry will lead to new opportunities for relationships. "The real task is to be in harmony with the larger plan that is trying to happen here," he says. "Goals can sometimes get in the way of progress. There is a process of *listening*, which is about surrender to guidance and to an idea that is trying to evolve. It's very important to keep our own ideas about how it *should* happen out of the way of what *is* trying to happen."

A good example of this principle, he says, was the first satellite linkup. "It was not anything anyone could have figured out or planned in advance. It was something that was meant to be if the conditions were right. The less we knew about it the better off we were. All the experts said it was completely impossible, but we didn't have time to start believing them before it just happened. We were willing to just allow it to come through, to be a midwife to an expression of the real need to have a new way of contacting one another."

Another principle illustrated by the first space bridge, says Hickman, is that "You don't have to force Soviet officials to say 'yes' or 'no' right away when you propose something unprecedented. If you don't force them, and if they like the idea, they'll play along until someone tells them to stop. When we first proposed the idea to the Gosteleradio official, we didn't want him to have to say 'yes' or 'no'—all we asked for were visas so that we could return and continue discussing it. Right up to the time of the broadcast itself, there was never a point at which anyone said yes. There was just never a point at which anyone said no."

Someone did briefly attempt to say no—on the American side. Several hours before the two-way rock 'n' roll exchange, Hickman and Lukens braodcast a twenty-five-minute show from Moscow to the California festival, introducing the concept of the space bridge and showing some prerecorded clips of the Soviet bands that would perform that night. But rock promoter Bill Graham, who was handling many of the performers at the festival, pulled the plug on the Moscow transmission after about ten minutes "because he was convinced this was a KGB disinformation plot originating in some Los Angeles basement," says Hickman. "He made an announcement saying that he knew that rock 'n' roll was banned in the Soviet Union because he, Bill Graham, had tried and failed to bring rock bands to Moscow. Therefore he knew this event was impossible. He even offered a ten-thousand-dollar reward to anyone who could prove that the space bridge actually originated in Moscow." Steve Wozniak and other concert officials managed to restrain Graham from interfering further in the satellite broadcasts, but meanwhile Hickman and Lukens had their hands full explaining this turn of events to Gosteleradio officials who were still uneasy about the two-way transmission that night. "We finally convinced them to go ahead with the program," says Hickman, "but Bill Graham almost destroyed this whole thing because of his prejudice about what couldn't be done."

The next space bridge, between a second US Festival in California and a studio audience in Moscow, was in many ways more difficult to organize than the first. Hickman and Lukens negotiated two transmissions, one of which would be interactive: panels of citizens in both countries would be able to talk to each other, and audiences would be free to ask questions. Gosteleradio officials, all of whom were now back from vacation, were impressed by the success of the first simulcast, but several were quite nervous about the notion of a spontaneous discussion beaming through space. Hickman patiently worked out guidelines, lists of participants, and other logistics.

On Saturday, May 28, 1983, an audience of two hundred Americans, breezily dressed in shorts and T-shirts, crammed into a sweltering ninety-five degree tent set up on the rock concert's grounds. About four hundred Soviets crowded into the considerably cooler Moscow studio. (While newspaper accounts later characterized the Soviet crowd as being "selected students from various Moscow institutes," Hickman says that he was given a hundred tickets to distribute to Soviet friends and that none were screened or inhibited from coming.) On the US side, moderator Sam Keen, a contributing editor of *Psychology Today*, briefed the audience on the positive, nonpolitical goals of the space bridge. "We don't want it to be challenging," he told them. "We don't want to guilt-trip them. We don't want to say, 'What are you doing in Afghanistan?' "

When the audiences first glimpsed one another, there were several minutes of foot-stomping, kiss-blowing pandemonium before they settled down to listen to the panelists—astronaut Rusty Schweickart, US Representative George Brown, computer entrepreneur Steve Wozniak, and communications specialist Maurice Mitchell on the US side, and cosmonaut Vitaly Sevastianov, vice-president of the Soviet Academy of Sciences Yevgeny Velikhov, and academician Zoya Malkove on the Soviet side. Velikhov drew a standing ovation on both sides of the earth when he declared: "People think that nuclear weapons are the muscles of a nation while in fact they are a cancerous tumor on a nation's body. We have to perform an operation as quickly as possible. . . . We should have the courage to undergo this operation; we should build bridges."

During one of the hour-long broadcast's more serious moments, Vitaly Sevastianov asked Schweickart, "How do you feel about our future? Are we going to die by the year 2000?" Schweickart joked that given the amount of "lubrication" he and Sevastianov tended to consume whenever they visited each other, the two of them might well indeed die by the year 2000, but added, "I know that both of us are working to see that life for thousands of generations will continue on the planet." Through interpreters, audience members asked each other chatty questions about rock bands, current movies, the status of women, college entrance requirements, video games, and favorite sports. The *Los Angeles Times* headlined their article about the linkup the next day, "A US-Moscow Hot Line for the Fun of It."

Eight hours later, Moscow and the southern California festival linked up a second time, this time for a musical exchange that involved all two hundred thousand concert goers and the main stage of the festival. "That is Russia and the kids there want to be like us—wear jeans and T-shirts and shorts and most of all they want rock 'n' roll," shouted an announcer as the cheering Soviet audience appeared on the huge outdoor Diamond Vision screen and both crowds began dancing to the rhythms of Arsenal, a Soviet jazz-rock band. Next, the Australian band Men at Work entertained the two audiences. Then Hickman and the other space-bridge planners held their breath as Soviet and American musicians prepared for an ambitious finale—an attempt to play together. Would the transmission signals' complicated twenty-two-thousand mile path and the three-second time delay hopelessly muddle the sound?

Arsenal cranked out another tune, complete with a wailing soprano saxophone solo, and American pop singer John Sharino and guitarist Joel Nelson started improvising to the Soviet rhythm. To everyone's amazement, the two audiences appeared to be clapping their hands and dancing to an identical beat, in perfect unison. The intercontinental jam session lasted a full five minutes. After a few more songs from the Australian rockers, the audiences waved good-bye.

Five weeks later, in early July, Gosteleradio broadcast an hour-long documentary of footage from the second satellite linkup. The day after the broadcast, according to Hickman, Sergei Lapin, the head of Gosteleradio, "who was very, very nervous all along and almost vetoed the whole thing," was standing next to Foreign Minister Andrei Gromyko as a bevy of Soviet dignitaries waved West German Chancellor Helmut Kohl good-bye at the Moscow airport. "I saw your program last night," Gromyko remarked to Lapin, "and the satellite linkup was one of the best things I've ever seen." "Oh, yes," Lapin replied, "we worked very hard on it." The satellite broadcasts were now firmly established as being in the realm of the possible, and Hickman, his mission accomplished, gradually phased himself out of direct involvement with subsequent linkups, preferring to let "the experts in two-way satellite communication do them all."

More within the Esalen Institute's purview is its Soviet-American "health promotion project," directed by Dulce Murphy, which grew out of Esalen's long-standing interests in holistic health and "the idea of neglected human potentials—aspects of the human psyche, mind and body that have not yet been fully explored by modern science," explains Hickman. In the Soviet Union, some healing strategies that are often considered "alternative" in the United States are accepted parts of the health-care system. Acupuncture, acupressure, and hypnosis are routinely used, and herbal medicines are sometimes prescribed. There is widespread public interest in psychic healing and faith healing, and articles on these subjects appear in the official press. Especially in remote areas, such as some parts of Siberia and Uzbekistan, traditional healers still work alongside mainstream medical personnel. Controversy over the efficacy of such techniques rages, much as it does in the United States. According to Michael Murphy, "*Komsomolskaya Pravda,* the eleven-million-circulation journal for Soviet youth, made a formal proposal for a national institute of healing, which was attacked by *Literaturnaya Gazeta,* the Soviet literary gazette, for promoting superstition."

Although many Soviet officials scoff at these techniques and emphasize the leaps that have been made in improving "modern" medical care in the Soviet Union, there also seems to be a tendency to believe that whatever works is worth investigating. The Tashkent Institute of Medicine, for example, is studying seventy herbs used by traditional healers to discern what plant alkaloids they may contain that would explain their healing qualities. In 1986, the Soviet Academy of Sciences invited Michael Harner, an American anthropologist and practicing shaman, to give lectures and workshops at the Academy on how shamanic healing techniques—renamed "psychorhythmic therapy" for the occasion—can be used to rehabilitate alcoholics.

Dulce and Michael Murphy spent three months living in Moscow in early 1984 and were struck by how many of their Soviet friends suffered from the same health problems as Americans: cancer, heart disease, alcoholism, and stress. Here, it seemed, was a particularly fertile area for Soviet-American exchange and cooperation, and Dulce Murphy began envisioning a joint health promotion program that would attack such problems as diet inbalance, lack of exercise, declining longevity, the deterioration of physical attractiveness, and alcohol and drug abuse. "Good luck," said one American official who heard of her plans to present a proposal to a number of official Soviet institutes. "You must be some kind of masochist."

But coincidentally, during that same year the Soviet Ministry of Health, in a major policy shift, launched a national education campaign on health promotion. The climate was right, and by April 1984 Dulce Murphy had negotiated a contract with the Soviet Ministry of Printing, Publishing and Book Trade (Goskomizdat) for reciprocal book exhibitions in both countries of the best current literature on preventive medicine, wellness, and holistic health.

In January and February 1985 the Esalen team hauled to the Soviet Union two copies each of a thousand American books covering sports and physical fitness, child care, alternative therapies, stress management, psychology, and death and dying. They exhibited them for one week at the National Library of Medical Sciences in Moscow and one week at the National Library of Science and Technology in Novosibirsk, Siberia; following the exhibitions, the books were donated to the libraries, which are mainly open to medical and scientific personnel.

The exhibitions, however, were open to the general public. Each day, about five thousand people came to the exhibition halls, and many stayed for eight hours, hungrily reading as many books as they could. Others brought cameras and photographed the books, page by page; still others brought notebooks and patiently copied the books word for word. "The exhibition in Moscow had what a small bookstore would have in America," says Hickman, "but it was the biggest thing that'd ever happened in the Soviet Union on this particular subject." Of the two thousand books, Hickman estimated they probably gave about five hundred away to individuals who "asked in the most heartfelt way, or seemed to have the greatest need." The books were accompanied by an American delegation of physicians and psychologists, led by Harvard psychiatrist John Mack, who gave public lectures that were widely covered in the Soviet press.

In April 1985 the Soviets sent two copies of a thousand current Soviet books in the medical sciences and health fields to exhibitions held at the University of California at Los Angeles School of Nursing and the Fort Mason Center in San Francisco. A seven-member Soviet delegation, led by Dr. Aron Belkin, the director of the Soviet National Research Center on Psychoneuroendocrinology, delivered lectures, gave press interviews, and participated in private meetings with colleagues. The American response may not have been as effusive—"We're way ahead of them in health promotion and disease prevention, and 70 percent of their books were in Russian," says Hickman—but it was still congenial enough to clear the way for further exchanges.

In January 1986 Dulce Murphy signed a second contract, this time with the Ministry of Health, for a broader range of exchanges in the health-promotion field, beginning with a major Soviet-American conference on the mind/body relationship in late 1986 in Moscow and a reciprocal conference at the Esalen Institute in Big Sur the following year.

After the conferences, the Esalen Institute and the Soviet Union will publish a book on the subject coauthored by scientists from both countries.

Another proposal still to be negotiated is the establishment of a Soviet-American commission "that would develop a five-year program to examine the philosophy, the theory, and the research area of the human potential field," explains Hickman, "defined as broadly as possible in order to bring together Soviets who don't normally get to work together, since their system makes it very difficult for them to do interdisciplinary work." Dulce Murphy also plans to gather a team of Americans to help the Soviets expand their educational program in smoking and alcohol prevention. But Hickman prefers that the health promotion project not look too far ahead. "The main thing," he says, "is to get people like Aron Belkin and Norman Cousins together, and see what they think is the most important thing to do."

Perhaps Hickman's most unusual behind-the-scenes role was to help create an organization bringing together Soviet cosmonauts and American astronauts to share their experiences and feelings about flying in space. In 1980 Joseph Goldin had organized a day-long series of lectures and workshops in Moscow's Ismailov Park on various human potential ideas, and he invited Hickman to be a featured speaker. (Michael Murphy describes attending one of Goldin's park seminars: "We got together with psychics and physicists and groups of singers who sang pagan, pre-Christian songs—it was just a hell of a good time.") Among the four hundred people who came to the 1980 event was a Soviet cosmonaut, Georgy Grechko, to whom Goldin introduced Hickman. Hickman asked Grechko whether he and other cosmonauts would like to meet with some American astronauts in a private, informal setting. The cosmonaut replied that they would. But Hickman remembers that Grechko was skeptical of "this American from this strange institute in California who says he can get astronauts to come and meet with us."

A few months later, at a cocktail reception for two visiting Soviet diplomats in Sausalito, Hickman mentioned his meeting with the cosmonaut to Rusty Schweickart, the pilot of the Apollo 9 mission in 1969 and the backup commander for the first Skylab mission in 1973, and asked whether he would be interested in organizing an astronaut-cosmonaut get-together. Schweickart replied that he would. During the next few months, Schweickart brought up the possibility of creating an astronaut-cosmonaut organization with several astronaut friends, and found

mixed reactions. "Many feared that the Soviets would attempt and succeed in simply using such a group for narrow political goals, and that
we would be too naive to avoid that," recalls Schweickart. "On the other
hand, most were curious to know what effect space flight had had on
the cosmonauts. Who are they as people? Were their values changed?
What do they really care about? What concerns and values do we share
and is there anything reasonable (and safe) that we can do about it?"

Schweickart went to the Soviet Union for the first time on an Esalen
exchange in July 1982 and, thanks to Hickman's wangling, privately
met with three Soviet cosmonauts—Georgy Grechko, Vitaly Sevastianov,
and Alexei Leonov, the cocommander of the 1975 Apollo-Soyuz docking.
Schweickart and Hickman also spoke to a number of high-ranking Soviet
officials who would, as Schweickart later put it, have "something to say
about whether or not the cosmonauts would be able to pursue this exploration."

The light was sufficiently green for Hickman and Schweickart to bring
two other former American astronauts, Michael Collins and Edward
Mitchell, to an initial planning meeting held in April 1983 at Puschino,
a scientific center outside of Moscow. Cosmonauts Alexei Leonov, Alexei
Yeliseyev, Vitaly Sevastianov and Valery Kubasov attended; both Kubasov and Leonov were veterans of the 1975 docking of Apollo and Soyuz
spacecraft. "The most valuable thing about the Apollo-Soyuz Test Project
was that when both sides worked together on this flight, they not only
got to understand each other better, but also found deep respect," remarked Leonov. "I remember when we were getting ready for the flight,
Tom [Stafford], Don [Slayton], and Vance [Brand] kept saying over and
over again: 'Cooperation means friendship, and friendship means peace.'
These words are still very true today."

At this meeting, the astronauts and cosmonauts agreed to some basic
ground rules, including the need to avoid supporting or condemning
either nation's policies. Instead, they would stress the value of cooperative development of the space environment. They decided to try to
bring together thirty astronauts and cosmonauts in October 1985 to
launch a new organization, the Association of Space Explorers (ASE).
The theme of their first congress would be "The Home Planet," and
Jacques Ives Cousteau would be their keynote speaker and recipient of
their first "Planetary Award." Their kickoff project would be a joint art
exhibition by artist-astronauts Alan Bean and Alexei Leonov in Paris,
an idea which, according to Schweickart, "captured the essence of our

early determination to focus our activities on *doing* things together that supported our purpose, rather than falling into the old tired pattern of saying things profound."

After several delays, three astronauts, three cosmonauts, and the French "spacionaut" Jean-Loup Chretien held a final planning meeting in October 1984 at Edgar Mitchell's home in France. As they struggled to agree upon a joint press release that both sides were satisfied was sufficiently nonpolitical, Mitchell commented: "The task here is to maintain the perspective from our voyages outside the earth's atmosphere; a perspective that has impressed upon the world's population the interconnectedness of all life. Are we going to continue to be mired in the traditional rhetoric of the political struggle that is pointing us all toward destruction and nuclear war? Or can we preserve that view of the earth that keeps it whole for all people?" They finally hit upon a joint statement that pleased everyone—and the answer seemed yes.

But formidable logistical problems remained. Schweickart and Hickman had carefully kept the State Department, NASA, the White House and other government entities apprised of their activities. The State Department gave them mild encouragement and NASA told them informally that it had no policy toward the new organization. But as Schweickart began recruiting American astronauts, he found that, in addition to the difficulties created by the potential participants' demanding schedules, few active astronauts were willing to jeopardize their flight assignments by associating themselves with an event that included Soviet cooperation. "As soon we came back with an agreement from the Soviet side," remembers Hickman, "the Americans started dropping out."

A reliable source told Hickman that at a Houston briefing in 1984, a NASA official charged with assigning crews warned his astronauts that if they joined the Association of Space Explorers "they would never fly again." Hickman believes the warning reflected the official's personal views more than a coherent NASA policy, but it was not the only instance of pointed, if unofficial, discouragement. "One particular scientist who was very excited about coming, who works for Cal Tech and is not an employee of NASA," relates Hickman, "was called by NASA the day before he left for France and told that if he went it might jeopardize his chances of working on the space shuttle again." On the other hand, two other active "payload specialists" not employed by NASA were left unmolested and attended the October 1985 congress, with no apparent ill effects on their careers.

Schweickart was only able to muster six American astronauts and one Saudi Arabian astronaut who had flown in the American program, while the Soviets brought seventeen cosmonauts, eight from the Soviet Union and one each from Hungary, Czechoslovakia, the German Democratic Republic, Poland, Bulgaria, Rumania, Cuba, Mongolia, and Vietnam. "The only reason the Soviets had more representation was because US officials discouraged our people from going," Hickman says, "not because the Soviets were trying to stack the meeting."

The most moving moments of the congress, held in a ninth-century chateau near Cernay, France, were the intitial introductions. Each cosmonaut or astronaut spoke about how flying in space had personally affected him and what he thought the Association of Space Explorers might be able to accomplish. "The first day or so [of our flight] we all pointed to our countries," said Saudi Arabian astronaut Sultan Bin Salman Al-Saud. "The third and fourth day we were pointing to continents. By the fifth day we were aware only of one earth." Said Cosmonaut Sigmund Jaehn from the German Democratic Republic (East Germany): "Before I flew, I was already aware of how small and vulnerable our planet is; but only when I saw it from space, in all its ineffable beauty and fragility, did I realize that humankind's most urgent task is to cherish and preserve it for future generations."

By the end of the four-day meeting, the space veterans had launched an organization "with membership limited to the 150 people who have to date taken flights in space." They had discussed possibilities for cooperative programs in space, such as a joint mission to Mars and a more comprehensive space rescue program, and "programs that would educate the world public to a positive vision of space," such as an international children's "space art" competition and a book of essays by astronauts and cosmonauts.

The wording of their press announcements delicately skirted any references to Star Wars or military uses of space; even the term "peaceful uses of space" was banned as being too closely associated with Soviet proclamations. "Both sides agreed to all the wording on everything that has appeared in the press," says Hickman, adding that "Leonov and the other ASE cosmonauts have been interviewed by journalists and asked, 'What do you think about Star Wars?' And they have refused to answer those questions. They have refused to comment on something that the entire Soviet Union makes a statement about. All the experts told us we could never get the Soviets to do that, yet it has happened."

Hickman hopes he has made himself obsolete in the astronaut-cosmonaut organization. "Esalen is in the process of turning over all of the organizational activities—including fund-raising, negotiation with the Soviets, and follow-up activities—to the organization itself so that by next year we will no longer be involved except on a consultant basis," he says. "It will be up to the astronauts and the cosmonauts. Whether it works out or not will depend on their long-term commitment."

Another of Hickman's behind-the-scenes successes took place in November 1984, when pop-folk singer and guitarist John Denver became the first major American artist to tour the Soviet Union since the collapse of the cultural exchange agreement in 1979. Hickman managed to get the Soviet Union of Composers to invite him and Pepsico, Inc. to foot the bill. On his twelve-day trip, designed to test the waters for a public concert tour the following year, Denver informally met with a number of Soviet musicians. "It was like getting together with the equivalent of Stevie Wonder, Michael Jackson, Linda Ronstadt, and Pavarotti in one room," Denver later said. Along with the globe-trotting Muppet Kermit the Frog (who was in Moscow, said Kermit, to "visit Russian frogs"), he gave a concert for children at the American embassy in Moscow. Denver also crooned his songs about "peace, love, and family" to an invited audience of 350 officials and musicians at the Union of Composers and "passed his audition," as he put it—Goskoncert, the Soviet concert agency, invited him for a return engagement in summer 1985 that included nine public concerts in Moscow, Leningrad, and Tallinn.

As promised, the Soviets advertised the concerts on billboards and in newspapers, and the public was able to buy tickets at box offices and kiosks. But at least some members of the Soviet audiences, accustomed to watching artists cleverly skirt the bounds of the permissible through satire, metaphor, allegory and other techniques, were nonplussed by Denver's earnest, lengthy, and all-too-familiar homilies between songs about the need for peace. They responded to Denver's performances with warm but not tumultuous applause; according to American musicolgoist and Sovietologist Ted Levin, who accompanied Denver, "At least some in those audiences could not quite believe that the darker side of state authority was uninvolved in the whole affair. An artist whose means of expression reveals any conformity to official government policies and positions will be viewed by the more cynical as an agent of the forces of power. . . . Even an artist as sincere, as independent, and as well-meaning as John Denver can raise suspicions of having been co-opted."

The Esalen program is particularly interested in these kinds of psychological insights. Robert Bathurst, a former naval intelligence officer and an adjunct professor of National Security Affairs at the Naval Postgraduate School, has for several years led weekend seminars at Esalen on cross-cultural understanding between Soviets and Americans. With American businessmen, psychologists, and government employees, and Soviet émigrés who work or used to work in similar occupations, Bathurst leads "simulations and games" to explore the cultural patterns governing a nations' behavior in international relations: when it goes to war, how it negotiates, and how it conducts business and handles foreign proposals. "The purpose of the games is to identify underlying cultural patterns," Bathurst says, "and to have an interesting and amusing time doing it."

For example, invariably "the American players go through an extraordinarily complex process to select their representative. . . . Everyone has to have his or her input," explains Bathurst. "In contrast, on the Soviet side, a leader simply emerges out of what appears to Americans to be general chaos. The Soviets allow the strongest person to be the leader, even if this person takes positions the rest of them don't share. They don't argue about it, but instead get down to the business of organizing their strategy." He has noticed that during the games "the Russians are always sitting against the wall, protecting their backs. They convey a sense of vulnerability that we Americans don't seem to have."

As the simulation of a negotiating process continues, further patterns emerge: "The Soviet Union is a high-context culture, which means Soviets place more importance on the setting in which a message is received and less importance on the message itself. . . . They go for the big picture, emphasizing the general over the particular, stability over change, history over the concerns of the moment. Whereas the American cultural tendency is always to pay more attention to what's actually being said in a given message than to the larger context in which the message is given and received. Americans emphasize specificity of content, adaptability, change, and novelty of approach."

Despite the make-believe format, tensions during the games can get extraordinarily high. In one session, "the Americans, who started off with strong protestations of their desire for peace and understanding, ended up so angry and frustrated by the intransigence of the Soviet players that they started throwing pillows at them. In other words, there was war." Bathurst believes that real wars are also the product of frustrated expectations leading to anger: "Jimmy Carter, the most powerful man in the world, was totally unprepared for the invasion of Afghanistan, an act that for the Soviets, given the circumstances, followed as night follows day, while Brezhnev, the second most powerful man in the world, was absolutely dumbfounded that Carter couldn't understand the Soviet imperative to enter Afghanistan."

Esalen has sponsored a number of invitational conferences on Soviet-American citizen diplomacy and the political psychology of the Soviet-American relationship, and Hickman has authored several articles on the "psychological principles" of citizen diplomacy. Since Soviet society has "very different values about personal freedom, political rights, and social organization," write Hickman and Esalen colleague James Garrison, understanding and empathizing with the Soviet perspective "requires a high self-esteem, a highly developed sense of personal identity, and a high degree of individual security on the part of the citizen diplomat." They stress that it is important for "Americans to be Americans, to embody those ideals which for several centuries have characterized this country, namely freedom and equality—ideals that no other country has enjoyed in such bounty. . . . A fundamental component of citizen diplomacy, then, is the need to understand one's own psychology, not only in terms of how one is affected by the outside world, but also how one projects one's inner emotional state and political ideals onto others."

The Esalen program is now launching projects in still other fields. One is a writer's exchange, growing out of Michael Murphy's contacts in the literary world, to complement the Dartmouth writers' exchanges pioneered by Norman Cousins. In 1986 Esalen brought several Soviet writers to New York City and Big Sur for brainstorming sessions with American writers on ways to "educate Americans in a greater way about modern Soviet literature and vice versa."

But the government cultural exchange agreement signed in Geneva in November 1985 may obviate continuing some of Esalen's past activities, and Hickman believes the profusion of citizen diplomacy activities in all sectors in the past five years means it is time to reevaluate the program. Simply organizing Soviet-American exchanges may have become—well, too easy. "When we began, there was a whole field to develop on the citizen side, but a lot is going on now in the Soviet-American relationship," says Hickman without a trace of regret. He believes that the Esalen program should use its contacts and experience to "look creatively at what the official agreement *doesn't* cover, and look for the margins and edges where we can operate well and expand the relationship further. We have to assess where the relationship isn't developed and work to develop that aspect of it."

One such aspect, he believes, are exchange projects that reach beyond the scope of the nonprofit sector into the business world. Hickman is currently working with several partners to develop a company to assist American businesses, particularly in the entertainment industry, in arranging co-business ventures with Soviet agencies. With his help, Amitie Puppets, Inc., arranged for forty members of the Obraztsov Puppet Theater to come to the United States in February 1987 for a nine-week tour of three cities. Hickman is also currently helping two major American film studios negotiate the coproduction of three feature films that would be shot on location in the Soviet Union. He has recently discussed with Vice President George Bush and Secretary of State George Shultz the possibility of setting up a private foundation to underwrite a broad range of cultural exchanges with the Soviet Union—exchanges that would be negotiated under the terms of the new government agreement but financed by the American business sector. So far, he has found "a lot of support for this idea."

Hickman often relies on his Soviet friends for fresh direction and inspiration. Joseph Goldin continues to dream of a worldwide project called "The Mirror for Humanity," where large video screens set up in prominent public places all over the world could constantly broadcast images of people going about their daily lives in other countries. "It is not possible to change overnight the attitudes of people or even the textbooks they use," Goldin told Dusko Doder of the *Washington Post* in 1983. "But it seems that when you have large groups of people communicating with one another, their common sense will always prevail. Technically, this is possible to do without false illusions."

In the past three years, Goldin has gotten into hot water with Soviet authorities; although well-placed Soviet friends improvised several jobs that would "legalize" him but allow him to continue his creative work, Goldin turned them down, one by one, because they placed too many restraints on his freedom. Turning down employment that suits one's abilities is sufficiently maladaptive that Goldin was put under psychiatric observation; several weeks later he was released and declared totally sane. Charged with "vagrancy," Goldin went to trial and defended himself and his life-style so brilliantly, according to Hickman, that the judge set him free. Later, Goldin was again placed in a psychiatric hospital for twelve days until one of his influential patrons managed to get him released. Goldin still appears to do exactly what he pleases—writing a few screenplays here and a few articles there, spending most of his time galvanizing a half-dozen exchange projects and space bridges with Americans and other Westerners—but he has now been identified as something of a malcontent, and, for example, was picked up by local police and placed in a psychiatric hospital for observation during the July 1985 Moscow International Youth Festival.

Yet less than a year later Goldin was able to organize an extraordinary April Fool's Day open-air party on the old Arbat Street of Moscow, which had the official sponsorship of Komsomol. Thousands of young Soviets wore masks and costumes and danced wildly to the music of Alla Pugacheva, the number-one Soviet pop singer, in an event described as "a first" by seasoned American observers.

Goldin describes himself thus: "I am not a criminal. I am not a dissident. I am no spy. I am a neutrino. I pass through walls. I have no weight or mass." Explains Hickman: "He can't really be at peace living in Soviet society, which requires him to surrender to rule by a group of people who are far less intelligent and creative than he is. But he would never leave, because he loves his country and knows his impact is there, not here. He's so committed to helping resolve the problem in the Soviet-American relationship that he really wants to be where he can have the most impact."

What Hickman and other Esalen citizen diplomats call their "heart connections" with individual Soviets continue to renew their commitment to the movement. "When you're in Russia staying up until the sun rises with these wonderfully heartful people, you laugh louder, you cry harder, you exult more, you pound your fist more in anger—life has a sharper edge than it has anywhere else," says Michael Murphy. "The passion of the Russians is indescribable. They are flammable to ideas. . . . There is something wonderfully full-bodied about Russian spirituality. Once you get past Intourist and the big package tours and start meeting individual Soviets, it's an adventure to explore the questions that really count for them. I hope that more and more Americans will do that."

Meanwhile, communication between the "New Age" communities of the two countries remains peculiarly invulnerable to crackdowns by authorities or the vagaries of official Soviet-American relations. It is difficult to stop Soviets and Americans from burying quartz crystals in the earth around the Kremlin, the White House, and missile silos, and then meditating to send "positive healing energy" to these areas. It is hard to pass a law against communicating telepathically with Americans nine thousand miles away at the precise moment of the full moon in order to "visualize the web of light around the planet," as several meditation groups in the Soviet Union are now doing.

Hickman sees their work as being more about creating peace than about stopping war. "The world is held hostage to these weapons, and yet it's also not well designed to live without them. Our work is not about reducing the number of nuclear arms in the world next year, but rather creating the public and political environment in which arms control has permission to happen, and then creating a social environment, a way for humans to relate to each other, that guarantees that once the arms race stops it never starts again.

"What is peace really all about? Peace is now defined only in terms of war, but that definition undermines it. Peace is not just the absence of war. It is a process and an experience involving relationship and communication—involving the unfoldment of the human being. Peace is something that happens every day in our lives, and only when we have more peace than we do conflict in our daily lives are we going to have peace in the world. The external world is a reflection of the internal world."

Hickman took a sabbatical from the Esalen program in 1986, in part because twenty-two trips to the Soviet Union and five years of sixteen-hour days had exhausted him physically and emotionally, and in part because he wanted to explore further what the term "peace" could really mean. One place he is looking is the nonhuman world. For the past two years Hickman, his personal and professional partner Gigi Coyle, and several other humans have spent August living on a beach on the coast of British Columbia, kayaking next to the orcas (killer whales) who come into the large bays and experimenting with "some new sorts of communication technology involving music and underwater microphones and speakers." The purpose, he says, is "to develop relationships with killer whales in a way that has a significant impact on people."

Hickman and Coyle would like to extend such whale communication to the Soviet-American sphere. They've spoken to Soviet scientists about collaborative whale and dolphin research, although at present most Soviet research on these animals is classified. They dream of establishing a Soviet-American "peace park and wildlife sanctuary" in the Bering Strait, which is the main breeding ground for Hickman's favorite whale, the beluga, and a place where the countries nearly touch. "There are two islands that are three miles apart—one is ours and one is theirs—and the border is right in between," Hickman says. "Many of the polar bears in that area are born in the Soviet Union and they cross the ice at a certain age and live in Alaska." In the future he and Coyle would like to set up a program where American and Soviet "scientists, artists, and other sorts of professional and ordinary people" could communicate and interact with the beluga and each other.

Far-fetched? No more so than some of the other ideas he has helped midwife. If there are new precedents to be set and new opportunities for relationships to be developed, Hickman will take them on. And when negotiations for sharing the planet begin between whales and humans, it's a good guess that Hickman will be in the midst of them, quietly working behind the scenes, rolling between the two communities in his kayak, shuttling messages through the waves.

꧁ ꧂

CHAPTER SEVEN

THE SOVIETS' FAVORITE CAPITALIST:

ARMAND HAMMER

In June 1985 Armand Hammer, the chairman and chief executive officer of Occidental Petroleum, decided to take a three-week business trip. He boarded his personal Boeing 727 jet, the *Oxy 1*, and set off for Washington, DC, where he met with President Ronald Reagan and urged him to hold a summit meeting with Secretary Mikhail Gorbachev. Hammer then flew to Moscow and urged Secretary Mikhail Gorbachev to hold a summit meeting with President Ronald Reagan. Before returning to Los Angeles, Hammer also found time to land in Wales and have dinner with Prince Charles, hop over to Peking and meet with Deng Xiaoping and other top Chinese leaders, and chat in Budapest with Janos Kadar, the general secretary of the Hungarian Communist Party.

Armand Hammer is a citizen diplomat in a category by himself. Prime ministers, princes, presidents, dictators, revolutionaries—Armand Hammer has met, and does business, with them all. "If I see an opportunity, I start at the top," he once said, "and then I send my team in." His "team" is comprised of the executives and managers of one of the world's largest energy, food, and chemical conglomerates, Occidental Petroleum, a fifteen-billion-dollar-a-year company listed number nineteen in the Fortune 500 in 1986. Hammer bought Occidental as a tax shelter in 1957, when its main assets were eight nearly dry oil wells worth an estimated thirty-four thousand dollars.

Armand Hammer's life story is such a dizzying amalgam of fortunes made and lost, swashbuckling international wheeling-dealing, and interactions with the high and mighty that, as the *New York Times* once put it, "most writers of topical-events fiction would be embarrassed to put him in a novel." Fact, legend, political intrigue, scurrilous gossip, and startling contradictions weave through his life in strange and subtle ways. Few disagree that Armand Hammer is the quintessential American capitalist—entrepreneurial, shrewd, energetic, and forever in search of the "big deal." Yet in 1921, long before the word "détente" was ever applied to Soviet-American relations, Armand Hammer became, at the age of twenty-three, the first American to strike a major business deal with the Soviet Union—a deal arranged with Lenin himself that earned him, in addition to large profits, an inscribed photograph from Lenin reading "To Comrade Armand Hammer."

On May 21, 1986, he turned eighty-eight years old, but he claims that he still works "fourteen hours a day, seven days a week. It keeps me young, it keeps me excited, it keeps my glands functioning. I never feel my age, especially when I am about to make a deal." Aides say he never goes more than ten minutes without making a phone call, and his personal phone bill is rumored to be over one million dollars a year. He has homes in Los Angeles and New York, apartments in London and Moscow, two Rolls Royces, and a personal jet equipped with a master bedroom, a guest bedroom, a well-stocked kitchen and bar, three telephones, a video recorder, and a library of Charlie Chaplin films. He keeps fit by swimming every day, reportedly has a fantastic memory, and is skilled in the art of autohypnosis, waking up after fifteen-minute self-induced catnaps to continue working at all hours of the day and night.

As an executive he is known as ruthless and autocratic, firing associates so soon after he hires them that former Occidental presidents are known as "Hammer's Other Collection." Yet even one of his critical biographers, Edward Jay Epstein, admits that Armand Hammer does not fit the stereotype of the calloused and money-grubbing multimillionaire. "On a personal level, Armand Hammer is a modest and affable man, who far more closely resembles a country doctor than a corporate magnate. He peers at the world through thick Magoo-like glasses and is slightly hard of hearing," wrote Epstein in the *New York Times Magazine* in 1981. "In my presence at least, Dr. Hammer was almost always patient, polite, and generous in dealing with his associates and other businessmen."

Although Hammer graduated with top honors from a well-known medical school, he never practiced medicine. Although a lifelong Democrat, he nearly went to jail in the 1970s for making an illegal cash contribution to Richard Nixon's campaign and he now calls himself a "strong supporter" of President Reagan. He is serving his second three-year term as the chairman of President Reagan's Cancer Advisory Panel, yet he complains that administration aides sometimes block his access to the President. To those accustomed to a black-hats-and-white-hats view of the world, Hammer's breezy familiarity with leaders of both the Communist and non-Communist worlds is bewildering. Epstein reports that one "member of the President's inner circle, who asked not to be identified by name," told him: "We simply don't know which side of the fence Hammer is on."

Even though Armand Hammer is, to put it mildly, a publicity hound, he was the only citizen diplomat approached who declined to grant an interview for this book. After six months of requests and a good deal of string pulling, an apologetic letter at last arrived from his lawyer and close friend, Arthur Groman. "Please don't take this personally," Groman wrote, "because the same declination has been made to several other journalists." The letter gave Hammer's busy schedule as the reason. Other reasons are more probable.

Among them is that twice, in recent years, Hammer has gotten bad press when he allowed independent journalists to investigate his life. Epstein's article, "The Riddle of Armand Hammer," which appeared in the November 28, 1981, issue of the *New York Times Magazine*, detailed the activities of Hammer's father, Julius Hammer, an early supporter of the American Communist Party, and bluntly raised the question of whether Armand Hammer's single-minded pursuit of East-West trade was in fact helping the Soviet Union more than the United States. Even more trenchant was a July 1983 article in *Harper's Magazine*, "Dr. Armand Hammer's Medicine Show," by Joseph Finder, then a graduate student at the Harvard University Russian Research Center, which depicted Hammer as a diligent lackey for his father's devious Communist operations designed to supply hard currency to the struggling Bolshevik regime and allow it to consolidate its grip on Russia. Finder's article was an excerpt from a book appearing later that year, *Red Carpet*, which unflatteringly portrayed five American businessmen who have struck deals with Moscow.

This may shed some light on why Hammer did not leap at the chance to be interviewed for another book. There are also rumors that his remarkable health is beginning to fail, and that Hammer's advisors believe Occidental stockholders should learn such news in an organized fashion—not via a news leak sprung by an unfamiliar journalist. But an interview was not essential. There is no shortage of published accounts of his life—and no dearth of disparate interpretations of his motivations.

At one extreme are Hammer's own accounts, including a 1932 autobiography about his early years in the Soviet Union called *Quest of the Romanoff Treasure*, and the semicommissioned biographies which unabashedly glorify his name, including the 1975 *The Remarkable Life of Dr. Armand Hammer* by Bob Considine and the more recent *The World of Armand Hammer*, a glossy photo essay edited by John Bryson. Both of the latter are dedicated to demonstrating that Hammer is the ultimately successful, ultimately philanthropic American tycoon, someone who works constantly yet also seems to have unlimited time to socialize with the world's elite. Considine's account in particular is embarrassingly sycophantic, filled with chapters with titles like "Genesis of a Genius" and phrases such as "everything he touched turned to gold."

At the other extreme is *Red Carpet*, which, though generally well-researched, consistently reflects Joseph Finder's frustration at being unable to muster more hard evidence to support his thesis that Armand Hammer is, for all practical purposes, a stooge for the Kremlin. Edward Jay Epstein takes a more moderate position, preferring to raise more questions in his article than he answers. "Understanding the convictions and motivations that underlie these apparent contradictions is not a simple matter," writes Epstein, noting "how convenient it is that Hammer's convictions on world peace and international relations always neatly coincide with his self-interest." In response, Hammer wrote a letter to the *New York Times* quivering with indignation about the "misrepresentations . . . that by a pen stroke attempt to denigrate or destroy the very meaning of one's life. This I cannot tolerate in silence."

Even Hammer's name is controversial. Finder and Epstein point out that American socialist Bertram Wolfe recalled in his memoirs that his friend Julius Hammer named his eldest son for the arm-and-hammer symbol of the Socialist Labor Party. Hammer, however, says that he was named for the lover Armand in Alexander Dumas's novel *Camille*. One thing everyone does agree upon is that his name has nothing to do with the well-known baking soda company. Tired of hearing jokes calling him "The Baking Soda King," Armand Hammer made one desultory attempt in the 1950s to buy the Church and Dwight Company, the producer of Arm and Hammer baking soda, but its owners refused to sell. (In October 1986, however, Hammer gleefully announced that he had managed to acquire an interest in the company.)

Armand Hammer's paternal grandparents were Russian Jewish merchants who emigrated from Odessa to the United States in 1875 with their one-year-old son Julius. Finding the streets of America were not paved with gold, the Hammers moved to France and tried selling art and antiques; some years later, when Julius was a teenager, they moved back to the United States and took up residence in Bradford, Connecticut, where Julius found work in a foundry. Here he, like many other dissatisfied workers, joined the Socialist Party and began campaigning for workers' rights. A few years later the family moved to the Lower East Side of Manhattan and Julius was apprenticed to a druggist. Within a few years he had bought the drugstore, acquired several others, and was running a small pharmaceutical plant on the Upper East Side. He married a young widow, Rose Robinson, and a few years later, in 1898, Armand was born. Julius soon started medical school at the Columbia College of Physicians and Surgeons.

Julius Hammer became a general practitioner in the Bronx, opening a combination home and office on Washington Street and often giving free health care. Armand Hammer recalls that his father would frequently visit a poor patient's home and surreptitiously leave money on the bed stand to pay for the prescriptions he would write. Julius Hammer also continued to support the Socialist Party, attending meetings and donating funds, and was a leader in what became known as the "Left Wing" of the party, which eventually joined with other factions to become the American Communist Party. In 1907, he went to the International Socialist Congress in Stuttgart, Germany, where he apparently met Lenin, the leader of the Russian Bolshevik Party. Like many other American leftists, Julius Hammer was thrilled by the success of the Bolshevik revolution in 1917, but unlike most he was in a position to offer the war-ravaged nation concrete help. Circumnavigating the French and British blockades, he managed to send, on credit, a shipment of medical supplies and pharmaceuticals to Bolshevik Russia.

By this time Armand Hammer was enrolled in medical school at Columbia University. Hammer says that his father approached him during his sophomore year and asked him to take over the family's faltering pharmaceutical business—a dishonest partner had left it on shaky foundations and Julius Hammer, between his medical practice and his political activities, did not have time to nurse it back to health. Armand Hammer did not drop out of medical school, but instead hired a classmate to take notes for him, which he memorized at night after spending all day working to boost the business. His aggressive marketing strategies soon paid off, with his most shrewd move based on a hunch that the price slump in medical supplies immediately after World War I was strictly temporary. Armand Hammer bought up all of the supplies he could find at depressed prices and several months later sold them at a brisk profit. He had made his first fortune—by some accounts, as much as a million dollars. And he still managed to graduate from Columbia Medical School in 1921 in the top ten of his class.

In the meantime, Julius Hammer had become still more involved with Communist causes. Although the US government steadfastly refused to recognize the fledgling Soviet government (and did not until 1933), the Soviets sent a diplomatic representative to New York anyway, a man named Ludwig Martens, who set up a quasi-legal office in New York City called the Soviet Bureau. Martens had two missions—to persuade the US government to extend diplomatic recognition, and to try to foster American trade with the Soviet Union, which was rich in natural resources but desperately needed food and manufactured supplies of all kinds. Martens asked Julius Hammer for help with the latter task, and as a "commercial attaché" for the Soviet Bureau Hammer took one trip through several Western states attempting to persuade businessmen to sell to the Soviet Union. By all accounts, his efforts failed, and Julius Hammer soon returned home.

But his activities had attracted a good deal of attention from New York's Tammany Hall politicians, and Julius Hammer fell victim to the Red Scare of that era. In July 1919 the wife of a Russian diplomat at the Czarist embassy in Washington, DC, came to him pleading for a therapeutic abortion because of her heart condition. Julius Hammer performed the abortion; the woman died several days later; Hammer was promptly charged with manslaughter and convicted after a long and sensational trial, even though substantial evidence indicated that the woman probably died of the Spanish influenza then sweeping the country. Julius Hammer may have been framed. He was sentenced to a minimum of three and a half years and a maximum of fifteen years at Sing Sing. Twenty-one-year-old Armand Hammer was furious and distraught, blaming the conviction on incompetent defense lawyers and political graft.

With his father in jail, Armand Hammer took on an even more prominent role in the family business. Hammer's biographer, Bob Considine, says that Armand took over the business so thoroughly that Julius Hammer sold all of his shares to Armand before entering jail and played

only a minor role in events of the next few years. *Red Carpet* author
Joseph Finder speculates that Julius Hammer remained the mastermind
of the pharmaceutical business, now called the Allied Drug and Chemical
Company, and orchestrated its subsequent dealings from prison. The
evidence on both sides is sketchy.

What is clear is that Armand Hammer graduated from Columbia
Medical School in June 1921 and was awarded a prestigious internship
at Bellevue Hospital that was to begin in January 1922. Hammer decided
to travel during the intervening six months to the Soviet Union, where
few foreigners had dared venture for nearly five years. He has consistently
stated that his main reason for going was to help combat a typhus
epidemic then raging there. As a young doctor with an interest in bac-
teriology and the money to purchase and bring his own Army surplus
"field hospital" filled with medical and surgical supplies, he was in a
good position to do volunteer work for a few months. In the 1932 account
of his early Soviet adventures called *Quest of the Romanoff Treasure*,
Hammer also states that another goal for his trip was to meet with Soviet
officials, persuade them to pay the debt incurred from Julius Hammer's
early shipment of medical and pharmaceutical supplies to the Soviet
Union, and explore the possibility of further trade deals between the
Hammer firm and the Soviets.

In *Red Carpet*, Joseph Finder declares that the second, less altruistic
purpose was in fact Armand Hammer's main mission, that he was little
more than an emissary for his father Julius, and that the story of wanting
to help fight a typhus epidemic was simply a cover for a secret agenda:
bolstering the economic basis of the Bolshevik state and helping finance
the spread of world Communism. Even the seventy-five-thousand-dollar
investment in the field hospital and medical supplies, Finder claims,
was simply a means of bolstering his "alibi." Finder's evidence, however,
is largely circumstantial. Armand Hammer does avoid mentioning his
father's Communist Party affiliations in his accounts of his early Soviet
experiences; Finder interprets this to mean that he had something to
hide about his own ideological loyalties. Another, possibly more plausible explanation is that Hammer was uncomfortable with his father's
political convictions and made a concerted effort to distance himself
from them.

Twenty-three-year-old Armand Hammer crossed the Soviet border on
a lurching train and arrived in Moscow in July 1921, to be greeted by
a representative from the Soviet foreign office and deposited in a hotel.

"Never in my life have I seen a hotel that less deserved the name, 'Savoy,' " Hammer later wrote, describing with fascinated horror the peeling wallpaper, bedbugs, and roaches, as well as the rats and mice that lived in the bathroom.

Prepared for food shortages, Hammer had prudently brought a supply of cheese, sardines, butter, jam, bread, and biscuits from Germany. After three days of this fare, however, his stomach rebelled and he lay on his bed, too sick to move, until a Soviet official discovered his plight and persuaded a doctor to write him a medical prescription for fresh vegetables, bread, and meat. Armed at last with a *payok*, a ticket that would allow him to go to the front of the food rationing lines in Moscow, Hammer went to buy food. As hungry and bedraggled men, women, and children standing in the food lines stared mutely at his new English tweeds, Hammer recalls feeling so ashamed that "I decided that I would rather starve than deprive a single one of them of the precious handful of food." Only his discovery, a few days later, of a "food speakeasy" run by a German matron saved him from returning to a sardines-and-cheese diet.

Hammer's first impressions of Moscow reveal the tremendous ravages left by World War I, the civil war, and the famine in the countryside: "The people seemed clad in rags; hardly anyone wore stockings or shoes but had wrappings of dirty cloth around their feet and legs. . . . No one seemed to smile, everyone looked dirty and dejected." Whether or not he originally intended to provide humanitarian relief to the Soviets, he appears to have been moved to do something to help. He met with Dr. N. A. Semashko, the Soviet Minister of Health, who thanked him for the field hospital and medical supplies, and, according to Hammer, referred him to a subordinate who could arrange for his volunteer work. But when Hammer tried to contact this subordinate, he was told the man was out of town and would not return for a month. Hammer despaired of accomplishing anything in this chaotic country, and considered heading for home. Then Gregory Weinstein, an American acquaintance of his father, who had been deported in 1920 along with Emma Goldman, Ludwig Martens, and other radicals, and who was now an official in the Commissariat of Foreign Affairs, arranged for Hammer to join a "mixed group of observers" on a month-long trip to the Ural Mountains, an area in the heart of Russia heavily hit by the famine.

The journey, which Hammer describes as being "lightly undertaken as a relief from the boredom of Moscow," was to change his life. Evidence of the famine, grimly hinted at in Moscow, now surrounded him. From his train window Hammer saw "children with their limbs shriveled to the size of sticks and their bellies horribly bloated . . . clustered 'round our windows begging piteously for bread—for life itself—in a dreadful ceaseless whine." He saw corpses piled high and unburied near train platforms, their precious clothes stripped from them, and crows circling above. He heard stories of cannibalism and saw frantic, weakened masses of peasants fleeing their homes on trains, hoping to find food in cities and dying of starvation and disease on the way. Everywhere the land was parched from the drought and "everywhere we went we met with the same condition—tremendous mills, factories and mine works standing idle and the workers hanging about, hungry and despairing."

Near one village, he and several other expedition members came upon an old man in the woods energetically sawing wood into planks. Such purposeful industry was a rare sight in the famine area, and one of the observers asked what he was doing. "Sawing wood," the old peasant replied shortly. Pressed for an explantion—the planks were too big to fit into a stove—the old man told them his situation in a resigned voice that sent chills down Hammer's spine. The old man was alone; he had only food left for three more weeks; after that he would surely die, and he was building his coffin with his remaining strength "so that I shall not be buried like a dog in the bare ground."

Hammer was appalled by the contradiction—great piles of precious metals, jewels, furs, and other goods lying around in warehouses while food was unobtainable. Hammer was also aware that American farmers had had a bumper year's crop of wheat, the world price of wheat had dropped to a dollar a bushel, and farmers were burning the wheat rather than selling it at such a low price. Why don't you sell these goods in exchange for food from other countries? he asked an official in Ekaterinburg (now called Sverdlovsk). It is impossible, the official replied—the European blockade has just been lifted, it would take too long to organize such a trade, and the quantity of food needed would require the exchange of nearly a million dollars worth of goods. Hammer reportedly replied: "I have a million dollars—I can arrange it. Is there anyone here with authority to make a contract?"

In a meeting with the hastily convened Ekaterinburg Soviet, Hammer offered to ship a million bushels of American wheat to the Soviet Union in exchange for one million dollars worth of furs, hides, metals, precious stones, caviar, and other goods. Although his proposal included a 5 percent commission for his company, Hammer claims that "my heart had been so wrung by what I had seen that the thought of doing business, or making a profit, did not enter my head at that time." The officials in Ekaterinburg cabled Moscow to inform their superiors of the plan and Hammer continued on his journey.

The rumor that this short, dark-haired young American was in fact a millionaire who was going to send them food was soon circulating through the villages and towns he visited, and Hammer found himself being treated as a hero. In one town, when hundreds of peasants gathered around him calling for a speech, Hammer tried out the few Russian words he had taught himself while lying sick in the Hotel Savoy. His speech met with tumultuous applause, and Hammer sat down feeling very pleased with himself, until he noticed that the crowd seemed to be waiting expectantly for more. "They understood nothing," a Soviet acquaintance explained with a grin. "They thought you were talking English, and now they're waiting for a translation."

In Alapayevsk, north of Ekaterinburg, Hammer was shown an enormous, empty asbestos mine, with its huge amphitheaters of gray rock and machinery standing idle. Perhaps Hammer would be interested in taking a concession for running the asbestos mine, an official with him suggested. Hammer knew no more about asbestos mining than he did about grain shipments, but he was intrigued by what looked like easy profits for the taking.

By the end of September 1921, Lenin had heard of Hammer's willingness to do business. Lenin's New Economic Policy, just adopted, specifically called for encouraging foreign investors to take concessions on faltering businesses within the Soviet Union and help rebuild them with their capital and technology. Lenin hoped that if Hammer could be persuaded to take a major concession such as the asbestos mine, other American businessmen would follow suit. In the first of fourteen references to Hammer found in Lenin's *Complete Collected Works*, Lenin told V. V. Kuibyshev, a member of the Presidium of the Supreme Economic Council, that "We must conclude with Hammer very soon . . . the agreement on the concession."

Hammer returned from the Urals to Moscow in early October and began negotiating with officials for a grain contract and an asbestos concession. In a letter dated October 14, 1921, addressed to members of the Central Committee, Lenin optimistically referred to Hammer and his offer to send "one million poods [36 million pounds] of grain on very easy terms (5 percent) and to take Urals valuables on commission for sale in America. . . . [and] to help rehabilitate the Urals industry." If Hammer could not be persuaded to take on the asbestos mine, Lenin told colleagues, perhaps the grain contract could be drawn up in the *form* of a concession. "Agreements and concessions with the Americans are of exceptional importance to us," wrote Lenin. "We almost have something with Hammer." But Hammer proved no easy bargainer, and Lenin wondered nervously on October 19, 1921 whether "Hammer is in earnest. . . . and [whether] the plan is not just so much hot air."

When negotiations stalled, a Soviet official named Boris Reinstein—another former American and friend of Julius Hammer—arranged a personal interview with Lenin in hopes that the Big Chief could break the deadlock. Armand Hammer and Lenin met for an hour in Lenin's office on October 22, 1921. "Lenin rose from his desk and came to meet me at the door," recalled Hammer. "He was smaller than I had expected—a stocky little man about five feet three, with a large, dome-shaped head, wearing a dark grey sack suit, white soft collar and black tie. His eyes twinkled with friendly warmth as he shook hands and led me to a seat beside his big flat desk." They spoke in English. For the hour that followed, Hammer says, "I was completely absorbed by Lenin's personality."

After opening pleasantries, including conversation about Julius Hammer and Armand's stay in Russia, they discussed the terms of the asbestos agreement. Hammer found "The Red Dictator," as he called him in his memoirs, far more agreeable on terms than his subordinates, and they quickly came to an understanding. According to Hammer, Lenin expressed gratitude for his offer to help with medical relief efforts but said: "We have plenty of doctors. What we want here is American businessmen who can do things as you are doing. Your sending us ships with grain means saving the lives of men, women and little children who would otherwise helplessly perish this winter. To the gratitude of these agonized people I add my humble thanks on behalf of my government." Tears came to Lenin's eyes when he spoke of the suffering caused by the famine, recalls Hammer, who came away from the interview deeply impressed by the Soviet leader's compassion for common people. "Lenin has been called ruthless and fanatical, cruel and cold. I refuse to believe it," Hammer has written. "It was his intense human sympathy, his warm personal magnetism and utter lack of self-assertion or self-interest that made him great."

Before leaving, Hammer presented Lenin with a gift, a twenty-inch-high bronze statue of a monkey bemusedly holding a human skull that he had purchased in Britain. According to Hammer, Lenin studied the statue for several minutes, pondering what it might mean. "If wars will someday wipe out all civilization," he finally commented, "there will only be monkeys left, and somewhere the monkey will pick up a human skull and wonder where it came from." Lenin placed the monkey on his desk and left it there. Today, when Soviet guides give tours of Lenin's meticulously preserved office, they routinely point out the bronze monkey statue given by "Armand Hammer, the well-known American capitalist."

The hour-long meeting with Lenin elevated Armand Hammer to the status of a Very Important Person, and he was soon moved out of the disagreeable Hotel Savoy to a government guest house known as the Sugar King's Palace (named for its former owner, a wealthy Ukrainian merchant who made his fortune in sugar beets). "Suddenly I found myself in a palatial suite with bathroom attached," Hammer recalls. "There were well-trained servants, excellent cuisine, and if need be, a bottle of old French wine from the well-stocked cellar. . . . Such was the magic of Lenin's name, and my new status as a concessionaire."

Hammer hastily summoned Boris Mishell, the European manager of his Allied Drug and Chemical Company, to Moscow, and on October 27, 1921, Hammer and Mishell signed the grain contract with the Soviet government. A few days before signing the asbestos contract, Hammer casually mentioned to Mishell: "Lenin told me that if there was anything else I wanted to be sure and let him know." Mishell hastily drew up five more conditions for the asbestos contract, including provisions for offices, an agreement that Red Army soldiers would protect their property, the right of their employees to travel freely about Russia and leave the country at will, the placement of radio and telegraph stations at their disposal, and the facilitation of trains moving freight.

The stipulation involving protection by the Red Army necessitated a meeting between Hammer and Leon Trotsky, the Commissar of War. "He greeted me quite cordially," Hammer recalls, "but his glance was cold and piercing." To Hammer's astonishment, Trotsky spoke calmly of America's coming revolution and offered the "curious argument" that the Soviet Union was a stable place for capitalists to invest because the Soviet Union had already had its revolution. Hammer's meeting with Trotsky was productive but disconcerting—later he described "the Red War Lord" as "a man of remarkable, but imperious, character, with great ability and unflinching will, but with a degree of fanaticism of which Lenin had given me no sign."

The asbestos contract signed on November 2, 1921, granted Hammer's company mining rights for twenty years, with the Soviet government receiving a 10 percent commission. Hammer was also given another kind of "concession"—he was granted the right to act as an agent for American companies who might wish to sell products to the Soviet Union. Word of the agreement was soon splashed across the front page of the *New York Times*, and the US Department of Justice promptly began an investigation into the Allied Drug and Chemical Company.

Hammer stayed in the Soviet Union another month, busily making arrangements for these unexpected business ventures. On November 3, 1921, Lenin sent him a letter in English apologizing for his inability to meet with him again. On November 10, Lenin sent an autographed photograph of himself inscribed "To Comrade Armand Hammer." On November 17, the first shipment of grain arrived at the port of Reval (now Tallinn), and Hammer supervised the unloading of wheat and the reloading of the ship with sables, minks, hides, decorative metal castings, paintings, and nearly a ton of Russian caviar in fifty-pound wooden kegs. The ship left for New York in early December, with Hammer aboard.

Back in the United States, Hammer turned away from a medical career. He dissolved the old Allied Drug and Chemical Company, reconstituted it under a new name, the Allied American Corporation, and spent several months traveling around the United States talking enthusiastically about his Soviet experiences and persuading American companies to let him represent them in Moscow. By spring 1922 he was the official representative for no less than thirty-eight major American companies, including US Rubber, Allis-Chalmers, the National Supply Company, Ingersoll-Rand, US Machinery, Underwood Typewriter, and Parker Pen. A meeting with Henry Ford in Dearborn, Michigan, resulted in the Ford Company being added to his list, and Ford agreed to allow Soviet engineers to come to Dearborn and be trained in the "Ford Method." Hammer returned to the Soviet Union in late March 1922 and began traveling through the Ukraine and southern Russia collecting orders for Fordson tractors. (By the end of the 1920s, despite his fiercely anti-Bolshevik public statements, Ford had sold twenty-four thousand tractors and a few thousand automobiles to the Soviet Union.)

Hammer was present when the first shipment of fifty tractors was unloaded on the docks of Novorossiisk on the Black Sea. After the tractors were uncrated, gassed, and oiled, Hammer and several Ford-trained Soviets drove the tractors into the city. But the inhabitants of Novorossiisk, panicked by what appeared to be an invasion by a bizarre new type of American tank, swiftly called out the local militia and made preparations to defend their city until it was explained that the odd noisy machines were being delivered to help grow food. Hammer traveled with the tractors through a hundred miles of Ukrainian countryside, helping to give demonstrations, and in the city of Rostov-on-Don he met Anastas Mikoyan, then the twenty-eight-year-old head of the local soviet (city council) who would one day become the Soviet Minister of Trade.

Hammer also went to Alapayevsk to check on his asbestos mine, but to his dismay found the workers in a state of enraged mutiny. Food had been promised to them two weeks before, but it had not arrived and the workers were threatening to shoot Hammer's Soviet manager. Hammer discovered that the shipment of food he had dispatched by railroad had been diverted to a siding north of Ekaterinburg while a railroad official smugly asked for half a carload of food as a bribe. Hammer, outraged, cabled Lenin immediately. In short order, the unfortunate railroad official was shot by Trotsky's soldiers and the shipment went through.

Hammer brought in automated equipment such as four-bladed automatic saws, compressed air drills, and mechanical rock crushers, and the mine was soon in full operation. The workers were made happy with not only food but also a shipment of surplus American army uniforms to wear as clothing. "Everyone thought the American army must all be millionaires if they could wear clothes like that," remembers Hammer. He built houses, schools, and a hospital for the workers. But the asbestos mine was never the golden goose that Hammer hoped it might be—a glut of asbestos on the world market in the early 1920s dropped prices drastically, and labor, logistical, and bureaucratic delays continued to plague him. Not until the end of 1925 did the mine begin to show a profit.

But this did not seem to daunt Hammer, who foresaw that he would make plenty of money in the Soviet Union in other ways—primarily as an agent for other American manufacturers. Lenin welcomed him back to the Soviet Union in a letter dated May 11, 1922: "Excuse me please, I have been very ill; now I am much, much better. . . . [I wish you] full success of your first concession: such success would be of great importance also for trade relations between our Republic and the United States." On May 24, Lenin wrote a letter to Stalin about Hammer, urging him to "give these persons and their enterprise particular support. This is a small path leading to the American 'business' world, and this path should be made use of in every way."

Hammer returned to New York in mid-June, 1922, and gave a dinner for prominent American businessmen to promote the idea of Soviet-American trade. He insisted that his doing business with the Soviet Union did not mean he was sympathetic to Communist ideology, telling the *New York Times:* "When I conferred with officials of the [Soviet] government, I told them that I was a capitalist, that I was out to make money." He spent the summer buying machinery for his asbestos mine and signing contracts for the import of goods to the Soviet Union. He also orchestrated a vigorous letter-writing campaign to New York Governor Al Smith for the release of his father from prison. Julius Hammer was paroled on January 23, 1923, and pardoned by Governor Smith not quite two years later.

Armand Hammer persuaded his younger brother, twenty-two-year-old Victor, to come to the Soviet Union in the fall of 1922 and work with him. By May 1923, the Hammer family—Julius, Rose, Victor, and Armand—was comfortably settled in a late-nineteenth century mansion in a posh section of Moscow. The Brown House, as they called it, became a lively center of Moscow social life for the next seven years, with parties and dinners bringing together Soviet officials, commissars, intellectuals, and artists with distinguished Western visitors such as Mary Pickford, Douglas Fairbanks, John Dewey, Will Rogers, and E. E. Cummings.

In a one-year contract signed on July 14, 1923, Hammer's Allied American Company officially became the Soviet Union's sole export-import agent for transactions with the United States. The contract allowed the company to handle the import of two hundred thousand gold rubles worth of agricultural and mining equipment and other goods, and the export of an equivalent value of Soviet goods. Hammer's main Soviet export was asbestos, but he quickly set up a subsidiary firm, under the name Allied Furs Sales, to export minks, sables, and hides.

But there were already signs that the days of Lenin's New Economic Policy were numbered. After suffering a debilitating series of strokes and partial paralysis for a year and a half, Lenin died of a final massive stroke on January 21, 1924. In the summer of 1924, when his one-year agenting contract was up for renewal, Hammer was summoned to the office of Leonid Krassin, the Minister of Foreign Trade, and told that from now on Soviet exports and imports with the United States would be managed by a new government agency called Amtorg. Hammer listened in dismay while his lucrative agreements with Ford, Allis-Chambers, Underwood, and many others evaporated in a few sentences. Krassin carefully pointed out, however, that the Soviet government was still eager to offer a manufacturing concession to Hammer's company.

According to Hammer, he got the idea for what to manufacture while trying to buy a pencil in a stationery store in Moscow. He was startled to find that all regular graphite pencils were imported, expensive, and hard to obtain. A pencil that cost two or three cents in the United States cost fifty kopeks (about twenty-six cents) in the Soviet Union. Hammer soon returned to Krassin's office and asked for a manufacturing concession to make pencils. In what Hammer refers to as record time for a Soviet bureaucratic transaction—three and a half months—and over the vociferous protests of the fledgling state-run pencil factory, which had yet to produce any pencils, Hammer closed the deal in 1925. Now all he had to do was find out how to make pencils.

He swiftly invaded the pencil-making empire of the Faber company in Nuremburg, Germany, luring a number of disgruntled employees well versed in the art of pencil making away from their jobs with promises of housing, high wages, and free education for their children. In a similar fashion, he spirited away pen-making experts from factories in Birmingham, England, and soon returned to Moscow, where he found an abandoned soap factory on the banks of the Moscow River to renovate. By the end of its first year of operation, Hammer's new pencil factory had produced fifty-one million pencils and ten million pens, and by the end of the next year it had turned out an additional seventy-two million pencils and ninety-five million pens.

Hammer chose a blatantly patriotic motif for his new company—the Statue of Liberty set against a waving American flag. Each pencil was embossed in silver letters: HAMMER. Older Soviet citizens today can remember walking into stationery stores and asking for "Three Hammers, please." To increase production, Hammer instituted a profit-sharing and piecework system among his employees. As production—and wages—rose, Hammer was besieged with applications for jobs at the factory, which soon employed eight hundred workers. Hammer began exporting pencils to England, Turkey, Persia, and China, and he was lauded in the Soviet press for turning the Soviet Union into an exporter of a manufactured product.

The praise was not unmixed, however. Officials at the state pencil factory complained bitterly about "foreign capitalists who try to exploit Russia's wealth." After Hammer's balance sheet was published in the Soviet press, revealing first-year earnings of over a million dollars, editorials complained that the pencil prices were too high and the Soviet Union's gold was being siphoned out of the country. Hammer took the hint and lowered his prices.

But as Stalin began consolidating his power, Hammer's position grew more and more precarious. In 1928, during a dinner at the Hammer mansion, Minister of Education A. V. Lunacharsky leaned over to Hammer and whispered, "I have been following the attacks on you in the newspapers; don't pay any attention to them. You know, some of the comrades have to let off steam periodically, and since they haven't local capitalists to train their guns on, you have to be the goat." Hammer, only partly reassured, apparently began making plans to move himself, his family, and his profits out of the Soviet Union in the late 1920s.

Hammer was by this time a settled resident of Moscow, fluent in Russian, and had a Russian wife, a singer named Olga Vadina, and a young son, Julian. His brother Victor was also married and had a child. As a "hobby," says Hammer, he and Victor had collected paintings by Russian and European masters being sold at bargain prices at second-hand stores and auctions, as well as Romanoff era sculpture, china, silverware, furnishings, and other knick-knacks—some of it dross, some of it priceless art. They had decorated the Brown House until it resembled a lavish and disorganized museum. In early 1930, Hammer began formal negotiations to sell his factories to the Soviet government and get out. A good portion of his profits were stored in the form of rubles in Soviet banks, which were impossible to export. But Hammer ingeniously bargained for a clause in his termination contract which allowed him to take his "household effects" out of the country—including his entire art collection, which by now filled not only his house but also several warehouses.

In early 1930 Hammer and his wife and son left the Soviet Union, spending a year in Paris before moving to the United States, where he and Olga were soon and apparently amicably divorced. Victor, who was by this time estranged from his Russian wife, was not as lucky in family matters: his wife refused to leave the country, and by Soviet law this meant Victor could not take his son, Armand Victorovich, with him to the United States. (Armand Victorovich, whose American name is rumored to have landed him a four-year sentence in a labor camp during the Stalin years, still lives in the Soviet Union and works at a publishing house; now that his uncle Armand Hammer is once more in the good graces of the Soviet government, he occupies an odd position of privilege, holding a special passport that allows him to travel abroad whenever and wherever he likes.)

Armand Hammer arrived in New York City in 1931 with what seemed, in the depth of the Great Depression, to be a completely unsalable collection of Russian art and artifacts. As his biographer Bob Considine puts it, "Nobody wanted a forgotten czarina's ruby-studded swizzle stick." But through what Considine calls "proper merchandising" and Joseph Finder calls "lowbrow huckstering," Hammer managed to make his Romanoff art "move" by setting up special sales in American department stores. He threw lavish parties to win over Russian émigrés who might otherwise make a stink about an ancestor's china service being sold at Bullock's for $299.95. Some émigrés, however, could never quite forgive him for cutting up richly brocaded Russian Orthodox vestments and turning them into pillows and handbags. The department store approach was sufficiently successful that when publishing mogul William Randolph Hearst decided to liquidate about eleven million dollars worth of his personal art collection to obtain some needed cash in 1940, he contracted with Hammer Galleries to manage the sale.

During the Stalin era, Hammer's contact with the Soviet Union effectively ceased. "I could not do business with Joseph Stalin," Hammer says simply. Joseph Finder claims in *Red Carpet* that Hammer continued to import Soviet art throughout the 1930s in a secret deal that helped the Soviet government convert its czarist treasures into hard currency, but he offers scanty documentation for this assertion. Hammer did strike one deal with the Soviet government in 1933, to import a shipment of Russian white-oak barrel staves. Correctly predicting that the end of Prohibition was near at hand and that the sudden revival of alcohol production would create a shortage of barrels, Hammer briefly cornered the market on barrel staves. This is the only documented contact between Hammer and the Soviet government for a period of almost thirty years, until well after Khrushchev had assumed power.

Hammer instead concentrated on making his fortune in the United States. In the mid-1930s, Hammer got into the whiskey business, beginning with alcohol made from surplus rotten potatoes (called "neutral vegetable spirits" on the label). When restrictions on the use of grain for alcohol production eased, Hammer began buying distilleries to make high-quality bonded bourbon, building J. W. Dant Bourbon into a top-selling whiskey and finally selling it for $6.5 million in 1953. In 1943 he married New Jersey socialite Angela Zevely and took up the genteel pastime of raising prize-winning Angus cattle, finally selling his herd "for tax reasons" in 1954 for about one million dollars.

Hammer also began cultivating relationships with influential Americans. An avid supporter of Franklin Delano Roosevelt, he paid for a series of campaign radio ads in the 1940s and became an acquaintance of Eleanor Roosevelt and her son, Elliot. Eleanor Roosevelt once appeared in court as a character witness for Hammer in a tax trial. In 1952, Armand and Victor Hammer bought Campobello, the Roosevelts' retreat on an island near the Maine-Canada border, and in 1962 they donated it to the United States and Canadian governments as an international park. Hammer met former president Herbert Hoover and President Harry Truman once each, in connection with famine relief efforts in Europe after the war, and added their signed photographs to his growing collection of "famous people I have known."

In the mid-1950s his personal life became complicated when his marriage to Angela came to a stormy dissolution after a long and sensational divorce trial. Hammer hired a battery of top lawyers and got the better end of the settlement, but Angela, in a fit of pique, stole Hammer's treasured personal letters from Lenin. They have never been found, although Hammer offered a reward for their discovery after Angela's death in 1965. In 1956, Hammer apparently decided to make a fresh start in life. He sold his businesses, moved to southern California, married an heiress named Frances Tolman, and attempted to retire.

But at the age of fifty-eight, Hammer was not yet ready to be put out to pasture. "I tried water-skiing. I even took flying lessons. But there's no substitute for running a big business once you've had the experience," he later said. A friend advised him to invest in the oil business as a tax shelter, and Hammer, along with his wife and several other partners, decided to loan a faltering California-based company named Occidental Petroleum fifty thousand dollars to drill two do-or-die wells. Chartered in 1920, Occidental had not paid a dividend since 1934; in 1956 its stock was selling at eighteen cents a share on the Los Angeles Stock Exchange.

To Hammer's astonishment, both of the new wells struck oil. Hammer began buying shares of Occidental in the open market, and invested one million dollars in the company so that it could acquire leases on eleven oil fields near Los Angeles. By 1957, he had become the company's largest shareholder and its president. He hired one of California's most respected oil engineers, Gene Reid, to work for Occidental, and in 1961 the company hit a major oil field in the San Joaquin Valley east of San Francisco. Hammer began acquiring fertilizer and other petroleum-related companies, including the Best Fertilizer Company, the International Ore and Fertilizer Company, and the Jefferson Lake Sulphur Company. By 1963 Occidental was more a fertilizer conglomerate than an oil company, with $22.3 million of its profits coming from fertilizer sales and only $2.7 million from oil and gas sales.

Sometime in the late 1950s, Hammer once again became intrigued with the possibility of trading with the Soviet Union. Khrushchev, unlike Stalin, appeared to be someone with whom he could do business. In January 1961 Hammer arranged through Senator Albert Gore of Tennessee, an old cattle-breeding acquaintance and confidant of the newly inaugurated President Kennedy, to travel to eight countries, including the Soviet Union, as an unofficial trade emissary for the US Commerce Department.

In Moscow Hammer met with Anastas Mikoyan, the Soviet Minister of Trade whom he had met nearly forty years earlier during the Fordson tractor demonstrations in the city of Rostov-on-Don. Hammer later told the *New Yorker:* "It was really a nice meeting. [Mikoyan] got kind of sentimental." They also talked business—Mikoyan was preoccupied with the United States government's boycott of Soviet crab meat because of the alleged use of slave labor to process it. Mikoyan insisted that there had been no slave labor in the Soviet Union since Stalin's death. "Why don't you ask your Japanese friends?" he said. "They crab side by side with our vessels. They would surely know, and tell you, if we were using slave or forced labor." (A few months later, after US intelligence verified that Mikoyan was right, the boycott was lifted.)

Hammer was about to leave for India and a meeting with Prime Minister Jawaharlal Nehru when word came, two days later, that Nikita Khrushchev wished to speak with him. Khrushchev, Mikoyan, and Hammer met for over two hours and discussed a variety of topics, including the crab controversy, Soviet repayment of a World War II lend-lease debt, and the Soviet steel and natural gas industries. According to Hammer, Khrushchev spoke glowingly of a steak served to him during his American visit and told him: "Unless Russia can bring its steak up to American size and quality, Communism is sure to fail." (Hammer later presented a prize Angus bull and two cows to Khrushchev as a gift.) Although he kept this part of the meeting secret for several years, Hammer also proposed to the Soviets a potential billion-dollar fertilizer deal; Occidental would help the Soviet Union construct fertilizer plants near their huge natural gas fields in return for receiving the final products of ammonia, urea, and potash.

At the conclusion of the meeting, Khrushchev gave Hammer an engraved gold automatic pencil and an inscribed photograph reading, "To Mr. Hammer, the first concessionaire who talked to Lenin." (Nikita Khrushchev never met Lenin.) Hammer mentioned to Khrushchev that he would like to visit the old pencil factory on the Moscow River. Hours later a Soviet limousine took him to the plant, now renamed the Sacco and Vanzetti Pencil Factory, where Hammer had a champagne, vodka, and caviar reception with the employees, including several old-timers who recognized him.

Hammer and his wife Frances went back to the Soviet Union in the summer of 1964, and he met with Khrushchev a second time on July 12, 1964, to continue his fertilizer deal discussions. While in Moscow he also met with Minister of Culture Ekaterina Furtseva and arranged an unprecedented private art exchange: the Pushkin Museum in Moscow would show paintings of Grandma Moses provided by Hammer Galleries, and Hammer Galleries in New York would exhibit the icons of Russian artist Pavel Korin. This, the first of several Soviet-American private fine-art exchanges organized by Hammer, went off without a hitch—large crowds gathered at the exhibitions in both countries.

Like many of his other art exhibition arrangements, this one was probably designed to enhance his business position. At a press conference in London on September 26, 1964, Hammer announced that "relatively soon" he would sign a contract with the Soviet Union to build ten chemical-fertilizer plants in Siberia that would produce ammonia fertilizer from Soviet reserves of natural gas in Kamchatka. Since the United States government refused to consider authorizing credit for the deal, the financing would be done through British banks. But Khrushchev's ouster nixed Hammer's plans, and Armand Hammer was left to go looking elsewhere for his "big deal" for several more years.

Hammer's instinct for money-making opportunities took him to Libya, a small desert country with vast oil reserves and a notoriously corrupt government under the rule of King Idris. Hammer bid on Libyan oil concessions, delivering his bids on sheepskin scrolls tied with ribbons of red, green, and black—Libya's national colors—and sweetening his offer with a clause promising to search for water near King Idris's desert birthplace. Occidental received two concessions in March 1966 and sank five million dollars into three dry holes before hitting oil one hundred miles from the Mediterranean. Hammer built a pipeline to the sea and soon Occidental's stock rose precipitously.

When the revolutionary regime of Colonel Muammar al-Qaddafi seized power in 1969, it threatened to nationalize the operations of the large multinational oil companies. Qaddafi decided to first put pressure on Occidental, the smallest of the companies and the one most dependent on Libyan oil. On September 4, 1970, Hammer acceded to Qaddafi's demands, reaching a compromise of 51–49 percent ownership and $136 million compensation in order to stave off 100-percent nationalization. The "common front" of the oil companies was broken, leading to profound changes in the price of oil and the world energy market. "Some critics say Oxy's move helped OPEC get a stranglehold on the Western world," concedes Hammer, "but we had no choice."

With the dawning of Soviet-American detente in the early 1970s, Hammer once again revived his plans for a huge trade deal with Moscow. To help grease the wheels, he made a secret $100,000 cash contribution to Richard Nixon's campaign in 1972, but in an apparent miscalculation did not deliver the cash until a few days after April 7, 1972, when a new campaign financing law outlawing such contributions went into effect. On March 4, 1976, Hammer appeared in court in a wheelchair, surrounded by a bevy of cardiologists. He pleaded guilty and spoke contritely of his misdeed in faltering tones while his lawyers described him as "a sick old man [who] lives four blocks from the office, goes in late, goes home for lunch and takes a nap in the afternoon." The judge gave him a suspended sentence and fined him three thousand dollars. A few months later he had miraculously recovered and was again flying around the world on his private jet.

In the meantime, his Soviet deals were progressing. In July 1972 Hammer met for five days with the heads of eighteen Soviet ministries. On July 18, 1972, he announced a series of preliminary agreements with the Soviets for Occidental and several other US companies to provide patents and technology for oil production, chemical plants, and waste reclamation in exchange for Soviet oil, gas, nickel, chrome, and chemicals. Occidental would also oversee the construction of a chain of Holiday-Inn-style motels in the Soviet Union and a skyscraping "world trade center" in Moscow. (Only one of these deals eventually materialized: the World Trade Center, a grandiose building complex resembling a Hyatt Hotel, now stands near the banks of the Moscow River and is informally known as "Hammer's trade center.")

And there were yet more rabbits in Hammer's hat. On April 12, 1973, Hammer modestly announced "the deal of the century"—an eight-billion-dollar twenty-year fertilizer barter with the Soviet Union. Occidental's $700 million phosphate mining operation in Florida would deliver annually, from 1978 to 1998, $200 million worth (approximately one million tons) of superphosphoric acid to the Soviet Union and buy from it an equivalent amount of ammonia, urea, and potash, produced by Soviet fertilizer plants that Occidental would help construct. The deal hinged on the granting of $180 million in credits from the US Export-Import Bank to the Soviet Union, which President Nixon personally authorized after meeting with Hammer on July 20, 1972.

On May 9, 1973, Hammer told the Society of American Business Writers: "I am a capitalist, and anyone who knows me knows what an ardent supporter of capitalism and America I am. But I think a capitalist can deal with a Communist. . . . The Hot Line, my friends, is no longer only in the basement of the White House. The hottest communication right now is the steady flow of negotiations between American businessmen and Russian commercial representatives."

Once again Hammer pulled off a major art exchange with the Soviet Union at the same time that his business deal was being consummated. In 1972 Hammer sent a collection of 104 oils, watercolors, and drawings by American and European masters on tour in the Soviet Union. In return, Minister of Culture Ekaterina Furtseva sent forty-one French Impressionist and Post-Impressionist paintings belonging to the Hermitage and Pushkin Museums, which had never before been seen in the United States, to exhibitions at Hammer Galleries, Knoedler's Galleries (a venerable art dealership that Hammer acquired in the early 1970s), and the National Gallery of Art.

On October 22, 1972, in the midst of his phosphate negotiations, Hammer gave a Goya painting valued at close to a million dollars to the Soviet government. Five days later, he presented two original manuscript letters written by Lenin, which he had acquired from an art dealer, as an "unconditional gift to the government and people of the USSR." Party Secretary Leonid Brezhnev wrote him a thank-you letter on November 10, 1972. The painting and letters apparently helped pave the way for Hammer's first meeting with Brezhnev, on February 15, 1973. Hammer spoke with Brezhnev for two hours in the Kremlin and later reported that he found him "a man of great humanism and vast warmth and understanding, enormously intelligent and sophisticated in the ways of the world. . . . I told him, 'You remind me very much of Lenin, whom I met in this very building fifty-two years ago.' His eyes filled with tears, which showed that he is a very human person who is trying to do good for his people just as Lenin tried." Brezhnev gave him a gold watch, which Hammer delightedly told reporters "keeps very good time," and which he was fond of displaying next to the set of presidential cuff links Nixon had given him.

During a state dinner held at the White House in June 1973, Nixon, Brezhnev, and Hammer held up the receiving line for five minutes while chatting in English and Russian. Hammer's relationship with Brezhnev blossomed into perhaps the coziest of all his friendships with Soviet leaders. For a 1974 NBC documentary about his Soviet dealings called "The Russian Connection," Hammer arranged with apparent effortlessness a filmed interview with Brezhnev, something other television correspondents had attempted to obtain for years without success. Hammer said in the documentary: "I think that these two great nations have to live together, and if they trade together, I think that they'll maintain the peace of the world. . . . I think if you trade with somebody, it's pretty hard to fight with them." Brezhnev added: "We have formed a very solid basis for good relations between our two peoples. Armand Hammer has expended considerable effort. I help him, he helps me. It is mutual. We do not discuss secrets—just business."

During the Brezhnev era Hammer acquired a reputation as "the Soviets' favorite capitalist"—a title he adores. "Hammer knew Lenin, damn it," Joseph Finder quotes a rival American businessman who deals with the Soviet Union. "How the hell are we supposed to compete with that?" Since 1972 Hammer has had the rare privilege of being allowed to fly into the Soviet Union on his personal jet. In 1976 Brezhnev gave Hammer a private apartment in Moscow to stay in during his business visits. When he arrives, his Soviet maid greets him. The walls are decorated with Russian masterpieces that Hammer has willed to the Soviet government. Soon after moving in Hammer discovered that the electrical system was inadequate for his fully equipped kitchen, including a dishwasher and large freezer, and, at his request, the Soviet government tore up the streets and installed new wiring. On Hammer's eightieth birthday, on May 21, 1978, Soviet officials gave a banquet in his honor and pinned a bright red-and-gold medal on his lapel—the Lenin Order of Friendship Among the Peoples, an award generally given to foreign Communists and never before to a businessman.

Brezhnev and Hammer met at Yalta on August 25, 1978, and Hammer asked for the Hermitage to loan him "The Benois Madonna" by Leonardo da Vinci, which had only left Leningrad once before, for an American tour. Brezhnev agreed, and an exhibit called "The Legacy of Leonardo" toured Los Angeles, New York, and Washington DC in 1979. "Whether the collection is shown in Moscow or Houston, Tokyo or Denver, the public's response is the same," says Hammer about his own peripatetic art collection, now worth an estimated $53 million. "Enthusiastic and eager viewers line up for the opportunity to view works of artistic genius. To my mind, this common response demonstrates that all our planet's passengers are *joined* by more concerns than separate them. . . . I have come to believe that international understanding is possible through artistic exchanges."

But in contrast to his successful art swaps, Hammer's fertilizer deal ran into unexpected trouble. After numerous start-up delays, in 1979 about 1.3 million tons of ammonia were shipped to the US and half-a-million tons of superphosphoric acid were shipped to the Soviet Union. Then Soviet troops invaded Afghanistan, American dockworkers refused to unload Soviet ships in protest, President Jimmy Carter imposed a Soviet trade embargo, and the fertilizer shipments ceased.

Hammer apparently concluded that saving his fertilizer deal required nothing less than an attempt on his part to end the war in Afghanistan. And for more than a year he shuttled around the world trying to get the major players to negotiate a settlement. He met with Brezhnev in Moscow on February 27, 1980, and announced at a press conference afterwards that Brezhnev had told him he would withdraw troops as soon as "the US and the countries surrounding Afghanistan" stopped supplying arms to rebels across the Pakistan border. Brezhnev gave Hammer a letter to give to Carter. Hammer then flew to Pakistan and conferred with General Mohammad Zia ul-Haq about halting arms shipments, at the same time temptingly dangling the prospect of Occidental drilling an offshore oil field and building a new oil refinery in Pakistan. In rapid succession Hammer also met with Senator Charles Percy, Secretary of State Alexander Haig, Britain's Lord Carrington and United Nations Secretary General Kurt Waldheim to present his Afghanistan "peace proposal": a phased withdrawal of Soviet troops in return for a stop to the arms traffic over the Pakistan border.

Then, on April 24, 1981, President Reagan lifted the trade embargo with the Soviet Union for other reasons. Hammer wrote a letter to Reagan praising his "courageous decision" and immediately went to Moscow to get his phosphates deal rolling again. As far as can be discerned, he also abruptly ceased his Afghanistan peacemaking efforts. "In that light," comments Edward Jay Epstein, "it perhaps becomes clear where his highest priorities lay."

Yet it was also during this period that Hammer first began actively justifying Soviet-American trade in terms of its contribution to stopping the arms race. In 1982, he told a reporter that if Reagan and Brezhnev could simply meet one another as human beings, they would find common ground. "[Brezhnev] is a man with a warm heart. He's a sentimental and emotional man. When he talks about peace, tears come to his eyes. . . . And I know Reagan is a fine man, a very genial man. He's also a very warm man with a lot of charm, and I think that these two fellows would like each other and that would be so important because they would cut through all the red tape, all the bureaucracy and all of the people who are trying to keep the two countries apart. I know we don't buy their ideology and they don't buy ours, but there's no reason why we can't trade with them, have cultural exchanges with them, and why we can't let history decide which society is the best for mankind. That is better than dropping bombs on each other."

In the 1980s Hammer apparently decided to take advantage of his access to both American and Soviet leaders to push for renewed arms control talks. "If we can survive the next several years without an accident of some sort," he said in March 1984, "I believe we will find a new spirit of accommodation in which the two greatest powers can live together on this planet in peace." For the past four years, Hammer has publicly urged both superpowers to adopt a no-first-strike pledge for both conventional and nuclear weapons, and he has consistently advocated a policy of regularly scheduled summit meetings every eighteen months between American and Soviet leaders. "With regularly scheduled meetings, neither country has to worry about face or hurriedly adjusted agendas," he said in 1984.

On November 28, 1984, Konstantin Chernenko invited Hammer to Moscow to discuss Soviet-American relations and to pave the way for talks in January 1985 between Andrei Gromyko and George Shultz. Hammer suggested in a *New York Times* opinion on September 22, 1985, that if President Reagan were sincere about his plan to share Star Wars research and development with the Soviets at a later stage, then it would make both political and practical sense to offer to share that technology now. Hammer told reporters prior to the November 1985 Geneva summit that he worried that the President "will bow to hard-line advisors and take the position that you can't trust the Russians, that you've got to be tough and intimidate them. That won't work in my opinion."

Hammer has been accused of exaggerating his own importance in world affairs and using that cultivated image to further his company's deals. Certainly Hammer goes to great lengths to foster the impression that he is on intimate terms with the world's most powerful leaders, and he tends to use the word "friend" rather loosely in describing his relationships with well-known people. In an article about Hammer's latest glossy biography, *The World of Armand Hammer,* Michael Kinsley, the editor of the *New Republic,* wrote: "Hammer's whole 'world,' in fact, seems to be one of cynical mutual exploitation. He is a man who measures his self-worth by the size of his airplane, who is attracted to people solely because they are rich or powerful or famous, and who is unaware or indifferent that his so-called 'friends' are attracted to him for the same reason."

Yet Hammer's philanthropic endeavors hint at a genuinely more complex "world" than mere ego gratification. "I have two dreams," he announced in 1985, "peace between East and West and a cure for cancer." In April 1970 he gave five million dollars to "my friend Jonas Salk" to establish a cancer biology research center at the Salk Institute in San Diego. In December 1981 Hammer announced that he would give a million dollars to whomever discovered a cure for cancer "similar to that discovered by Dr. Jonas Salk with the polio vaccine." In 1982 he pledged to give one hundred thousand dollars each year to the scientist who had done the most that year to further efforts to find such a cure. In May 1986, he personally arranged and paid for Dr. Robert P. Gale and other American physicians to travel to Moscow and perform bone marrow transplant surgery on victims of the Chernobyl nuclear power plant disaster.

His chairmanship of President Reagan's Cancer Advisory Panel is only one of dozens of such positions that he holds with private and governmental organizations, ranging from the National Symphony to the Planned Parenthood Association to the Georgetown Center for Strategic and International Studies. One of his pet projects is the American branch of United World Colleges, based in New Mexico, where several hundred young people come from more than fifty countries to live and learn in an environment that stresses cultural diversity and international harmony. In November 1985 Hammer threw a charity ball in Palm Beach, Florida, to raise money for the United World Colleges; the star attractions were Prince Charles, who is the international president of United World Colleges, and Princess Diana. The ball got off to a rocky start; many arrangements were bungled by the Occidental staff, and miffed local society people complained that Hammer was a "known sympathizer of Communist causes" and refused to attend. Hammer, nonplussed, paid an unidentified Palm Beach charity seventy-five thousand dollars to get his ball permit and raised four million dollars in one evening.

Although he seldom speaks about it, it is also known that since the early 1970s Hammer has privately lobbied Soviet leaders on the behalf of Soviet Jews. "I tried to help whenever I could," is all he will say. In 1978 Hammer began initiating and funding an annual "Armand Hammer Conference on Peace and Human Rights—Human Rights and Peace," which attracts delegates from more than thirty countries. "It's the only conference of its kind where the Soviet Union sends delegates from all the socialist countries," says Hammer proudly. "They sit there with delegates from the United States, France, and Germany, and they have to hear criticism."

Hammer is sometimes criticized in the business community for letting his fondness for flashy deals take priority over cautious and prudent management. A case in point might be his recent coal-mine deal with China. In 1979 Deng Xiaoping, Communist Party Vice Chairman of the People's Republic of China, met Hammer at a Houston barbecue while making a brief US tour. According to *Time* magazine, Deng reportedly said: "No introduction is necessary. We know Dr. Hammer as the American who helped Lenin. Why don't you come to China and help us as well?" Hammer said he would love to, but his advanced age made it imperative that he travel in the comfort of his own jet, and he understood that private jets were not permitted to land in China. Deng replied: "It can be arranged. You send me a cable when you are ready to come."

Two months later, Hammer was chatting with Chinese leaders in Peking, and in May 1984 he signed a $580 million agreement to develop one of the largest open-pit coal mines in the world in the Shanxi province some three hundred miles west of Peking. At peak production, the mine will produce fifteen million tons of coal a year, 70 percent of which will be exported to Japan, Korea, and other Far Eastern countries. *Time* called it "the largest Sino-US deal yet," but it nearly collapsed several times during the four years of negotiations, and was rumored to have been saved by the personal intervention of Deng Xiaoping. "I never doubted it would happen as long as Deng was behind me," gloated Hammer after the deal was finalized. Others were less impressed. In late 1984 *Fortune* magazine called the Chinese venture "chancy" in view of the fickle world price of coal.

The most likely and consistent explanation for why Hammer has spent sixty years promoting Soviet-American trade is that he likes to make money. Yet his only significant Soviet deal to reach the implementation stage since the 1920s—the fertilizer swap—has not been that lucrative. Hammer guessed wrong in 1973 about future world phosphate prices, and now has to deliver superphosphoric acid to the Soviet Union at a market price 40 percent lower than he expected. Occidental is rumored to have sunk $90 million into the deal; while Hammer insists that it has consistently shown a profit, other sources say that Occidental lost thirty million dollars from 1981 to 1983 on the barter, and in 1984 *Fortune* magazine referred to it as "a money loser."

"Business is business," begins Hammer's 1932 book, "but Russia is romance." Some of his aides suggest that he is drawn to the Soviet Union by sentimental nostalgia, others that he has never quite given up hope of repeating his thrilling successes of the 1920s. Still other observers point out that he obviously has fun playing the role of world statesman, and a few even credit him with altruistic motives. All of these explanations seem more plausible than the inevitable grumbling in some circles that Hammer is a Soviet henchman. "Does Hammer merely take advantage of his contacts with the Russians to advance his business interests? Or does Hammer take advantage of his business contacts to serve Moscow's interests?" asks Edward Jay Epstein in the *New York Times*. A third question might be: "Does Hammer, by advancing his business interests, also serve the interests of the United States, the Soviet Union, and the rest of the world?"

Hammer's "what's-good-for-Occidental-is-good-for-the-world" philosophy sets him apart from other citizen diplomats whose primary motivation is creating peace. Yet his accomplishments—his steadfast advocacy of East-West trade, his art exchanges, his aid to Chernobyl victims, and his role as a personal liaison between world leaders—have merit independent of his motivations. Historians may someday conclude that Hammer has done the right things in Soviet-American relations for the wrong reasons. But his legacy of "right things" may remain long after the reasons have faded.

Perhaps the most revealing decoration in Hammer's sixteenth-floor Los Angeles office is a plaque with a quote from Abraham Lincoln. "If I were to try to read, much less answer, all the attacks made on me, this shop might as well be closed for any other business. I do the very best I can; and I mean to keep doing so until the end. If the end brings me out all right, what is said against me won't amount to anything. If the end brings me out wrong, ten angels swearing I was right would make no difference."

❖❖❖

CHAPTER EIGHT

RIDING IN TANDEM:
CHRISTOPHER SENIE

When his train rolled into Moscow on the morning of July 4, 1983, Christopher Senie had a lot on his mind. The long, restless ride from Finland had given him too much time to think. What if the Soviets didn't meet them at the station? What if the Soviets were insulted because his Americans were not top-quality athletes? What if someone got injured? What if the visas didn't come through? What if . . .?

It didn't help that what they were attempting to do was, at first glance, a little ridiculous. What would it really mean if a group of American, Soviet, and Scandinavian riders bicycled all the way from Moscow to Washington, DC? Would it change anything? Would the world care?

For the next five weeks they were riding into the unknown. Never before had Western bicyclists toured so extensively in the Soviet Union. Never before had Soviet bicyclists toured in the United States. It was a long, grueling, mysterious road before them, a road no one had yet taken. The miles—twelve hundred of them—stretched to the imagination's limit and beyond. And all of the Americans, it seemed, were depending on him.

What if . . . "The train just stopped all of a sudden, and I heard this voice on the loudspeaker calling out my name," remembers Senie. "I didn't have my shoes on, it was raining, there was all this commotion. Then I saw all these beautiful Russian women ready to give us flowers, and a huge sign that must have been fifty feet tall saying, 'Welcome to Bike for Peace 1983' in English and Russian. And the next thing I know I have a bouquet of roses in my arms and the head of the Soviet Peace Committee is shaking my hand and wishing me Happy Independence Day."

According to Russian folklore, rain during arrivals and departures of great significance is a sign of good luck. If so, then the thirty-two participants in Bike for Peace '83 were blessed more times than they care to remember. It was raining when the train carrying the American and Scandinavian riders arrived in Moscow. It was raining two days later, when it was time to board their bikes. To the bikers, bogged down in wet ponchos, Washington, DC, seemed very far away.

A crowd of several hundred Muscovites huddled under umbrellas at the headquarters of the Soviet Peace Committee with soggy banners of encouragement. Christopher Senie, who had been tending to last-minute administrative details at the American embassy all morning, had jumped into a taxi and arrived at the starting point, just in time to be buttonholed for a speech. Soon the first bikers escaped from the crowd and were out of sight. Bike for Peace '83 was under way, and so far as Christopher Senie was concerned, there was only one detail still unresolved: his own bicycle was nowhere to be found.

Sudden visions of headlines—"American Leader, Bikeless, Left Behind in Moscow" appeared with startling clarity in his mind. Panicked and breathless, Senie ran to his partner Tore Naerland, the Norwegian originator and primary organizer of Bike for Peace, who was just about to ride away. Little did Senie know that Naerland had arrived in Moscow with a plot in mind. Like Christopher Senie, Tore Naerland is thirty-one years old and a deep believer in the power of long-distance bicycle rides to teach both participants and bystanders the value of cooperation. Unlike Senie, Naerland is 90 percent blind and thus does all of his bicycling from the back seat of a tandem. Tore Naerland had been thinking about what a powerful living symbol it would be to have an American and a Soviet team up on a tandem for the duration of Bike for Peace 1983.

"Take the tandem! Take the tandem!" Senie heard Naerland yell as he rode out of sight on his own tandem.

Mystified, Senie searched the group's supply bus and found a white Peugeot tandem bicycle. He had just swung a leg over it and was about to ride away when he heard a voice in the crowd call out, "Christopher! Christopher!" A young, muscular Russian ran up to him, introduced himself as Vladimir, and climbed on the back seat. It was soon apparent that Vladimir spoke no English and Senie spoke no Russian. It was also soon apparent, when it came time to shift gears, that Senie had never before ridden a tandem. This embarrassed him then; it embarrassed him still more when he found out that his tandem partner was Vladimir Semenets, 1972 Olympic gold medalist in the tandem sprint.

Two days later, it had stopped raining as they approached Kalinin, a small city north of Moscow. As the number of houses by the road increased, so did the number of people who came running from their gardens, fields, and homes to wave at the colorful flock of riders in their red (USSR), white (Scandinavia) and green (USA) Bike for Peace T-shirts. An enthusiastic crowd of nearly three thousand people awaited them in a parking lot near the city center.

The bikers walked through the door of a large sports complex and "three thousand more people stood up and started applauding. The crowd outside was just the crowd that couldn't get inside," recalls Senie. A huge banner with a white outline of a dove hung on the back wall. Senie took the microphone and began explaining why Semenets had begun riding in the front seat by pointing to Semenets's sturdy legs and comparing them to his own skinny ones. "Today while riding on the tandem, I leaned back, closed my eyes, and listened," he told the crowd. "I heard the wheels coming off the pavement, and the gears changing, and the voices shouting back and forth in many languages. Pretty soon I noticed the Americans are shouting *vnimanie* instead of 'attention' when they see a hole in the road, and the Soviets are shouting 'attention' instead of *vnimanie*. I listened very carefully, and I heard a very exciting sound—the sound of peace. Today it was louder than it was yesterday, and by the time we get to Washington it's going to be loud enough to be heard by hundreds of thousands of people."

Christopher Senie thinks of Bike for Peace as a performance, an event capable of provoking the same kind of emotional response that good theater can provoke. "When you go to see a play, you go with a certain willingness to believe in the actors, and to let them bewitch you a little and work their magic on you. And sometimes you come away from the theater with tears in your eyes and a lump in your throat, because that play has *done* something to you. That's the kind of emotional event we're trying to trigger."

Thus it doesn't faze Senie to hear Bike for Peace '83 described as "merely symbolic." He would only quarrel with the word "merely," for he is a believer in the power of symbolism. "Bike for Peace may have registered a tiny, unmeasurable impact on the emotions of an awful lot of people, who might go through the thought process: 'Well gosh, to ride twelve hundred miles together must have been difficult, I can't ride over to George's house without getting tired, how the heck did they do that, they speak different languages, they must've gotten to be pretty good friends, well, maybe it is possible to be friends with the Soviets.' And that little accomplishment is what Bike for Peace is all about."

At first glance, Christopher Senie could be fairly described as a Yuppie. Tall, rangy, with disorganized curly brown hair and emphatic eyebrows, he appears as comfortable wearing a buttondown shirt and tie as he does a T-shirt and cycling shorts. For four years he has practiced law with the firm of Senie, Stock, and LaChance in Westport, Connecticut, where he is now a junior partner specializing in criminal drug and alcohol cases and civil litigation. His office, at first, appears unremarkable with its shiny broad desk, boxes of files, and diplomas on the wall. Gradually, though, as he begins to talk about Bike for Peace, other features of his office, before unobtrusive, become noticeable, such as the numerous photographs of Soviet children and bicycle riders, the large framed felt appliqué reading "We Are the Impossible Dream," and the white Peugeot tandem bicycle parked along the back wall.

Senie's office is on the top floor of a three-story brick building called "The Marketplace," located on Main Street not far from the library, the town bank, the YMCA, and the cinema. Westport, Connecticut, is the kind of town real-estate agents describe as a good place to raise a family, and "The Marketplace" is a family affair. His father Alan Senie (a senior partner) and sister Kathryn also practice law with Senie, Stock, and LaChance. Downstairs, his mother Susan Senie runs a real-estate business.

Also downstairs, tucked in a corner of a corporate art gallery, is the office of Teamworks, Inc., the nonprofit corporation that Senie created to run the American portion of Bike for Peace '83. The office is not, at the moment, prepossessing, consisting as it does of a couple of file cabinets, a desk, and a bulletin board. But the Teamworks, Inc. brochure exudes confidence and energy. The word "Teamworks" itself has become a tandem bicycle; the "A" and the "O" have sprockets and pedals. Teamworks, Inc., according to the brochure, is "aimed at improving international, intercultural, and intercommunity relations . . . by sponsoring challenging 'teamwork' projects, which bring people of different backgrounds and perspectives together to work toward shared goals." Among the projects listed are an annual Soviet-American Bike for Peace, an "international construction company" of students from East and West, and "The New Century Musical," a touring show designed to "serve as a dramatic and colorful kickoff to the final fifteen years of this century."

Succinctly stated over the background of a photograph of smiling bikers giving a circular group massage is the essence of the Teamworks philosophy:

GOAL	Improved working relations	International, intercultural, intercommunity
OBJECTIVE	Increased understanding	Between people of different backgrounds, perspectives
APPROACH	Inspiration	Emotional appeal as opposed to political pressure
METHOD	Teamwork projects	Symbolic side-by-side work toward shared goals
TOOL	Recordings/communications	Publications of books, films, slide shows
TARGET	General public	Through distribution of publications
THEME	Upcoming turn of the century	Artificial time frame within which to improve relations

This is Christopher Senie's nutshell formula for breaking down prejudice. For much of his life, he has been applying these techniques to dissolving racial prejudices in his own community. Bike for Peace was his first attempt at applying this method to ameliorating what, in his view, is a similar case of blind, systemic prejudice between Americans and Soviets. In his race relations work, Senie learned the value of the aphorism: "You can't reason prejudice out of a person because it didn't get in that way." He learned that rational arguments have little effect on gut-level bigotry and fear. But he also learned that seemingly miraculous shifts of perception and attitude can be achieved when the two groups of people are brought face to face in situations that allow them to work and play together.

Senie believes that his Teamworks formula is applicable to any situation where widespread prejudice dominates the relationship between groups of people, and he has dreams of eventually trying it on other schisms (young/old, rich/poor). But for now, he says, the most serious prejudice he encounters as he walks down Main Street is the pervasive American prejudice against the Soviet people. "Any project that brings Soviet and American people together to meet one another is doing something good," he maintains, "whether it's bike trips, or musical performances, or exchanges where people meet their professional counterparts. It doesn't even matter much what topics are on the agenda. What matters is that people's preconceived ideas about one another are eroding; the ignorance, which supplies the prejudice, is reducing."

In the front yard of his parents' home on the shores of the Saugatuck Bay is a small blue-hooded sailboat, in the back a private dock. The four Senie children, who all live in the Westport area, still gather for family dinner every Sunday. Christopher Senie credits his parents with imbuing him with an awareness of the existence of prejudice and injustice in the world. "When I was ten we had the typical conversation at the dinner table—'eat your brussels sprouts because there are children starving,' " remembers Senie. In most families, this would have been simply rhetoric, but in the Senie family, it led to becoming a foster family to a child in Venezuela. Soon a black child about Christopher's age from the Bedford-Stuyvesant ghetto began spending summers with the Senies. When Senie was fifteen he and his family joined a local battle to bring black children into Westport's all-white schools; Senie made one of his first speeches to the local Board of Education.

During his senior year in high school Senie invented a program that brought Westport seniors and juniors into the hallways of Bridgeport elementary schools to tutor black children in reading, writing, and math skills. The program was so successful that school administrators continued it after Senie graduated. For three summers, he and other members of his family volunteered as counselors at a multiracial community day camp. The fourth summer he organized a camp program for older children that included numerous bicycle trips. At the end of that summer, a fellow counselor gave him a mug that is still his favorite; painted on it are the words "Follow your heart, wherever it takes you," and a homely, serviceable bicycle.

Senie went on to study education at Hampshire College, where he dreamed of organizing a multiracial teenage bicycle trip across the United States called the "Magic Circle Summer." In June 1975 Senie and five other young people drove a used van seventy-two hours to Seattle, Washington, sold it for about what they paid for it, and started pedalling east. They rode more than three thousand miles in ten weeks. The cross-country journey taught Senie "that you can take almost any group of people from different backgrounds and perspectives, give them maps, put them on bicycles, and make it a success."

After graduation, Senie worked for two years as program director for the Youth Adult Council in Westport. He organized canoe races, drama workshops, musical productions, concerts, a youth-center construction project, and, of course, bicycle trips for teenagers in the community.

The job allowed him to hone his ideas about how to bridge barriers between groups of people. Teamworks, Inc., he admits, is really a grander, more personal version of the Youth Adult Council, aimed at bringing together estranged nations instead of estranged teenagers.

Senie claims he "had no interest whatsoever" in the Soviet Union until January 1981, the beginning of his last semester of law school at the University of Bridgeport, when he took a course in Soviet law because it happened to fit his schedule. "I became fascinated after the second or third class, when I realized I knew *nothing* about the Soviet Union—I didn't even know they *had* a legal system." At the end of the course his professor announced that he was organizing an August 1982 trip of American lawyers and judges to meet their Soviet counterparts. Senie was the first to sign up. "At that time it was news to me that it was even possible to *go* to the Soviet Union."

Senie decided to make a film or videotape on the Soviet legal system, and in March 1982, five months before his trip, he attended a meeting near Boston of a group called American-Soviet Cultural Exchange group to ask for help. There he heard someone speak about an unsuccessful citizen diplomacy project called Tennis for Peace. Senie drove home thinking about bicycles instead of lawyers. Visions of American and Soviet bikers riding together danced in his head. "I knew this was just a magic idea," he says, "and that this kind of inspirational, emotional event wasn't going to take any warheads off of any missiles right away, but would be fun and exciting and have that emotional appeal."

Senie approached the Citizen Exchange Council (CEC), the New York-based group sponsoring the lawyers' trip, with a proposal for a dozen Americans and Soviets to spend one summer cycling through the Soviet Union and one summer cycling through the United States. The CEC agreed to sponsor the trip if he could obtain permission from the Soviets. In August 1982, during the lawyers' trip to the Soviet Union, Senie brought along a zoom-lens camera and a tape recorder for his videotape on the legal system ("I have the honor of having been kicked out of two Soviet courtrooms," he laughs) and a proposal for what he then called "Bike Ride for Peace." In Moscow he met with officials of the KMO, the Soviet Committee on Youth Organizations, and "they all said it would be a marvelous project," recalls Senie. "But then I never heard from them again. I kept writing and writing and I was obviously getting nowhere." Still, he was convinced it was a sound idea and only a matter of time before he could pull it off.

Then in March 1983 Howard Frazier, director of a Connecticut-based group called Promoting Enduring Peace, told him that three young Norwegians had organized a very similar project, called Bike for Peace, and had already obtained Soviet permission for American, Scandinavian, and Soviet cyclists to ride from Moscow across Scandinavia to Oslo, and fly from there to the United States. The Norwegians were coming to the United States the following week to arrange the American leg. Frazier invited Senie to meet them at a press conference in New Haven.

On a wall in Senie's office is a photograph of a smiling blond man with a handlebar mustache, a blond woman with a baby in her arms, a tall young man with unruly hair, and Senie, all standing behind a tandem bicycle. Tore Naerland's numerous long-distance bike trips, including one across the United States and several to publicize rights for the disabled, have earned him the nickname "The Biking Viking." In 1982 Tore and his wife Bjoerg had organized a Bike for Peace trip from Oslo to Bucharest, Rumania. While on that ride they dreamed of an even more spectacular Bike for Peace which would connect Moscow and Washington, DC. After a flurried exchange of letters and proposals, Tore Naerland and Andrew Kroglund, an Oslo University student, went to Moscow in January 1983 and persuaded the Soviet Peace Committee and the Soviet Sports Committee to cosponsor the event.

Christopher Senie had anticipated many problems with his Bike Ride for Peace idea, but never that someone else would think of it first. "I was really, honestly crushed," he says. "All my enthusiasm was gone and I decided to abandon my project." He went to the press conference in New Haven and watched gloomily as the American press swarmed around the Norwegians and their novel idea. Afterwards he introduced himself to Naerland and Kroglund, and even though he had told himself that he was just going to wish them good luck and walk away, he couldn't quite bring himself to leave the Norwegians' side. He drove them to New York, where at a meeting "I criticized their program as being too big and too political. They wanted to have two hundred people riding and big mass rallies and banners everywhere. I kept saying, why dilute the impact of the event itself with slogans that will alienate various people and be abused by others? I also told them they were way behind schedule. What are you doing here fifteen weeks before you start riding? My proposal had been for a whole year later, in 1984. And we had quite a discussion, with raised voices."

He pauses. "I think it was my hurt coming out. I was hung up on the idea of being the founder of Bike for Peace. At this point, I was still thinking, well, I'm giving them the benefit of my perceptions, but

I'm not going to have any part of it." He couldn't quite bring himself to tell that to the Norwegians, however, who hinted that perhaps he could organize the American portion of their trip. They agreed to meet with Senie again before returning to Oslo.

"It was really my family who sat me down and said look, Chris, stop sulking," he says. His mother Susan remembers a long discussion "where we agreed that the fact two people had the same idea at the same time must mean it's a darn good idea and the time is right." Senie realized that the Norwegians badly needed his experience and energy to organize the American segment, and that by becoming their American coordinator, "I would have a hand in making the first Bike for Peace happen, and still enjoy this ego-boosting thing of being some kind of trailblazer. But that was one of the most maturing experiences in my life, having to accept being number two, and learning that it's okay to be number two, you can still do what's important to you."

Senie arrived at Kennedy Airport at 5 P.M. on March 16, 1983, only a few hours before Naerland and Kroglund were to board their plane. The Norwegians looked worn out: Naerland's mustache appeared to droop, and Kroglund's face showed the effects of a week of driving in American traffic. But their enthusiasm was undampened, and they began pulling out folders and enumerating contacts in Baltimore and Philadelphia before pausing, almost as an afterthought, to ask Senie to be the American coordinator. Senie said yes. "There we were, all of us already exhausted, with a glass of wine in our hands," remembers Senie, "toasting Bike for Peace and feeling as though our lives were about to take on a new and very important dimension."

Two days later, Senie went to the Westport Bank and Trust Company and borrowed thirty-two thousand dollars. He formed a nonprofit group called Bike for Peace, Inc., applied for tax-exempt status, set up an office in "The Marketplace," arranged for secretarial, phone answering, and telex services, printed stationery, obtained insurance, and began assembling a staff. An old friend between jobs, Kim O'Neill, became his executive director. David Emerson, a student from Maine with extensive long-distance bicycling experience, was in charge of arranging routing and logistics for the leg between New York and Washington, DC. Senie's younger sister, Allyson, who had just graduated from Ithaca College with a degree in political science, moved to Washington, DC, and began drumming up congressional support for Bike for Peace, using as a base the office of a local congressman, Bruce Morrison.

Senie began working sixteen-hour days to fit in his full-time law practice with Bike for Peace. "Things just started happening," he says. "We started to have weekly staff meetings and volunteers started dropping by. It resembled what I imagine a congressional campaign to be like. A little bit on the shoestring, but really quite effective." Soon his whole family was drawn in: his brother Matthew, who ran a nearby restaurant, became a press spokesperson; his sister Kathryn and mother Susan began fund-raising to pay for overhead and staff salaries (riders were expected to pay for their travel, food, and accommodations) by designing a brochure asking for sponsors to contribute a "penny a mile." Using the in-house phones for Congressional offices, Allyson Senie was able to generate more than thirty letters from Congressmen, support that proved invaluable when it came to persuading the US State Department, which has a history of looking askance at letting Soviets into the US for anything resembling a peace demonstration, to grant entry visas to the Soviet cyclists.

Senie knew that his concept of Bike for Peace differed slightly from the Norwegians' and the Soviets'. On a brief trip to Moscow and Oslo in May 1983, Senie signed a protocol with the Norwegians, identical to one that the Soviets had signed, which laid out the principles of Bike for Peace and dedicated the ride to the United Nations' World Disarmament Campaign. Included in the protocol were four trip slogans:

- "Yes to Freeze!"
- "No to Nuclear Weapons in the East and West, North and South!"
- "Let None Be the First to Use Nuclear Weapons!"
- "Yes to Disarmament and Peace!"

Senie feared that these slogans might give Bike for Peace too leftist an image for mainstream American tastes. But he knew that he had to sign the protocol to participate, and he figured that as the American coordinator he would have opportunities to tone down the political aspects of the trip.

For example, when the American press asked what Bike for Peace was trying to accomplish, Senie avoided talking about nuclear weapons and instead gave a "sore muscles and flat tires rap," emphasizing the trip's symbolism. "We did a reverse PR campaign in this country to draw attention away from those slogans. And the local press basically gave the Senie family the benefit of the doubt on this one," he says. "It all happened so fast—before anyone had really figured out that we were actually cooperating with the Soviet government, and started asking too many questions, it was all over."

Senie knew that many who did realize that the Soviet government was not only sanctioning but participating in Bike for Peace would instantly consider it a propaganda ploy. There's no question, he says, that the Soviets enthusiastically supported Bike for Peace. The Soviet Peace Committee, an ostensibly private organization supported by voluntary donations that nonetheless has close and obvious ties to the Soviet government, had sponsored a highly successful 1982 Women's Peace March from Stockholm to Minsk, and they were looking for a similar project for 1983. Bike for Peace fitted the bill.

Senie concedes that the Soviets endorsed Bike for Peace to "help build their image at home and abroad as a government that wants peace. We were used by the Soviet government to some extent." What he does not accept is that this invalidates the event's significance. "If you want to make things happen, if you want to take a step forward, sometimes you have to be willing to be used. Sure, it would be purer to have four Americans and four Soviets bicycling together in the Soviet Union without either government knowing about it. But that's *impossible*. You have to be willing to play by some rules, to become partners *with* them, to let them help you shape it. And that's not such a frightening thing."

Senie also believes that the Soviet desire to avoid war goes much deeper than any propaganda line. In Moscow, before the bikers began riding, they were taken to a formal room in the Kremlin to meet Bahken Sarkisov, Deputy Chairman of the Presidium of the Supreme Soviet. All of the riders were a little nervous about this encounter with Soviet officialdom; Senie remembers feeling particularly self-conscious "because I had made a pact with myself not to wear a tie for seven weeks and had not even brought one along." Then the doors opened and this "very warm fellow" with dark bushy eyebrows and gray hair appeared. Naerland presented him with a Bike for Peace flag and T-shirt, and Sarkisov joked that he would give the T-shirt to his grandson but keep the flag for himself. "He gave a rather standard speech about peace," says Senie, "but it was *sincere*, and here's where I challenge critics who say we were just dupes of the Soviet government. There was warmth and genuineness in him, and it wasn't, 'Oh, boy, these people are going to help us trick the Americans,' but rather: 'This is really important.' You have to be there to know how sincere it is."

The American delegation was made up of people who "just surfaced naturally" when they heard about Bike for Peace by reading the newspaper or by word of mouth. Five of the nine Americans came from the Westport area; others came from Pennsylvania, New Hampshire, and Vermont. Senie did not bother to screen applicants for their biking skills and took people mostly on the basis of enthusiasm, trusting that only experienced bikers would volunteer.

Only after the Americans arrived in Oslo on June 26 and went out with the Scandinavian delegation for a sixty-mile "practice ride" did Senie realize how green his Americans were. One had only a dim notion of how to shift gears. Few could keep up with the Scandinavian delegation, which included seven other Norwegians besides Naerland and Kroglund, one Swede, and one Finn. (Bjoerg Naerland was not among them; on May 23, 1983, the Naerlands' first child, Fred Christoffer, was born. Fred's first name means "peace" in Norwegian and his middle name was chosen in honor of Christopher Senie.) Senie began wondering how they would survive riding fifty-five miles a day for twenty-four days out of the next month, and how the Soviets would react to such amateurism.

All of the riders were introduced at a Soviet press conference soon after their arrival in Moscow. Senie had expected the Soviet delegation to consist of top-notch athletes, but he was not prepared for "Olympic champion followed by national champion followed by this guy who was the first to climb Mt. Everest, and so on," says Senie. "And here I had to get up there and say, well, here's a bartender from Norwalk." Publicly, he did his best to make it sound as if all his Americans were superior bikers. Privately, he took the Soviet leaders aside and confessed that he had some novices along. To his surprise, the Soviets told him not to worry about it.

In retrospect, says Senie, the greenness of the American group was a blessing. "If we'd had better riders it would have been harder to establish that this was not a competition," he says. "But we took ourselves out of any competition right away—it was all we could do to just keep up. The Soviets never tried to make fun of us, though, and they couldn't have cared less that we didn't give them a good run for their money athletically." Most of the Soviets worked in sports-related jobs and many were professional athletes. Among them were fifty-nine-year-old Dr. Yuri Filimonov, a physician in sports medicine from Astrakhan; Lydia Chislova, a sports commissioner and one of two women Soviet riders; and nineteen-year-old Yevgeny Zamulin, a professional bicycle racer and the only Soviet rider not married. Two officials of the Soviet Peace Committee, Vladimir Kokashvili and Eugene Oskolsky, led the Soviet delegation and rode in a car instead of on bicycles.

It was soon clear that the Soviet Peace Committee had whole-heartedly thrown itself into Bike for Peace; the riders were astonished to discover that traffic had been stopped for them on a major highway leading out of Moscow. They were accompanied by a police escort, a "sag wagon" full of supplies and gear, a van with two capable Soviet mechanics at their beck and call, and several hundred additional Soviet riders, many of them children, who wanted to ride a portion of the trip with the thirty-two-member core group. Before they set off, the Soviet press had featured photographs and stories about Bike for Peace; many Soviet citizens thus knew their route and lined up to wait for them. Farm workers in baggy shirts, old women in blue headscarves, and children in rubber boots left their field work to gawk at the riders. In the towns, "people came running from their houses to wave and throw us flowers," says Senie. The bikers became adept at steering with one hand.

From the newspaper photographs, many Soviets recognized Allyson Senie, who has a distinct pearly smile, dark eyes and eyebrows, and curly brown hair. Often they chanted her name as the bikers whizzed past. "Allyson has a very wholesome, all-American face, and the Russian papers really picked up on her," says her brother. "I'm sure there will be a wave of Russian babies named Allyson." Allyson Senie has another explanation: "I was a center of attention because I was Christopher's sister. The family bond is really important in Russia and they really liked the fact that we were brother and sister."

The cyclists usually rode about twenty miles in the morning before a "technical stop." Sometimes refreshments were simply served from the back of the sag wagon; at other times Soviet women in white coats administered food and drink. At lunch there would invariably be a reception and speeches, often by the mayor of the town. Children were given time off from school or camp and appeared with balloons and hand-painted banners. Girls in white kneesocks and boys in blue blazers shyly asked for autographs and presented flowers. The bikers learned to travel with flowers tucked in their handlebars, in their shorts, wherever they could be fit. Often Senie used such breaks to add his own touch of theater by selecting a young boy or girl from the crowd and giving them a spin around the town square on the back of the tandem.

When they arrived at their destination, there would again be a reception, speeches, food, and sometimes entertainment. The town mayor would then sign the bikers' petition, which urged "the leading politicians of the greater powers to take the responsibility for the people of the world so that humanity, and the basis for all life on earth, will not be destroyed by nuclear war." The petition was written in three languages and carried in a *budstikka*, a gold-colored quiver with a shoulder strap that Norwegians once used to deliver important messages (it has a spike on one end so that the *budstikka* can be implanted in a wooden door).

Traditionally dressed Soviet women in jeweled headdresses offered the bikers bread and salt on embroidered cloths as a symbol of friendship. Then the bikers were treated to feasts on long wooden tables, concerts of balalaika music, and, once, a taste of rock 'n' roll. In Kalinin more than two hundred young singers and dancers performed a dramatic musical show written for the bikers that had an anti-nuclear-weapons theme.

At first the Westerners were suspicious of all this pageantry. But it was soon evident that the warmth and friendliness of the people greeting them were unmanufactured. Long after the official receptions ended, local people lingered to talk with the bikers and shower them with gifts of pins, flowers, and food. By the end of the trip the bikers' T-shirts were so laden with badges and pins of groups, towns, and schools that they resembled the back bumpers of well-traveled Winnebagos. Some Soviets who didn't have paper on hand asked the bikers to autograph their clothing. Frequently, they asked them to take a message back to their home countries that the Russian people want peace.

Although they were not exactly unchaperoned while riding, the cyclists were free to wander the villages and towns at night, and often were spontaneously invited into people's homes. The evening after their first day of riding, Allyson Senie and four other riders met a man on the street who became very agitated when he saw Allyson, pointing to her shirt and speaking rapid Russian. Finally she realized that he had given her a pin at a reception earlier that evening. The man gestured that he wanted to invite the bikers to his home. Although aware that he was a little drunk, the riders followed him for about half an hour until they arrived at the door of a tiny, rundown apartment. The man excused himself and left them in the hallway, where they heard a vigorous, incomprehensible dressing-down given by his mother—who was, says Allyson Senie, "furious that he should come home drunk at 10 P.M. with five strangers in tow." Then the door opened, they were welcomed in with smiles, and tea, wine, and children were brought out. The man was a musician, and the five riders all had a turn at attempting to play his trumpet before he gave a brief concert. "They just wanted to talk to us, even though none of them knew English," remembers Allyson Senie. "They couldn't believe that Americans were sitting in their home. We were there for hours."

While still in Moscow, all of the riders had stayed in one hotel, but at meals the Soviets had sat at one table while the Scandinavians and Americans clustered around another. "It was kind of segregated, and rather uncomfortable," recalls Allyson Senie. Riding together changed that quickly. Allyson, who had never before done any long-distance bicycle riding and who had not had much of a chance to train, remembers hitting the first hill outside Moscow and wondering what she was doing on a bicycle in the pouring rain, in the Soviet Union, trying to keep up with world-class athletes. "Then I just felt this hand on my back, and it was one of the Soviets *pushing* me to help get me up that hill." Allyson Senie wasn't the only one to get a helping hand that day, and from then on, the stronger riders habitually pushed the weaker riders up hills. It was never discussed, she says, but it was clear that the Soviets each adopted particular riders as their "buddies." "I'd say 90 percent of that awkward feeling at the beginning was gone after that first day, because we were touching each other, and pushing each other up hills, and saying 'thank you,' and we were smiling and sweating and cold together."

The only Soviet rider who spoke English was journalist Alexander Gigoryev, who, predictably, was much in demand on the road. Although all the Scandinavians spoke English, none of the Scandinavians or Americans spoke Russian. Says Christopher Senie, who is a great believer in learning languages and has been taking Russian ever since the trip: "In a way it was great we didn't know each other's languages. We were forced to find nonverbal ways of communicating. You'd see these great little conversations going on around the group, with people only half-understanding each other."

The cyclists often sang while riding, sometimes accompanied by tapes blaring from the black lead car (a favorite tape was a Beatles medley, which lacked, however, the song "Back in the USSR ") Yuri Filimonov, the oldest Soviet rider, took the lead in teaching the others Russian folksongs. Another favorite tape was the Bike for Peace theme song, written by American pop songwriters Tom O'Neill and Michael Terry, called "Riding for Peace:"

People together, on their way
Riding forever with something to say
Leaving a light in the hearts of the people behind.

Strangers behind got a glow in their eyes
Spreading the word as the riders go by.
Setting the stage for the dream that tomorrow will bring

The farther we go, the more we believe
Keeping up hope, we're riding for peace.

The song's driving beat may have helped keep the riders pedaling at least a few times when some of them could have been forgiven for wondering if the "riding forever" part was the most telling of all.

Allyson Senie soon taught the Soviets how to use her frisbee. Other games, ranging from cards to spin the bottle, kept the riders amused. At one rest stop, some of the local Soviet riders decided to show the group a game of circle tag "that was not taught in any language," says Senie. "They just physically moved people around until we caught on." Circular group massages became a popular between-riding activity, as did frequent group saunas.

Saunas were segregated by sex, but it didn't take long before the clothes barrier went the way of the language barrier. At a lunch stop on one particularly hot day, Allyson and Rannveig, one of the Norwegian women, threw off their clothes and went skinny-dipping in a nearby lake. "I thought, oh my God," says Senie, "but the next thing I knew everyone had their clothes off and was in the water." "It wasn't complete skinny-dipping, we had our underwear on," Allyson hastily adds. "But the funniest thing was seeing Vladimir and Eugene, the big Soviet bosses, out there in their little boxer shorts running into the water."

In the evening, the bikers often explored local bars and discotheques. Tired muscles were shaken out with enthusiastic dancing, and long conversations with local young people were initiated over vodka. Wrote Norwegian leader Andrew Kroglund about the encounters: "Forgotten are the last tough kilometers; forgotten are the swollen knees and the threatening cramps; forgotten are the minor disputes which always seem more important than they deserve to be. You sit there totally at ease letting your eyes glide from American to Russian to Scandinavian—and you feel the brotherhood of man pulsating in your veins; you feel you are a part of something important; you feel love."

Christopher Senie and Vladimir Semenets developed a particularly close friendship. "Even though it was in many ways a coincidence that Vladimir and I ended up on the tandem together," explains Senie, "it was interesting that we had very similar personalities—kind of reserved, kind of sensitive, but in our own way, tough. He can ride a bicycle up and down mountains all day to train for the Olympics, and I can keep working on a project like Bike for Peace for as long as it takes."

Semenets handled the steering and gearing, while Senie, in back, tried to contribute half of the muscle power. This prompted Semenets, "who had spent more time on a tandem than I had driving an automobile," to try to teach Senie that sheer might was not the only trick to successful tandem riding. "He used to turn around and motion with his hand saying 'Like a cat, like a cat'—which he learned how to say in English—to try to get me to lighten up on the pedals." It became a standard joke among the bikers that the world would be a much safer place if super-power leaders would have a go at riding a tandem. Western newspaper cartoonists picked up on the idea and sketched tandem bicycles with two empty seats marked: "Reserved for Ronald Reagan and Yuri Andropov." The first rule of riding a tandem, says Senie, is that if you don't work together, you crash.

The hours spent staring at Semenet's back were, oddly enough, much-needed times of rest for Senie. While riding, he could close his eyes and try to relax; as soon as he dismounted from the bicycle, all of his responsibilities as the leader of the American delegation would reappear. The five leaders—Tore Naerland, Andrew Kroglund, Vladimir Kokashvili, Eugene Oskolsky, and Senie—met several times daily to handle all of the decisions that arose during the trip. "We used to joke that the Norwegians had the only democracy," says Senie. "The Norwegians would always run back to their delegation and put everything to a vote, and the Soviets seemed to want to make it look like their delegation was a democracy. But I came right out and said, 'This is a dictatorship. I'm running the American delegation.' " Control had its price, though: Senie, who had been working double-time for fifteen weeks before the ride began, became more and more rundown during the trip, until "by the time we got to New York I was running on one out of eight cylinders."

After arriving at their destination, the first thought of the Soviet leaders, who had spent a sedentary day riding in the lead car, would be to call a meeting. Senie's first thought would be to lie down on a patch of grass and catch his breath. "For months after the trip I couldn't get off my bicycle without looking around and sort of cringing, thinking

I'd hear someone scream out, 'Christopher Senie! Christopher Senie!' "
Kokashvili and Oskolsky were not oblivious to Senie's exhaustion, however: in the Russian town of Kresttsy, where all the bikers were treated
to a sauna, the Soviet leaders reserved the hottest and most relaxing
seat for the American leader. In this particular sauna, tradition had it
that beating each other with small leafy birch branches added to the
sauna's effectiveness. "Here we are, grown men, stark naked, and acting
like little kids," remembers Senie, "running in and out of this sauna
throwing cold water on each other and hitting each other with these
birch leaves for an hour and a half."

At other times, the Soviets leaders did not seem fully aware of the
bikers' need to relax and recuperate after a long day's ride. When they
arrived in Leningrad, the bikers were immediately taken to the solemn
memorial commemorating the victims of the nine-hundred-day siege of
Leningrad during World War II. Some of the Americans and Norwegians,
not understanding the memorial's significance, kept their bike helmets
on, took their shoes off, whispered, giggled, and acted in other ways
the Soviets considered disrespectful. Later, the Americans and Norwegians apologized for their behavior; the Soviets agreed to give more
advance warning next time; and matters were additionally amended when
all of the bikers participated in a solemn wreath-laying ceremony at
another World War II memorial in Leningrad.

"I underestimated the pressure of this trip," says Senie. "It's one
thing to ride a long way and then get off your bike and go lie down in
a park, and it's another to have to be gregarious, be social, give autographs, make speeches, and respond to these demanding and enthusiastic crowds." One night one of the American women, exhausted and
homesick, started to cry and said it was because she had not had a Coke
for more than a week. "Vladimir Kokashvili and Eugene Oskolsky got
into a taxi with her and went racing around Leningrad trying to find her
a Pepsi," recalls Senie (Pepsi is manufactured in the Soviet Union). The
next day, at the morning technical stop, there were hundreds of bottles
of Pepsi waiting for them on long tables. "Word had gotten out—the
Americans want Pepsi—and it just appeared," he chuckled.

The Soviets also at times found the ride stressful. At the border
between Finland and the Soviet Union, where it was raining (their Russian good luck was holding), the Soviets nervously clustered around their
leaders as they tried to fill out the Finnish customs forms. Their uneasiness, says Senie, was exacerbated by the "somewhat overzealous ex-
clamations" of a few Scandinavians and Americans of how glad they

were to be back in the West. "I remember Allyson and I both noticing that the Soviets seemed a little intimidated, and mentioning to each other that we should take special care of them for a few days. It's easy to underestimate the fears that a Soviet might have about crossing the border and leaving the protection of the home country."

The biggest strain on the riders was caused by the US State Department. Vladimir Semenets told a crowd of nearly ten thousand people in his hometown of Leningrad: "If Christopher and I are able to ride our tandems all the way to Washington, DC, that victory will mean more to me than winning the gold medal." But it then appeared unlikely that the US State Department would grant entry visas to the Soviet riders. During the spring, before the trip, Senie had traveled to Washington, DC, to meet with State Department officials; he had received assurances that Bike for Peace should pose no visa problems and that the Soviets should apply for visas through normal channels. But when the Americans left for Oslo in June, the US entry visas for the Soviets had yet to be granted. Senie made several last-minute phone calls in the United States and was told that he could pick the visas up at the American embassy in Moscow. When he arrived in Moscow, he was told they were still being processed. No reason was given for the delay. Two days later, when the bikers began riding, the visas had still not been issued. Back in the United States, Senie's father began calling the State Department several times a day. "I don't know whether this was a facetious remark or what," says Alan Senie, "but at one point someone in the State Department told me that they thought there were enough Russian tourist groups in the United States and we didn't need another one."

Upon arriving in Leningrad, Senie immediately went to the American consulate. Still no visas. "By this time we had all gotten so close that the Americans and the Scandinavians could not conceive of what it would be like to do the last leg without the Soviets," says Senie. The Soviet leaders refused to make plane reservations for their riders to fly between Oslo and New York until the visas had been cleared. Only two days before they were scheduled to leave the Soviet Union, Senie watched the rest of the riders set off from Leningrad while he and Vladimir Kokashvili stayed behind to wrestle with American officials one more time. To their amazement, the visas were at the consulate when they arrived that morning. No explanation was given for this sudden turnaround, either, although Senie noticed that the visas were marked "special exchange."

The nagging uncertainity of the visas put all of the leaders under stress and magnified minor disputes. One issue they repeatedly confronted was speech making. The riders took turns giving short speeches at the frequent receptions, and all had a chance to speak at least once during the trip. While Senie and the Soviets wanted to keep their message upbeat and nonpolitical, concentrating on the potential for friendship and cooperation that Bike for Peace symbolized, the Norwegians felt that speeches should be straightforward calls to action against the arms race. Senie feared, however, that politicizing the bikers' messages with explicit denouncements of Pershing IIs, cruise missiles, and SS-20s would divide the group over which superpower was more at fault. "The Americans and the Soviets had a very similar philosophy—we both had something to be defensive about," he says. "The Soviets wanted to be political, but in a different way from the Norwegians. The Soviets wanted to have slogans and speeches saying how bad nuclear weapons are, but not how bad Americans and Soviets are. Instead of the Norwegians being in the middle, as you might expect, lots of times it was the American and Soviet leaders arguing with this youthful Norwegian group."

After one of the Norwegians made what both Senie and the Soviets felt was too barbed a speech, the five leaders convened what they later called the "let's-not-point-fingers-at-anyone talk." When things became heated, says Senie, the language differences produced humorous results. Kroglund and Naerland spoke to each other in Norwegian, Kokashvili and Oskolsky in Russian, and Kroglund and Oskolsky in German—all while Senie waited for them to tell him what they had concluded. Bike for Peace, they eventually agreed, was a joint effort, and their speeches should concentrate on the perspectives that united them. As private individuals, they could disagree as much as they liked; as members of Bike for Peace, they had to speak as a team.

Only a few days after this talk, a young woman student greeting the riders at a reception in the Soviet city of Novgorod said in her speech, "We will not allow the Americans to use Europe as a launching pad for their missiles." Senie heard Eugene Oskolsky let out a groan. Immediately several of the Norwegians came over to Senie and lobbied him to rebut this comment. "They told me, 'You must tell her and this audience that the only reason the United States is using Europe as a launching pad is that the Soviets are using Eastern Europe as a launching pad for the SS-20s.' I said, 'No, I'm not going to mention it.' And they were *furious* at me," he says. "They told me, 'You can't let a comment like that go by.' " Senie told them he could, and that this was not the time or the place to get into a debate over Euromissiles.

When his turn came, Senie spoke about a girl he had met in Novgorod during the 1982 lawyers' tour, with whom he had shared his vision of Bike for Peace. She had given him a friendship ring that he had worn during the year. Waving a small velvet pouch in the air, he told the audience, "I have a friendship ring from the United States for this young girl, to whom I spoke about Bike for Peace when it was still only a dream. And less than a year later, we have ridden bicycles into her city. I want to find this young lady tonight and exchange this gift with her." The crowd roared its approval. (The girl was not in the crowd, but her friends told her about the speech; she later found Senie outside of his hotel and took him home to meet her family.) Senie did not mention the SS-20s, cruise missiles, or Pershing II missiles. "Even though something had been said that shouldn't have been," he recalls, "it was better to leave it unanswered. The Norwegians were very upset with me, although I think later they recognized that this was a good speech. It was typical of the different goals we all had, yet our goals were similar enough that it all held together."

One night in Finland, the bikers had a chance to share their thoughts about Bike for Peace with each other. A young Finnish woman had brought three dozen white candles and arranged them in a circle on the floor of the gymnasium where the bikers were to sleep that night. She lighted one candle, dripped some wax on the floor, positioned the candle, and softly explained that every person should tell the others what it was about Bike for Peace that held the greatest meaning for him or her. When a person wished to speak, he or she could come to the center, take a candle, and light it; that person's turn would be next.

The bikers hesitated at first. Then one of the Soviets took a candle and began speaking in Russian while someone else translated. Others followed, one by one, Americans, Norwegians, Finns, Soviets, filling the gymnasium with their stories and with the soft flickering tapers. "I tried to say something, but I didn't get too many words out before I just started to cry," remembers Senie.

But politics arose again when the riders arrived in Stockholm drowsy after an all-night ferry ride from Abo, Finland. Members of a Swedish peace group greeted them and told them that visits to both the American and Soviet embassies were scheduled for that day. The bikers rode to the American embassy, but found, instead of an official welcome, a small Swedish demonstration against the deployment of the Euromissiles. Senie and Alexander Grigoryev went up the steps and spoke with an American attaché who had come out to investigate the commotion. They were not invited inside and they did not ask the official to sign their petition. The group then rode to the Soviet embassy, where they were treated to a huge reception with elegant drinks and food. Swedish national television was there to record the inequity of the greetings, and Senie was infuriated by the none-too-subtle message he felt the Swedes had deliberately engineered: the Soviets want peace, the Americans, well. . . .

That night he called the head of the Swedish peace group, demanding an explanation. It turned out that the Swedes had not intended the receptions to be one-sided, and had written and called both embassies in advance. But there was no follow-up correspondence from the Americans, while the Soviet embassy officials invited the Swedish organizers to help plan the reception. The organizers thus knew that the Americans might not welcome Bike for Peace with open arms, but, in light of their general frustration with what often appears to be insensitivity on the part of American officials for European concerns about peace, they were not particularly worried about the American embassy's image. "It is peculiar in many ways that the Americans are seldom as PR-minded as are the Soviets," says Andrew Kroglund. "It is not that they do not need it these days in Europe!" "I'm not saying the US embassy staff wasn't partly at fault here," adds Senie. "The State Department has a philosophy about interaction with peace groups which is a little bit stiff in my opinion. But still, it bothered me a great deal."

A few days later, the issue flared again when one of the Soviet riders, Valery Chaplygan, told about five hundred people in Karlsskoga, Sweden: "Isn't it a shame that the only person who has refused to sign our petition is the American ambassador to Sweden." Senie walked away from the group and lay down on some grass, feeling that these fault-finding political references were fraying the unity of Bike for Peace. "I was watching the group become divided in ways the critics would love to see, just to prove we couldn't do it," he says. Several people, including Eugene Oskolsky, came over to apologize for Chaplygan's comment. Their Swedish hosts took them to lunch in a room hung with chandeliers and filled with tables set with fine silver and crystal. Senie approached Vladimir Kokashvili and said he had to address the group immediately. Would he translate for him? Of course, said Kokashvili, but he pointed out that the mayor of the town was present. Was it necessary to speak right then? Senie said yes.

"I made what I considered to be the most important speech of the whole trip," he says. "First I said that no one asked anyone at the

American embassy, much less the ambassador, to sign our petition. Then I said that if we think our slogans and our petition are going to be as enthusiastically embraced in the West as they have been in the East, we're really fooling ourselves. I spoke about what I thought Bike for Peace was about and what we'd done together. We'd ridden nine hundred miles together, we had told stories, we had drunk vodka at night together, we'd patched flat tires for each other, we had gone to each other's homes, we had *lived* together for two weeks, and there was no reason why we had to start arguing with one another over what these governments are doing. That's not what Bike for Peace is about. Bike for Peace is about compassion, the compassion of ordinary people, and the possibilities that exist for ordinary people to work together and to advance to the point where our governments will stop these things. And I went on and on and I was in tears." When he sat down, there was a burst of applause. Later, Valery Chaplygan apologized to Senie and they hugged each other.

By the time they arrived in Oslo, the group felt the need for a rest. "Even the Soviets were getting tired," remarks Allyson Senie. The Americans worried about how the other riders would react to the East Coast megalopolis after days of riding in serene countryside. "Before they boarded the plane, Senie passed out "survival kits" of dimes, phone numbers, and instructions on how to call the various embassies. Because of the visa imbroglio, the Soviets had to take a different flight to New York that arrived an hour earlier, and the Americans feared that the Soviets might get lost in Kennedy airport. When they were reunited, "there was all this hugging and kissing like we hadn't seen each other for years, even though we'd only been apart for ten hours," recalls Allyson Senie. Bike for Peace had successfully crossed the ocean, and their good luck seemed destined to hold: it was pouring rain.

But the healthy working relationship among the five leaders was soon to be severely tested. Senie had made arrangments for the group to ride into the United Nations Plaza and hold a reception and press conference with officials from the United Nations Disarmament Office. The night before, Vladimir Kokashvili and Eugene Oskolsky rounded up Senie, Naerland, and Kroglund for an emergency meeting. They suggested canceling the next morning's reception because the staff of the Soviet Permament Mission to the UN had managed to arrange a meeting for Bike for Peace with United Nations Secretary-General Javier Perez de Cuellar. Senie protested that he and his staff had worked hard to set up the next day's reception and it seemed too late to be switching plans. Also, he didn't think it was a good idea for the Soviet leaders to be arranging their activities in the United States. "All the American press needs to hear is that the Soviet Union is controlling this event in this country, and we're going to be finished," he recalls saying.

Up to this point the five leaders had made every decision by consensus. For the first and last time, they took a vote. The vote was four to one in favor of scrapping the Disarmament Office reception; Naerland and Kroglund were excited by this opportunity to present their petition to Cuellar. Senie's vehement opposition fell on deaf ears. Kokashvili and Oskolsky told him that the Soviet UN staff would cancel the next morning's meeting. Senie went to bed thinking the matter out of his hands.

The next morning Senie, Grigoryev, and Kroglund were interviewed on CBS morning news, their biggest splash in the American press. That night Senie called his Westport office. "My staff told me that the United Nations had been on the phone three times that day, and that they were absolutely furious at me, because we had stood them up. The Soviets hadn't canceled the reception. There were over forty officials and press people waiting for us, with buns and drinks and signs and cameras, and we simply never showed up." Senie's normally calm, even voice crescendos at the memory. "And I was *absolutely* as angry as I'd ever felt. I was on a pay phone, and Vladimir Kokashvili was standing next to me. I reached into my pocket and pulled out some change, then I hung up the phone and I swore and I threw that change against the wall. And Vladimir just walked away. I didn't throw it at Vladimir," he adds hastily. "I was just screaming that this was a stupid, stupid decision. And that was it. Those were the last words that I said to the Soviet leaders until we got to Philadelphia."

Senie shakes his head. "The emotions had just reached the level where I had had it. I was tired, I had been bicycling, I had planned this meeting, they'd wanted to cancel it, I was voted down, then they didn't cancel it, my name is mud at the United Nations, which is the last thing in the world I wanted—and I left the negotiating table. I was absolutely not going to talk to them, I was so furious." He stares at his hands as he remembers the tangle of emotions and events that created the crisis. "You have to understand that I have always felt that people should never leave the negotiating table, that that's the worst thing you can do," he says after a pause. "And here I was in the middle of Bike for Peace, choosing to stop talking to my partners. Something I am completely opposed to, and have never been able to understand in others. And here I was doing it. And now I know how people can do it. You can get *so mad*. I went to the American participants, and I said, we are not going to see the Secretary-General on the ninth of August, and I want you to back me up, and they all said yes."

A pall fell on the formerly jolly group. Although many of the bikers didn't fully understand what was going on, they knew that their leaders were arguing, and that, added to the heat and congested highways, put everyone in a cranky mood. The Norwegians suddenly found themselves in a position corresponding to their geographical location: the middle. They began shuttling messages back and forth between Senie and Oskolsky and Kokashvili. Tore Naerland had more inspiration than the audience could have known when he spoke in front of the Liberty Bell about the need for communication and understanding.

The next morning, the Philadephia Art Museum treated the bikers to a gourmet breakfast on its terrace, and the five leaders gathered for the first time since the spat. Senie tersely told the others that he and the other Americans would have no part of the meeting with the Secretary-General. Between Philadelphia and Newark, Delaware, the Norwegians and Soviets lobbied him to change his mind. Apologies, proposals, and counterproposals flew back and forth. "Eugene Oskolsky, a really warm and compassionate man, volunteered to take the rap from me. He told Andrew that he would write a telegram to the head of the Disarmament Office saying that it had been his mistake not to cancel the reception. And as it turned out it wasn't his fault. Somebody they had told at the Soviet mission to cancel it didn't do it." The telegram was sent and Senie's mood mellowed somewhat. But when the bikers arrived at Newark, Delaware, and were treated to an outdoor potluck dinner—the mayor declared it Bike for Peace Day and gave them a key to the city—"I was still absolutely mad and still feeling sorry for myself," says Senie,

As he sat alone after dinner, "listening to this lousy jazz," Vladimir Kokashvili came up to him and offered to take him to his hotel room so that they could settle some financial matters; the Soviets had yet to pay Senie for all of the Soviet delegation's food and lodging. "I said, 'I don't feel like doing that now, Vladimir, let's do it another time.' He came back about ten minutes later and said the same thing. I said, 'Look, Vladimir, we can do it *tomorrow*.' Then he came back a third time, and I said, 'Okay, okay, let's go to the hotel room and take care of the money.' "

When they arrived, Oskolsky was in the room, but he quickly excused himself. After settling the money, Kokashvili asked Senie if he wanted a drink. Senie said yes. They started talking. "I said to him, Vladimir, why is it that on this entire trip you have never said the words 'I'm sorry?' I have never heard those words come out of your mouth. And I am apologizing left and right for things." They kept talking. "It was the most amazing meeting I've ever had," recalls Senie. "We started talking about Vladimir, and his father, and his life-style and his personality, and why he wasn't very good at saying 'I'm sorry.' Then we started talking about my background and my personality. And after forty-five minutes of talking about what makes us tick, we wound up hugging each other in tears."

Kokashvili and Senie went into the adjoining room to look for Oskolosky, and found the entire Soviet delegation tensely waiting for them. "Those Soviets wouldn't go to bed that night until their bosses and me had made up. They were so upset that I was angry at their leaders that everybody was out of sorts, and they really wanted to clear the air." Senie and all of the Soviets then did the only logical thing under the circumstances: they had a party. "We sat there until the early hours of the morning drinking vodka and eating dried fish until we were all friends again. And I agreed to go meet the Secretary-General."

This brush with disaster illuminated the importance of what they were trying to do with Bike for Peace; for a few days they had fallen into the same trap as government leaders who are not on speaking terms. "The situation with those five leaders was a little mini-microcosm of the situation of government leaders trying to negotiate arms agreements," says Senie. "That experience convinced me that the one ingredient that's been missing so far in negotiations is *desire*. The governments have not really wanted to make those agreements yet. They would like to get military superiority first and then reach agreements. And now I understand that you have to really *want* to get there. Because it's hard. It's harder than I ever thought it was. Emotions get involved, feelings and pride get involved, you get defensive, you feel the other guy did something just to hurt you, things do break down. And now I know that you've got to care a lot, because it's hard. The Soviets brought me back in, by wanting so much to make me feel better. But the tension, the pressure we were all under. . . ." He pauses. "There was even a time when Andrew hit Vladimir. That's how tough this whole project was. I'm telling you this because I think it makes it all that more brilliant an experience. It shows how deeply we were all committed to a common goal, or things would have simply fallen apart. It was like an acting company who fights with one another, but when the curtain goes up they put on a beautiful performance anyway."

All the riders were relieved that peace had been restored among the leaders. Nevertheless, the last day of the trip—August 5, 1983—was hot, humid, and frustrating. Many of the bikers got lost on Baltimore's surburban streets, and flat tires were epidemic as they rode through construction areas. Then, only five miles from the Capitol Building, the rear axle on Senie and Vladimir Semenets's tandem broke. It was impossible to fix with available tools; they had to find a new wheel. There were no shortage of bicycle wheels in the anxious crowd of bikers, but all were being used. In desperation, Senie went up to a teenaged boy who had ridden with them from New York and asked him to give up his rear wheel. He is still not sure that was the right thing to do. "It was so important that that tandem ride into Washington, I felt some sacrifice had to be made," he says. "But that kid was crushed. He had to ride the most exciting part in the back of a van." Like a flock of confused birds, the bikers circled Senate Park in front of the Capitol Building and met their last welcoming crowd and press conference. And as a sign that their good luck had held, it started raining.

The next night, Congressman Bruce Morrison of Connecticut honored the bikers at a dinner in Washington, DC, and the following day they took a bus back to Westport, Connecticut, for a final farewell dinner on the grounds of a local church. As they disembarked, they formed a circle, held hands aloft, and sang "We Shall Overcome." Reporters interviewing the bikers heard the word "family" reiterated by nearly every participant. That night the staid walls of "The Marketplace" reverberated with the sounds of Soviet songs and American rock 'n' roll dancing as the bikers celebrated with a last party.

"Bike for Peace was successful in ways that were never discussed in the newspaper," muses Senie. "The success that was always talked about was that we rode twelve hundred miles, and we all became buddies, and it all seemed so easy. The real success story is that we did it even though it was hard. Our ultimate goals were the same, but our surface-level goals were slightly different, and that caused tensions. We had come at it from slightly different angles, for slightly different reasons, yet we hung in there even when we went through very bitter times, when there was a lot of anger and a lot of hurt feelings. Those five leaders struggled through this thing together. And at the end, we were saying good-bye to family."

A few days later, Senie, Kokashvili, Kroglund, and Oskolsky presented their petition to Secretary-General Cuellar at a United Nations ceremony. "You are all truly an important part of our diplomatic corps," wrote Senator Gary Hart in one of the many notes and telegrams of congratulations that poured in. "None of us really believed we would revolutionize the world. We do believe, though, that we have done just as good a month's job as have the professional diplomats and negotiators in Vienna, Geneva, and Madrid," wrote Kroglund in his journal. "We worked as a team and got beyond the language of diplomacy. We spoke our minds and thus could respect each other. When we finished, our biggest victory was that we could each go our own way with a raised head and know that we succeeded where governments fail."

Bike for Peace caused quite a stir in Westport, Connecticut, and for awhile, Senie was a hometown celebrity. The local paper editorialized: "Although many of us are in no shape to hop on a bicycle and pedal twelve hundred miles, perhaps the trip can serve as an example to all of us that it is within our power to do more than talk about peace. . . . It may be naive to think anything can make Soviet and American leaders stem the tide of increasing weaponry and abandon their nuclear stockpiles for peace, but happily there are those who try anyway."

Senie, though, was on the verge of collapse. And now that he put his T-shirt and cycling gloves away, and put back on his tie, the reality of the sixty-thousand-dollar debt Bike for Peace had accumulated, before a theoretical figure, suddenly took on an awful three-dimensional reality. "There is always a letdown after a project like this but mine lasted a year," he says. "It has been very difficult and emotionally very exhausting for me to carry personally this kind of debt. I had said at the beginning of this project that if it cost me a hundred thousand dollars that was fine. I really wanted to do this and it was going to be my first house. So nothing happened that I hadn't set myself up for. But facing that reality is very hard. I'm not making enough money to buy a house even if it was one I could live in and build equity in. Of course, I have built equity—a lot of equity in the form of personal growth and very rewarding contacts in the Soviet Union. But it has been exhausting, and I think Allyson Senie is the only person in the world who knows what I've been through."

After the ride was over, Allyson Senie became the sole staffperson of Bike for Peace, Inc., and she and her brother met for breakfast and dinner every day to discuss next steps. Both knew that the only real way to get Bike for Peace out of debt was to do it again in 1984 and begin fund-raising anew. "We kept meeting like that every day, I think, because we were frightened of losing the relationship we had developed over the summer," says Allyson Senie. "It was the only thing we had left of Bike for Peace."

In November Senie sent a telex to Kokashvili and Oskolsky proposing that his sister come to Moscow to discuss a potential Bike for Peace '84. They telexed back that she was welcome to come talk about it, but they didn't seem overly enthusiastic. "They said something about not being able to pay for the hotel this time. We could tell they were hesitant, but we felt desperate and decided to push it anyway," says Allyson Senie. Official Soviet-American relations, in the aftermath of the Soviet shooting of the Korean airliner and the collapse of the Geneva arms control talks, were just then hitting new lows. Still, Allyson Senie flew to Moscow in early December 1983 for four days of meetings.

The first day went reasonably well. Oskolsky and Kokashvili appeared receptive to repeating Bike for Peace on a different route, and went so far as to call their secretary to check on train fares for a section of the trip through Poland. The next day, however, Allyson Senie was told that instead of meeting with Yuri Zhukov, the head of the Soviet Peace Committee, she would meet with his deputy. "Vladimir tried to warn me before we went in," she recalls. "He and Eugene were very uptight, but I figured that was just because this guy was their boss."

First Deputy Haharbin, "a big, Soviet-looking gentlemen," proceeded to launch into a forty-five-minute lecture on the state of the world in general and Soviet-American relations in particular. "He told me, 'You just deployed your Pershing II and cruise missiles,' and I thought, 'My God, is this what this is all about?' He said, 'How can you expect us to cooperate with you when you've just deployed your missiles? You go home and you tell your President to remove your missiles. I'm not closing the door on further joint projects, but right now we cannot work together.' " Allyson Senie sat silently in her business suit with her hands folded, fighting back tears, trying to feel older than her twenty-two years, and wondering what she was going to say. "I had a long time to think because he just kept going on and on. But all I could think of was Bike for Peace is over, we've got this debt, we can't do another project, we can't raise money, what am I going to tell Christopher? And at the end he said, 'I know it may seem to you like this is an even more opportune time to work together on joint programs. But it's just not right.' "

He finished and looked at her expectantly. Allyson Senie took a deep breath. "I said, 'First Deputy Haharbin, you have found my only argument, and that is I think this *is* an opportune time to work together, and I believe we need now more than ever to have these joint programs. But I understand your position and I hope in the future we can work together.' " She wipes a tear that has surfaced from the memory. "He was really ready for me to come at him, but I was so humble. If I had been one of the Norwegians, I would have fought. If I had been Christopher Senie, I would have said exactly what I did say. I just intuitively knew to back down and say we had completely miscalculated."

Then a remarkable change came over the Peace Committee official. "It's like it dawned on him suddenly that he was talking to a young woman, not the United States incarnate," recalls Allyson Senie. "It was obvious that he felt terrible for having harangued me. And he went to his safe and pulled out a beautiful little painted box as a personal gift to me. It shows a little boy reaching up to grab the tail of a big bird that looks like a peacock. There is an old story in Russian folklore that if you can pluck a feather from this bird, all your wishes will come true."

Allyson and Christopher Senie made the difficult decision to close down the Bike for Peace office for six months. In spite of their disappointment, they were able to joke that Allyson had gotten herself fired. "It's so hard not to think that if Christopher had gone it wouldn't have turned out this way. But I think the missiles were a bigger issue than my age or sex," says Allyson Senie. She applied to the Columbia School of International Affairs, where she is now enrolled in the master's degree program. Senie, meanwhile, was taken out to dinner by his parents and counseled as to how he would be able to manage his now seventy-five-thousand-dollar debt.

But during that spring, when he was supposed to be resigning himself to Bike for Peace's demise, Senie conceived the idea of Teamworks, Inc., and began drafting its statement of purpose. He changed the name of his nonprofit group both to reflect the broader scope of programs he envisioned and as a gesture recognizing that the Bike for Peace name and concept properly belonged to Tore Naerland.

Things were beginning to look up by summer 1984. He had stayed in touch with Vladimir Kokashvili and Eugene Oskolsky, although they had yet to mention doing any more projects together. Then, on August 30, 1984, Kokashvili called him at home "completely out of the blue" and suggested that they work together on a Bike for Peace '85. Senie met with Kokashvili and Yuri Zhukov in New York in October, and they agreed to a plan for 1986 instead of 1985 to give everyone more time to organize and raise funds. In February 1985, Senie flew to Moscow and signed a preliminary agreement for Bike for Peace '86, a similar odyssey connecting Kiev to New York City via Prague and Montreal. His equity, and his patience, were paying off.

"Teamworks is really going to take off now," enthuses Senie. "I have a sense that the Peace Committee appreciates the risks that were taken over here; I think they know this project happened a little bit by magic. And I think they greatly overestimate my pull in the United States, since we managed to get the visas approved." He can describe a vision for a full-fledged Teamworks, Inc., "down to the color of the carpet. Five years from now it will be quite an operation. What I really long for is the day when I know that Teamworks is advancing forward everyday, whether I do something on it or not, and I am free to do the law work that I'm not now doing very well." Hiring a professional staff, and engaging in the kind of businesslike marketing and fund-raising necessary to maintain high-quality staff salaries, he believes, is key to the success of small, focused citizen diplomacy groups like his own.

Also key to making his other projects materialize will be steadfastly refusing to become more overtly involved in politics. "I'm really doing good work if both the Soviet government and the US government appreciate and are not offended by my projects," he says. "And you can fit into that narrow center line if your real purpose is lowering the wall of ignorance and prejudice that exists, which is something that everyone at least in theory agrees with.

"In a hundred years or so, we're going to look back and say, how could we ever have been spending so much of our talents and time and resources on the military? I think that of the two approaches to peace right now—the political approach, with banners and rallies and arguments, and the emotional approach, with symbolic events like Bike for Peace—the emotional work is at the real cutting edge. The American people have to *like* the Soviet people more than they do. To do that, they've got to know how warm they are, and how compassionate, and that they have similar frustrations and hopes and dreams and problems. We have to win emotional support for efforts to bring about peace so that those political arguments can be heard."

He believes it will be a slow, gradual process, and that there is a ten-to-fifteen-year lag time before these new attitudes are likely to be translated into policy. The one hitch, he admits, is that these kinds of efforts presuppose that there is time for this admittedly slow process of education and change to take effect. "It's a race with time," he says. "Will we mature quickly enough to avoid annihilating each other?

"You know," he continues, "I didn't start doing this work because of any immediate fear of nuclear destruction. I'm in it because of this tremendous wall of prejudice that I see, like the one between blacks and whites that I grew up with. I just wanted to bring a little compassion into the hearts of people who don't know what it is that they're saying when they say, 'Oh those Russians, we should blow them up.'

"We've got to keep working and keep learning about each other. The one thing an American should do if he or she really wants to do something for world peace is go to the Soviet Union. Borrow the money and go to the Soviet Union. When the American people and the Soviet people want to shake one another's hands, to meet each other, and to realize that there are common bonds too numerous to mention, that is when the United States and the Soviet Union are going to want to get the dangerous situation we have now under control."

✤✤✤

CHAPTER NINE

THE INNOCENT ABROAD:

SAMANTHA SMITH

Samantha Smith caught cynics unawares. She could not have been more unlike the traditional diplomats she unintentionally provoked. She made no postures. She struck no negotiating positions. She did not try to reassure disparate constituencies of her middle course. She did not let the fact that she was not an expert keep her from speaking out. She refused to accept that "difficult" meant impossible. She did not believe we could afford pessimism. She set the world in a tizzy.

When she was killed in a plane crash on August 25, 1985, millions of people all over the world grieved as if for their own child. For, in a way, she was a child of the world—a symbol of childhood itself, a guardian of our dreams and hopes for children everywhere. Now she will be a child forever. Her voice will remain high and pure, her vision unobscured by shades of gray, by comprehensive but disempowering "buts" and "on the other hands." Her dreams are intact, but it is now up to the rest of us to carry them out. What she did for the world will never be measurable, but that she did something is incontrovertible.

The heads of the two most powerful nations on earth sent condolences to her mother, Jane. "Everyone in the Soviet Union who has known Samantha Smith will remember forever the image of the American girl who, like millions of Soviet young men and women, dreamt about peace, and about friendship between the peoples of the United States and the Soviet Union," said Mikhail Gorbachev in a telegram. President Reagan, who never publicly acknowledged Samantha while she was alive, wrote: "Perhaps you can take some measure of comfort in the knowledge that millions of Americans, indeed millions of people, share the burdens of your grief. They also will cherish and remember Samantha, her smile, her idealism and unaffected sweetness of spirit."

Samantha and her father, Arthur, were on their way back from a two-

week filming session in England for a television series featuring Samantha called Lime Street. *The Beechcraft 99 skimmed the tops of trees, crashed, and burst into flames on its approach to the Lewiston-Auburn airport, killing everyone aboard. Three days later, more than a thousand people gathered for a memorial service in Augusta, Maine. Though Augusta is an off-limits area for Soviet officials, the State Department hastily granted an exception to Vladimir Kulagin, the first secretary for cultural affairs of the Soviet Embassy in Washington, DC, and a personal friend of the Smiths. After reading Gorbachev's telegram, Kulagin put aside his notes and told the crowd in English, "You should know that millions of mothers and fathers and kids back in Russia share this tragic loss. The best thing would be if we continued what they started with good will, friendship and love. Samantha shone like a brilliant beam of sunshine at a time when relations between our two countries were clouded."*

US Senators Mitchell and Cohen of Maine have introduced a bill that would establish and fund a two-million-dollar "Samantha Smith Memorial Exchange Program" to promote youth exchanges between the United States and the Soviet Union. The Soviet Union is helping keep her memory alive by issuing a special commemorative stamp in her honor and announcing that a newly discovered Siberian diamond of rare beauty will be named after her. A two-way television space bridge between children in Minneapolis and Moscow in December 1985, organized by the Peace Child Foundation, was dedicated to Samantha's memory.

And Jane Smith is making a determined and gutsy commitment to carry on her daughter's and husband's work. She has organized the Samantha Smith Foundation to promote Soviet-American youth exchanges. In 1986 the Foundation cosponsored, with Ted Turner's Goodwill Games project, an international youth art competition for Soviet and American children and a journey to the Soviet Union for twenty of Samantha's eighth-grade classmates from Manchester, Maine.

I interviewed Samantha and her parents in their home in April 1985, and wrote the following chapter in May 1985. Not wanting to hide Samantha behind the screen of an obituary, I have left the chapter as it was before she died. Some of it is painful, now, to read. But perhaps that pain will help awaken us to the preciousness of life, which Samantha so well understood, and inspire us to work for her dreams.

—G. W.

On a banner behind the makeshift stage, in handpainted, childishly askew letters, is a quote from Mahatma Gandhi: "If we are to reach real peace in this world and if we are to carry on a real war against war, we shall have to begin with the CHILDREN." About two hundred parents and children are sitting in a dormitory lounge at the University of Southern Maine in Gorham, Maine, whispering to each other about the television cameramen maneuvering in the background. Soon Samantha Smith bounds to the microphone like a young cat released from a cage.

"I thought I'd read a few selections from my book, if you guys don't mind," she begins, beaming a winsome smile at the audience and tossing her head to one side. "Actually, the whole thing started when I asked my mother if there was going to be a war. There was always something on television about missiles and nuclear bombs. Once I watched a science show on public television and the scientists said that a nuclear war would wreck the earth and destroy our atmosphere. Nobody could win a nuclear war. I remember that I woke up one morning and wondered if this was going to be the last day of the earth."

Samantha Smith is now nearly thirteen years old. Under her fashionable blue-and-white checked blouse and skirt are incipient signs of puberty. The girl who so impressed hard-bitten reporters as a "gangly-legged bundle of energy" and charmed them with her penchant for softball is growing up. Her straight brunette hair, once held back in a hair band, has now been clipped into a stylish page-boy. Her lips are tinged with lipstick and mascara highlights her wide blue eyes. Still, despite the attention, despite the instant fame, despite the book, despite Hollywood, Samantha has held on to her charming lack of professionalism. When she occasionally flubs a word she shakes her head and glances up at the audience with a self-deprecating grin. She reads quickly and decisively. She appears to have a good deal to say.

"I asked my mother who would start a war and why. She showed me a newsmagazine with a story about America and Russia, one that had a picture of the new Russian leader, Yuri Andropov, on the cover. We read it together. It seemed that the people in both Russia and America were worried that the other country would start a nuclear war. It all seemed so dumb to me. I had learned about the awful things that had happened during World War II, so I thought that nobody would ever want to have another war. I told Mom that she should write to Mr. Andropov to find out who was causing all the trouble. She said, 'Why don't *you* write to him?' So I did."

Dear Mr. Andropov,

My name is Samantha Smith. I am ten years old. Congratulations on your new job. I have been worrying about Russia and the United States getting into a nuclear war. Are you going to vote to have a war or not? If you aren't please tell me how you are going to help to not have a war. This question you do not have to answer, but I would like to know why you want to conquer the world or at least our country. God made the world for us to live together in peace and not to fight.

Sincerely,
Samantha Smith

Samantha wrote on a lined piece of notepaper in the careful, looping script of ten-year-olds everywhere. Her father Arthur helped her mail the letter to "Mr. Yuri Andropov, The Kremlin, Moscow, USSR." Samantha was impressed that it cost so much to mail—forty cents. Her expectations were not high. "I thought I'd just get a form letter, like I did from the Queen of England"—to whom, at the age of five, she wrote a fan letter. Her father's expectations were zero. Samantha and her parents soon forgot about the letter.

Four or five months later, Samantha was summoned to the secretary's office of her elementary school and told that there was a reporter from the Associated Press on the telephone who wanted to speak with her. Samantha protested that there must be some kind of mistake. "Mrs. Peabody said, 'Well, did you write a letter or something to Yuri Andropov?' She practically dragged me into the office and got me on the phone. And the reporter told me that there was an article in *Pravda* that talked about my letter, and there was even a picture of it."

Samantha managed to overcome her surprise and spoke with the reporter for a few minutes. A story went out over the news wires and the Associated Press sent a photographer to Manchester to take a picture of a grinning Samantha next to her father's manual typewriter. Meanwhile her father, a professor of English at the University of Maine, located a copy of *Pravda* and asked some colleagues in the Russian department to translate the article. *Pravda* indeed quoted excerpts of Samantha's letter and said, in reference to her question about why Andropov might want to conquer the world: "We think we can pardon Samantha her misleadings, because the girl is only ten years old."

Samantha was understandably pleased that *Pravda* had printed her letter. But she was miffed that no attempt had been made to answer her questions. So she wrote a second letter, this time to the Soviet Ambassador to the United States, Anatoly Dobrynin. She asked him whether

Mr. Andropov was planning to answer her questions, and added that "I thought my questions were good ones and it shouldn't matter if I was ten years old."

Apparently, that did it. A week later the Soviet embassy called Samantha at home to say that a reply from Yuri Andropov was on its way. Within a few days, the postmistress of Manchester, Maine, called to say that a peculiar envelope had arrived via registered mail for Samantha. The letter, typed in Russian on cream-colored paper and signed in blue ink, was dated April 19, 1983, and was accompanied by an English translation.

Dear Samantha,

I received your letter, which is like many others that have reached me recently from your country and from other countries around the world.

It seems to me—I can tell by your letter—that you are a courageous and honest girl, resembling Becky, the friend of Tom Sawyer in the famous book of your compatriot Mark Twain. This book is well-known and loved in our country by all boys and girls.

You write that you are anxious about whether there will be a nuclear war between our two countries. And you ask are we doing anything so that war will not break out.

Your question is the most important of those that every thinking man can pose. I will reply to you seriously and honestly.

Yes, Samantha, we in the Soviet Union are trying to do everything so that there will not be war between our countries, so that in general there will not be war on earth. This is what every Soviet man wants. This is what the great founder of our state, Vladimir Lenin, taught us.

Soviet people well know what a terrible thing war is. Forty-two years ago, Nazi Germany, which strived for supremacy over the whole world, attacked our country, burned and destroyed many thousands of our towns and villages, killed millions of Soviet men, women, and children.

In that war, which ended in our victory, we were in alliance with the United States; together we fought for the liberation of many people from the Nazi invaders. I hope that you know this from your history lessons in school. And today we want very much to live in peace, to trade and cooperate with all our neighbors on this earth—with those far away and those near by. And certainly with such a great country as the United States of America.

In America and in our country there are nuclear weapons—terrible weapons that can kill millions of people in an instant. But we do not want them ever to be used. That's precisely why the Soviet Union solemnly declared throughout the entire world that never—never—will it use nuclear weapons first against any country. In general we propose to discontinue further production of them and to proceed to the abolition of all the stockpiles on earth.

It seems to me that this is a sufficient answer to your second question: "Why do you want to wage war against the whole world or at least the United States?" We want nothing of the kind. No one in our country— neither workers, peasants, writers nor doctors, neither grown-ups or children, nor members of the government—wants either a big or a "little" war.

We want peace—there is something that we are occupied with: growing wheat, building and inventing, writing books and flying into space. We want peace for ourselves and for all peoples of the planet. For our children and for you, Samantha.

I invite you, if your parents will let you, to come to our country, the best time being the summer. You will find out about our country, meet with your contemporaries, visit an international children's camp—"Artek"— on the sea. And see for yourself: in the Soviet Union—everyone is for peace and friendship among peoples.

Thank you for your letter. I wish you all the best in your young life.

Y. Andropov

Andropov's letter arrived at 8 A.M. on Monday, April 26, 1983. When Samantha got home from school that afternoon, the lawn in front of her house was blanketed with reporters and cameramen. Before the night was out, she and her mother, Jane, were on a jet chartered by CBS and NBC to New York City for a round of appearances on the *Today Show*, *CBS Morning News*, and *Nightline*, as well as more interviews with major newspapers, radio stations, and wire services. A few days later, Samantha and her mother were off to California for an appearance on the *Tonight Show*. Samantha's prior traveling experience had been limited to visiting her grandparents in Florida and Virginia. Her reaction? "It was different," giggles Samantha, "but it was *fun!*"

Samantha flips through the pages of her book, *Journey to the Soviet Union*, to her favorite part of her trip: her visit to Camp Artek on the Black Sea. She describes the elaborate welcome the Soviet children gave her; the Young Pioneers' swimming contests and games; her late-night whispers with her best friend, thirteen-year-old Natasha, and the other girls in the camp dormitory. "The kids had lots of questions about America—especially about clothes and music," reads Samantha, her index finger tracing the words. "They were all interested in how I lived and sometimes at night we talked about peace, but it didn't really seem necessary because none of them hated America, and none of them ever wanted war. Most of the kids had relatives or friends of their families die in World War II, and they hoped there would *never* be another war. It seemed strange even to talk about war when we all got along so well together. I guess that's what I came to find out. I mean, if we could be friends by just getting to know each other better, then what are our countries really arguing about? Nothing could be more important than *not* having a war if a war would kill everything."

Now it is time for questions. A dozen seventh and eighth graders from Gorham Junior High School take turns stepping to a floor microphone and reading queries from slips of paper. Samantha stands with her hands folded a little stiffly on the podium, her face intent as she concentrates on hearing each question. Her answers are brief and to the point.

"How have your attitudes toward Russia changed?"

"At first, when I hadn't gone over there, some of my parents' friends said it was sort of gray and dull. And the news was always saying that it wasn't nice at all, and that they were mean and truly wanted to be enemies and stuff. But when I got there I found out that the people were really friendly and very down-to-earth. They certainly didn't want war at all because they had gone through such tragedies earlier in their lives."

"Do you have any message to give people in the United States?"

"Well, I feel that one of the reasons we are having problems with them is that many of the people in the United States government have not actually gone over there for a tour, or to actually meet any of the children or other adults in the Soviet Union. Half the adults seem to think that they are our enemies, but they haven't even been over there to experience meeting people in the Soviet Union to see what they are like. I have experienced that and I have found out that the people of the Soviet Union are very friendly and they're trying as hard as we are to have peace."

"Would you like to visit the Soviet Union again?"

"If anybody wants to invite me, I'd be happy to go."

"What do you see for our future? Do you think it's possible to have world peace?"

"I think there's a way we can have peace among children. As for the adults—I think it's possible. But, well, I can't exactly do that much about it, because I'm a kid. I would like to be able to do something about it, but I can't. I think we can achieve peace if we try hard enough."

The questions end, the audience gives her a grateful ovation, and Samantha exits to a chair on the side of the room. While other children make presentations, her young-lady chic disappears as she sprawls across her father's lap like a giant kitten. Samantha is tired. It is already an hour past her usual bedtime. But she and her father can't slip away just yet; a short photo session is scheduled after the program. Then they must drive nearly two hours from Gorham back to Manchester, for tomorrow is a school day. Samantha Smith is in the seventh grade.

One would never suspect that a connection had been forged between Manchester, Maine (population 1,940) and Moscow upon driving into this sleepy one-stoplight hamlet just west of Augusta. Though a sign says the town was founded in 1775, it still has a certain raw, almost frontier look, with its general stores clustered around a highway intersection and clapboard houses scattered amidst surrounding farms, woods, and orchards. The Smiths live down one of many curving lanes, in a two-story white house with dark green shutters and a backyard of mixed pine-birch woods. It is quiet and peaceful; evening grosbeaks come to the feeder at their kitchen window.

A week after the Gorham speech, Samantha lounges on the couch reading a "Garfield the Cat" book and good-humoredly waiting for the interview to begin. It is hard not to gasp at first sight of her. She is wearing hot pink fuzzy socks, pink nylon running shorts, and a yellow sweatshirt with "California" scripted across it in electric blue. Her lips and fingernails are fulgent pink. And her straight brunette hair has been cramped into the thin tendrils of a brand-new perm.

She stands up and puts aside her book to shake hands. It is an adult gesture, but she steps much closer than adult body language would dictate. The effect is breathtaking. After delivering a dazzling smile, she reclines again on the pillows, one shaved leg stretched insouciantly across the couch, one hand touching her unfamiliar curls.

Looking at Samantha is an exercise in cognitive dissonance. There on the sofa, she is a sophisticated little aristocrat, her makeup impeccable, her manner urbane; she is also a twelve-year-old girl who doesn't question her father's right to decide what she wears in public and who goes to bed at 8:30 P.M. in her lavendar flannel pajamas. Her voice has lowered since her early talk show days; she can now sound like a teenager if she chooses, or she can suspend that maturity and trip lightly through her words in flawless little-girl-speak. Is she a girl, or is she a young woman?

It is not only the contradictions inherent in her age that make meeting Samantha somewhat disconcerting. Like the people of the country she became famous for visiting, Samantha is not who one would expect her to be based on newspaper accounts. One expects to find an earnest, studious child who regularly peruses the *New York Times* and keeps up with the latest debates on arms control. One expects a prepubescent Helen Caldicott. "Some people think that because of what's happened to me I'm a real superperson peacemaker," says Samantha with a tiny inhalation of breath before she speaks. "But I'm not really into politics that much. I'm just *concerned*, and this just sort of happened."

One expects a prodigy, but instead finds a normal twelve-year-old girl with typical twelve-year-old interests and perspectives. Samantha watches a fair amount of television. She giggles a great deal—fine-tuned, highly-modulated giggles that can convey intricate shades of meaning. She watches—and giggles at—Bugs Bunny shows in the morning while she eats her Cheerios. She chews gum and has a weakness for popsicles. She is at the age when boys have become intriguing, and when few things can keep her in the bathroom longer than getting ready for a Friday night school dance.

Once the initial surprise is over, though, one also realizes that it is her very normality that has made her such an effective symbol of her generation. In a culture jaded by hothouse-grown child performers, Samantha is reassuringly genuine. Her brand of childish directness, bereft of learned and fuzzying complexities, has made many an ideologue wince. Going to the Soviet Union allowed her to come to her own conclusions— a fact that delights her fans and irritates her detractors.

"All the children here, and all the children over in the Soviet Union, are not enemies," declares Samantha. "For some really strange reason, the grown-ups that rule don't get along. Whenever you want to do something at home, and you ask your parents if you can, they always say, 'Give me two good reasons.' But here the grown-ups never give any good reasons for why they don't get along. Maybe it's time we did a little back talk," she says, impishly eyeing her father, who has just settled in an armchair.

Because she so obviously lacked a political ax to grind, public interest in Samantha's conclusions was keen. She could be trusted to tell things the way she saw them. Within a few weeks of the letter's arrival, Andropov's invitation was confirmed: the Soviets offered to provide an all-expenses-paid two-week sojourn for Samantha and her parents. And so as Samantha's July 7, 1983, departure date drew near, the Smith family packed bags full of Maine College T-shirts and pennants as gifts for their Soviet hosts, and the Western press prepared to record her every impression.

Immediately after her Aeroflot jet from Montreal arrived in Sheremetevo Airport, Samantha was besieged by reporters asking her what she thought of Moscow. Blinking sleepily under the bright camera lights, she said she thought the airport looked a lot like American airports, and soon she was whisked away to bed in a deluxe suite in the Sovietskaya Hotel, which is normally reserved for visiting dignitaries. The next day, she rode in a black limousine accompanied by a full police motorcade to Red Square, where she toured the palaces and churches of the Kremlin, visited Lenin's tomb and study ("Lenin," she explains, "is sort of like their George Washington") and laid flowers at the Tomb of the Unknown Soldier. Samantha's summary: "Moscow was pretty exciting, we got to go to all these tourist places. But after awhile it started to get boring, and my feet started hurting because the shoes that looked best on me were too small."

Much more to her liking, and her favorite part of the trip, was her visit to a large youth camp called Artek in the Crimea. Samantha was met at the airplane by a busload of Young Pioneers her own age and welcomed to Artek by a cheering bleacherful of uniformed children with balloons and banners, mostly in Russian, but one in English: "We are glad to meet you in our Artek." Older children in folk costumes presented her with a traditional bread-and-salt welcome. "I didn't know whether I was supposed to eat it at first or not," says Samantha, "but finally I did and it was delicious."

Samantha donned a Pioneer uniform (white blouse, turquoise skirt, and white knee socks) and the white chiffon bow that Soviet girls often wear in their hair, but eschewed wearing the red Pioneer neckerchief, which symbolizes devotion to Communism. According to Samantha, "The Young Pioneers are a little like Boy Scouts or Girl Scouts except that their activities teach them about Communism instead of democracy."

She had expected, though, that the camp would be "more wildernessy, with tents and stuff."

Samantha opted to spend the night in one of their dormitories instead of in the hotel with her parents. A thirteen-year-old blue-eyed blonde named Natasha, who spoke fairly good English, soon became her best friend. They played together on the beach, took a boat ride to nearby Yalta (where Samantha dangled her legs in President Roosevelt's chair), and tossed wine bottles stuffed with messages from the deck of the boat into the Black Sea. "Hopefully we will all have peace for the rest of our lives," read Samantha's message. By this time she knew enough "adolescent Russian," as her father puts it, to be able to sing Russian songs on the boat with the other children, arms locked together as they swayed back and forth.

Samantha would have liked to stay longer. "They have hundreds of tons of jellyfish that don't sting in the Black Sea, and you can have jellyfish fights. It's wonderful. They're about the size of your palm, and kind of gooey." But the camp session was ending, and after a final evening of closing ceremonies that included a parade, fireworks, skits, dancing, and costume shows, the campers went home and Samantha flew to Leningrad.

There her every move continued to get prime-time coverage in the American, European, and Soviet press as photo opportunities unfolded. Samantha in a colorful Russian folk costume made for her by other children. Samantha eating enormous raspberries on a collective farm. Samantha at the Kirov Ballet trying to put on a signed pair of toe shoes given her by the prima ballerina, Alla Sisova. Samantha accepting flowers from a Soviet sailor on the ship *Aurora*, which fired the first shot of the Russian Revolution. Samantha laying a wreath at the Piskarevskoye Memorial to the nearly half-million citizens of Leningrad who died in the nine-hundred-day siege by the Nazis during World War II. Samantha was on "every other night on Soviet TV," says her father Arthur, "and probably has greater public recognition there than she does here."

Then it was back to Moscow on an overnight train for a final whirlwind of activities, including visits to the Toy Museum, the Moscow Circus, and the Puppet Theater; a chance to try out a racing bicycle in the Velodrome of the Krylatskoye Olympic Center; and a lesson from expert gymnasts on how to twirl ribbons.

"Kids have written to say they think she was very brave to go to the Soviet Union, but she doesn't think she was, and I would have to agree," says Arthur Smith. "But what she did that *was* very difficult was to carry off that trip. Two weeks of twelve-hour days, and she greeted everyone everywhere with enthusiasm, eagerness, and good humor. God only knows I wasn't in good humor for twelve hours a day for two weeks."

"I'll vouch for that," interjects Samantha's mother, Jane, who has also joined the interview.

"And Samantha, I thought, did a helluva good job of doing that, and I don't think people realize what an effort that was. It looked like a lot of fun, and it *was* a lot of fun for her, but I also think very few people could've done what she did."

In addition to her hectic tourist schedule, Samantha's appointment calendar would have made a visiting dignitary envious. Valentina Tereshkova, the first woman in space and the current president of the Soviet Women's Committee, invited Samantha and her family over to her office for tea. US Ambassador to the Soviet Union Arthur Hartman and his wife Donna also had the Smiths to their house for an American lunch of hamburgers and French fries—which, after a steady diet of Chicken Kiev, tasted great to Samantha. And suspense built in the Western press about the possibility that Samantha might meet in person with Andropov, who had been out of public view for some time.

Although the Soviets never made any promises one way or the other, the Smiths held out hope that they might see Andropov until the last day of their trip. Then one of Andropov's deputies, Leonid Zamyatin, came to Samantha's hotel room bearing gifts with Andropov's calling card—a silver samovar (teamaker), a china tea service, and a hand-painted laquered box *(palekh)* with a painting of Red Square and St. Basil's Cathedral. Samantha, in turn, presented him with the gift she had brought for Andropov: a book of Mark Twain speeches. "I'm sure we would have met him if it had been at all possible," says Arthur Smith. "But it wouldn't have been particularly suitable to have somebody who was in dialysis and too frail to stand up be forced to endure a photo session. They said he was busy, but we just assumed he was sick."

Samantha flew home with scrapbooks of photographs of her visit, seventeen suitcases filled with gifts, and some very strong opinions. "Things are just the same over there. I mean, they're just people. There's nothing wrong with them, they're just like us."

"Well, things *are* a little different there," cautions her father.

"Well, yeah, it's a lot stricter there, but that's nothing to *accuse* them of. It's just a different way of living. It doesn't hurt us, and it's not like the Nazis or anything."

Before she wrote her letter, Samantha says, "I really think I got [the Soviets] mixed up with Hitler a little bit. Because in my letter I said why do you want to conquer the world? So at that point I thought [Andropov] was Hitler and I thought he was mean and he wanted to just bomb us all off." She has since learned a great deal, she confides. And while she's never heard of the term "citizen diplomacy," she has great faith in what it can do. "People should know that peace is always possible if we try hard enough. Us kids have made friends, and we're really no different, just smaller versions of grown-ups."

Samantha has a scheme in mind to take advantage of the friendliness of young people. She calls it the Granddaughter Exchange. The idea is to take the granddaughters—and, she supposes, the grandsons too—of the world's heads of state "and just scatter them all over the place," she says with a wave of her arms. "Then they could come back and tell people what the place was like, and hopefully, usually, most of the news would be, these other people are nice people."

But while Samantha has not forgotten about the concerns that launched her into the public eye, she believes that solving the grown-ups' problems is primarily a job for grown-ups. She admits that she does get tired of being asked the same questions over and over again about world peace. Asked if she feels a strong urge to speak at peace symposiums like the one in Gorham, she pauses for a moment and her forehead wrinkles. "I don't feel a *need* to go and speak, but I mean it's nice to go and do it. It's a good idea. But there's nothing necessarily *pushing* me to do it."

A few grumblers suspect that Samantha's parents are pushing her. But Arther and Jane Smith have, to all appearances, resisted the temptation to become stage parents. Arthur Smith is a tall, unruffled, laconic man, who prefers nodding his head to saying the word "yes." When he really intends to praise someone, Samantha's father calls them "down-to-earth," an adjective that fits him nicely. He refers to Samantha's letter to Andropov and subsequent invitation to the Soviet Union as her "experience." The events that followed her return—a plethora of talk shows, a children's conference in Japan, a television special of interviewing Democratic presidential candidates, a visit with the children of Soviet diplomats in Washington, DC—he refers to as her "adventure."

Arthur Smith quit his post as an English professor at the University of Maine to handle Samantha's busy schedule. "I wanted to make sure there was somebody there to make order and sense" out of the offers that were pouring in, he explains. Her mother, Jane—a thin, pretty woman who, like Samantha, transforms when she smiles—works as an administrator in the Maine Department of Health and Human Services in an agency that finds placements for abused and neglected children in state custody. Samantha's television and book fees are barely covering the loss of income from Arthur's former job. But "she enjoys it," says her father, "and I wanted to make this experience available to her."

When Samantha's letter was published in *Pravda* and the first trickle of news stories began, her father was quick to caution her not to let this attention go to her head. "Dad said, 'Oh, it'll last a couple of days,' " giggles Samantha. Arthur Smith sighs. "All through this I'm saying to Samantha, now remember, this is all going to be gone next week." "Then the letter gets here," continues Samantha, "and it's like ZOOM, everyone's here, it's like a magnet. It's like, Daddy, you *lied*."

The press was delighted by the fairy-tale quality of this unlikely pen-pal relationship and curious about this unexpected glimpse into the character of the new Soviet leader. Anyone in Samantha's shoes would doubtless have become famous for awhile. Reporters sopped up every detail of her all-American girlishness with glee. Yes, she has freckles. Yes, she plays softball. Yes, she doesn't like homework. Yes, she sleeps with stuffed toys and likes Michael Jackson and has a Chesapeake Bay retriever for a best friend.

But the press's fascination was kept alive by Samantha's own "production values." Her aplomb at handling microphones and her ability to look directly into the camera and encapsulate her thoughts into a single line soon endeared her to network news producers. About what good her letter and trip might do: "I really hope it made the heads of state think it would be better not to have bombs, because there might be a mistake." About whether she favored a nuclear freeze: "I suppose so. It would be better if we had destroyment [of nuclear bombs], but I'm for a freeze, too." Samantha's opinions were soon being solemnly broadcast to the world.

The hot pursuit of the press at first astonished, then amused Samantha. "It got to be kind of funny, you know? At how *strange* these people can be. They're so desperate, for what? Does it really make a difference?" Samantha is an equanimous child, but she found some of the reporters' questions tiresome, and she developed a fine disregard for the logic of competitive news businesses. "People kept asking me the same questions over and over again, and I asked them, why can't you ask me a question, and then pass around the answers? I mean, how stupid can you get? Here it costs a fortune to come talk to me, when they could simply get it from another reporter."

In Montreal, as she was about to board the plane for Moscow, the Canadian Mounted Police were unable to restrain a gaggle of reporters, who shoved so many microphones into her face that she inadvertently bit metal. Samantha once told David Hartmann on ABC news that she had dreamed about a cameraman "walking backwards who stepped on my big toe and broke my whole foot." But she says the occasional inconvenience caused by the press has been far outweighed by how much fun she has had from all the hoopla. "Sometimes I'd think, I wish this wasn't happening, because of the reporters and stuff, but then I'd think about getting to California and doing the other things that come with it, and I'd think, on the other hand, I *like* this."

But even as millions of people on both sides of the Cold War were falling in love with Samantha, others were plainly irritated by this pip-squeak who had dared infiltrate the adult world of diplomacy. Even as the staff writers of *People* Magazine were scrambling to get to Manchester and find out the names of Samantha's dog and cats, scores of editorials chastised the American people for being duped into believing that Andropov's message might be sincere.

While no editorialists went so far as to suggest that Samantha herself was devious, the Soviets were castigated for taking advantage of Samantha's naïveté. *U.S. News and World Report* ran a story by Nicholas Daniloff bluntly headlined: "Samantha Smith: Pawn in Propaganda War." Opined the *Cleveland Plain Dealer*, "Although the letter surely provided Samantha with an enormous thrill, it nevertheless was a manipulative and exploitative thing to do to an innocent ten-year-old." A Japanese newspaper cartoon portrayed Samantha as Little Red Riding Hood and Andropov as the Wicked Wolf.

The entire correspondence, went a prevailing theory, had been orchestrated by the Soviets to help lull the American people into believing that the Soviets desire peace, while designs to take over the world proceed apace within the Kremlin. Some speculated that the letter and invitation were the results of months of planning; KGB agents snooping around Maine had profiled the Smiths, decided that Samantha had just the right combination of poise, pulchritude, and peaceful rhetoric, and then sent word to pluck her letter from the pile. Others took a less extreme view, saying that the Soviets had probably had nothing so grandiose in mind when they first printed Samantha's letter in *Pravda,* but, noting the Western press's response to the letter's publication, had smelled a good public-relations move, and were simply lucky to have picked a child so capable of handling the media blitz.

Not everyone was quite so ready to write off Andropov's gesture as meaningless, though. While his letter was "excellent propaganda," said the *Lewiston Daily Journal* of Maine, "at the same time it contained within it a hint of sincerity." A few other editorialists pointed out that propaganda or no, it was encouraging that the Soviet Union wished to underscore an image of itself as a nonaggressive, peace-loving nation. In the elaborate morass of diplomatic hinting, it could perhaps be taken as a positive signal of Soviet interest in improved relations.

If it was such a hint, it was one the Reagan administration chose to ignore. President Reagan conspicuously refrained from publicly acknowledging Samantha's letter. "Our contact with the Reagan administration has been, on their part, furtive," remarks Arthur Smith. "The White House called the town of Manchester to verify her existence, and George Bush's people made an inquiry, but it seems to me that Reagan has tried to avoid Samantha."

When she was first interviewed on the NBC *Today Show,* Jane Pauley asked her in a voice and manner nearly as sweet as Samantha's own: "Samantha, do you know what the word 'propaganda' means?" Samantha did not. But she certainly does now. After tightening her face into an exaggerated blink, she opens her eyes and replies in her lilting little-girl voice, "Well, I think they were using me, but it was propaganda for peace. I mean, what were they doing it for, so that they could have a war? It doesn't exactly fit together. So it was propaganda for peace, to get me over there so I could see what it was like, and come back and tell people how nice it was."

Her parents, too, are aware that Samantha's trip emphasized a rosy picture of Soviet life. But they believe that the American press usually presents only the dark side of the Soviet Union and that Samantha's trip provided a healthy counterbalance. "The Soviets certainly wished to be seen as something other than what the Western press often portrays them as," says Arthur Smith. "But the truth is that the Soviet Union is a nation of 270 million people, and these people have families, and aspirations for their children, and that's a side we almost never hear about. The very idea," he shakes his head, "that they could have *engineered* Samantha's experience is absurd. My feeling is that this kind of thing comes from those junk spy novels, which used to be about the Nazis and now are about the KGB, in which the Soviets are seen to be the most manipulative exploiters of the human psyche you can imagine."

Arthur Smith has evidence against such a conspiracy theory. Before forwarding Andropov's letter to Samantha, the Soviet embassy called Arthur to ask permission to release it to the press. If he had said no, he believes, the Soviets would have kept it quiet. And he and Jane dismiss as ridiculous the notion that the KGB investigated them in advance. "My response to that," he says, "is that Samantha's reaction to all this could not even have been predicted by her own parents." Indeed, the KGB would have been inept to have chosen as their public relations pawn a girl who was too bashful to try out for the fifth-grade play. "I was really shy," confirms Samantha. "I *hated* to meet new people. When my mom had friends of hers over it was like, 'Hi, um, I'm going to my room now,' and they'd never see me again."

And even if it was primarily meant as a good public-relations move, her father points out, it could have backfired rather spectacularly. "They took an enormous risk in issuing this invitation to a ten-year-old, who could very well have, even with the best of intentions, headed off on such a journey and after three days said, 'I hate this, I want to go home,' right in front of the cameras. And since the American press was always tailing us, the Soviets would not have been able to guard against that.

"The press kept saying, 'You only saw what they wanted you to see.' Well, the truth is we saw exactly what we asked to see," he adds. Prior to their journey, the Soviets asked the family to write or call the Soviet embassy in Washington whenever they thought of something they might like to see or do. Once they arrived in Moscow, the Soviets went over each item in their itinerary with them and asked them if they wanted to make any changes.

"Some people ask," says Samantha, " 'Well, don't you think they set it all up?' Well, *of course* they did," she says in her somewhat exasperated, almost-adolescent voice. "I mean, what are they going to do, show me the grossest parts of all, or just let me wander around on my own? Of *course* not. If I had a new friend come over to my house I wouldn't take them down in the basement where it was all cluttered. Here it's an invitation from the Soviet premier, and what are they supposed to do, tell me to get lost or something? I'm sure they're going to say, here are some tickets, go have a good time, 'bye."

Nor could the Soviets have prevented Samantha from announcing a sudden change in her itinerary. At the top of the stairs in their house is an original cartoon by MacNelly from the *Chicago Tribune* that the Smiths say is their favorite. It shows a pigtailed and pouty Samantha tugging on the sleeve of an enormous and stern-looking Andropov.

Reprinted by permission, Tribune Media Services

"Obviously," says Arthur Smith, "the Soviets put themselves in the kind of position where Samantha could have said, okay, we want to see the silos outside of the such-a-place, in front of all the cameras, including all of the Western journalists, and terrifically embarrassed our hosts. What the American journalists never seemed to catch on to was that the Soviets were really at great risk in this whole enterprise. We could have been ready for some kind of stunt activity, and the child certainly could have been very unpredictable."

Indeed, there were some who urged the Smiths to use Samantha's trip to pull a surprise political move on Andropov. Before leaving, they were besieged with letters, telegrams, and phone calls from Soviet Jewish émigrés in Europe, Israel, and the United States pleading with Samantha to hand-deliver emigration requests for relatives in the Soviet Union. The Smiths, perplexed at suddenly finding themselves in the middle of one of the stickiest aspects of Soviet-American relations, finally decided to take the letters and deliver them to an official in the Soviet Foreign Ministry.

A number of the reporters who tailed Samantha through the Soviet

Union couldn't resist taking jibes at the Soviets to demonstrate that *they* weren't being fooled. The *Boston Globe*, for example, called Camp Artek "a symbol of Soviet socialist hypocrisy . . . an exclusive summer camp for the sons and daughters of the Soviet elite." Official Soviet descriptions of Artek describe it as a competitive merit camp, with selection based on scholastic, athletic, and leadership abilities. According to Arthur Smith, the truth is probably something in between—some children get there because of pull, others because of merit. But implying that admission to Artek was solely a matter of political privilege is about as accurate, he says, "as a Soviet journalist describing Stanford University as a place reserved for the children of the ruling capitalistic elite."

To offset all that footage of smiling, laughing Soviet children in skits and swimming contests, a CBS correspondent assured viewers that "Artek is putting on its happiest face for Samantha." The network dug up a Soviet film showing Young Pioneers going through paramilitary training: learning to assemble submachine guns, patrolling beaches at night with automatic weapons, and enduring rigorous obstacle courses. The editorial message was clear: under Artek's smiling and sunny surface lurks a Communist boot camp. "There will be no night patrol for Samantha," the correspondent ominously concluded.

Arthur Smith shakes his head. "My view of the press has altered more than my view of the Soviets. You understand a lot more about journalism when it's you they're writing about." He recalls passing out Russian copies of Andropov's letter to reporters and telling them with a straight face that the Russian alphabet was just like English, only it has to be read in a mirror. "And you know a couple of them actually *believed* me for awhile," he says with a sigh.

Arthur worries that the American people are not really aware of who makes the decisions that affect what news they hear. "You know exactly what to expect from *Pravda*, and most Russian citizens do too, and they're good at reading it and understanding what it means between the lines. However, I don't think a lot of Americans understand how complicated the distortion of the information they're receiving can be."

When Samantha first returned from the Soviet Union she was, as one commentator put it, "hotter than a patty melt in a microwave." Appearances on the *Tonight Show*, the *Phil Donahue Show*, and *Nightline* followed in rapid succession. "It was a little like a weary Dorothy returning from the land of Oz" remarked one television station, "only in this case she never met the Wizard." In December 1983 she and her mother were invited to Japan, where she met local officials and told six hundred of her peers at a children's symposium on science, technology, and the future: "The year 2010 can be the year when all of us can look around and see only friends—no opposite nations, no enemies, no bombs."

Meanwhile, the Disney Channel had approached the Smiths with an offer for Samantha to do her own ninety-minute television special interviewing the Democratic presidential candidates about issues of concern to children. The program, which aired in February 1984, was called "Samantha Smith Goes to Washington," and it unleashed a fresh torrent of sarcasm from editorial commentators. "In other times, such a lovely child would have wanted to be Shirley Temple. Now she wants to be Dan Rather," lamented an editor of the *New Republic*.

Nonetheless, all of the Democratic candidates except for Walter Mondale and Gary Hart took Samantha and her constituency seriously enough to agree to be interviewed. Dressed in preppy tweed blazers and skirts, Samantha found life on the other side of the interviewing process to be a bit nerve-racking, and more work than she anticipated. "I had to stay up every night writing up my questions, and it took *so* long. I couldn't even watch television." Samantha was most nervous with her first subject—Reubin Askew—but she relaxed by the time she got her final interviewees. Most of the candidates used her questions as springboards for avuncular replies about the dangers of the current administration's economic, environmental, and foreign policies.

Samantha's early flush of enthusiasm for journalism soon faded, however, and she began drifting away from her Dan Rather role toward the Shirley Temple end of the television spectrum. Offers from Hollywood continued to pour in and she played a bit part in a sitcom the following fall. In March 1985 she made a pilot for a television series starring Robert Wagner called *Lime Street*. A member of the "adventure-detective" species, the show features an insurance investigator with two loving daughters, a princess, and a parachute escape from a plane that catches on fire. Samantha plays the oldest daughter. Does she want the show to become a series—which means that the family will have to move for at least six months to an apartment in Los Angeles? "Yeah!" she replies. "I really like California."

Acting, though, has not exactly been a lifelong dream. In her preletter days, she wanted to be a veterinarian. Even now, her parents have steered Samantha away from placing too many hopes on a Hollywood career. She describes with enthusiasm her latest Christmas present, a camera: "If my acting career doesn't follow me, I'll probably become a free-lance photographer." Has she thought about how acting might fit in with her concerns about nuclear war? "No, I don't think they do fit together," says Samantha, wrinkling her nose. "It's really weird. They don't at all." Are Jane Fonda and Ed Asner possible role models? Samantha doesn't know who Jane Fonda and Ed Asner are. "Ed Asner's the head of the union you just joined," her father tells her. Samantha's expression signals a noncommittal "Oh."

The dangers of being immersed in Hollywood culture at such an impressionable age have not been lost on the Smiths, and "to a certain extent it's already happening," says Jane Smith. "She wants to have her hair changed every week and to wear the Hollywood fashions. But you can't tell how much of it is her age, and how much of it is Hollywood."

Samantha's parents are keeping a sharp eye out for any possible ill effects on their daughter. They are strict about her keeping up with homework. But the way they see it, Samantha's letter and trip have given her options that her parents could never have provided for her. They hope that Samantha's show-biz career will earn enough to pay for a good college education. In the meantime, culture-minded Arthur—a Shakespeare buff—would "like to see Sam get to Europe." But Samantha doesn't hesitate when asked where she would next like to travel. "Africa," she says.

It is past nine o'clock, and Samantha has already left, come back in pajamas (still wearing the hot pink socks, and with a blue kerchief now wrapped around the perm) to give good-night kisses to her parents, and tripped off to bed. Around the kitchen table, the discussion with her parents—about how Samantha has affected their lives, how she may have affected the world—goes late into the night.

"It remains to be seen what the total effect of her journey was," says Arthur Smith. "But I think Samantha's efforts were most helpful in causing people to think about the Soviet Union in a more human light. The more people who understand the Soviet Union in even somewhat objective terms the better, so that we can begin to think of them as people, not just as the evil empire—as a different system in the world, and not just an opposing system."

The Smiths were not active in the disarmament movement before Samantha wrote her letter. "But I certainly was in some sympathy with the freeze movement, and with the idea that it was more important to talk to the Soviets than to blow the world up in a nuclear war," recalls Jane Smith. "It made sense to me that we should talk to them and learn to get along with them before we should expect them to change, rather than waiting for them to become like us before we will talk to them, which seemed a little absurd."

Arthur Smith points to two enormous orange filing cabinets in his study, both filled with Samantha paraphernalia. "We have a complete archive of anything you might want, from the *New Republic* to *Barbie Magazine*." Also in the file drawers are numerous video clippings of Samantha's television appearances. Her father pulls out a few and plugs them into their television.

One shows Samantha on the *Tonight Show* just after the letter from Andropov arrived. She wears jeans and wriggles with excitement in her chair. "Well, congratulations!" begins Johnny Carson. "Are you getting tired of answering all the questions that people like myself, and people on the news shows, are asking you?" "Yes," giggles Samantha. The audience roars. During her second appearance with Carson, after her trip to the Soviet Union, Samantha perches rather stiffly on the edge of her chair because "her friends at home," explains her mother, "had made fun of her for looking like a little girl dangling her legs the first time."

Watching the clips, the way other parents watch home movies of their kids, the Smiths are amazed at the difference between her first and second shows; her giggly nervousness is replaced by an almost frightening self-possession. Even her parents don't understand why Samantha has such an aptitude for the airwaves. Samantha is walking the high wire of stardom all by herself, and though her parents are ready to catch her at a moment's notice, they follow her progress with an amused, bewildered respect.

Samantha's mail indicates that she is still inspiring and provoking people to clarify their thoughts on Soviet-American relations. About six thousand letters have arrived for Samantha in the last two years, many from children throughout the world, including a hefty number from Soviet children. Frequently they send pictures of themselves and postcards of their towns or cities. Several hundred have yet to be translated. Arthur Smith has kept them all, bundled in rubber bands in boxes under his desk. Most are simply fan letters, but not all.

One letter, postmarked Portland, Maine, from a "Mrs. John Smith" with no return address, says: "You lovely, sweet people *must* wake up and smell the coffee! You are all as gullible as two-year-olds taking candy from strangers. The Russians say the word 'peace' and you grab at it, and at them, like candy. Yes, they want peace—but how? Under *their* terms! They want to dominate the world and that includes us. Doesn't that frighten you? They will never change. They have used you poor people and my heart aches for you because you have been so blind."

Samantha pays little attention to the dozen or so letters that arrive every week; she obviously considers the mail to be Daddy's territory. Her father attempted to answer them at first with a thank-you card bearing Samantha's signature, but he gave up after the first six hundred or so, when he discovered that such answers only encouraged people to write for extra autographs, signed photographs, and other special requests. Ironically, the girl who has made something of a career out of getting a reply from a famous person has no time or interest in answering all of *her* mail. The exception is her regular correspondence with Natasha, her best friend in the Soviet Union.

Arthur Smith is saving those letters for a reason. One day, Samantha will go into the study, pull out those boxes, and start reading those letters herself. She will think about what has happened to her from a new perspective. She will have lost some of her childhood perspicacity, but she will have learned other things in the meantime.

Samantha is growing up. Any snapshot of her will soon be dated. Perhaps she will someday start perusing the *New York Times* and keeping up on the latest arms control debates. Perhaps she will someday become a "superperson peacemaker." Or perhaps she will remain only "concerned." Who Samantha Smith will become is very much an open question, but she appears quite capable of deciding that for herself. And if we are all lucky, the adult Samantha will be just as direct and original as she is now.

"It all seemed so dumb to me," Samantha said. Millions of people on both sides of the Cold War have thought the same thing. The difference is that Samantha acted. She and her journey to the Soviet Union will continue to intrigue, inspire, and infuriate the grown-ups. For her brilliance, or her crime, was to ask the questions that persist in hovering around the superpower conflict. Why are the Russians our enemies? Why must we have nuclear weapons? Why can't the grown-ups get along? Why . . . ?

❧❧❧
APPENDIX:
WHAT YOU CAN DO

Citizen diplomacy is more than just a concept—it is a network of thousands of individuals and organizations looking for your involvement. Your options are manifold. You can participate in an existing project or create one of your own. Travel to the Soviet Union is helpful, but there's a lot you can do in your own backyard: you can write to a Soviet pen pal; you can host Soviets through your school, church, business, or civic organization; you can get your community to develop a sister-city relationship with a Soviet city; and you can educate yourself, your neighbors, your family, and your friends about the Soviet Union. For a useful guide on the basics of getting started, you might consult the Center for Innovative Diplomacy's *Having International Affairs Your Way: A Five-Step Briefing Manual for Citizen Diplomats*.

In the following thirty-eight sections, we describe hundreds of citizen diplomacy activities now under way and supply addresses and telephone numbers to help you find out more. Much of this information has been synthesized from the publications of the Institute for Soviet-American Relations (ISAR), a clearinghouse for citizen diplomacy information run by Harriett Crosby and Nancy Graham. In cooperation with the Friends Committee on National Legislation, ISAR publishes a journal three times a year called *Surviving Together* that reports on the leading events, personalities, articles, and views in the field. Beginning as a photocopied, ten-page collection of odds and ends in 1983, the journal has since swelled to nearly one hundred pages per issue. Citizen diplomats throughout the country regard past and current issues of *Surviving Together* as basic texts.

Another key resource drawn upon is a handbook published by ISAR called *Organizations Involved in Soviet-American Relations*. The new 1986 edition describes 232 organizations representing 1,313 staff members and 89 exchange projects; its appendix contains much useful information, including the full text of current government exchange agreements, addresses and phone numbers of Soviet agencies and organizations, recommended reading lists, and guidelines on how to develop exchange projects.

While most of the activities we describe represent purely private initiatives from American citizens, a few enjoy partial support, financially and organizationally, from the American government. Following the November 1985 Geneva summit meeting, President Reagan appointed Stephen Rhinesmith, former President of the American Field Service International Scholarship Program, to be special coordinator of his US-Soviet Exchange Initiative. Rhinesmith's office, part of the United States Information Agency (USIA), can provide assistance for some citizen exchange initiatives.

The following sections are organized by key words starting with ANIMALS and ending with YOUTH:

Most of the subjects—like *BUSINESS*, *JOURNALISM*, and *LAW*—are self-explanatory. But because overlap between some categories is unavoidable, a few of the finer distinctions warrant explanation:

- *CHILDREN* primarily covers activities involving preteens, while *YOUTH* covers nonacademic activities involving high school and college students.
- *UNIVERSITIES* covers college-level academic exchanges as well as college-level programs in Soviet studies, while *TEACHING* covers exchanges between Soviet and American primary and secondary school teachers. *LANGUAGE* describes programs for learning Russian available for both high school students and adults.
- *GENERAL EXCHANGE* refers to organizations promoting many types of citizen diplomacy that are often good places to begin.

TO LEARN MORE:

The Center for Innovative
  Diplomacy
424B Cole St.
San Francisco, CA 94117
(415) 552-6819

Friends Committee on National
  Legislation
245 Second St., NE
Washington, DC 20002
(202) 547-6000

The Institute for Soviet-American
  Relations
1608 New Hampshire Ave., NW
Washington, DC 20009
(202) 387-3034

The President's US-Soviet Exchange
  Initiative
The US Information Agency
301 4th St., SW
Washington, DC 20547
(202) 485-1548

ANIMALS

Linda Tellington-Jones is an animal trainer known in equestrian and zookeeping circles throughout the world for her Tellington-Jones Equine Awareness Movements (TEAM), a method of training and healing horses through bodywork and awareness exercises for both horses and riders. In 1984, after reading about five American psychologists who interviewed Soviet children on their attitudes toward peace, she decided to go to the Soviet Union to meet with "horse people." She was particularly interested in trying to heal Aswan, a famous Arabian stallion who was suffering from arthritis.

By the time Tellington-Jones arrived in the Soviet Union, Aswan had already died. Undaunted, Tellington-Jones told her Intourist guide about her interest in horses and the Moscow "Hippodrome," where her grandfather had ridden and trained horses for the Czar between 1902 and 1905. The Intourist guide, an amateur horse trainer herself, decided to help Tellington-Jones visit the Hippodrome, but officials told them it was "quarantined" and off-limits to Western tourists. Then Tellington-Jones met Soviet impresario Joseph Goldin through their mutual acquaintance Jim Hickman (*see* chapter 6). Goldin sneaked her into the Hippodrome and arranged for her to give an impromptu demonstration of her TEAM to several Soviet trainers, who were so impressed that they invited her back the next day for a second demonstration for fifty of their colleagues. Tellington-Jones returned several months later and gave two weeks of workshops to more than 150 trainers, amateur riders, and veterinarians, spending her days working with small groups of veterinarians and her evenings giving public lectures to Soviets who had heard rumors of her unusual healing powers.

Tellington-Jones's work has enjoyed the support of Yelena Petushkova, a Soviet Olympic gold medal winner in dressage and president of Soviet Athletes for Peace. At the Bitsa Olympic Sports Complex, Tellington-Jones has helped Petushkova work with the Soviet jumping and dressage teams and plan their development program for riders. Whenever she is in the Soviet Union, she stays with the veterinarians in their special quarters. The head veterinarian at Bitsa, Dr. Nina Khanzhina, now regards the two most important aspects of her veterinary training program as sports medicine and TEAM.

Tellington-Jones has also applied her "TEAM touch" to the broken elbow of Vladimir Pozner, the Moscow radio commentator who frequently appears on ABC's evening show *Nightline*. After his treatment, Pozner quipped that his dream is now to be reincarnated as a horse so that she can work on him more.

Tellington-Jones believes that "animals are great ambassadors. They open doors for us—creating open avenues for communication between peoples of nations that have had a lack of understanding." Following this philosophy, she has devised an "Animal Ambassadors" program, in which American animal lovers can exchange pictures or drawings of their whole families—animals included—with animal-loving Soviet families. Helping to get this project underway is the Club Healthy Family, a large organization based in Gorky Park in Moscow.

Appendix

TO LEARN MORE:
TEAM Club/Animal Ambassadors
Box S-999
Carmel, CA 93921
(408) 624-2623

ART

In 1983, Patty Winpenny, a mother of two in Pawlet, Vermont, was at a loss. She had studied Russian at Swarthmore, lived in Leningrad for over a year while directing a language program for the Council on International Education Exchange (*see* "Universities"), and gotten a masters degree in Soviet and Eastern European political economy, but she found limited opportunities for using her skills in her community. She read Russian stories to children in the town library, ordered Soviet childrens' books at the local bookstore, gave lessons on Soviet geography and history as a substitute elementary school teacher, and lectured on Soviet political economy at a community college, but somehow, it was not enough. Then, in 1983, the Citizen Exchange Council (*see* "Travel and Tourism") asked her to lead a cross-country ski trip in the Soviet Union. When she returned, a local peace group sought her advice on how it could help children learn more about the Soviet Union. With her guidance, the group decided to focus on a form of communication that transcended the language barrier—art.

What later became known as the Children's Art Exchange launched its program by borrowing art from a longstanding collection of the Boston-based Organization for American-Soviet Exchanges (*see* "General Exchange"). The exhibit was kicked off by a gala reception featuring Vermont Senator Patrick Leahy and Edward Malayan, an assistant to Soviet Ambassador Dobrynin. In April 1985 Winpenny set out for the Soviet Union, "personally knocking on doors" of schools, art clubs, the Children's Writers Union, and the Children's Publishing House and delivering hundreds of pieces of American children's art. Her visits netted several agreements for ongoing exchanges as well as several hundred pieces of Soviet children's art in return. Within a month she was back in the Soviet Union carrying more American art and bringing back more Soviet art.

Winpenny was determined that the Children's Art Exchange be more than just a simplistic "peace project" where kids "learn about postage costs to the Soviet Union and that's about all." In her view, art from foreign cultures contains more than just colors and shapes—it also contains ideas. If American kids are to appreciate a Soviet kid's drawing of a camel in the desert, for example, they need to know about the Central Asian republics of the Soviet Union. Winpenny decided to write an elementary school curriculum to accompany the art exchanges that has since been introduced in a number of Vermont primary schools

309

and published under the title *Soviet Studies for the Elementary and Junior High Grades: An Integrated Arts Approach*.

Winpenny is now putting her collection of Soviet art on display in schools and museums throughout the United States, assisted most recently by the Smithsonian Institution's Traveling Exhibits Program. Participating schools may keep a few pictures permanently (as well as accompanying postcards and essays), but Winpenny prefers loaning the art work or handing out color Xerox copies to ensure their widest possible circulation. In all, the Children's Art Exchange has connected twenty-five American schools with more than a dozen cooperating schools, art clubs, and Young Pioneer clubs in Moscow, Leningrad, Tallinn, Frunza, and elsewhere. The Children's Art Exchange is looking to double the number of participants on both sides in 1987 and can be contacted if you would like to involve your school in the program.

Another organization promoting the exchange of Soviet and American children's art is the Minneapolis-based Consortium on New Educational and Cultural Ties with the Soviet Union (CONNECT), which was started by Paula DeCosse, a forty-three-year-old children's nonfiction book writer. In 1984, while traveling to the Soviet Union on a tour led by Cynthia Lazaroff (*see* chapter 2), DeCosse decided to set up art exchanges with the Moscow Central Pioneer Palace (a youth center involving thousands of Soviet children), the Moscow Central Children's Theater, the Children's Art Museum in Yerevan, and schools in Moscow, Tbilisi, and Yerevan. When she returned to the United States, she put the hundred pieces she had collected on display in nine cities, including in San Francisco the Democratic National Convention and an art gallery in Sitka, Alaska. For the American contribution to the exchange, DeCosse collected children's art from forty states and sent three hundred of the best pieces to the Soviet Union. The Children's Museum in Yerevan was so pleased that it asked to keep several for its permanent collection and sent a hundred more of its own paintings to the United States.

CONNECT then organized a contest in which American and Soviet children submitted art based on the theme of "Cooperation in Space." The winning paintings were exhibited at the Moscow Children's Theater and the young artists each received special congratulatory letters from three astronauts and three cosmonauts. DeCosse is now making arrangements to bring these paintings to the United States.

CONNECT is also arranging a wider variety of exchanges—of essays, photographs, and "video letters," for example—between schools in Minnesota and the Soviet Union. In the near future, it plans to bring to the United States Soviet posters, photography, puppets, dancers, art professors, and children (*see* "Children").

Other children's art exchange groups have sprung up around the country as well. The Boston-based Children Are the Future brought twenty-one artists—

eleven of them children and teenagers—from Afro-American, Hispanic-American, and Armenian-American communities to Yerevan to work with Soviet artists, young and old, and create a seventy-foot, four-paneled peace mural on the wall of a housing project. In Tennessee and Georgia, Bernice Massey, a schoolteacher and visual artist, helped her students prepare a friendship mural for the children of Soviet diplomats attending a Washington, DC, school. Massey also initiated a project called "Soviet Landscape of Dreams," in which she weaved baskets "inspired by landscapes of the Soviet Union and the traditional dome-shaped architecture there." A Nashville television station captured the exhibit and her message in a film called "Baskets for Peace," which Massey later showed in the Soviet Union.

Another way to get involved in Soviet-American art exchanges is to support official exchanges of paintings and sculptures. The fruits of such support were evident after the Geneva summit in 1985, when each country agreed to loan forty Impressionist and Post-Impressionist paintings to one another, giving many American art lovers their first glimpse of the Soviet-owned classics of Cézanne, Monet, Renoir, Gauguin, Van Gogh, Rousseau, Matisse, and Picasso.

TO LEARN MORE:

Children Are The Future
P.O. Box 1063
Brookline, MA 02146
(617) 232-4222

Children's Art Exchange
RR2 Box 3400
Middlebury, VT 05753
(802) 545-2224

CONNECT
4835 Pennsylvania Ave. S.
Minneapolis, MN 55409
(612) 922-4032

Bernice Massey
590 BonAventure Ave.
Atlanta, GA 30306

BOOKS AND MAGAZINES

In August 1983 Anya Kucharev and Gwendolyn Grace, both then working for the Esalen Soviet American Exchange Program (*see* chapter 6), were helping several Americans and Soviets to set up a "space bridge" between the University of California at San Diego and the Moscow International Book Fair, a major cultural event that has taken place every other year since 1977. In three weeks, Kucharev and Grace lined up a booth space, authors, and books on such topics as the antinuclear, environmental, holistic health, and human potential movements. A week before the fair began, Korean Airlines Flight 007 was shot down and so was the space bridge. Kucharev and Grace nevertheless decided to go ahead with their exhibit. "We were in tears and in shock," Kucharev recalls, "at the number of people who came, clutching these books, reading them, taking notes for three or four days. . . . People wanted these books."

When Kucharev and Grace returned, twenty-eight-year-old Jocelyn Stoller, another Esalen associate and an expert in cross-cultural education, decided to try transforming the project into a commercially viable business that would help expose Soviets and Americans to one another's books—a venture that became known as the Soviet-American Book Exchange (SABE). Kucharev and Stoller have since introduced Soviet editors, translators, and writers to their American counterparts and tried to develop joint Soviet-American publications and book exhibitions. In 1985 they helped get Soviet publishers interested in translating and publishing American books on environmental studies, the writings of native Americans and other ethnic minorities, and alternative health-care methods. Later in 1985 SABE returned to the next Moscow Book Fair, where as many as seven thousand people each day waited for hours in the rain to see 200,000 books from 104 countries. This time SABE exhibited 800 books and journals from 176 publishers on such varying subjects as computers, music, hunger, nuclear war, and underwater photography.

Unlike the 1983 fair, the 1985 fair attracted many American publishers, including the Association of Jewish Book Publishers, whose participation was demanded by other American publishers in 1977. One elderly Soviet Jew came to the Association's booth every day, carefully copying a large volume of Hebrew into a notebook. By far the most popular exhibit was the Association of American Publishers' "America through American Eyes," which displayed 312 books chosen by a committee of American writers, editors, and librarians. The bilingual catalogue of these books became one of the most sought-after items at the fair; more than five thousand were given out each day. A number of academic presses also attended the fair. "It is the memory of those teeming crowds," reflects Hunter Cole of the University of Mississippi Press, "that transcends all else for me. In them I sense the power of books and the hope that books can engender."

The Library of Congress has been exchanging books, government documents, periodicals, and newspapers with Soviet libraries on and off since the 1920s. It now has sixty-two Soviet exchange partners, including Moscow's Lenin State Library. Many major US university libraries also have ongoing exchanges with Soviet libraries; Columbia University alone shares materials with forty Soviet libraries.

If you are interested in buying Soviet books, you can write for a free catalogue to Imported Publications, which for fifteen years has sold English, Spanish, and Russian editions of Soviet children's books, general fiction, cookbooks, magazines and newspapers, as well as Soviet textbooks in engineering, art, and political theory. Kamkin Books is the largest US distributor of Soviet books, and is also the sole US agent for the Soviet record agency Melodiya. Another source of information about Soviet publications is *The Current Digest of the Soviet Press*, which publishes a weekly compendium of translated articles from more than ninety Soviet newspapers and journals. And you can now subscribe to daily English translations of *Pravda* from Associated Publishers.

You can also receive English translations of a wide variety of Soviet journals covering technical, scientific, and medical fields. Every year, the Soviets publish more than thirty US journals and Americans translate and publish more than a hundred Soviet journals. The most popular US magazine published in the Soviet Union is *Scientific American;* fifteen thousand Soviets subscribe to it and another five thousand copies are sold at kiosks.

Under the government cultural agreement, both countries also exchange monthly national magazines, *America Illustrated* and *Soviet Life*. The US Information Agency distributes sixty thousand copies of *America Illustrated* in the Soviet Union through subscriptions and newsstand sales; if the long queues at kiosks selling the magazine and the high black-market price of back issues are any indication, the magazine is extremely popular. While the Soviets are allowed to sell up to sixty thousand copies of *Soviet Life* in the United States, the American public purchases perhaps half this number. The Soviets have made it clear that they will only allow more copies of *America Illustrated* to be distributed when more Americans subscribe to *Soviet Life*.

TO LEARN MORE:

Associated Publishers
2408 Territorial Road
St. Paul, MN 55114
(612) 646-2548

Association of Jewish Book
    Publishers
838 5th Ave.
New York, NY 10021
(212) 249-0100

The Current Digest of the Soviet
    Press
1480 West Lane Ave.
Columbus, OH
(614) 422-4234

Imported Publications
320 W. Ohio St.
Chicago, IL 60610-4175
(312) 787-9017

Kamkin Books
12224 Parklawn Dr.
Rockville, MD 20852
(301) 881-5973

The Soviet-American Book
    Exchange
3268 Sacramento St.
San Francisco, CA 94115
(415) 567-2663

Soviet Life Magazine
1706 18th St. NW
Washington, DC 20009

BUSINESS AND TRADE

Donald Kendall, sixty-five, opened Soviet markets to an American product now consumed by millions of Soviets—Pepsi-Cola. Kendall joined Pepsi-Cola, Inc. (later PepsiCo, Inc.) as a bottle line worker and a fountain-syrup salesman in 1947 and quickly moved up the corporate ladder—to national sales manager in 1949, to vice president for national accounts in 1952, to vice president of marketing in 1957, and to president of the international division in the same year. In 1959 Kendall decided to test the possibility of selling Pepsi in the Soviet Union by setting up a booth at a Moscow trade fair after Coke had turned down the chance to have a booth. Ridiculed by his associates for believing that a soft drink could be sold in the Soviet Union, Kendall knew he was taking a major risk. The night before the trade fair—and the night before Vice-President Richard Nixon was to have his famous "kitchen debate" with Nikita Khrushchev—Kendall told his old friend Nixon, "I've got to get a bottle into Khrushchev's hand, or I'm in the doghouse." The next day, Nixon steered Khrushchev over to the Pepsi booth. "I told Khrushchev," recalls Kendall, "that I wanted him to try a Pepsi made in New York and one made in Moscow. I knew which one he would like the best." Khrushchev found the "Moscow Pepsi" so appealing that he downed seven bottles—all while Kendall's promotional photographers clicked away.

By 1963 Kendall had climbed into the presidency of the company, and through his persistence, PepsiCo reached an agreement in 1972 to provide the Soviets with soft drink concentrate, bottling equipment, and assistance with quality control in Soviet production of the soda. In return, the Soviets agreed to sell Stolichnaya Russian vodka and wine to PepsiCo (which is distributed through its subsidiary, Monsieur Henri). The first Pepsi plant opened in May 1974 in Novorossiisk, a city on the Black Sea, and sales soon skyrocketed. The Soviets began advertising Pepsi by proclaiming that "a drink of Pepsi-Cola will put you in a good mood and will refresh you."

A decade later, fourteen Pepsi plants were operating in the Soviet Union, serving Soviet stores, restaurants, kiosks, and other retail outlets. PepsiCo now appears to be one of the principal beneficiaries of General Secretary Gorbachev's antivodka campaign; a new two-billion-dollar, five-year deal aiming to double sales of Pepsi there by 1991 was signed in 1985. Kendall is a stalwart advocate of increased trade with the Soviet Union, calling it "one of the main means of solving the problems between the United States and the Soviet Union."

Kendall is one of thousands of Americans who have taken their business to the Soviet Union since Armand Hammer's first business exploits in the early 1920s (*see* chapter 7). Business activity expanded rapidly when Richard Nixon and Leonid Brezhnev signed an agreement on trade in October 1972. A flurry of protocols, visits, and business negotiations followed, but the honeymoon was short-lived. In 1974, the US Congress tacked the "Jackson-Vanik Amendment" onto the Trade Reform Act, which required that the Soviets ease their restrictions on emigration before the President could give the Soviet Union "most favored nation" trade status, new trade agreements, or Export-Import Bank financing. The result on trade was devastating. Without access to Export-Import Bank financing, which between 1972 and 1974 provided half a billion dollars in assistance, the Soviet Union had much more difficulty raising the hard currency necessary for buying goods from the United States. In addition, without a "most favored nation" trade status, the Soviet Union had to pay tariffs three-to-five times larger than the United States' "normal" trading partners.

Other problems befuddled US-Soviet trade as well. In 1978, the US Department of Commerce required all US firms exporting oil and gas equipment to the Soviet Union to get special licenses; eighteen months later it refused to issue these licenses. In 1980 President Carter sought to punish the Soviet Union for its invasion of Afghanistan by embargoing most grain and phosphate exports, suspending the licensing of all high-technology exports, and imposing restrictions on Soviet ammonia imports. When President Reagan came to office in 1981, he relaxed some of these controls, but reimposed them later in reaction to Soviet complicity in the repression of Poland. In the years since, many of these controls have gradually been lifted, but the damage to the US trade balance was significant; one estimate is that remaining trade limitations have deprived the United States of more than two billion dollars in sales to the Soviet Union since 1980. Today, the level of Soviet-American trade is roughly comparable to that of US trade with Algeria.

US exports to the Soviet Union are mostly wheat and corn. But the composition of US exports is beginning to diversify. Agricultural exports now include cotton and almonds. In 1985 US firms received $185 million worth of new machinery and equipment orders from the Soviet Union—twice the order level of 1984. And some of these orders were for whole factories; Owens-Illinois, for example, built for the Soviet Union two plants producing glass face-plates, funnels, and solderglass for television set manufacture.

While the United States exports more to the Soviet Union than it imports, some American consumers have found certain Soviet products extremely valuable:

- More than five thousand Soviet Belarus tractors, reputed for ruggedness and reliability, are now operating on American farms; in 1985, there was a 40 percent increase in US purchases. New Orleans uses a hundred Belarus tractors to pull the floats in its Mardi Gras parade.
- Soviet surgical stapling guns have become an important new medical technology distributed by US Surgical Corp. and 3M.

• Soviet technologies for metal working have attracted numerous US firms. The rails for the Washington, DC, Metro were welded using Soviet equipment. Olin Brass of East Alton, Illinois, is using a Soviet-devised electromagnetic metal shaping process for casting copper alloys. Multi-Arc Vacuum Systems, Inc., of St. Paul, Minnesota, is marketing a Soviet-developed process for coating metals. J. R. McDermott Inc. of New Orleans, Louisiana, holds a license from the Soviet Union to build flash welding machines for large-diameter offshore pipelines.

One recent boon to Soviet-American trade has been the sudden availability of private credit. Even though the Export-Import Bank continues to be snarled in the Jackson-Vanik restrictions, ten US banks agreed in 1985 to lend the Soviet Union as much as $2.4 billion to help finance grain imports. Overall, the Soviet Union currently has a trade surplus with Western nations.

If you are interested in promoting or getting involved in Soviet-American trade, one place to begin is the US-USSR Trade and Economic Council. Established in 1973 as a nongovernmental organization run jointly by Soviets and Americans, the Trade Council facilitates trade, banking, insurance, shipping, and technology transfer between the two superpowers through annual conferences and exhibitions. In December 1985 it brought to Moscow 415 Americans representing more than 340 corporations, trading companies, and law firms to meet with the top Soviet trade personnel, including General Secretary Gorbachev, Prime Minister Nikolai Ryzhkov, and Minister of Foreign Trade Boris Aristov. It also unanimously approved a resolution declaring its support for granting the Soviet Union "most favored nation" trade status and allowing it Export-Import Bank credits, which, it argued, could lead to sales of more than ten billion dollars. To keep its members apprised of recent developments in US-Soviet trade, the Trade Council bimonthly publishes *The Journal of the US-USSR Trade and Economic Council*.

Several other organizations also promote Soviet-American trade. The American Committee on US-Soviet Relations (formerly The American Committee on East-West Accord) published a 1983 book entitled *Common Sense in US-Soviet Trade*. Business Executives for National Security (BENS) has arranged for a number of high-level American business executives to visit the Soviet Union. Taking a more academic approach, the Center for Corporate Economics and Strategy at Duke University has charted economic reforms under way in the Soviet Union and their implications for East-West trade. And the Institute on Strategic Trade has analyzed Soviet-American trade and technology transfer and educated the public, businesses, and government agencies through publications, seminars, and conferences.

You can keep up with recent developments in the field through various publications. The most comprehensive compendium of information is *Interflo:*

An East-West Trade News Monitor. Also available is the *Research on Soviet and East European Agriculture Newsletter*, which provides current information on Soviet agricultural policy. Other useful journals are *PlanEcon, The Journal of Commerce*, and the US State Department's *Business America*.

Another indispensable tool for doing business in the Soviet Union is *US Information Moscow*, a "yellow pages" of necessary contacts, addresses, and telephone numbers.

TO LEARN MORE:

American Committee on US-Soviet
   Relations
109 11th St., SE
Washington, DC 20003
(202) 546-1700

Business Executives for National
   Security (BENS)
21 Dupont Circle, NW #401
Washington, DC 20036
(202) 429-0600

Center for Corporate Economics and
   Strategy
Fuqua School of Business
Duke University
Durham, NC 27706
(919) 684-2494

Institute on Strategic Trade
499 S. Capitol St., #404A
Washington, DC 20003
(202) 484-5033

Interflo: An East-West Trade News
   Monitor
P.O. Box 42,
Maplewood, NJ 07040
(201) 763-9493

PlanEcon Journal
Plan Economy
1156 15th St., NW
Washington, DC 20005
(202) 939-8968

Research on Soviet and East
   European Agriculture
University of Southern Maine
96 Falmouth St.
Portland, ME 04103
(207) 780-4306

US Information Moscow
3268 Sacramento St.
San Francisco, CA 94115
(415) 922-2422

US-USSR Trade and Economic
   Council, Inc.
805 Third Ave.
New York City, NY 10022
(212) 644-4550

CHILDREN

In 1981, British documentary filmmaker David Woollcombe created a minor hit in London when his play *Peace Child* was performed in the Royal Albert

Music Hall. Adapting Bernard Benson's *The Peace Book*, then a best-seller in Europe, and using David Gordon's music, Woollcombe's play is set in the year 2025 and describes how American and Soviet children in the 1980s led the world's children on a successful crusade for peace. Woollcombe and Rosey Simonds, his wife and coproducer, decided to bring the play to America, and, with the assistance of John Marks, director of an organization called The Search for Common Ground, they were able to premiere *Peace Child* at the Kennedy Center in Washington, DC, in 1982. Since then, Woollcombe and Simonds have put on more than 350 performances throughout the United States and in eleven other countries. The play has also been performed with American and Soviet child actors in several Soviet cities, in a dozen American cities, and via a Moscow-Minneapolis "space bridge." Woollcombe and Simonds are now planning more Soviet-American performances, trying to produce a joint Soviet-American recording of all of the play's music, and preparing a film of the play with a joint Soviet-American cast.

If you are interested in having *Peace Child* performed in your town, either their production or yours, you can write to the Peace Child Foundation. Available are a book, a study guide, and a video, all of which encourage children to rewrite parts of the play with their own scenes.

The play *Peace Child* is one of many projects involving American and Soviet children. A good place to get an overview of these projects is CONNECT, based in Minneapolis, Minnesota, which serves as a clearinghouse of information from schools, churches, and other organizations involving youth in the exchange of letters, art, photography, and video letters (*see* "Art"). Another key source of information is the Samantha Smith Foundation, directed by Samantha's mother Jane G. Smith (*see* chapter 9), which in 1986 cosponsored, with the Turner Broadcasting System, an International Youth Art Competition for Soviet and American children and gave the winners free trips to the 1986 "Goodwill Games" in the Soviet Union (*see* "Sports"). In spring 1986 the foundation convened a small gathering of the leading citizen diplomats working with children that offered five hundred children displaced by the Chernobyl nuclear power disaster an opportunity to spend a summer in American camps—an offer the Soviets have thus far declined. The foundation is now working on several media outreach projects, including a book, a documentary, and a TV movie about Samantha, and in fall 1986 it began publishing a lively national children's newsletter aimed at keeping children and teachers up-to-date on US-Soviet children's exchange opportunities.

In 1982 Pat Montandon started a San Francisco-based organization called Children As The Peacemakers because, she says, "I wanted children to have a voice in their future. Kids will never want to declare war if they see each other as people at a young age." With this philosophy, Montandon has taken delegations of children, ages five to eleven, to meet with heads of state around the world. On three separate trips, she has brought more than a hundred children to the Soviet Union, one of which was received by the Kremlin's leaders. In 1986, the organization sponsored an essay competition, whose winner, ten-year-old Star Rowe, accompanied an eleven-year-old Moscow girl, Katerina Lycheva, on a goodwill tour throughout the Soviet Union and the United States; the duo's itinerary included a brief visit with President Ronald Reagan.

Also formed in 1982 was the New York-based Kids Meeting Kids Can Make a Difference. After introducing New York City children to the children of Soviet diplomats at a United Nations reception, the organization collected more than twenty thousand friendship letters from American children and sent them to children in the Soviet Union, beginning a number of pen-pal relationships. In 1986 the program sent ten American teenagers to Soviet Pioneer camps and hosted ten Soviet teenagers in the United States.

Another organization bringing Soviet children to the United States is the Holyearth Foundation/Earthstewards Network, directed by Danaan Parry, a physicist who once worked with the US Atomic Energy Commission, and Diana Glasgow. In 1985, the group brought twenty children to tour the Soviet Union and meet with Soviet children in schools, private homes, Pioneer Clubs, discos, and parks. In the small city of Cherkassy, Parry and Glasgow helped Soviet and American children plant birch trees for peace—a ceremony they repeated when twenty Soviet youths interested in computers visited the United States in October 1986.

The Boston-based Children Are the Future (*see* "Art") has taken American children to the Soviet Union for tours of schools, parks, summer camps, and children's hospital wards. The trips have enabled American children to work with Soviet children on joint projects involving murals, animated films, puppets, and musical instruments. Young Storytellers for Peace, a group based in Bellevue, Washington, trained children from Montana and Washington in the art of storytelling and then gave them a chance to try out their skills on audiences in Moscow, Leningrad, and Odessa during an April 1986 tour.

If you are interested in educating children about the Soviet Union, you might want to use the curricula available from Educators for Social Responsibility (*see* "Teaching"), the Children's Art Exchange (*see* "Art"), and the US-USSR Youth Exchange Program (*see* chapter 2 and "Youth"). Another resource is the National Foundation for the Improvement of Education's book of Soviet children's art and creative writing entitled *The Soviet Union as Seen by Its Children*. And the Ground Zero Pairing Project (*see* "Sister Cities") has produced a package of booklets, videotapes, and audio tapes on *Elementary School Educational Material on Russian Geography, Language, Literature and Children*.

TO LEARN MORE:

Children As The Peacemakers
999 Green Street
San Francisco, CA 94133
(415) 775-2323

The Holyearth Foundation/
    Earthstewards Network
6330 Eagle Harbor Dr., NE
Bainbridge Island, WA 98110
(206) 842-7986

Kids Meeting Kids Can Make a
    Difference
Box 8H
380 Riverside Dr.
New York, NY 10025
(212) 662-2327

National Foundation for the
    Improvement of Education
1201 16th Street, NW, Rm. 628
Washington, DC 20036
(202) 822-7840

Peace Child Foundation
3977 Chain Bridge Rd., Suite 204
Fairfax, VA 22030
(703) 385-4494

Samantha Smith Foundation
Box 60
Manchester, ME 04351
(207) 623-1306

Young Storytellers for Peace
1075 Bellevue Way NE
Bellevue, WA 98004

ENVIRONMENT

The Wisconsin-based International Crane Foundation (ICF) has been working with Soviet scientists for more than ten years to save the nearly extinct Siberian Crane. After hearing about the successes of an American captive breeding program for whooping cranes and other endangered cranes, Soviet scientist Dr. Vladimir Flint began corresponding with Dr. George Archibald and other scientists at ICF. In 1977, Dr. Flint brought four Siberian Crane eggs, carefully packaged in a plywood box, to Moscow and handed them to ICF scientists, who then brought them back to Wisconsin for incubation. Two of the eggs hatched, the first of which the Wisconsin team affectionately named Vladimir, incognizant that the crane was really a female. Since then, ICF has imported more eggs and slowly developed a population of nineteen Siberian Cranes. In 1983 and 1985, ICF brought eggs laid in captivity back to the Soviet Union to be hatched by common cranes acting as foster parents. Meanwhile, Dr. Flint and other Soviet scientists traveled to the Wisconsin facility and, based on what they learned, established their own crane breeding facility at the Oka Nature Preserve, two hundred miles from Moscow.

David Blair, an environmental educator from New Hampshire, is now preparing to use these crane exchanges as the basis for an environmental education curriculum for Soviet and American children. By writing essays and drawing pictures about each other's endangered cranes, whales, and seals, participating children, Blair hopes, will learn to appreciate both nature and one another.

Russell Peterson, former Republican governor of Delaware, used his position as president of the National Audubon Society to work with Soviet scientists in the International Union for the Conservation of Nature and Natural Resources (IUCN) on studying the possibilities of a nuclear war triggering a nuclear winter. Under the auspices of the IUCN, American and Soviet specialists have also met in Moscow to discuss how to reintroduce the almost-extinct Przewalki's horse into its natural range in Central Asia.

At Dartmouth College, Dennis and Donella Meadows, the principal authors of *Limits to Growth,* started the Resource Policy Center, which has brought together American and Soviet resource management scientists to write textbooks, develop curricula, and train environmental teachers and analysts. Along with similar groups in the Soviet Union, Hungary, and Bulgaria, the Center has formed the International Network of Resource Information Centers, which annually meets for a week at Lake Balaton in Hungary to design joint research programs.

In a project called Salmon for Peace, Arthur Hasler of the University of Wisconsin-Madison is working with Soviets and Chinese to restore depleted populations of sockeye salmon in the Amur River system of the Soviet Union and northeastern China. In July 1986, Trout Unlimited signed an agreement with the Soviet fish and game agency, Rosohotrybolovsoyuz, to work together to protect wildlife and fishing resources and to allow Soviet and American anglers to fish in each other's waters.

Under the leadership of Nicholas Robinson, the International Committee of the Sierra Club has also exchanged delegations, literature, and information with the All-Russia Society for the Protection of Nature. Similar exchanges have been undertaken with David Brower through his Earth Island Institute.

All of these initiatives have rested in part on the 1972 Agreement on Cooperation in the Field of Environmental Protection. This agreement was renewed after the 1985 Geneva summit with commitments on both sides to begin cooperative projects in fields ranging from monitoring global air pollution to exchanging of wild animals.

TO LEARN MORE:

David Blair
Box 145
Dublin, NH 03444
(603) 827-3205

Earth Island Institute
13 Columbus Ave.
San Francisco, CA 94111
(415) 788-3666

The International Crane Foundation
Route 1, Box 230C
Baraboo, WI 53913
(608) 356-9462

National Audubon Society
950 Third Ave.
New York, NY 10022
(212) 832-3200

Resource Policy Center
Thayer School of Engineering
Dartmouth College, HB 8000
Hanover, NH 03755
(603) 646-3551

Salmon for Peace
c/o Arthur Hasler
University of Wisconsin
680 N. Park St.
Madison, WI 53706
(608) 262-2840

Sierra Club International Committee
730 Polk St.
San Francisco, CA 94109
(415) 776-2211

Trout Unlimited
501 Church St. NE
Vienna, VA 22180
(703) 281-1100

FILM AND PHOTOGRAPHY

In the spring of 1983, Marlow Boyer, a writer and photographer in his young twenties, joined a thirty-one-person delegation from Seattle to deliver goodwill letters signed by forty-two thousand city residents to their sister city in Tashkent. Boyer's photographs of the trip were so compelling that he received a ten-thousand-dollar grant to make them into a film called *People to People* (now available from the Educational Film and Video Project [EFVP]). While working on the film, Boyer was diagnosed as having a rare and virulent cancer, but he pushed on and completed the project.

"If there is one thing I would like to be remembered for—other than my good looks, charm, wit, impeccable driving record and paid-up library fines," Boyer wrote in an open letter to his friends, "it is the show *People to People*. [It] has more to do I think with life and hope and friendship than most of my other dubious 'accomplishments.' . . . [It] is of the utmost importance to try to do something useful, something that in some way will improve the world. In some small way, *People to People* just might do that. Not many 25 year olds get a chance at something like that. I was lucky." Boyer died two months later. Marlow's father David, a writer and photographer for *National Geographic*, has carried on his son's work; since Marlow's death, David Boyer has arranged for *People to People* to be shown to more than 150 audiences that have included top members of the Reagan administration, Kremlin officials, and the Pope.

Photographs are often a powerful and cost-effective means of exposing Americans to people and places in the Soviet Union they might otherwise never see. No one has taken this principle further than Dean Conger, a *National Geographic* photographer who recently selected photographs garnered from more than thirty trips to the Soviet Union since 1961 and prepared a multiprojector slide show and a book, *Journey Across Russia: The Soviet Union Today*.

Many citizen diplomats have also recorded their experiences on film and videotape. Bruce Rigdon, a citizen diplomat with a special interest in religion in the Soviet Union, worked with NBC to produce *The Church of the Russians* (available from John T. Conner Center [*see* "Religion"]). The Citizen Exchange Council (*see* "Travel and Tourism") has helped produce films about the Soviet legal system, Soviet women, and a young American woman dealing with her first impressions of the Soviet Union. Cynthia Lazaroff (*see* chapter 2) worked with filmmakers Jim Arnold and Lynne Joiner to document her trek in *Challenge of the Caucasus* (Coronet/MTI).

Danish filmmaker Samuel Rachlin, whose fluency in Russian has helped him to get Soviets to open up on camera, has made an extraordinary series of films about life in the Soviet Union. One of his films documents the career of Vladimir Vysotsky, a popular Soviet actor and balladeer, who was a folk hero to many Russians and whose death in 1980 brought nearly a hundred thousand Soviets to the Taganka Theater for a spontaneous street demonstration. PBS's *Inside Story* has already broadcast Rachlin's films on Vysotsky and *Jews in Moscow*, and will soon broadcast Rachlin's films on Soviet children, women, and nuclear power.

Other films available about life in the Soviet Union include: *A Soviet School Day* (EFVP); *On the Other Side*, which follows the National Council of Churches' 1984 trip to the Soviet Union (CJW Video Artists); *Soviet Students Speak to America* (The US-USSR Youth Exchange Program [*see* "Youth"]), *Big Red*, a puppet animation film about an American artist's journey on the Transiberian Railroad (Big Red Productions), and *We're Not in Kansas Anymore*, a documentary about a journey of American teenagers to the Soviet Union (Big Red Productions).

If you are interested in films exploring the arms race and East-West relations, among the best available are: *The First 50 Years: Reflections on US-Soviet Relations* (Quest Productions); *The Cold War* (Cine Information); *US vs. USSR— Who's Ahead* (EFVP); *What About the Russians?* (EFVP); and *What Soviet Children Are Saying About Nuclear War* (EFVP).

Many films made for American audiences often end up in Soviet hands as well. Since 1984, the Chicago-based Peace Productions has been taking peace-oriented films, geared mainly toward children, into the Soviet Union. Roald Z. Sagdeev, director of the Soviet Space Research Institute, showed *The Day After* to the general staff of the Soviet military. The 1958 cultural exchange agreement sought to regularize shipments of major feature films in both directions, but censorship on both sides as well as Americans' limited interest in most foreign films have presented difficulties. Still, the Soviet Union has purchased about five US films per year, including *Some Like It Hot*, *West Side Story*, and *Kramer vs. Kramer*, and many more American films enter through nonofficial channels. Meanwhile, American audiences seem to be getting interested in Soviet films; crowds recently flocked to see *Moscow Does Not Believe in Tears*, *Rasputin*, and *The Kindergarten*.

TO LEARN MORE:

Big Red Productions
495 Broome St.
New York, NY 10013
(212) 966-1757

Cine Information
215 W. 90th St. #9C
New York, NY 10024
(212) 595-2779

Dean Conger
National Geographic
17th & M St., NW
Washington, D.C. 20037

Coronet/MTI Film and Video
108 Wilmot Rd.
Deerfield, IL 60015
(800) 323-5343

CJW Video Artists
1112 Spring NE
Grand Rapids, MI 49503

Educational Film and Video Project
6511 Gwin Rd.
Oakland, CA 94611
(415) 654-6312

Inside Story
250 West 57th St., Suite 1905
New York, NY 10019
(212) 307-6280

Peace Productions
2500 North Lakeview
Chicago, IL 60614
(312) 929-0127

People to People
9406 Locust Hill Rd.
Bethesda, MD 20814
(301) 530-1578

Quest Productions/Catticus
    Corporation
2600 10th St.
Berkeley, CA 94710
(415) 548-0854

FISHING

After Marianne Clarke, twenty-eight, tried unsuccessfully to use her Russian degree from Stanford to teach English in the Soviet Union, a friend offered her a position with a Seattle-based firm called Marine Resources Co., a venture jointly owned by the Soviet Fisheries Ministry and Bellingham Cold Storage. Within weeks, Clarke found herself aboard a floating fish-processing factory with seventy-two Soviet men and eight Soviet women, working as a liaison between the Soviet processing ship and American fishing trawlers and, as the *Los Angeles Times* later reported in a profile, "knee-deep in a mess of fish entrails." The day Clarke arrived on board, she became terribly seasick and was nursed back to health by a Soviet crewman, who later told her, "That night I held you in my arms, I looked up at the sky and said, 'Thank God for sending us a woman.' " Throughout the remainder of her stay, her shipmates regularly sent her packages of candy, beer, or fresh-baked black bread. "It was such a stimulating environment," says Clarke. "Just being able to speak Russian every day was very exciting. I was always learning."

Clarke's experience is just one part of an expanding web of cooperation between American and Soviet fishermen in harvesting Pacific hake. American trawlers once ignored the hake because they lacked facilities for processing and quick-freezing it. But in 1977, the Soviets convinced the Marine Resources Co. that their floating fish factories were perfect for the job, and American trawlers agreed to deliver their hake catch to Soviet ships floating just outside the United States' territorial waters. The Soviets get extra fish for Soviet consumers, while the Americans get extra employment and income.

TO LEARN MORE:

Marine Resources Co.
192 Nickerson, Suite 307
Seattle, WA 98109
(206) 285-6424

GENERAL EXCHANGE ORGANIZATIONS

If you are unsure about where to begin, you might contact the handful of organizations that are eager to help create exchange programs in virtually any field. Particularly experienced and well connected are the Citizen Exchange Council (*see* "Travel and Tourism"), Delphi Research Associates (*see* "Hosting Soviets"), the Esalen Soviet-American Exchange Program (*see* chapter 6), the Holyearth Foundation/Earthstewards Network (*see* "Children"), and the Organization for American-Soviet Exchanges (OASES), and US-USSR Bridges for Peace (*see* "Religion"). You also might contact the International Exchange Association, a coalition of thirty-five exchange groups that keeps track of the entire American network of exchange organizations.

TO LEARN MORE:

The Esalen Soviet-American
 Exchange Program
3105 Washington St.
San Francisco, CA 94115
(415) 563-4731

The International Exchange
 Association
1625 Eye St., NW
Washington, DC 20006
(202) 293-8998

Organization for American-Soviet
Exchanges
151 Coolidge Ave., Suite 609
Watertown, MA 02172
(617) 924-0713

or
1302 R St., NW
Washington, DC 20009
(202) 332-1145

HIGH TECHNOLOGY

When Joel Schatz, forty nine, fills out a Soviet visa application, he lists his occupation as "cultural repairman." Since 1983 Schatz, a former general systems theorist who has had his hands in everything from designing energy policy to directing mental health clinics, has shuttled between the Soviet Union and his San Francisco office to "wire up" Soviet-American communications through a variety of electronic technologies.

In 1984 and 1985, Schatz worked with the US Radio Network to hold three "global town meetings" connecting American and Canadian radio audiences via transcontinental telephone to such noted Soviets as poet Yevgeny Yevtushenko and healer Djuna Davitashvili (*see* "Parapsychology"). From thirty cities, listeners joined Schatz's studio guests by telephone in asking Soviet participants probing questions.

Schatz then added a visual dimension to Soviet-American conversations by introducing "slow-scan" video equipment, a twenty-five-year-old technology that sends live television snapshots over a telephone line every four seconds. After bringing a slow-scan machine to Moscow, Schatz orchestrated several Soviet-American discussions that enabled the participants to see one another at a fraction of the cost of satellite "space bridges" (*see* "Television").

Schatz also helped introduce high-level Soviet officials to his lap-held Radio Shack computer, which he carries the way most people carry a notepad. One of the Soviets most intrigued was Professor Oleg Smirnov, director of the Institute for Automated Systems, which was set up in 1982 to build networks among Soviet computers and between these computers and the outside world. Schatz developed a working relationship with Smirnov and other Soviet scientists by plugging his Radio Shack computer into a nearby telephone line and sending electronic mail to them—for approximately twenty cents per page. Ultimately Schatz succeeded in connecting these Soviet scientists with American computer scientists through the Electronic Information Exchange System (EIES) in New Jersey.

When Schatz informed the US Department of Commerce of his activities, they effected what he has called a "computerectomy," disconnecting the Moscow-EIES computer link. "This is free speech," he protested, "planetary communication among consenting adults!" Schatz hired a lawyer, convinced the

Department of Commerce to concede that the EIES computer network was only "exporting" words, and got the US government to issue a written go-ahead for all unclassified Soviet-American computer communications.

Since then, the Soviet Union has been deluged with requests by Americans for computer linkups between scientists, astronauts and cosmonauts, alcoholism therapists, children, and numerous other special interest groups. One important user has been Dr. Robert Gale of the University of Southern California in Los Angeles, who, with Schatz's assistance, intends to follow up his medical treatment of victims from the Chernobyl nuclear accident and learn more about the long-term consequences of radiation by conversing with the Soviet Ministry of Health via computer and videophone.

To help the Soviets deal with these new communications projects, Schatz has interested the Soviet Academy of Sciences in building a Moscow-based communications "teleport," an integrated communications facility enabling cost-effective "up-loading" and "down-loading" of high-quality digital satellite communications. Meanwhile, back in the United States, he has begun constructing an analogous communications facility in San Francisco that will be linked to the Moscow teleport through permanent dedicated circuits. Once connected, Schatz envisions these two teleports continually facilitating Soviet-American communication through electronic mail, computer-based conferences, telephones, and videophones. Schatz also hopes to hook up another high technology called compression video, which is a low-cost method of sending full-motion color television signals across digital lines.

Schatz believes that at first much of this high technology will remain only in the hands of privileged Soviets. But in time, he contends, more and more Soviets will be given access, fostering millions of new daily dialogues between Soviets and Americans. "With the proliferation of decentralized communication linked by satellite technology," says Schatz, "the focus of interactive human communication is expanding beyond national boundaries to the planet as a whole."

If you are interested in applying these high technology tools to your own projects, you can contact Schatz, the US Radio Network, Internews (*see* "Television"), or Spacebridge Productions, Inc., which specializes in interactive global television communications.

The Soviets have recently made computer education a top priority for primary and secondary school students, and in 1985 the Carnegie Corporation of New York and the Soviet Academy of Sciences sponsored discussions in Moscow on computer education. The discussions led to an agreement to exchange programmers and computer teachers.

TO LEARN MORE:

The Carnegie Corporation
437 Madison Ave.
New York, NY 10022
(212) 371-3200

Joel Schatz
c/o San Francisco-Moscow Teleport
3278 Sacramento St.
San Francisco, CA 94115
(415) 931-8500

Spacebridge Productions, Inc.
212 High St., Suite 201
Palo Alto, CA 94301
(415) 322-1414

US Radio Network
P.O. Box 1899
Burbank, CA 91507
(818) 344-4389

HOSTING SOVIETS

Interested in bringing Soviets to your city, school, church, or home? One helpful reference is *Inviting and Sponsoring Soviet Guests: A Handbook for American Hosts*, which addresses such basic issues as finances, visas, formalities, program planning, translation, and manners. The handbook was sponsored by ISAR (*see* opening section of appendix) and prepared by Delphi Research Associates, an established agency promoting high-quality exchanges with the Soviet Union. Under the leadership of Paul von Ward, Delphi has helped arrange both the Association for Humanistic Psychology's three-year scientific exchange agreement with the Soviet Institute of Psychology of the Academy of Sciences and the US Department of Housing and Urban Development's participation in the Soviet-American Agreement on Housing and Other Construction.

The largest official organization for hosting foreign officials is the National Council for International Visitors, which works with ninety-nine locally based world-affairs organizations. To bring over Soviet officials, the Council works closely with the US Information Agency and helps obtain endorsements from the American embassy in Moscow. If you already have made arrangements for Soviets to visit the US, the Council can help plan their itineraries, including home stays.

If you want to host any of the roughly two hundred Soviets who come to the United States each year as tourists, you can contact the National Council of Soviet-American Friendship, which has twenty-five affiliated local chapters to help you.

If your hosting desires run to the scale of conferences, you might contact Meridian House International, which since 1960 has helped bring foreign visitors to the United States (only a handful, however, from the Soviet Union) and involve them in seminars, colloquia, forums, and roundtable discussions. For further information on how to organize conferences with Soviet officials, you might also contact the facilitators of the Dartmouth Conferences (*see* chapter 5) at the Charles F. Kettering Foundation.

TO LEARN MORE:

Dartmouth Conference
Charles F. Kettering Foundation
5335 Far Hills Ave.
Dayton, OH 45429
(513) 434-7300

Delphi Research Associates
1750 K St., NW
Suite 1110
Washington, DC 20006
(202) 466-7951

Meridian House International
1630 Crescent Place, NW
Washington, DC 20009
(202) 667-6800

National Council of American-Soviet
   Friendship
85 East 4th St.
New York, NY 10003
(212) 254-6606

National Council for International
   Visitors
1623 Belmont, NW
Washington, DC 20009
(800) 523-8101
(202) 332-1028

HUMAN RIGHTS

Israel Singer, the forty-three-year-old Secretary General of the World Jewish Congress (WJC), has traveled to the Soviet Union "countless times" since 1980 to secure better treatment of the two and one half million Jews living there, thirty to fifty thousand of whom have asked for permission to emigrate and have been refused (hence the term "refusenik"). Along with Edgar Bronfman, President of the WJC and Chairman of Seagram Company, Singer has developed contacts with high-level party officials in the Soviet Union. Because Bronfman advocates better trade relations with the Soviet Union as well as better human rights policies—he's a leading member of the US-Soviet Trade Council (*see* "Business")—the Soviets have been particularly eager to have serious talks with him. "It's difficult to explain to [some human rights] activists," says Singer, "but there is a correlation between detente and an easing of both emigration and rights [for Jews] in the Soviet Union." In advocating rewards for better Soviet human rights policies rather than punishments for Soviet infractions, the WJC, says Singer, is "opposed to the hard-line positions. . . . We believe that moderation brings many more results." Other American Jews who have initiated dialogues with Soviet officials on the government's treatment of Jews are Rabbi Marvin Hier of the Simon Wiesenthal Center in Los Angeles and Morris Abram, Chair of the National Conference on Soviet Jewry.

Several of the organizations trying to monitor, publicize, and eliminate human rights abuses worldwide focus some of their attention on the Soviet Union. Amnesty International seeks the release of all "prisoners of conscience"—those detained for their beliefs, color, sex, ethnic origin, language, or religion, provided they have neither used nor advocated violence. If you join one of its 3,400 neighborhood groups, you can "adopt" political prisoners in the Soviet Union and write letters in support of fair trials and early releases.

Helsinki Watch is concerned with human rights abuses in the thirty-five European and North American countries that signed the 1975 Helsinki accords on security and cooperation in Europe. The so-called "third basket" of those accords guarantees a host of human rights, including the freedom to choose one's place of residence, the freedom to leave and reenter one's country, and the right to receive a fair trial. In 1976, eleven Soviets organized an ad hoc group to monitor their government's adherence to the Helsinki accords, but Soviet officials swiftly quashed the group and put most of its original members in jail. Since then, "watch committees" comprised of prominent opinion leaders have sprung up throughout Europe and in New York. Today, Helsinki Watch keeps in touch—unofficially—with the remnants of the original Soviet group and continues monitoring Soviet violations of the Helsinki Agreement.

Some organizations combine their advocacy of human rights with their search for ways to prevent nuclear war. Humanitas, founded by folksinger Joan Baez, encourages its members to promote human rights in the Soviet Union by establishing more people-to-people contacts and reducing Cold War tensions. The World Without War Council believes that Americans should establish contacts primarily with dissidents, refuseniks, members of persecuted religious communities, and independent peace activists; it is now completing a handbook aimed at encouraging such contacts. And Soviet independent peace activists who have left the Soviet Union and resettled in New York City have formed the Trust Group Center Abroad. The Peace Activists East and West Coordinating Committee seeks to link US peace activists with independent peace and human-rights groups in the East bloc.

Each of these organizations is eager to have newcomers join its ranks and amplify its voice and each will keep you informed about the human rights situation in the Soviet Union. Two other helpful sources of information are the annual reports of the Human Rights Internet and Freedom House.

TO LEARN MORE:

Amnesty International
322 8th Ave.
New York, NY 10025
(212) 807-8400

Freedom House
20 West 40th St.
New York, NY 10018
(212) 473-9691

Helsinki Watch
36 West 44th St.
Suite 911
New York, NY 10036
(212) 840-9460

Humanitas
P.O. Box 818
Menlo Park, CA 94026
(415) 324-9077

Human Rights Internet
1338 G Street, SE
Washington, DC 20003
(202) 543-9200

The National Conference on Soviet
  Jewry
10 East 40th St., Suite 907
New York, NY 10016
(212) 679 6122

Peace Activists East and West
Coordinating Committee
154 State St.
Northampton, MA 01060

Simon Wiesenthal Center
9760 W. Pico Blvd.
Los Angeles, CA 90035
(213) 553-9036

Trust Group Center Abroad
528 Fifth St.
Brooklyn, NY 11215
(718) 499-7720

World Jewish Congress
1 Park Ave.
Suite 418
New York, NY 10016
(212) 679-0600

The World Without War Council
1730 Martin Luther King, Jr., Blvd.
Berkeley, CA 94709
(415) 845-1992

JOURNALISM

In late 1981, Catherine Menninger became concerned about how poorly American and Soviet journalists covered one another's societies and suggested to Tom Winship, editor of the *Boston Globe*, that Soviet and American newspaper journalists should meet and discuss how they might improve their reporting. Winship immediately liked the idea and convinced one of his editors, Frank Grundstrom, who was also the President of the New England Society of Newspaper Editors (NESNE), that NESNE should take on the project.

For the past five years, Grundstrom, fifty, has been developing an exchange program between NESNE editors and members of the Union of Soviet Journalists. From bureaus throughout the Soviet Union and in New York and Washington, DC, about ten Soviet journalists have come to week-long NESNE meetings held at various college campuses in New England since 1982. Ten NESNE journalists, all editors, traveled to the Soviet Union to meet Soviet journalists in 1983 and 1985. The meetings focused on the problems journalists in both countries face in trying to portray each other's societies accurately.

Out of these conferences have emerged several specific collaborative projects. One, a joint exhibit of the best of each nation's photojournalism, traveled throughout both nations in 1986. In a second project, the journalists have published samples of one another's "human interest" stories. The NESNE journalists, for example, published a Soviet story about how Soviet doctors successfully reattached the arm of a little girl that was torn off by an animal at a zoo. A third project will allow two young American journalists to work three months for the *Moscow News* (a Soviet paper with an English edition for American tourists) and two young Soviet journalists to work for two New England newspapers.

Several other organizations of journalists have also developed exchanges with the Soviet Union. Pointing to the success of NESNE, Catherine Menninger persuaded a group of West Coast journalists—including Mel Wax, a San Francisco television newsman, and Jack Burbe, an editor of the *Los Angeles Times*—to hold several week-long meetings with Soviet journalists in a program called the Committee of California Printers and Broadcasters. Members of the American Society of Newspaper Editors met twice with Soviet journalists in 1984, once in Moscow and once in Princeton, New Jersey, and, despite the occasionally harsh words traded at those meetings, they met again in 1986. Sixteen African-American journalists from the Black Press Institute have also traveled to the Soviet Union and participated in a conference with Soviet journalists.

Taking a somewhat different tack, Robert Karl Manoff, former editor of the *Columbia Journalism Review* and managing editor of *Harper's* magazine, and David M. Rubin, professor of journalism at New York University, have founded the Center for War, Peace, and the News Media, which critically studies media coverage of the Soviet Union and the nuclear arms race. The Center's bimonthly bulletin, *Deadline*, contains careful analyses of media omissions, distortions, and misreporting. In May 1986, the Center cosponsored, with the Netherlands-based Alerdinck Foundation Center for East-West Communications, a one-day conference in New York City for American and Soviet journalists. During the conference, representatives from NBC News and Gosteleradio critiqued one another's coverage of the November 1985 Geneva summit based on videotapes they had exchanged prior to the conference. Soviet and American journalists also discussed clippings exemplifying American and Soviet reporting; American samples came from the *Los Angeles Times*, the *New York Times*, and the *Washington Post*, and Soviet samples came from *Izvestia*, *Sovietskaya Rossia* and *Literaturnaya Gazeta*.

TO LEARN MORE:

Alerdinck Foundation Center for
East-West Communications
Alerdinck Foundation
Den Alerdinkweg 5
8055 PE Laag Zuthem (Zwolle)
Netherlands
(0) 5290-822

American Society of Newspaper
Editors
P.O. Box 17004
Washington, DC 20041

Black Press Institute
7917 S. Exchange
Chicago, IL 60617

Center for War, Peace, and the
News Media
1021 Main Building
New York University
New York, NY 10003
(212) 598-7804

Committee of California Printers
and Broadcasters
c/o Mel Wax
Port of Oakland
66 Jack London Square
Oakland, CA 94607
(415) 839-7488

New England Society of Newspaper
Editors
P.O. Box 3030
Worcester, MA 01602
(617) 754-5131

LABOR

Some of the earliest contacts between Americans and Soviets were through labor unions such as the Industrial Workers of the World. Over the years, however, US labor unions, responding to emerging anti-Communism, all but severed their ties with Soviet unions. Today a small number of American unions such as Association of Machinists and Aerospace Workers have restored some ties. In 1985, for example, a delegation of editors from American trade union newspapers and journals, led by Robert John Kolasky, President of the International Association of Trade Union Journalists from the AFL-CIO and the chief editor of the journal *Machinist*, traveled to the Soviet Union at the invitation of the All-Union Central Council of Trade Unions.

If you are interested in bringing members of your union or work association in contact with ordinary Soviet workers, Counterpart Tours, a division of Labor Research Association, is your best bet. In 1984, it sponsored trips to the Soviet Union and Greece for electrical workers, teachers, occupational safety and health workers, trade unionists, sociologists, and health care professionals.

TO LEARN MORE:
Counterpart Tours
250 West 57th St.
Room 1428
New York, NY 10107
(212) 391-0035

LANGUAGE

Armen Dedekian knows how serious the language barrier can be between Americans and Soviets; he's had to break it twice. After World War II, Dedekian was uprooted from Boston at the age of four when his family moved to Soviet Armenia. He learned Russian and lived in Yerevan until 1965, when he, his parents, and his sister returned to the United States, forcing him to learn English once again.

In 1971 Dedekian began teaching Russian at the prestigious Buckingham, Browne, and Nichols Secondary School, which became one of the first American schools to offer Russian to its students in 1954 and today has several faculty members teaching courses in Russian literature, history, and foreign policy. Since then, Dedekian has led the school's Russian Chorus and Russian Dance Ensemble on numerous trips to the Soviet Union, and he has organized the New England region of the American Council of Teachers of Russian's annual "Olympiada," in which high school kids compete in conversational Russian, "area studies" (geography, history, and literature), and poetry recitation; one of his students went on to the 1981 International Olympiada finals in Moscow and won a gold medal. Dedekian has also organized an annual trip for forty high school and college students called "August in the USSR," which is preceded by an optional six-week intensive course in Russian. Next year, Dedekian—once the tennis champion of Armenia—plans to bring the leading tennis players from American high schools and colleges to compete against leading Soviet players.

Dedekian sits on the board of the American Council of Teachers of Russian (ACTR), which links America's Russian teachers and which has various programs, newsletters, books, and exchanges to help students learn Russian. The task ACTR faces is staggering. Only one in five thousand American high school students is learning Russian. "The US is the only industrialized country without a universal foreign language requirement in its high schools," laments Frederick Starr, President of Oberlin College, "and the only one that would allow its population to remain almost wholly ignorant of the language in which its chief adversary thinks."

If you would like to do your part to help bolster America's literacy in Russian, you might consider enrolling in the special summer language programs offered at a number of universities, including Boston University, Duke University, Johns Hopkins University, Indiana University, Middlebury College, North-western University, Norwich University, Ohio State University, UC Berkeley, UC Santa Cruz, University of Texas, and Yale. You can also spend a summer learning Russian *in* the Soviet Union through programs offered by Anniversary Tours (*see* "Travel and Tourism"), Associated Academic Programs in Leningrad, the State University of New York, Middlebury College, the Council on International Educational Exchange, and the ACTR (*see* "Universities").

If you prefer diving into the language on your own, various tools are available. The more serious can choose among hundreds of books (such as *Russian in Ten Minutes a Day*, available from Bilingual Books), the Soviets' own Russian guides (available from Kamkin Books), tapes (among others, Audio-Forum), and even videotapes (available from EMC Publishing). For the more light-hearted, Maxim Books enables you to learn Russian through underground jokes and humorous short stories.

Once you learn Russian, you can adapt your word processor to the Cyrillic alphabet with software available from Gutenberg Software (for Apple Computers) or from University Microcomputers (for IBM PCs).

If you are teaching Russian and wish to improve your proficiency, courses and materials are available from the Baltimore Friends School.

Learning Russian not only is good for citizen diplomacy, it can culminate in a career. Job opportunities for Russian speakers can be found in lists put out by the Modern Language Association, the American Association for the Advancement of Slavic Studies (*see* "Universities"), and the American Association of Teachers of Slavic and Eastern European Languages.

TO LEARN MORE:

American Association of Teachers of Slavic and Eastern European Languages
Dept. of Foreign Languages
Arizona State University
Tempe, AZ 85287
(602) 965-6391

American Council of Teachers of Russian
815 New Gulph Road
Bryn Mawr, PA 19010
(215) 525-6559

Associated Academic Programs in Leningrad
Murkland Hall
University of New Hampshire
Durham, NH 03824
(603) 862-3522

Audio Forum
Language Division
Guilford, CT 06437

Baltimore Friends School
5114 N. Charles St.
Baltimore, MD 21210
(301) 435-2800

Bilingual Books, Inc.
Box C19000
Seattle, WA 98150

Buckingham, Browne and Nichols
School
Gerry's Landing Road
Cambridge, MA 02138
(617) 547-6100

Council on International
Educational Exchange
205 East 42nd St.
New York, NY 10017
(212) 661-1414

Duke University
Dept. of Slavic Languages and
Literature
314 Languages Building
Durham, NC 27706
(919) 684-3975

EMC Publishing
300 York Ave.
St. Paul, MN 55101
(612) 771-1555

Gutenberg Software
47 Lewiston Road
Scarborough, Ontario
M1P 1X8 CANADA
(416) 757-3320

Kamkin Books
12224 Parklawn Dr.
Rockville, MD 20852
(301) 881-5973

Maxim Books
Box 48051
Los Angeles, CA 90048

Middlebury College
Russian Department and Russian
School
Middlebury, VT 05753
(802) 388-3711, ext. 2532

Modern Language Association
10 Astor Place
New York, NY 10003
(212) 475-9500

State University of New York
Office of International Education
New Paltz, NY 12561
(914) 257-2233

University Microcomputers
665 Monte Rosa Drive, Suite 915
Menlo Park, CA 94025
(415) 854-8845

LAW

In the late 1970s, Attorney General Griffin Bell signed a "communiqué" with the Chief Justice of the Soviet Supreme Court, L. M. Smirnov, commencing the American Bar Association's (ABA) exchange with the Association of Soviet Lawyers. Since then, prominent American lawyers, law professors, and jurists have traveled to the Soviet Union and their counterparts have traveled here to learn about one another's legal systems, exchange views on international law, and develop legal tools for helping the superpowers cooperate in environmental protection, trade, joint publications, and scientific experiments. These exchanges, in turn, have helped the ABA's Committee on Soviet and East European Law prepare books and seminars that lawyers and businesses can use to navigate the intricate, ever-shifting shoals of American and Soviet trade laws.

Another program involving top legal scholars from both the United States and the Soviet Union has been initiated by the Lawyers Alliance for Nuclear Arms Control (LANAC). In meetings in both Moscow and Washington, DC, LANAC has brought together esteemed Soviet and American legal scholars and produced joint papers on the nuclear freeze, treaty verification techniques, nonproliferation, and principles for future cooperation. Among the Americans involved were former Harvard Law School Dean Erwin Griswold, former federal judge Shirley Hufstedler, former Iowa Senator John Culver, and Harvard Law School professors Roger Fisher and Abram Chayes.

TO LEARN MORE:

American Bar Association
Committee on Soviet and East
    European Law
1800 M St., NW
Washington, DC 20036
(202) 331-2239

Lawyers Alliance for Nuclear Arms
    Control
43 Charles St., #3
Boston, MA 02114
(617) 227-0118

MEDICINE

If you are interested in meeting Soviet doctors, one option is attending the annual congresses of the International Physicians for the Prevention of Nuclear War (IPPNW), which are open to members of its affiliate organizations (see chapter 1). The US affiliate of IPPNW is Physicians for Social Responsibility (PSR); non-physicians can join PSR as associate members. One to two thousand people from fifty to sixty countries—including the Soviet Union and most socialist-bloc countries—usually attend these four-day congresses. The 1987 congress will take place in Moscow and the 1988 congress in Montreal.

PSR has sponsored several post-congress trips to the Soviet Union that have included visits to medical institutes and meetings with Soviet physicians active in the Soviet Committee of Physicians for the Prevention of Nuclear War. PSR has also sponsored several reciprocal physician exchanges, involving small groups of Soviet doctors touring the United States and small groups of American doctors touring the Soviet Union in order to lecture on the medical consequences of nuclear war and related issues.

In 1985 and 1986, medical students working with IPPNW arranged to tour the Soviet Union and visit informally with Soviet medical students. Harvard Medical School student David Kreger made a slide show based on the 1985 trip and took a year off from medical school in order to present it to more than one hundred audiences in eleven states. Kreger then organized a 1986 IPPNW backpacking expedition to the Caucasus Mountains for two dozen American, Swiss, and Soviet doctors and medical students, which was modeled after the Caucasus treks for teenagers pioneered by Cynthia Lazaroff (*see* chapter 2). The mountaineering medics buried on the summit of Mt. Elbrus a "message to the world" signed by IPPNW co-presidents Dr. Bernard Lown and Dr. Yevgeny Chazov which read in part: "In the nuclear age, the nations of the world are all climbers on a mountain, depending for their survival on the rope of tolerance."

Various other medical exchange opportunities are available. IPPNW medical students established an East-West pen pal program in 1985. A consortium of medical students and faculty at Harvard, Case Western Reserve, and the University of California at San Francisco are planning a long-term Soviet-American exchange of medical students, in which the students would have the opportunity to spend several months studying in one another's country. Anyone interested in helping facilitate or participating in such an exchange can contact David Kreger for more information. The American Medical Student Association sponsored a "study tour'" to the Soviet Union in 1985 and will sponsor another in 1987 or 1988. And Professional Seminar Consultants, Inc., organizes numerous trips to the Soviet Union for American health professionals that emphasize visits to Soviet hospitals and medical institutes.

Many citizen diplomats believe that Soviet-American medical exchanges not only will build good relations but also improve the world's health. The Esalen Health Promotion Project sponsors Soviet-American book exchanges, professional conferences, and joint studies on innovative approaches to health care (*see* Chapter 6). Recent collaboration between fifteen American medical centers and five Soviet medical centers led to new findings about the effectiveness of aspirin in treating juvenile rheumatoid arthritis. Senate Resolution 227, passed in November 1985, calls on the superpowers to undertake a joint project, similar to the successful East-West joint efforts in the 1970s to eradicate smallpox, to immunize the world's children by 1990.

TO LEARN MORE:

American Medical Students
  Association
1910 Association Drive
Reston, VA 22091
(703) 620-6600

Esalen Health Promotion Project
3105 Washington St.
San Francisco, CA 94115
(415) 563-4731

International Physicians for the
  Prevention of Nuclear War
225 Longwood Avenue
Boston, MA 02115
(617) 738-9404

David Kreger
27 Inman Street
Cambridge, MA 02139
(617) 868-4301

Physicians for Social Responsibility
1601 Connecticut Ave., NW
Suite 800
Washington, DC 20009
(202) 939-5750

Professional Seminar Consultants,
  Inc.
3194 Lawson Blvd.
Oceanside, NY 11572
(516) 536-7292

MILITARY

At the end of World War II, the armies of the United States and the Soviet Union met and shook hands together in victory at the river Elbe. Forty years later, seven Americans present at the Elbe meeting traveled to the Soviet Union and met with Soviet Elbe veterans. The reunited Elbe veterans were treated to hero's welcomes by the mayors of Moscow, Volgograd, Kiev, and Leningrad. A number of Soviet Elbe veterans then toured the United States.

American and Soviet military personnel also occasionally meet under more official circumstances. American and Soviet naval officers usually meet once each year to discuss ways to prevent dangerous incidents at sea. In 1986, Congress authorized one hundred thousand dollars for the Secretary of Defense to prepare a plan for a pilot program that would exchange visits between American and Soviet high-ranking military officers.

Retired US military personnel have also tried to influence Soviet military policy through unofficial contacts. Members of the Center for Defense Information, for example, a private arms control group run by retired Rear Admiral Gene R. LaRocque and more than a dozen other former high ranking US military officers, have traveled to the Soviet Union and met with various Soviet officials to discuss arms control. Retired Air Force Major General Jack Kidd is the president of Bridges Worldwide, which sponsors a variety of exchange projects and has designed a strategy to end the arms race called the Strategic Cooperation Initiative (SCI), or "Star Light."

TO LEARN MORE:

Bridges Worldwide
Box 223730
Carmel, CA 93922
(408) 372-0515

Center for Defense Information
1500 Massachusetts Ave., SW
Washington, DC 20005
(202) 862-0700

Elbe Anniversary Journey for Peace
P.O. Box 1776
Lawrence, KS 66044

MOUNTAINEERING

On August 22, 1985, William Garner, thirty-six, an independent consultant on Soviet affairs in Washington, DC, and Randy Starrett, forty-three, a trial lawyer from suburban Fairfax County, Virginia, reached the summit of the most challenging mountain in the Soviet Union—Pik Pobedy or Victory Peak. The feat made them the first non-Soviets to receive the coveted "Order of the Snow Leopard" for climbing all four of the Soviet Union's peaks higher than twenty-three thousand feet: Pik Kommunizma, Pik Korzhenevskaya, Pik Lenina, and Pik Pobedy.

Pik Pobedy has been scaled only by 150 people; fifty others have died attempting it. When they reached the top, Garner, Starrett, and their Soviet colleagues left a message in both Russian and English: "We . . . have climbed this mountain to illustrate for the people of our two countries how much greater value there is in our learning to take risks together than in our continuing to put the world at risk through mutual confrontation." In May 1986, Garner and Starrett organized a joint Soviet-American ascent of the west rib of Mt. McKinley.

In 1975 several members of the Soviet Mountaineering Federation—including Sergei Bershov, the Soviet speed climbing champion—came to the United States to climb as guests of the American Alpine Club. As the Soviets prepared to climb the Salathe Wall of El Capitan in Yosemite National Park, they decided they could use the expertise of seventeen-year-old climber Michael Warburton and invited him along. Warburton and Bershov, neither of whom spoke the other's language, took turns leading the climb and managed to pass ropes and backpacks with code words like "Santa Claus," "superman," and "cowboy." Accompanying the Soviet team was Vitaly Abalakov, the "father of Soviet mountaineering," who remarked, after watching Warburton and Bershov clowning around, "You and Sergei are two of the same boot."

The next year, Warburton and Valentin Grakovitch, another Soviet climbing companion, tried climbing an uncharted route in the Caucasus Mountains that they later named "the route of friendship." Despite bitter cold weather, a food shortage, and Grakovitch's injured ankle, the twosome decided to forge ahead. Just before reaching the top, however, Warburton fell 140 feet, severely injuring his head. He remained unconscious for five days while more than a hundred Soviets—including Sergei Bershov—worked to evacuate him from the mountain to a nearby Soviet hospital, where he recuperated for several weeks. In the

340

years since, Warburton and Bershov have corresponded and once were reunited at a base camp on Mt. Everest. Warburton has continued traveling to such countries as Austria, Australia, Czechoslovakia, Denmark, Germany, Great Britain, Japan, and New Zealand, not only to climb mountains, but also to present a slide show about his climbs with Soviets called "Roped to Each Other."

If you are interested in climbing mountains in the Soviet Union, you can contact Mountain Travel, an agency that specializes in Soviet wilderness trips and is one of the official US representatives of the Soviet Sports Committee, or Cynthia Lazaroff's US-USSR Youth Exchange Program (*see* chapter 2 and "Youth").

TO LEARN MORE:

William Garner
1330 21st St., NW
Washington, DC 20036
(202) 467-6713

Mountain Travel
1398 Solano Ave.
Albany, CA 94706
(415) 527-8100

Michael Warburton
2146 University Ave.
Mountain View, CA 94040
(415) 968-2194

NEGOTIATION

On June 27, 1978, seven Soviet Pentecostalists slipped past a Soviet guard and ran into the American embassy in Moscow seeking asylum. Having experienced years of religious discrimination, they felt they had exhausted all conventional avenues for emigration. American officials gave them living quarters in two basement rooms and the seven wrote open letters to Secretary Brezhnev and President Reagan. Negotiations for their release, however, soon reached an impasse. The American government, under public pressure to protect them, demanded they be allowed to emigrate, while the Soviet government, eager not to set a precedent for other refuseniks, demanded their removal.

The man the United States brought in to break the impasse was Olin Robison, the president of Middlebury College. As a former Air Force chaplain, an administrator in the Peace Corps, and coordinator for a government-funded program exchanging young American and Soviet political leaders, he was respected by the United States government. As a scholar whose research on religion in the Soviet Union made him a familiar presence in religious circles there, he was trusted by the Pentecostalists. And as an American whom the Soviet Institute of the US and Canada Studies consulted about President Carter's religious views, he was well known in the Soviet Union.

Five years after the Pentecostalists entered the embassy, Robison's quiet diplomacy succeeded; the seven peacefully left the embassy and, within a month, they and their families had permission to leave for Israel. Although Robison remains publicly silent about the details of his activities, he has written extensively on how American leaders should negotiate with Soviets. "[The] solution [to bigger issues such as arms control], if any, will come slowly and with difficulty. . . . The children's game of 'pick-up sticks' is a useful metaphor. You soon learn to do the easy ones first. Then, and only then, are some of the harder ones possible."

Techniques of successful negotiation with the Soviets have also been a long-standing interest of the Harvard Law School Nuclear Negotiation Project, directed by William Ury, which studies how Americans and Soviets can help prevent crises leading to nuclear war through such innovations as an improved hot line and a crisis control center staffed by both Americans and Soviets. The project's best-selling book on the "do's and don'ts" of negotiation, *Getting to Yes*, cowritten by Ury and Roger Fisher, is a useful tool for every citizen diplomat.

TO LEARN MORE:

Nuclear Negotiation Project
Harvard Law School
500 Pound Hall
Cambridge, MA 02138
(617) 495-1684

Olin Robison
Office of the President
Middlebury, VT 05753
(802) 388-3711

PARAPSYCHOLOGY

Since the early 1980s physicist Russell Targ, fifty-two, and his daughter Elisabeth, twenty-five, a medical student at Stanford who is fluent in Russian, have exchanged information and conducted joint experiments with the Soviet Academy of Sciences on the phenomenon of "remote-viewing," the ability of a person to see an unknown object or location over a long distance. In October 1984 the Targs met Djuna Davitashvili, an associate of the Soviet Academy of Sciences whose healing talents are said to have helped Soviet General Secretary Leonid Brezhnev in his final years. After agreeing to participate in their remote-viewing experiment, Davitashvili was told that in six hours, Keith Harary, an associate of the Targs, would be going to "an interesting place" in San Francisco. The Targs asked her to describe this place and Davitashvili stated that she "saw" a rectangular plaza at the end of a long road, a "cupola in the center of the plaza, many low buildings with pointed roofs in a long line, a large building with a trapezoid-shaped roof," "a profile of an animal's eye, and pointy ears," and a "white couch or divan."

Six hours later, as scheduled, Harary awoke ten thousand miles away, randomly picked one of six possible locations—none of which either the Targs or Davitashvili knew about—and went there for half an hour. The location he chose was the merry-go-round on a pier, where horses and white couches rested under a cupola, a location that subsequent blind judging found to correspond with Davitashvili's description. For the Targs, Davitashvili's description confirmed not only that remote viewing could work over very long distances but also that it could work over time—that is, a person may have the ability to "see" into the near-term future.

Russell Targ hopes to continue pursuing their joint research projects with the Soviets, "not only because of the increased resources and brain power such a collaboration creates," but also to help the superpowers avoid "the potentially destabilizing force in [any] perceived technological imbalance" in their psychic abilities. The Targs are trying to use their joint work with the Soviets to ensure that remote viewing is used for such stabilizing purposes as verifying that neither side is cheating on arms control treaties.

TO LEARN MORE:

Delphi Associates
1010 Harriet St.
Palo Alto, CA 94301
(415) 326-5271

PEACE GROUPS

Kent Larrabee, a sixty-eight-year-old social worker from Philadelphia, decided one day that he needed to tell the Soviet people his views on peace. In 1982, after walking 2,300 miles throughout Western Europe on a Quaker peace march, he visited the Soviet Union. On his last day there, he handed out twenty peace pamphlets in downtown Leningrad that said, "I must speak up to my government about getting rid of all nuclear weapons. And you must speak up to your government. If we don't do that, we are all going to perish."

Within an hour, his peace pamphlets had created a curious crowd of more than a hundred, and four police officers soon hauled him off to a local police station. The police called in several English translators and went off to confer in a private room about Larrabee and his pamphlets. "I stood there wondering," recalls Larrabee, "Would I spend a night, or maybe a week, in a Russian jail? Would I be deported?"

The police returned, handed Larrabee his papers, and told him he was free to go. Larrabee, nonplussed, told the nearly twenty police officers surrounding him, "I want to congratulate the police department of Leningrad for doing a good job. You did the right thing. I was causing a big commotion in your city and blocking traffic." Suddenly, the policemen smiled and relaxed. They told Larrabee that they had read some of his poetry in the back room and added that they liked it so much that they wanted autographed copies.

When Larrabee returned from the Soviet Union, he spent the next year and a half conveying this and other stories to more than five hundred television, radio, and live audiences. He also put together a slide show of his experiences called *The Russians Are People Too*.

Today, more than five thousand self-described "peace groups" are trying to improve Soviet-American relations as part of their mission to prevent war. For a comprehensive listing of these groups and their activities, you can consult either of the following references:

- *The Peace Resource Book* by the Institute for Defense and Disarmament Studies (Cambridge: Ballinger, 1985)
- *The Peace Catalogue* by Duane Sweeny, ed. (Seattle: Press for Peace, 1984)

Virtually every peace group has pamphlets, articles, books, slide shows, films, or videotapes about the Soviet Union. Some organizations, such as the Arms Control Association, the Institute for Policy Studies, the Coalition for a New Foreign & Military Policy, Peace Links (*see* "Women"), SANE, and the World Policy Institute, produce materials analyzing Soviet military forces and suggesting new possibilities for arms control. Other organizations, such as the American Friends Service Committee, the Ark Communications Institute, the Committee for National Security (*see* "Women"), Educators for Social Responsibility (*see* "Teaching"), and Fellowship of Reconciliation (*see* "Religion"), produce materials aimed at dispelling myths about Soviet history, culture, and people. Both kinds of information can be heard regularly on two nationally syndicated weekly radio programs—the SANE Education Fund's *Consider the Alternatives* and the Stanley Foundation's *Common Ground*.

Many peace groups travel to the Soviet Union and meet with members of the official Soviet Peace Committee, which has local chapters in most Soviet cities. Among the groups that hold regular meetings with the Soviet Peace Committee are Continuing the Peace Dialogue USA-USSR (*see* "Women"), the US Peace Council, and the World Federalist Association. Since 1982 Promoting Enduring Peace, a Connecticut-based organization directed by Howard Frazier, has used its relationships with the Peace Committee and the Soviet Friendship Society to take between 120 and 165 Americans on two annual "peace cruises" down the Volga River. In the summer of 1986, Frazier organized the first "peace cruise" in the United States, in which a diverse geographic and professional cross-section of 53 Soviets and 127 Americans made a week-long steamboat trip down the Mississippi.

Members of both the Institute for Policy Studies and the American Committee on U.S.-Soviet Relations (*see* "Business") have had ongoing discussions with top members of the Soviet Institute for US and Canada Studies on new ways of controlling arms and halting military intervention in other countries. The International Center for Development Policy has worked with several Soviet institutes and prepared joint papers with them on regional conflicts in the Third World. The Consortium on Peace Research, Education, and Development has exchanged its academic publications with various Soviet peace research institutes. Since 1969, the US United Nations Association (UNA) has had a "Parallel Studies Program" with the Soviet United Nations Association and the Soviet Academy of Science, which each year brings together internationally experienced Americans—including political scientists, directors of research institutions and foundations, heads of corporations and banks, and former diplomats—with high-level Soviets to discuss a wide range of security and economic issues. In September 1986 220 American citizens, including several senior Reagan administration officials and well-known musicians, journeyed to Riga, Latvia for a "Chautauqua style town meeting" that was covered extensively in the American and Soviet press.

TO LEARN MORE:

American Friends Service
   Committee
1501 Cherry St.
Philadelphia, PA 19102
(215) 241-7156

Ark Communications Institute
250 Lafayette Circle, Third Floor
Lafayette, CA 94549
(415) 284-3350

Arms Control Association
11 Dupont Circle, NW
Washington, DC 20036
(202) 797-6450

Chautauqua Institution
Box 1098
Chautauqua, NY 14722
(716) 357-6233

Coalition for a New Foreign &
   Military Policy
712 G Street, SE
Washington, DC 20003
(202) 546-8400

Consortium on Peace Research and
   Development
University of Illinois at Urbana-
   Champaign
911 West High St., Room 100
Urbana, IL 61801
(217) 333-2069

Institute for Policy Studies
1901 Q St., NW
Washington, DC 20009
(202) 234-9382

International Center for
   Development Policy
731 Eighth St., SE
Washington, DC 20003
(202) 547-3800

Promoting Enduring Peace
Box 5013
Woodmont, CT 06460
(203) 878-4769

SANE Education Fund
711 G St., SE
Washington, DC 20003
(202) 546-7100

The Stanley Foundation
420 East Third Street
Muscatine, IA 52761
(319) 264-1500

United Nations Association of the
   USA
Eighth Floor
300 East 42 St.
New York, NY 10017
(212) 697-3232

US Peace Council
1123 Broadway, Suite 513
New York, NY 10010
(212) 989-1194

World Federalist Association
418 7th, SE
Washington, DC 20003
(202) 546-3950

PEN PALS

In January 1932, Steve Scott, a thirty-year-old employee of the Army Corps of Engineers in Boston, began volunteering for the International Friendship League, which has been matching Americans with pen pals abroad since 1948. When he discovered that there was no program for pen-pal'ing with Soviets, he decided to start a program himself and by the end of the year had matched ten Americans with ten Soviets. Soon he had arranged many more—100 in 1983, 500 in 1984, 625 in 1985, and nearly 1,000 in 1986.

Most of Scott's Soviet pen pals are students in their twenties who are studying English. Some Soviet students have heard of his project and write asking for American pen pals; other names come from Soviet teachers or from Czechoslavakian and Hungarian youth magazines with pen-pal listings. His biggest sources of names are youth organizations in Yugoslavia and India that have names of Soviets who want to be pen pals. At any one time, Scott has fifty to a hundred new names ready for distribution. Most will write in English.

Scott himself has had four pen-pal relationships—only one of which was interrupted when he broke what he calls his golden rule: "never talk about politics in your letters." But generally, as his brochure says: "Whether you want to learn more about life in the Soviet Union, practice your Russian, or just like to make new friends in faraway lands, having a pen pal in the USSR can be an interesting and rewarding experience." The ultimate value, Scott believes, is that "the country is no longer only missiles and KGB agents—there's a human aspect to it. When you hear of the Soviet Union, you think, 'What's happening to my friends? How are they doing?' "

Interested pen-pal'ers can also contact Letters for Peace, which provides a kit for the quick preparation of personalized goodwill letters that has been used to send nearly twenty thousand individual letters to the Soviet Union since 1982—some of which have led to reciprocal pen pal relationships. If you want pen pals but hate to write, CONNECT in Minneapolis, Minnesota (*see* "Art") is trying to get Soviets and Americans to send "videotape letters" to one another.

TO LEARN MORE:

Letters for Peace
59 Bluff Ave.
Rowayton, CT 06853
(203) 853-8038

Russian Pen Pal Project
International Friendship League
55 Mt. Vernon St.
Boston, MA 02108
(617) 523-4273

THE PERFORMING ARTS:
MUSIC, DANCE, AND THEATER

Paul Winter is a jazz saxophonist who draws inspiration for his music from the "harmony of the natural world." In his recent albums, Winter and his fellow musicians have brought their music and recording instruments to the ocean to accompany whales and to the Grand Canyon to harmonize with coyotes. Now he has turned his attention to the wilderness and wildlife of Siberia. Remembering the enthusiastic response of a Soviet audience when he was still a novice musician, he has always considered the Soviet Union "part of my audience." In 1984 he traveled to the Soviet Union and met a man he had long regarded as his Soviet soul mate—poet Yevgeny Yevtushenko. He and Yevtushenko immediately hit it off and they toured the United States together in June 1985, blending their music and poetry.

Inspired by the magnificent wildernesses of the Soviet Union, Winter is now putting together what he envisions will be a seven-album series called "A Song of Russia," with each album focusing on the music, wildlife, and culture of a different region of the USSR. The first album is about Lake Baikal in Siberia, the largest freshwater lake in the world. With the assistance of the Union of Soviet Composers, Winter is recording the sounds of "nerpa," a freshwater seal found only at Lake Baikal. The official Soviet concert ministry, Goskoncert, sponsored a seven-city tour for Winter during August 1986.

Winter is one of a growing number of American musicians who have sought to perform for and with Soviets in the United States or the Sovet Union. Others have included Pearl Bailey, Bob Dylan, Tom Paxton, and John Denver (*see* chapter 6). Denver recently signed a preliminary agreement with the Soviet company Melodiya Records to produce an album and a songbook.

But you need not be famous to harmonize with musicians in the Soviet Union. Ted Everts, a recent graduate of UC-Berkeley, combined his interests in jazz and Soviet affairs to set up East-Wind Trade Associates, which has an agreement with Melodiya Records to distribute Soviet jazz records in the United States. Twenty-five members of the Balalaika and Domra Association of America arranged with the Glinka Conservatory of Minsk to spend a week studying traditional Russian folk instruments, and then brought their teachers back to the United States for concerts in Atlanta, Houston, Philadelphia, and New York. In Sudbury, Massachusetts, forty adults and high school students formed a community project called "Sharing A New Song" and toured the Soviet Union singing American folk and show tunes. Working through the Organization for Soviet-American Exchanges (OASES) (*see* "General Exchange"), the San Francisco Bay Area Slavyanka Male Russian Chorus arranged performances with Soviet choral groups for late 1986. Alaska Performing Artists for Peace arranged a 1986-1987 exchange of Alaskan and Siberian musicians and dancers that featured a performance of the Bladder Festival, an ancient Eskimo ritual of reunification.

In the theater world, the Am-Russ Agency has encouraged the translation and production of Soviet plays in the United States. In 1984, it also brought American theater personalities to the Soviet Union to meet and exchange scripts, theories, and techniques with Soviet playwrights, directors, actors, and managers. Another group organizing theater exchanges is Performers and Artists for Nuclear Disarmament (PAND), which in September 1984 sponsored a Leningrad concert involving talent from sixteen nations, including singer Harry Belafonte (President of PAND International), French mime Marcel Marceau, jazz player Dizzy Gillespie, singers from the New York Metropolitan Opera, and the "Magnificent Force Breakdancers."

If you are interested in bringing your dance, music, or theater ensemble to the Soviet Union, you can contact the Friendship Ambassadors Foundation, which specializes in setting up free performances there. Organizations listed under "General Exchange" can also be helpful.

TO LEARN MORE:

Alaska Performing Artists for Peace
1991 Hughes Way
Juneau, AK 99801

The Am-Russ Literary Agency
25 West 43rd St.
New York, NY 10036
(212) 921-1922

Balalaika and Domra Association of
America
2225 Madison Square
Philadelphia, PA 19146
(215) 935-4678

East-Wind Trade Associates
2141 Pacific Ave.
San Francisco, CA 94115
(415) 931-8858

Friendship Ambassadors Foundation
273 Upper Mountain Ave.
Upper Montclair, NJ 07043
(201) 744-0410

Paul Winter
Living Music
Box 68
Litchfield, CT 06759
(203) 567-8796

Performers and Artists for Nuclear
Disarmament
225 Lafayette St.
New York, NY 10012
(212) 431-7836

Sharing a New Song
Lincoln-Sudbury Regional High
School
Lincoln Road
Sudbury, MA 01776
(617) 443-9961

POLITICIANS

As director of the Federation of American Scientists (FAS) for sixteen years, Jeremy Stone has lobbied, written articles, and given speeches in an attempt to persuade members of the US Congress and Senate to visit "the object of their anxiety," the Soviet Union, and to persuade members of the Supreme Soviet to visit the United States. Today, three-quarters of Congress and half of the Senate, including many who hold key foreign policy making positions, have never been to the Soviet Union.

In 1971 Senator Mike Gravel from Alaska, with Stone's assistance, rounded up enough votes in the Senate for a resolution funding Senators, Congress members, state governors, and big-city mayors to travel to the Soviet Union. Members of the Nixon administration, however, successfully killed the bill in the House. "They didn't want their lieutenants fooling around with foreign policy," recalls Stone.

More than a decade later, when a friend asked Stone what she could do for peace, Stone suggested that she and a dozen others go to the office of every Senator and Congressman who had not traveled to the Soviet Union and ask them, "Why not?" The women went door-to-door to over three hundred offices, met with staffers, held luncheons and, by early 1986, succeeded in deluging the Soviet embassy with requests for "official visits."

Once national politicians travel to the Soviet Union, they are often eager to get their colleagues to go as well. In 1986, when Senators Pell, Long, Bumpers, Leahy, Metzenbaum, Riegle, Sarbanes, and Sasser returned from the Soviet Union, they introduced resolutions that would have established nongovernmental offices in Washington, DC, and Moscow to facilitate bilateral travel and contact between national leaders; invited all Politburo members to visit the United States; and funded a program exchanging up to five thousand students per year.

State and local politicians have also met with their Soviet counterparts through National League of Cities tours. In August 1985 the First World Conference of Mayors for Peace, which was sponsored by the mayors of Hiroshima and Nagasaki, brought together more than two hundred local officials from a hundred cities in thirty countries, including the United States and the Soviet Union. Through behind-the-scenes negotiations, Mayor Anne Rudin of Sacramento, California, and Mayor Charlotte Townsend of Carmel-by-the-Sea, California, got local leaders from Kiev, Leningrad, Volgograd, and Vilnius to agree to a joint statement urging a comprehensive test ban that went beyond the positions of both President Reagan and General Secretary Gorbachev.

If you think your politicians need a more constructive outlook on Soviet-American relations, ask them if they have been to the Soviet Union. If not, urge them to go. And if they are still uncooperative, urge their challengers to go. You might also suggest to your national representatives that they attend the Congressional Roundtable on US-Soviet Relations and the Arms Control and Foreign Policy Caucus, both of which expose time-pressured politicians to some of the best thinkers in the field.

TO LEARN MORE:

Arms Control and Foreign Policy
  Caucus
US Congress
501 House Annex 2
Washington, DC 20515
(202) 226-3440

Congressional Roundtable on US-
  Soviet Relations
2700 Virginia Ave., NW #807
Washington, DC 20037
(202) 226-3440

Federation of American Scientists
307 Massachusetts Ave., NE
Washington, DC 20002
(202) 546-3300

PSYCHOLOGY

In 1961 Fran Macy, now fifty-nine-year-old father of three, abandoned his government career in Soviet affairs to put behind him, once and for all, what he termed "Cold War employment." He returned to his "old interest in Soviet affairs" in 1982 when, after working for the Peace Corps and establishing a new career for himself in counseling, he was hired to be executive director of the Association for Humanistic Psychology (AHP). With the help of Paul Von Ward of Delphi Associates (*see* "Hosting Soviets") and Harriett Crosby of the Institute for Soviet-American Relations, Macy identified and contacted Soviet counterpart institutions for AHP and developed one of the most impressive exchange programs for professionals in the country.

Every autumn since 1983 the AHP has sent a delegation of twenty-five to thirty psychologists, psychotherapists, educators, and "organizational development" management consultants to Moscow, Leningrad, and Tbilisi to consult with their counterparts. Since 1985 the AHP has gotten the Soviet Ministry of Education to send several Soviets to participate in its US conferences and the Soviet Academy of Pedogogical Studies to give short-term teaching appointments to American scholars, including noted psychologist Carl Rogers. The AHP is also exchanging book and journal subscriptions with various Soviet institutions and encouraging mutual publication of one another's work. Macy suspects that the AHP's first full-fledged joint research project with Soviet counterparts will be on the role of psychologists and psychology in averting nuclear war, especially in dealing with the fears of war in both Soviet and American children.

Through these exchanges, American psychologists have learned that today's Soviet psychotherapy is essentially at the stage of American psychotherapy in the 1950s—performed almost entirely by MD psychiatrists. Increasingly, however, the Soviets are relying on "nondoctor" psychotherapy, much as Americans now do, and they consequently have a strong interest in American teachings in humanistic psychology, such as Carl Rogers's *Freedom to Learn for the 80s*.

The Center for Psychological Studies in the Nuclear Age of Cambridge Hospital, an affiliate of Harvard Medical School, has researched the attitudes of youths in the United States, the Soviet Union, and elsewhere about nuclear weapons and the people they define as "the enemy." The program has also produced and distributed a film, *What Soviet Children Are Saying about Nuclear War*. Most recently, it has gotten schools in Moscow and Cambridge to exchange videotapes about a "typical day" in each school and ultimately plans to discuss its research findings at a joint Soviet-American conference on "ideologies of enmity."

If you are a psychologist interested in working with Soviets or in Soviet-American affairs, you can contact either the AHP or the Harvard Nuclear Psychology Program. Alternatively, you might contact Psychologists for Social

Responsibility, which is now bringing together American and Soviet psychologists to do joint research relating to peaceful conflict resolution, improved communications, and overcoming people's images of "the enemy."

TO LEARN MORE:

Association for Humanistic
  Psychology
325 Ninth St.
San Francisco, CA 94103
(415) 626-2375

Center for Psychological Studies in
  the Nuclear Age
Cambridge Hospital
1493 Cambridge St.
Cambridge, MA 02139
(617) 497-1553, 1554

Psychologists for Social
  Responsibility
1841 Columbia Rd., NW, #209
Washington, DC 20009
(202) 745-7084

PUBLIC EDUCATION

If you happen to be in Boston at the right time and the right place, you might stumble upon a unique educational program, where instead of the books, pencils, and papers you will find *zakuski*, Russian-style hors d'oeuvres such as black bread, smoked fish, and pickles. The program called *Krug Druzei* (Circle of Friends), brings together Soviet emigrants with local Soviet scholars and other interested neighbors to indulge in Russian eating, dancing, and singing while sharing stories, slides, and travel tips.

Krug Druzei is one of dozens of groups springing up around the country that are trying to educate their local communities about the Soviet Union. Other examples include the Beyond War USA-USSR Task Force, the Center for US-USSR Initiatives (*see* chapter 4), the Center for Improving US-Soviet Relations, the Chicago Center for US/USSR Relations and Exchanges, Project Harmony, and Continuing the Peace Dialogue (*see* "Women"), which present the public with cultural events, slide shows, speakers, debates, and discussion groups. Supplementing these programs are various well-established community organizations on foreign affairs such as the World Affairs Councils of San Francisco, Chicago, Boston, and New York. The national organization coordinating these chapters, the National Council of World Affairs Organizations, has initiated a Soviet-American "dialogue on common problems" such as alcoholism, environmental protection, and the social responsibility of youth.

Several national organizations with local contacts and affiliates provide books, pamphlets, films, and videotapes about the Soviet Union in an effort to break through stereotypes and lay a factual basis for stronger relations. These include the American Friends Service Committee (*see* "Peace Groups"), the Committee for National Security (*see* "Women"), the John T. Conner Center for US-USSR Reconciliation (*see* "Religion"), the Friends Committee on National Legislation, the National Council of American-Soviet Friendship (*see* "Hosting Soviets"), Focus on Soviet Reality, and Institute for a Future.

If you are looking for materials that can be used in a high school, college, or adult-ed classroom, several groups supply curricula, readings, slides, videotapes, and films about life in the Soviet Union: Educators for Social Responsibility (*see* "Teaching"), the US-USSR Youth Exchange Program (*see* chapter 2 and "Youth"), Focus on Soviet Reality (which publishes translations of contemporary Soviet fiction, drama, and humor), and the National Education Association's National Foundation for the Improvement of Education (which is publishing a book of children's art and creative writing entitled *The Soviet Union as Seen by Its Children*).

If you're after higher-brow material, the following academic or quasi-academic "think tanks" regularly publish books, articles, and pamphlets about specific issues dealing with the Soviet Union: the American Committee on US-Soviet Relations (progressive) (*see* "Business and Trade"), The American Enterprise Institute (conservative), The Aspen Institute's US-Soviet Relations Project (moderate-to-progressive), the Atlantic Council of the United States (conservative), the Brookings Institution (moderate), the Carnegie Endowment for International Peace (moderate), the Council on Foreign Relations (moderate), the Foreign Policy Research Institute (conservative), the Hoover Institution on War, Revolution, and Peace (conservative), the Institute for Defense and Disarmament Studies (progressive), the Institute for East-West Security Studies (moderate to progressive), the Kennan Institute for Advanced Russian Studies (moderate), the Public Agenda Foundation (progressive poll data), and the Roosevelt Center for American Policy Studies (progressive). A number of these organizations sharpen their information through regular exchanges with Soviet scholars. The Foreign Policy Research Institute, for example, has annual meetings with high level officials in the Soviet Institute for US and Canada Studies.

TO LEARN MORE:

American Enterprise Institute
1150 17th St., NW
Washington, DC 20036
(202) 862-5800

Aspen Institute's U.S.-Soviet
    Project
1333 New Hampshire Ave., NW
Washington, DC 20036
(202) 466-6410

Atlantic Council of the U.S.
1616 H St., NW
Washington, DC 20006
(202) 347-9353

Beyond War USA-USSR Task Force
222 High Street
Palo Alto, CA 94301
(415) 328-7756

Brookings Institution
1775 Massachusetts Ave., NW
Washington, DC 20036
(202) 797-6010

Carnegie Endowment for
    International Peace
11 Dupont Circle, NW
Suite 900
Washington, DC 20036
(202) 797-6400

Center for Improving US-Soviet
    Relations
930 Henryton Rd.
Marriotsville, MD 21104
(301) 442-2808

Center for US-USSR Initiatives
3220 Sacramento St.
San Francisco, CA 94415
(415) 668-3083

Chicago Center for US/USSR
    Relations and Exchanges
55 E. Monroe St.
Chicago, IL 60603
(312) 236-0825

Council on Foreign Relations
58 East 68th St.
New York, NY 10021
(212) 734-0400

Focus on Soviet Reality
P.O. Box 46
New York, NY 10113
(212) 684-0491

Foreign Policy Research Institute
3508 Market St., Suite 350
Philadelphia, PA 19104
(215) 382-0685

Hoover Institution on War,
    Revolution, and Peace
Stanford, CA 94305
(415) 723-0603

Institute for a Future
173 Fairlawn Dr.
Berkeley, CA 94708
(415) 841-7923

Institute for Defense and
    Disarmament Studies
2001 Beacon St.
Brookline, MA 02146
(617) 734-4216

Institute for East-West Security
    Studies
360 Lexington Ave.
New York, NY 10017
(212) 557-2570

Kennan Institute for Advanced
    Russian Studies
The Smithsonian Institution
955 L'Enfant Plaza, SW
Suite 7400
Washington, DC 20560
(202) 287-3105

Krug Druzei/Circle of Friends
c/o Stephen Scott
10 Lancaster Street, #24
Cambridge, MA 02138
(617) 492-3606

National Council of World Affairs
    Organizations
1750 K St., NW
Suite 1200
Washington, DC 20006
(202) 362-7435

354

National Foundation for the
Improvement of Education
1201 16th Street, NW, Rm. 628
Washington, DC 20036
(202) 822-7840

Project Harmony
4 State Street
Montpelier, VT 05602
(802) 223-6648

Public Agenda Foundation
6 East 39th St., 9th Floor
New York, NY 10016
(212) 686-6610

The Roosevelt Center for American
Policy Studies
316 Pennsylvania Ave., SE
Washington, DC 20003
(202) 547-7227

RELIGION

For William Fowler, forty-four, pastor of the First United Methodist Church in Bristol, Tennessee (pop. 45,000), adding Soviet history, philosophy, and culture to his sermons and religious classes is a natural way to promote good Christian living. Growing up in Pulaski, a mid-southern Tennessee town where the original Ku Klux Klan was organized and where "unreconstructed rebels were still stewing in Civil War hatreds," Fowler learned the value of emphasizing people's similarities instead of their differences. Today, Fowler urges the six hundred members of his congregation to look "for a oneness, a unity" in people. "You don't like the Yankees," he probes, "how do you think the Russians are going to feel about the Germans?" Since 1983, Fowler has taught an in-the-church Russian history course to several dozen parish members, including attorneys, doctors, businesspeople, and housewives. "My method of teaching," he says, "is to find access points." In a Bible study group that included several grandmothers, for example, Fowler introduced them to Russian life by talking about the Russian tradition of swaddling infants—"All of a sudden, every one of them tuned in. That was their access point."

Fowler describes his parishioners as being "conservative politically" and admits "I keep waiting for a backlash [from them]. But it's interesting—they're kind of proud that other people in the city come to their church to hear their preacher." Moreover, Fowler believes his preaching has influenced his parishioners to respond to events such as the Chernobyl nuclear accident with cogent questions instead of immediate condemnation. "All of us," preaches Fowler, "are God's people and we're all trying to make it to the mountaintop. We don't have to throw rocks at each other on the way up."

The First United Methodist Church in Bristol, Tennessee, is one of hundreds of churches with programs on Soviet-American relations. The nondenominational Riverside Church in New York City has developed a syllabus and reader for a six-week course on the Soviet Union and Soviet-American relations. The

Episcopalian Trinity Church of New York City has sponsored a "Russian Discovery 1984" summer tour for twenty-five laypeople and clergy. The National Council of Churches' (NCC) US-USSR Church Relations Program has promoted contact between American churches and such Soviet organizations as the Russian Orthodox Church, the All-Union Council of Evangelical Christians-Baptists, the Lutheran Churches of Estonia and Latvia, and the Soviet Council on Religious Affairs. In 1982 the United Presbyterian Church passed "A Call for Reexamination and Reconciliation," urging its followers to reexamine their attitudes towards the Soviet Union, to seek more personal contacts with Soviet citizens, and to promote better cooperation between the Soviet and American governments. Other churches with programs educating their members about the Soviet Union and sometimes sponsoring trips there include the Baptists, the Church of the Brethren, the Lutheran World Ministries, the United Church of Christ, and the Unitarian Universalist Association of Congregations.

Support for citizen diplomacy has also come from private religious organizations. Various Jewish organizations promote greater contact between Soviet and American Jews to encourage better treatment of Soviet Jews (*see* "Human Rights"); the Long Island Committee for Soviet Jewry, for example, has gotten thousands of Jewish children to "twin" their Bar Mitzvahs with Soviet Jewish children through written correspondence. The Catholic Peace Mission, sponsored by Global Concepts (*see* "Travel and Tourism"), has enabled American Catholics to visit the churches and homes of Soviet Catholics. The Fellowship of Reconciliation (FOR), an interfaith pacifist organization, has programs encouraging Americans to relate to ordinary Soviets with photographs, "peace pledges," essays, packets of seeds (the "Seeds of Hope" project), children's art, and citizen exchange. FOR has also produced curricula, slide shows, and written materials on life in the Soviet Union, with a focus on religious practice there. US-USSR Bridges for Peace, a coalition of more than fifty church, civic, and peace groups, has sponsored a "Religious Leaders Exchange" with the Russian Orthodox Church and distributes a "Resource and Organizing Guide" for citizen diplomats. And the Connor Center, run by Bruce Rigdon, a specialist on religion in the Soviet Union, has two detailed readers "On Reconciliation between the United States and the Soviet Union."

Among the other major religious groups promoting greater Soviet-American contact through educational programs or trips are the Center of Concern, the Christian Peace Conference, the Churches' Center for Theology and Public Policy, a New Call to Peacemaking (a coalition representing the Society of Friends, the Church of the Brethren, and the Mennonites), and World Peacemakers.

TO LEARN MORE:

Center of Concern
3700 13th St., NE
Washington, DC 20017
(202) 635-2757

Christian Peace Conference
777 UN Plaza
New York, NY 10017
(516) 223-1880

Church of the Brethren
1451 Dundee Ave.
Elgin, IL 60120
(312) 742-5100

Churches' Center for Theology and
    Public Policy
4500 Massachusetts Ave., NW
Washington, DC 20016
(202) 885-9100

The Conner Center
320 North St.
W. Lafayette, IN 47906
(317) 743-3861

Fellowship of Reconciliation
P.O. Box 271
Nyack, NY 10960
(914) 358-4601

First United Methodist Church
322 Vance Dr.
Holston Hills
Bristol, TN 37620
(615) 764-7108

Long Island Committee for Soviet
    Jewry
1 Old Country Rd.
Suite 393
Carl Place, NY 11514
(516) 294-8181

Lutheran World Ministries
360 Park Ave. South
New York, NY 10010
(212) 532-6350

National Council of Churches
US-USSR Church Relations
    Program
475 Riverside Drive, Room 880
New York, NY 10115-0050
(212) 870-2429

New Call to Peacemaking
Box 1245
Elkhart, IN 46514
(219) 294-7536

Riverside Church Disarmament
    Program
490 Riverside Dr.
New York, NY 10027
(212) 222-5900, ext. 238

The Trinity Church
74 Trinity Place
New York, NY 10006
(212) 602-0700

Unitarian Universalist Association
    of Congregations
100 Maryland Ave., NE
Washington, DC 20002
(202) 547-0254

United Church of Christ
110 Maryland, NE
Washington, DC 20002
(202) 543-1517

United Presbyterian Church, USA
475 Riverside Drive, Room 1244H
New York, NY 10115
(212) 870-2137

US-USSR Bridges for Peace
Box 710
Norwich, VT 05055
(802) 649-1000

World Peacemakers
Massachusetts Ave., NW
Washington, DC
(202) 265-7582

SCIENCE

In his five trips to the Soviet Union since 1983, Frank von Hippel, a forty-eight-year-old physicist at Princeton's Center for Environmental Studies, and his Princeton colleagues Robert Socolow and Robert H. Williams, have helped persuade Soviet scientists to begin studying energy efficiency, initiated discussions with the leaders of the Soviet nuclear energy program on how to undertake and verify a cutoff in the production of all fissionable nuclear weapons materials, and launched parallel studies on the technical requirements of "deep reductions" in nuclear weapons stockpiles. In May 1986, Von Hippel, Tom Cochran and Adrian DeWind of the Natural Resources Defense Council (NRDC), and Charles Archambeau, a seismologist at the University of Colorado at Boulder, persuaded the Soviet government to allow NRDC to set up three high-accuracy seismic measurement stations around the Soviet nuclear test site at Semipalatinsk near the Chinese border to demonstrate the feasibility of setting up seismic stations to monitor a comprehensive test ban. In exchange, the Americans agreed to set up three of these stations near the Nevada nuclear test site. All six stations will be jointly run and operated by the Natural Resources Defense Council and the Soviet Academy of Sciences. This unprecedented agreement was made possible by the relationships built over the years between American and Soviet scientists, especially with Yevgeny Velikhov, vice-president of the Soviet Academy of Sciences.

Von Hippel's initiatives are merely the latest in a long tradition of American scientists working behind the scenes with their Soviet counterparts on the technical questions involved in arms control and nuclear war prevention:

- The American Academy of Arts and Sciences (AAAS) has undertaken parallel studies with Soviet scientists on new treaties dealing with ballistic missile defenses and antisatellite weapons. Since 1957, AAAS has served as the American sponsor for the annual International Pugwash Conferences that have brought together scientists from throughout the world—including Soviet and American scientists—to discuss various global problems, especially how to prevent nuclear war. Past meetings have helped lay the groundwork for the Limited Test Ban Treaty, SALT I, and the Biological Weapons Convention.

- Back in the 1960s, Jeremy Stone (*see* "Politicians"), Executive Director of the Federation of American Scientists, traveled five times to the Soviet Union to help convince officials there that antiballistic missile technologies were strategically destabilizing and technically flawed— an understanding the Soviet Union ultimately accepted in the 1972 SALT I Treaty.
- Thomas Malone, Chair of the National Academy of Sciences' Board of Atmospheric Sciences and Climate, Walter Orr Roberts, President Emeritus of the University Corporation for Atmospheric Research, astronomer Carl Sagan of Cornell, and numerous other scientists exchanged data with Soviet scientists to help determine whether nuclear war could trigger a "nuclear winter." In November 1983 both American and Soviet scientists presented their conclusions to one another in a "space bridge" between Washington, DC, and Moscow.

Large-scale scientific cooperation between Soviets and Americans in other areas began in 1959, when the NAS signed an agreement with the Soviet Academy of Sciences. Between 1972 and 1974, various Soviet and American government agencies signed additional bilateral agreements to increase cooperation in the fields of health, artificial heart research, space, environmental protection, atomic energy, agriculture, world oceans, transportation, energy, housing, and science and technology. This last agreement led to working groups being established, under the auspices of the National Science Foundation (NSF) and the NAS, in chemical catalysis, microbiology, forestry, physics, heat and mass transfer, computer applications to management, science policy, corrosion, earth sciences, polymer sciences, electrometallurgy, water resources, and metrology. With these agreements, the annual number of Soviet and American scientists traveling to the other superpower grew to 2,284 by 1975. In addition, Soviet and American scientists increasingly found themselves working together in international scientific institutions such as the International Institute for Applied Systems Analysis in Vienna and the CERN particle physics facilities in Switzerland.

In 1977, a NAS review panel found that, of the 275 American scientists surveyed, nearly all deemed the exchange programs very successful in promoting international scientific cooperation, informing them about Soviet science, and helping to reduce political tensions. Roughly half believed that their exchanges had led to important scientific contributions. Among the exchanges often cited as particularly valuable for Americans were those in electrometallurgy, computer applications to management, and theoretical physics.

In the late 1970s, concern by American scientists over the arrest and imprisonment of Soviet human rights activists and scientists such as Anatoly Shcharansky, a computer specialist, and Yuri Orlov, a physicist, prompted a number of scientists to cancel their trips. In 1980, when Soviet physicist Andrei Sakharov was exiled to Gorky, the NAS suspended all of its bilateral meetings with the Soviet Academy of Sciences and cut its budget for continued exchanges. To underscore its long-term commitment to exchanges, however, the NAS simultaneously formed a Committee on International Security and Arms Control that has since met twice per year with officials of the Soviet Academy.

Since the Geneva summit of 1985, many of the scientific exchanges of the late 1970s have been resumed. The NAS is now trying to increase communication between American and Soviet scientists in the areas of resource management, environment, energy, weather, and arms control. Scientists at a doctoral level interested in working with Soviet counterparts can contact the NAS about its programs and subscribe to its free *Newsletter of the Soviet-East European Exchange Program*.

TO LEARN MORE:

American Academy of Arts and
  Sciences
136 Irving St.
Cambridge, MA 02138
(617) 492-8800

National Academy of Sciences
2101 Constitution Ave., NW
Washington, DC 20418
(202) 334-2644

Federation of American Scientists
307 Massachusetts Ave., NE
Washington, DC 20002
(202) 546-3300

Natural Resources Defense Council
1350 New York NW, Suite 300
Washington, DC 20005
(202) 783-7800

SISTER CITIES

For Steve Kalishman, thirty-two, a lawyer from Gainesville, Florida, the notion of pairing with the Soviet Union has had special significance. In 1976, while working as a sailor on an American merchant ship delivering grain to Novorossiisk, a Soviet port on the Black Sea, he met and fell in love with a Soviet woman named Natasha Andrukovskaya. On his next trip to the Soviet Union, they married and several months later Natasha emigrated to Florida with him, where she now lives and retains her Soviet citizenship.

Since then, Kalishman has become a matchmaker between his and Natasha's hometowns. In 1982, working with a coalition of local church and synagogue members eager to improve Soviet-American relations, Kalishman persuaded the Gainesville City Commission—by a unanimous vote—to invite the people of Novorossiisk to join them in "a long-standing friendship and association."

A delegation hand-delivered the resolution and a key to the city of Gainesville to the mayor of Novorossiisk, who agreed to try this unique approach to forming relations with an American city.

Three more Gainesville delegations followed, each led by a city commissioner and involving representatives of local news media, businesses, schools, and the school board. Each of the delegations received a warm welcome in Novorossiisk and was able to engage in frank, open discussions with nonofficial Soviets in their homes, parks, and restaurants.

These visits led to exchanges of medical information, pen pals, children's art, and photographs, as well as pointing the way to some local business deals; one Gainesville jeweler now has an exclusive agreement to import Soviet cut diamonds and jewelry based on nineteenth-century Russian designs. Novorossiisk has become such a regular part of Gainesville life that the annual homecoming celebration of the University of Florida now sports booths with Russian food and a Novorossiisk theme-float in the homecoming parade.

The Gainesville-based Cross Creek Cloggers and the Bucksnort Barndance Band, an Appalachian-style dance ensemble and string band, kicked off a one-year fund-raising drive to pay for a 1985 journey to Novorossiisk under the heading, "Ask Your Sister to Dance." Said one spokesman for the cloggers: "We plan to sit down with some people and play some music, do some dance steps, and make some friends. It's sort of like what we do here." After raising the necessary funds, forty-three of Gainesville's finest "dancing diplomats" stomped and whirled in both formal and impromptu concerts in Moscow, Kiev, Krasnodar, and Novorossiisk, with one spontaneous concert stopping traffic on a main street in Moscow as hundreds gathered around, and another one, in cahoots with the well-known Russian Folk Ensemble, lasting through the middle of the night. A video crew accompanying the group captured their more than eighteen hours of performances and their other encounters with Soviets in a documentary, *Ask Your Sister to Dance II*, which had a gala premier in Gainesville and was broadcast on PBS. During an interview after a performance at a collective farm, one of the Soviet farmers (who had never seen an American before) told the television crew: "We are just simple people. We don't know much about international problems. But we do know that we need more of this dancing and singing together."

To involve the greater Gainesville community and to help educate other communities, Kalishman is distributing videotapes, a bimonthly national magazine called the *Citizen Diplomat* that has articles about the Gainesville program and other citizen diplomacy initiatives, and a handbook, *American-Soviet Sister Cities: Bridge Towards Peace*, aimed at encouraging other cities to start their own ties with Soviet cities.

The Gainesville program—emerging entirely from the grass roots—represents an important new step in the evolution of Soviet-American city-to-city exchanges. Since 1956, Sister Cities International, an independent organization formed at the suggestion of President Dwight Eisenhower, has established government-sanctioned "sister city" relationships between more than seven hundred and fifty American cities and twelve hundred cities in eighty-six nations. No American cities were linked with Soviet cities, however, until 1972, when, in what were essentially shotgun marriages with little community input, President Nixon and General Secretary Brezhnev arranged five pairings—Houston-Baku, Jacksonville-Murmansk, Oakland-Nakhodka, Baltimore-Odessa, and Seattle-Tashkent. These relationships were based primarily on existing economic ties; all of the chosen cities except Tashkent were major ports. In the wake of the Afghanistan invasion, the Jacksonville mayor unilaterally suspended his city's relationship with Murmansk in support of President Carter's sanctions. The other sister-city programs also became moribund, with the outstanding exception of the Seattle-Tashkent program, which has benefited from the strong support of Rosanne Royer, who speaks fluent Russian and also happens to be the wife of the city's mayor. The "Target Seattle" program, featuring education about the arms race and the Soviet Union, was attended by more than twenty-five thousand Seattle residents. Partly because of its strong sister-city relationship, the Soviets agreed to designate Seattle as the site of the 1990 Soviet-American Goodwill Games (*see* "Sports").

As citizen diplomacy initiatives multiplied in the early 1980s, new grass-roots sister-city efforts sprang up throughout the country. The Soviets, however, frustrated that four out of five past sister-city relationships had fallen apart, initially allowed only one new formal arrangement—Detroit-Minsk. The sluggish response of the Soviet officials and resulting pessimism from Sister Cities International, in turn, prompted end-runs not only by Steve Kalishman but also by the Ground Zero Pairing Project, which created informal links between fifty-five American and Soviet cities.

After the Geneva summit in late 1985, however, Soviet officials began warming up again to the idea of new sister cities. In April 1986 the Soviets approved in principle the establishment of formal sister-city relationships for ten more cities: Boulder, Colorado; Cambridge, Massachusetts; Duluth, Minnesota; Gainesville, Florida; Madison, Wisconsin; Mobile, Alabama; Richmond, Indiana; Salem, Oregon; Tallahassee, Florida; and Worcester, Massachusetts. In addition, the Soviets have asked that six additional pairings be made, based on requests they have received from Soviet cities. In October 1986 Salem-Simferopol became the first of the ten new pairs to match officially, and the first Soviet-American sister-city relationship to be initiated entirely on the citizen level.

TO LEARN MORE:

Gainesville-Novorossiisk Sister City
  Program
408 W. University Ave.
Suite 303
Gainesville, FL 32601
(904) 376-0341

Ground Zero Pairing Project
P.O. Box 19049
Portland, OR 97219
(503) 245-3403

Salem-Simferopol Sister City Program
c/o David Hunt
894 Highland NE
Salem, OR 97303
(503) 364-1736

Seattle-Tashkent Sister City
  Program
Sister City Committee
630 Randolph Place
Seattle, WA 98122
(206) 324-6258

Sister Cities International
1625 Eye St., NW, #424-26
Washington, DC 20006
(202) 293-5504

SPACE

Space, one of the first battlegrounds for Soviet-American Cold War competition, has also been one of the most fruitful areas for Soviet-American cooperation. In 1972 the two superpowers signed an Agreement Concerning Cooperation in the Exploration and Use of Outer Space for Peaceful Purposes, which included plans for a 1975 two-day docking of Apollo and Soyuz spacecrafts. Leading up to the docking was a long process of joint planning and training involving hundreds of Americans and Soviets, who, according to Martin Caidin, author of the best-seller *Marooned,* developed friendships that transcended their national loyalties: "Pilots are pilots; astronauts, cosmonauts, call them what you want, they are pilots first of all." At one conference in Greece, writes Caidin, two astronauts and two cosmonauts got drunk in a hotel room while both CIA and KGB agents tripped over one another combing the city to find them.

The cooperative ties built by the Apollo-Soyuz mission led to a series of joint biological experiments performed on board Cosmos 782 in 1976 and a jointly prepared, three-volume treatise on *Foundations of Space Biology and Medicine*. In addition, discussions began on joint ventures to monitor air pollution from space and to develop a space platform that would combine the longevity of the Soviets' Salyut Space Station with the weight-carrying capability of the Americans' Space Shuttle. These plans were shelved as détente broke down, but other forms of Soviet-American space cooperation continued:

- In 1979, the Soviet Union and the United States joined Canada and France in launching a global Search-and-Rescue Satellite (SARSAT) program, which is credited with having saved more than four hundred lives. For example, on April 7, 1984, an Air Force helicopter used the system to brave forty-mph winds, swirling snow, and twenty-foot waves to carry a Soviet sailor suffering from appendicitis from his trawler to a hospital in Iceland.

- In December 1983 scientists from the Soviet Union, the United States, and Japan agreed to cooperate in studying Halley's comet. American radio antennae and other equipment enabled two Soviet VEGA spacecraft to get higher quality photographs. Says Boris Ragent, a senior staff scientist at NASA-Ames Laboratories, "We got all the data as if it were our project. The Russians were very open about everything. It worked out well for everybody. We had access to their data and they had the benefit of our experience and knowledge."

- Also in December 1983, NASA placed three pieces of medical equipment aboard the Cosmos 1514 spacecraft to study the blood system and biorhythms of monkeys and the fetal development of rats.

Today, Soviet and American scientists continue to cooperate in studying comets and the effects of space on animals. In early 1986, after seven US astronauts died in the explosion of the Challenger Space Shuttle, Soviet cartographers mapping the surface of Venus named two craters after Christa McAuliffe and Judith Resnik, the two female astronauts on the Challenger. Serious discussions have taken place at a National Academy of Sciences gathering of scientists, space officials, astronauts, and cosmonauts concerning Cornell astronomer Carl Sagan's idea to send a joint manned mission to Mars.

If you are interested in learning more about Soviet-American space cooperation, you can contact the Association of Space Explorers (*see* chapter 6), the Institute for Security and Cooperation in Outer Space, The Planetary Society, and the Young Astronaut Council. If the joint mission to Mars intrigues you, one organization promoting it is The Search for Common Ground.

TO LEARN MORE:

Association of Space Explorers/USA
3278 Sacramento St.
San Francisco, CA 94115
(415) 931-0585

Institute for Security and
    Cooperation in Outer Space
1420 16th St. NW
Washington, DC 20036
(202) 462-8886

The Planetary Society
65 N. Catalina Ave.
Pasadena, CA 91106
(818) 793-5100

Young Astronaut Council
1516 30th Street, NW
Washington, DC 20036
(202) 682-1986

The Search for Common Ground
1701 K St., NW
Suite 403
Washington, DC 20006
(202) 835-0777

SPORTS

With the US boycott of the Moscow Olympics in 1980 and the Soviet Union's reciprocal boycott of the Los Angeles Olympics in 1984, the original Olympic ideals of promoting peace through cooperation in sports have become thoroughly entangled in Cold War politics. On a citizen level, however, the ideals are alive and well. In 1982, after seeing Lawrence, Kansas, obliterated in the ABC television show *The Day After*, Phillip Shinnick, captain of the US track and field team at the 1964 Olympics, helped bring the Soviet track and field team to compete in annual relay races in Lawrence. The event was so successful that Shinnick persuaded two of his former Olympic colleagues—long-jumper Bob Beamon and high-jumper John Thomas—to help him form an organization called Athletes United for Peace (AUP) on the principle that "through intense competition, athletes have formed common bonds of brotherhood and sisterhood that point the way towards a world of cooperation and respect for differences."

AUP has since brought the Soviet Dynamos to play soccer with Team America in St. Louis, Missouri, and Soviet runners to compete in marathons in Cambridge and New York. It has also sent the US Junior Olympic Mens Basketball team to several Soviet cities and American runners to the annual Moscow International Peace Marathon and Ten Kilometer Race. Currently AUP is being directed by former National Football League player Guy Benjamin, who is planning to bring a Soviet basketball team to play the champion team from the University of San Francisco.

To create the televised Olympic-quality competition with Americans and Soviets that did not occur in 1980 or 1984, television magnate Ted Turner (*see* "Television") reached an agreement with the Soviet All-Union Association of Sports and Gosteleradio to organize and broadcast "Goodwill Games" in Moscow in July 1986 and in Seattle in 1990. The 1986 games involved 3500 athletes from the Soviet Union, the United States, and fifty-three other countries competing in track and field, gymnastics, swimming, boxing, cycling, basketball, wrestling, and figure skating. "The Goodwill Games," says Turner, "offer a step in the right direction. . . . Not only will the participants compete together in the spirit of good sportsmanship, [but also] audiences worldwide will be able to see the harmony that can be fostered among nations."

If you are interested in getting involved in sporting events with Soviets, you can contact either AUP or Christopher Senie's Teamworks, Inc. (*see* chapter 8), which in 1986 organized a second successful Bike for Peace ride from Kiev to New York City. Alternatively, you might work through the US Olympic Committee, which in 1985 reached an agreement with Soviet officials to establish joint training camps, bilateral competitions, and exchanges of athletes, coaches, and sports officials.

TO LEARN MORE:

Athletes United For Peace
450 Harrison
Room 310
San Francisco, CA 94105
(415) 543-6671

Turner Broadcasting System, Inc.
1050 Techwood Dr. NW
Atlanta, GA 30318
(404) 827-1500

Teamworks, Inc.
125 Main Street
Westport, CT 06880
(203) 227-3223

US Olympic Committee
1750 E. Boulder St.
Colorado Springs, CO 80909
(303) 632-5551

TEACHING

If you're a primary or secondary school teacher and would like to meet or correspond with Soviet teaching counterparts, one contact is the International Academic and Information Exchange (IAIE). Founded by a group of Los Angeles teachers in response to Helsinki Final Accord, which invited "persons engaged in activities in education" to exchange ideas, methods, and materials, the IAIE has worked with the Soviet Teachers Trade Union to enable Soviet and American teachers to visit one another's schools. In addition, it publishes newsletters and teaching curricula and holds seminars to help American teachers understand Soviet teaching approaches.

Several other options are also available. The National Education Association is exchanging information on educational trends and teaching experiences with the Educational and Scientific Workers Union of the Soviet Union, primarily through personal contacts established among leaders of both organizations. The AFS International/Intercultural Program has enabled Soviets to teach in American schools while living in American homes and Americans to teach at special

English language schools in Moscow, Leningrad, and Kiev. Educators for Social Responsibility publishes excellent curricula and sponsors conferences aimed at helping teachers present material on the Soviet Union in an objective, thought-provoking manner.

TO LEARN MORE:

AFS International/Intercultural
  Programs
313 E. 43rd St.
New York, NY 10017
(212) 949-4242

Educators for Social Responsibility
23 Garden St.
Cambridge, MA 02139
(617) 492-1764

International Academic Information
  Exchange
P.O. Box 5523
Santa Monica, CA 90405
(213) 450-3620

National Education Association
1201 16th St., NW
Washington, DC 20036
(202) 833-4400

TELEVISION

In recent years, American television networks have made a small but growing number of high-quality shows about the Soviet Union. NBC produced a superb historic docudrama *Peter the Great*, which it filmed on location in the Soviet Union. PBS has shown Samuel Rachlin's remarkable essay films about the Soviet Union (*see* "Film and Photography"), produced a film about nine Soviets visiting the United States entitled *From Moscow to Chautauqua*, and is discussing several possible exchanges of shows with the Soviet Union. Home Box Office, Inc. produced *Sakharov*, which became the most honored show at the seventh annual cable television awards. And Phil Donahue's Multimedia Entertainment organized two "citizen summits" in 1985 and 1986, in which Donahue's American audiences could speak with Soviet audiences with Vladimir Pozner as moderator (copies are available from the Documentary Guild).

Perhaps the American who has most visibly committed himself to producing quality programs about the Soviet Union is entrepreneur, yachtsman, baseball owner, and television czar Ted Turner. "Recent trips to Cuba and the Soviet Union," Turner says, "have had a tremendous influence on my thinking about global relations. These trips have convinced me that the only way that humanity is going to continue to exist on this planet with our exploding technology is for us to engage in . . . global cooperation. In my opinion, there is absolutely no other course that we can take."

Turner's plans? "I'm desperately trying to hook the world together as quickly as possible so that we can share all the information and wisdom of our brilliant scientists and businessmen. I want to help the people who are working hard to improve relations between the two largest and most powerful nations on earth so that when the two of them get together, the rest of the world can come together as well."

Turner has formed an organization called the Better World Society that aims to produce top-notch documentary films and television shows highlighting and suggesting solutions to global problems, particularly those related to improving East-West relations. Its premiere show, *Challenge of the Caucasus* (*see* chapter 2), was broadcast on the eve of the November 1985 Geneva Summit and won a blue ribbon at the 1986 American Film Festival. The Better World Society is also considering producing several nights of alternative programs about the Soviet Union to compete with ABC's Cold War fantasy *Amerika*.

In May 1985 Turner signed a two-year agreement to exchange and jointly produce programming with Intervisions, a consortium of Eastern bloc broadcasting systems that includes Gosteleradio, the Soviet State Committee for Television and Radio. As a result, Turner's Superstation, which reaches thirty-four million households, will soon be showing news, entertainment, and sports programming from the Soviet Union. Among his first shows were broadcasts of the Goodwill Games, an alternative Olympics he organized in Moscow for July 1986 (*see* "Sports").

In other, less official ways, Americans and Soviets have been able to enjoy one another's television programs through videotape. Both Stanford University and Columbia University have set up special facilities for receiving and taping Soviet television. Creighton University has edited down forty hours of Soviet television and created a series called "Channel 3, Moscow." With more and more Soviets owning videocassette recorders—Moscow opened its first two video rental stores in late 1985—many are enjoying videotapes of American television recorded illicitly by households near the Finnish border.

Citizen diplomats eager to create their own television programs have set up "space bridges" between live American and Soviet audiences. Among the early pioneers of the concept were thirty-eight-year-old filmmaker Kim Spencer and thirty-five-year-old television producer Evelyn Messinger, who in 1982 created a production company called Internews. Spencer and Messinger have managed the technical end of the space bridges linking Soviets with Americans at the second US Festival in spring 1983 (*see* chapter 6), at the "nuclear winter" conference in autumn 1983 (*see* "Science"), at the Beyond War Award ceremony for IPPNW in autumn 1984 (*see* chapter 1), and at the 1985 Moscow-Minneapolis performance of the play *Peace Child* (*see* "Children").

Mainstream television is becoming increasingly interested in Soviet-American space bridges. In conjunction with PBS, Internews plans to link Carl Sagan and the US Jet Propulsion Laboratory with Command Control for the Soviet Manned Space Station to discuss the possibilities for a joint Soviet-American mission to Mars (*see* "Space"). ABC has also hired Internews to link a home in Philadelphia with a home in Leningrad so that both families can talk about their daily lives, and to produce a Soviet-American entertainment extravaganza during the next summit.

Internews is continuing to put together private dialogues as well. On September 11, 1986, Soviet and American scientists held a remarkably frank dialogue on "Chernobyl and Three-Mile Island: Implications for Cooperation in an Interdependent World" during a San Francisco-Moscow space bridge sponsored by the Esalen Soviet-American Exchange Program (*see* chapter 6), the American Academy of Arts and Science, and Internews. Thanks to an agreement ironed out by Yevgeny Velikhov, vice president of the Soviet Academy of Sciences, and Congressman George Brown from California, Internews will be creating closed-circuit space bridges between members of Congress and members of the Supreme Soviet starting in January 1987.

If you are interested in creating your own space bridge or in obtaining videotapes of previous space bridges, you can contact Internews or Spacebridge Productions (*see* "High Technology").

Finally, writer/producer Mark Gerzon is attempting to improve American television and film images of the Soviet Union and vice versa through a company called Mediators, Inc., which is catalyzing the coproduction of television feature films between Sovinfilm, the Soviet film agency, and major American networks Mediators, Inc. is also sponsoring an "entertainment summit" to bring together American and Soviet television bigwigs to discuss whether they are doing a good job of portraying the other side and how their programming could improve.

TO LEARN MORE:

The Better World Society
1140 Connecticut Ave., NW
Suite 1006
Washington, DC 20036
(202) 331-3770

The Documentary Guild
Shearer Rd.
Colrain, MA 01340
(413) 625-2402

Internews
One Lincoln Plaza
New York, NY 10023
(212) 877-4070

Mark Gerzon
Mediators, Inc.
20269 Inland Lane
Malibu, CA 90265
(213) 456-2512

TRAVEL AND TOURISM

The Citizen Exchange Council (CEC) is one of the few organizations arranging tours of the Soviet Union that comes highly recommended by both the US

Information Agency and the Soviet Friendship Society. In 1962, Stephen Dan James, a New York ad man, dreamed of getting Soviet and American leaders to swap their kids in a "hostage exchange for peace." By 1965, the idea had gotten lots of fanfare but few volunteer parents, and its promoters decided to concentrate instead on exchanging ordinary American and Soviet citizens. They named their new organization the Citizen Exchange Corps, modeling their name after the newly founded Peace Corps.

Today, the CEC, directed by Michael Brainerd, sends nearly a thousand Americans to the Soviet Union each year. Going far beyond the prearranged packages offered by the Soviet tourist agency, Intourist, the CEC gives every group a special focus—for example, "Educators Summer Seminar," "Photography Workshop in the USSR," or "Cross-Country Skiing." Every group has an American leader who is fluent in Russian and able to facilitate meetings with the group's Soviet counterparts. The CEC also hosts about fifty Soviets in the United States each year; in spring 1986, for example, it brought delegations of Soviets to meet with Americans to discuss theater, music, children's art, and children's literature.

For individual travelers and organizations such as churches, schools, or community groups eager for a high-quality, person-to-person first trip to the Soviet Union, brokers like CEC are the best bet. Pioneer Travel can help you arrange camping or driving tours to the seldom-visited rural regions of the Soviet Union. Several other travel agencies, listed below, have substantial experience arranging tours, often tailored to specific interests. Of course, if you wish to design your own tour—perhaps a railroad trip across Siberia, a horseback tour of Central Asia, or a desert tour by camel caravan—your travel agent can work directly with the New York representatives of Intourist. In 1985, 45,049 visas were granted to Americans for travel to the Soviet Union.

TO LEARN MORE:

Academic Travel Abroad
1346 Connecticut Avenue, NW
Washington, DC 20036
(202) 785-3412

Anniversary Tours/Voices of the
  Future
250 West 57th St.
New York, NY 10107
(212) 245-7501
(800) 223-1336

Citizen Diplomacy, Inc.
(East Coast Office)
Steve Kalishman
408 West University Avenue, Suite
  303
Gainesville, FL 32601
(904) 376-0341

(West Coast Office)
David Hunt
894 Highland NE
Salem, OR 97303
(503) 364-1736

Citizen Exchange Council
18 E. 41st St., Suite 1004
New York, NY 10017
(212) 889-7960

Enterprise Travel
270 Greenwich Ave.
Greenwich, CT 06830
(203) 629-3535

Foundation for International
  Cooperation
4909 Mohawk Road
Rockford, IL 61107
(815) 397-4599

Friendship Force
575 S. Omni International
Atlanta, GA 30303
(404) 522-9490

General Tours
711 Third Ave.
New York, NY 10017
(212) 687-7400
(800) 221-2216

Global Concepts
3004 Brockbank Ct.
Dallas, TX 75220
(214) 352-8416

Intourist
630 Fifth Ave.
Suite 868
New York, NY 10111
(212) 757-3884/5

Peace Odysseys
5250 Patriot Lane
Columbia, MD 21045
(301) 730-8296

People to People International
2420 Pershing Rd., Suite 300
Kansas City, MO 64108
(816) 421-6343

Pioneer Travel Service
203 Allston St.
Cambridge, MA 02139
(617) 547-1127

Russart Travel Services
3402 Geary Blvd.
San Francisco, CA 94118
(415) 668-4080

Russian Travel Bureau
20 East 46th St.
New York, NY 10017
(212) 986-1500

Tour Designs, Inc.
510 H St., SW
Washington, DC 20024
(202) 554-5820

World Peace Tours
Box 8910
La Jolla, CA 92038
(619) 942-7181

UNIVERSITIES

According to Allen Kassof, the fifty-five-year-old director of the International Research and Exchanges Board (IREX), which arranges Soviet-American exchanges among scholars, researchers, and scientists, "[IREX] is an organization focused primarily on professional concerns and only secondarily on people-to-people contacts." IREX trains researchers to work in the Soviet Union; exchanges individual scholars chosen in national competitions; organizes major Soviet-American collaborative projects in the humanities and social sciences; and disseminates the resulting research to the general public. "You can say quite accurately," observes Kassof, "that virtually everyone in the American professional research community concerned with Eastern Europe or the Soviet Union has at one time or another been in an IREX program."

IREX began in 1958, when the first Soviet-American cultural agreement was signed. To guard against politicization, the academic community formed an independent "interuniversity committee" to oversee its exchange programs. A decade later, the committee was given a more formal structure under the American Council of Learned Societies and the Social Science Research Council, and IREX was founded. The committee also appointed its first director, Allen Kassof, who was then teaching sociology and Soviet studies at Princeton.

Today, IREX, with staff of twenty-five and a budget of five million dollars—funded largely by the US Information Agency, the National Endowment for the Humanities, and the Department of State—oversees exchanges with the Soviet Ministry of Higher and Specialized Secondary Education (i.e., with Soviet universities) that involve doctoral candidates, junior faculty, senior scholars, and language teachers from both countries. IREX also has exchanges with the Soviet Academy of Sciences that have involved more than 1,250 Soviet and American humanities and social science specialists in such projects as crisis management, archeology, comparative literature, human longevity, and geography. IREX's programs have also occasionally funded research projects undertaken by government officials, business people, and independent scholars. Overall, IREX estimates that its exchanges have been responsible for more than four thousand books, articles, and dissertations.

Kassof has seen a real improvement in academic exchanges over the last twenty years, especially in joint projects: "There's a lot less nonsense. The early phases of the relationship involved a certain amount of fishing around. As the groups come to know and work with one another, professional standards are constantly improving."

In December 1985, IREX renewed its agreement with the Soviet Academy of Sciences to expand projects in such fields as international relations, law, history, philosophy, economics, geography, and psychology. For example, Soviet scholars are now prepared to provide access to their Moscow and Leningrad collections of ancient Hebraic manuscripts, which until now have been inaccessible to Western scholars.

In addition to the IREX-sponsored exchanges, some scholars and institutions have developed their own programs. Under the leadership of Dr. Irwin Weil, for example, the Department of Slavic Languages and Literatures in Northwestern University has linked American scholars interested in Russian literature with Soviet scholars from the Soviet Institute of World Literature. Duke University's Center for Corporate Economics and Strategy has sponsored ongoing exchanges between Soviet and American economists, computer scientists, and mathematicians.

If you are a university faculty member and wish to study or teach in the Soviet Union, you can find positions through the Council for International Exchange of Scholars (CIES). Affiliated with the American Council on Education, CIES has worked with the US Information Agency since 1973 to administer its senior scholar Fulbright grants in the natural, applied, medical, and social sciences. Several other faculty exchanges are also available. The University of Missouri at Kansas City, the State University of New York (SUNY), and the Mid-West University Consortium for International Activities (a consortium of seven universities headquartered at Ohio State University) all exchange professors with Moscow State University. In addition, the University of Lowell and the University of Massachusetts have had a small faculty exchange with Tbilisi State University.

If you are an undergraduate or graduate student wishing to study in the Soviet Union, you should contact SUNY, which has two programs open to students. One exchanges ten undergraduates and one faculty advisor each year for a semester of study with the Maurice Thorez Institute of Foreign Languages; the Soviets in this program are, in fact, the only Soviet undergraduates studying in the United States. A second program exchanges ten to twelve graduate students each year with Moscow State University.

There are also several "one-way" exchanges open to American students. Since 1966, the Council for International Education Exchange (CIEE), a consortium of twenty-eight American colleges and universities, has been sending about two hundred American students each year to learn Russian at Leningrad State University. Under three other programs run by Ohio State-Purdue, Middlebury College, and the American Council of Teachers of Russian (ACTR), another 150 American undergraduates study each year at Moscow's Pushkin Russian Language Institute. The CIEE, Ohio State-Purdue, and ACTR programs are all open to qualified students from any school in the country.

Another dimension of university involvement in Soviet-American relations is the growing number of programs in "Soviet studies." The principal centers for research in the Soviet Union today are Brown's Center for Foreign Policy Development, Columbia's W. Averell Harriman Institute, Harvard's Russian Research Center, Indiana University's Russian and East European Institute, Stanford University, the University of California at Berkeley, the University of Michigan Center for Russian and East European Studies, the University of Illinois Russian and East European Center, and the University of Washington at Seattle Russian and East European Studies Program. These universities not only publish prodigious amounts of research but also have vast collections of research materials and taped or videotaped lectures. Georgetown University's

Institute for the Study of Diplomacy is also noteworthy for its special interest in citizen diplomacy; in 1986, it published an academic book on the subject entitled *Private Diplomacy with the Soviet Union*.

Trying to enhance the whole field of Soviet studies has been the Social Science Research Council, which sponsors numerous grant programs, conferences, workshops, and research materials. A good way of keeping in touch with current Soviet studies programs is to join the American Association for the Advancement of Slavic Studies (AAASS), an organization with several thousand leading American scholars, researchers, public servants, and professionals. Its quarterly *AAASS Newsletter* lists, among other things, new opportunities for travel, study, research, and teaching in the field. Every year it also publishes an *American Bibliography of Slavic and East European Studies*.

TO LEARN MORE:

American Council of Learned
  Societies
228 East 45 St.
New York, NY 10017
(212) 697-1505

American Council of Teachers of
  Russian
815 New Gulph Road
Bryn Mawr, PA 19010
(215) 525-6559

The American Association for the
  Advancement of Slavic Studies
128 Encina Commons
Stanford University
Stanford, CA 94305
(415) 723-9668

Center for Corporate Economics and
  Strategy
Duke University
PO Box 10050, Duke Station
Durham, NC 27706
(919) 684-6774

Center for Foreign Policy
  Development
Brown University
Box 1948
Providence, RI 02912
(401) 863-3465

The Council for International
  Exchange of Scholars
11 Dupont Circle, NW, Suite 300
Washington, DC 20036
(202) 939-5400

The Council on International
  Education Exchange
205 East 42 St.
New York, NY 10017
(212) 661-1414

Fulbright Alumni Association
P.O. Box 1042
Bryn Mawr, PA 19010
(215) 645-5038

W. Averell Harriman Institute for
   Advanced Study of the Soviet
   Union
420 West 118th Street
12th floor, IAB
New York, NY 10027
(212) 280-4623

Harvard University
Russian Research Center
1737 Cambridge Street
Cambridge, MA 02138
(617) 495-4038

Indiana University
Russian and East European
   Institute
Ballantine Hall 565
Bloomington, IN 47405
(812) 335-7309

Institute for the Study of Diplomacy
Georgetown University
School of Foreign Service
Washington, DC 20057
(202) 625-3784

International Research and
   Exchanges Board (IREX)
126 Alexander St.
Princeton, NJ 08540-7102
(609) 683-9500

Midwest Universities Consortium for
   International Activities
Office of the Executive Director
Ohio State University
134 Derby Hall, 154 N. Oval Mall
Columbus, OH 43210
(614) 422-2755

Northwestern University Department
   of Slavic Languages and
   Literature
Evanston, IL 60201
(312) 491-8254

Ohio State University-Purdue
   Russian Language Program
Dept. of Slavic and East European
   Languages
Ohio State University
232 Cunz Hall
Columbus, OH 43210
(614) 422-8770

Social Science Research Council
605 Third Avenue
New York, NY 10158
(212) 661-0280

Stanford University
Dept. of Slavic Studies
Stanford, CA 94305
(415) 723-9668

State University of New York
International Program
State University Plaza
Albany, NY 12246
(518) 473-7909

University of California—Berkeley
   Center for Slavic and East
   European Studies
Berkeley, CA 94720
(415) 642-3230

University of Illinois
Russian and East European Center
1208 West California Street
Urbana, IL 61801
(217) 333-1244

University of Lowell
c/o Adolph Baker
17 Gage Rd.
Wayland, MA 01778
(617) 653-6252

University of Michigan
Center for Russian and East
    European Studies
220 Lane Hall
Ann Arbor, MI 48109
(313) 764-0351

University of Washington, Seattle
Russian and East European Studies
    Program
University of Washington, DR-05
Seattle, WA 98195
(206) 543-4852

University of Missouri-Kansas City
5100 Rockhill Road
Kansas City, MO 64110
(816) 276-1107

WOMEN

Since 1961 the Women's International League for Peace and Freedom (WILPF) in association with the Jane Addams Peace Association has been meeting with the Soviet Women's Committee to discuss not only such general "peace issues" as disarmament and the United Nations, but also issues of special concern to women, such as child rearing and the economic status of women. One woman involved in organizing these conferences has been Carol Pendell, mother of three sons and wife of a Methodist pastor, who has since traveled to the Soviet Union and met with women there numerous times and who has hosted Soviet women in her own home. In 1979 she started the USA-USSR Citizen's Dialogue to involve a wider spectrum of Americans and Soviets. In all of her activities, Pendell adheres to the basic credo of WILPF—that "women in countries whose governments do not see eye to eye should keep up relationships with one another."

Several other organizations have active exchange programs with the Soviet Women's Committee, including the American Association of University Women, Continuing the Peace Dialogue, Grandmothers for Peace, In Our Own Way, Mothers for Peace, Peace Links, and the Women's Action for Nuclear Disarmament. The US Corporate and Foundation Women's exchange with the Soviet Women's Committee has involved women from such diverse organizations as Radcliffe College, the *Christian Science Monitor*, and the Girls Club of America.

If you are searching for educational materials for women on Soviet-Amerian relations, the Committee for National Security (CNS) has extensive reports on two conferences it sponsored on "Women's Leadership on US-USSR Relations." Along with Peace Links, a network of thousands of American women founded by the concerned wives of several US Senators, CNS has been distributing an educational packet on the lives of Soviet women.

In an effort to weave—literally—closer relations between American and

Soviet women, a group of women from Boise, Idaho, have been sewing "peace quilts" and sending them, along with goodwill letters, to women in the Soviet Union. One massive quilt was a joint effort; American women weaved the main squares depicting portraits of Soviet and American children and Soviet women prepared a gold border and center. The joint quilt was presented to the arms control negotiating teams at Geneva in March 1986 before beginning a two-year tour of Soviet and American cities. Some of the wool for the Boise Peace Quilt Project has been provided by Peace Fleece, a cooperative effort by Soviet and American sheep farmers to produce and market wool products made from a blend of Soviet and American wool. Peace Fleece is also working with the Soviet Women's Committee on an exchange of knitted and crocheted articles.

TO LEARN MORE:

Jane Addams Peace Association, Inc.
777 UN Plaza
New York, NY 10017
(212) 682-8830

American Association of University
    Women
2401 Virginia Ave., NW
Washington, DC 20037
(202) 785-7700

Boise Peace Quilt Project
Box 6469
Boise, ID 83707
(208) 378-0293

Committee for National Security
1601 Connecticut Ave., NW
Washington, DC 20009
(202) 745-2450

Continuing the Peace Dialogue
Box 1710
Carmel Valley, CA 93924
(408) 659-3758
(408) 429-6584

Girls Club of America, Inc.
1030 15th St., NW
Washington, DC 20005
(202) 393-4554

Grandmothers for Peace
2708 Curtis Way
Sacramento, CA 95818
(916) 451-4969

In Our Own Way
2437 15th St., NW, Suite 400
Washington, DC 20009
(202) 483-0710

Peace Fleece
RFD 1
Box 57
Kezar Falls, ME 04047

Peace Links
747 Eighth St., SE
Washington, DC 20003
(202) 544-0805

USA-USSR Citizens Dialogue, Inc.
777 United Nations Plaza
New York, NY 10017
(212) 682-3633

US Corporation and Foundation
    Women
1133 Ave. of the Americas
New York, NY 10022

Women's Action for Nuclear
  Disarmament (WAND)
691 Massachusetts Ave.
Arlington, MA 02174
(617) 643-6740

Women's International League for
  Peace and Freedom
1213 Race St.
Philadelphia, PA 19107
(215) 563-7110

YOUTH

Convinced that today's youths are tomorrow's leaders, the American Council of Young Political Leaders began bringing together young leaders of the Democratic and Republican Parties (principally at the state and local level) with leaders of the Soviet Committee of Youth Organizations in 1971. By 1979 it had sent twelve American delegations with 165 participants to the Soviet Union and received sixteen Soviet delegations with 150 participants in the United States, each time arranging five days of intensive discussion. Much to the delight of the conference organizers, many of the early American participants in the program have gone on to become congressmen, governors, national political party officers, university presidents, and leading newspaper columnists.

The American Council of Young Political Leaders program, suspended in the early 1980s, was reestablished in August 1986. Other programs, working with the Soviet Committee of Youth Organizations, are also promoting dialogue between American and Soviet youths, including the Forum for US-Soviet Dialogue (which since 1972 has sponsored an annual conference, alternating countries yearly, of 80 Soviet and American young professionals and students), the American Field Service (AFS) International/Intercultural Program (*see* "Teaching") (overseen by the American Center for International Leadership), Project Luck, and Youth for Democratic Action (overseen by Americans for Democratic Action). International Student Pugwash has held biennial conferences bringing together students from the United States and abroad—including the Soviet Union—to discuss the public policy impact of science and technology with prominent international scholars. More contentious dialogues have been arranged by the Committee on International Discussion and Debate of the Speech Communication Association, which since 1974 has arranged for open debates on controversial issues between American and Soviet teams in both countries.

The National 4-H Council has run one of the oldest youth exchange programs, enabling Soviet and American youths to develop closer ties while studying each country's agricultural techniques.

Another way of meeting Soviets is at summer camp. Every year, the National Council of American-Soviet Friendship (*see* "Hosting Soviets") sends a group of young people, aged twelve to fifteen, to Camp Artek, the Soviet's international youth camp on the Black Sea. Since 1974, the YMCA has brought six to twelve Soviets in their twenties to serve as camp counselors at its camps and has sent an equal number of young Americans to serve as camp counselors at Soviet Young Pioneer Camps. Volunteers for Peace has organized international "work camps" in the United States focusing on peace, environment, education, and community development that have involved Soviet youths and, in turn, has sent American youths to workcamps in the Soviet Union. And the US-USSR Youth Exchange Program (*see* chapter 2) organizes annual wilderness treks for Americans and Soviets, ages seventeen to twenty-one, in the Caucasus Mountains of the Soviet Union.

A number of agencies arranging tours to the Soviet Union are oriented toward youth. Several are run by leading private prep schools, including the Buckingham, Browne, and Nichols School (*see* "Language"), the Phillips Academy at Andover (which will exchange twelve students and one teacher with an academy in Novosibirsk during the 1987–88 academic year), the Sidwell Friends School, and the St. Albans School. US Student Travel Tours also helps young Americans, ages eighteen to twenty-five, plan camping tours of the Soviet Union.

Several of the American youth organizations trying to improve Soviet-American relations are self-described "peace groups." Both the Student/Teacher Organization to Prevent Nuclear War (STOP), which focuses on high school students, and United Campuses to Prevent Nuclear War (UCAM), which focuses on undergraduates, distribute educational materials about the Soviet Union. Working with the Soviet Student Council, UCAM has also brought Soviet students to campuses in the United States.

Persuading the Soviets to allow youths under twenty-five years of age to come to the United States has traditionally been difficult, though not impossible. If you do manage to get permission to bring young Soviets here for educational or cultural exchange, you can ask the National Association for Foreign Student Affairs for help in arranging their US entry visas.

Even without travel, interesting joint ventures by American and Soviet youths are possible. Seattle's Lakeside High School recently became a sister school to Moscow School Number 20. By telex, they held an interscholastic swimming meet and chess match. Perhaps predictably, Seattle won at swimming and Moscow won at chess.

TO LEARN MORE:

American Center for International
  Leadership
522 Franklin St.
Columbus, Indiana 47201
(812) 376-3456

American Council of Young
  Political Leaders
1000 Connecticut Ave., NW
Washington, DC 20036
(202) 857-0999

Buckingham, Browne and Nichols
  School
Gerry's Landing Rd.
Cambridge, MA 02138
(617) 547-6100

Choate Rosemary Hall
Russian Studies Center for
  Secondary Schools
P.O. Box 788
Wallingford, CT 06492
(203) 269-7722

Committee on International
  Discussion and Debate
5105 Backlick Rd., Building E
Annandale, VA 22003

Forum for US-Soviet Dialogue
22 Hemlock Hill Rd.
Amherst, NH 03031
(603) 673-8639

International Student Pugwash
505 2nd Street, NE
Washington, DC 20002
(202) 544-1784

National Association for Foreign
  Student Affairs
1860 19th Street, NW
Washington, DC 20009
(202) 462-4811

National 4-H Council
7100 Connecticut Avenue
Chevy Chase, MD 20815
(301) 656-9000

Phillips Academy
Andover, MA 01810
(617) 475-3400

Project Luck
Box 397
South Weymouth, MA 02061
(617) 878-4299

St. Alban's School
Mass. & Wisconsin, NW
Washington, DC 20008
(202) 537-6400

Student/Teacher Organization to
  Prevent (STOP) Nuclear War
11 Garden St.
Cambridge, MA 02138
(617) 492-8305

United Campuses for the Prevention
  of Nuclear War
220 Eye St., NE
Suite 130
Washington, DC 20002
(202) 543-1505

US Student Travel Tours
891 Second Ave.
New York, NY 10019
(212) 867-8770

US/USSR Youth Exchange Program
3103 Washington St.
San Francisco, CA 94115
(415) 346-4234

Volunteers for Peace
Tiffany Road
Belmont, VT 05730
(802) 259-2759

YMCA International Program
  Services
356 W. 34th St., Third Floor
New York, NY 10025
(212) 563-4595

Youth for Democratic Action
1411 K St., NW
Suite 850
Washington, DC 20005
(202) 638-6447